Demanding the Land

Demanding the Land

Urban Popular Movements
in Peru and Ecuador, 1990–2005

Paul Dosh

Photographs by James Lerager

The Pennsylvania State University Press
University Park, Pennsylvania

Material from chapter 1 and the epilogue first appeared as "Tactical Innovation, Democratic Governance, and Mixed Motives: Popular Movement Resilience in Peru and Ecuador," *Latin American Politics and Society* 51, no. 1 (2009): 87–118. Reprinted with permission of *Latin American Politics and Society* and Wiley-Blackwell. Material from chapter 2 first appeared as "Surprising Trends in Land Invasions in Metropolitan Lima and Quito," *Latin American Perspectives* 33, no. 6 (2006): 29–54. Reprinted with permission of *Latin American Perspectives* and Sage Publications.

Library of Congress Cataloging-in-Publication Data

Dosh, Paul Gandhi Joseph.
    Demanding the land : urban popular movements in Peru and Ecuador, 1990–2005 / Paul Dosh ; photographs by James Lerager.
        p.   cm.
Includes bibliographical references and index.
Summary: "Examines the widespread Latin American phenomenon of illegal land seizures and squatter settlement development. Explains, based on case studies in Peru and Ecuador, how invasion organizations mobilize, why they succeed or fail, and why they endure or disappear"—Provided by publisher.
ISBN 978-0-271-03707-3 (cloth : alk. paper)
ISBN 978-0-271-03708-0 (pbk. : alk. paper)
1. Squatter settlements—Latin America.
2. Squatter settlements—Peru—Case studies.
3. Squatter settlements—Ecuador—Case studies.
4. Land tenure—Latin America.
5. Low-income housing—Latin America.
6. Social movements—Latin America.
7. Citizen participation—Latin America.
I. Title.

HD7287.96.L29D67 2010
307.3'36—dc22
                                2010002462

para Andrea

la cocinera

blending activism and artistry
stirring partnership and equality
seasoning our scholarship and pedagogy
with spices of justice and dignity

Contents

Figures and Tables

FIGURES

TABLES

Photographs

Acknowledgments

As a graduate of Lake Country School, a Montessori learning environment that fosters independence, I seem to depend on a surprisingly extensive network of colleagues and friends. With respect to this project, I relied heavily on my field research team. Andrea Galdames took the best interview notes of any of us, did extensive bibliographic research, and helped refine the project's conceptual innovations. Jesús Valencia made invaluable contributions to data collection and continued to monitor the Oasis, Encantada, Villa Mar, and Paraíso case studies after I had left Peru. César Flores co-interviewed the past and present neighborhood leaders of Pro, Sector C, and Rosales, and his inquisitiveness uncovered the hidden paramilitary past of these communities. Lastly, James Lerager shot four thousand photographs of land invasion settlements in Lima and Quito. His photographic work changed how we looked at and analyzed urban movements in Latin America, and his photographs are a vital contribution to this book. For an expanded selection of images, please visit http://webphotoessay.com/.

My love of Latin America began at age twelve with a Project Minnesota-León trip to Nicaragua during the Contra War. In the subsequent years, Larry Schaefer, Rosalba Murray, Sheila Malone-Povolny, Roy Grow, and Bev Nagel nurtured my interests in politics, Latin America, pedagogy, and social justice. It was Rich Keiser's inspiring classes at Carleton College, however, that sparked my interest in urban politics. After four years working with Rich, I told him I wanted to become a Macalester professor specializing in Latin American politics. He thought it was a good plan, and told me that attending Berkeley was the way to make it happen. Good advice.

I am deeply grateful for the guidance and support of my Berkeley mentors. As my principal adviser, David Collier helped me navigate shifts in my research agenda until I settled on the topic of land invasion settlements. David's 1976 study, *Squatters and Oligarchs: Authoritarian Rule and Policy Change in Peru*, was an inspiration for my work, and I hope this book lives up to the high standard set by that classic volume. While I conducted fieldwork in South America, David remained enthusiastic and encouraging about my discoveries on the ground, and during my final year at Berkeley his insightful feedback and confidence in me facilitated the prompt completion of this project. Ruth Berins Collier was my toughest and most effective critic, for which I thank her. I appreciate her humor and engagement with students, I enjoyed teaching with her, and I admire and applaud the collaborative spirit with which she recognizes students as colleagues and coauthors. Thankfully, Laura Enríquez coaxed me out of my political science shell and into the sociological study of social movements. She was always available and continued to provide excellent feedback on drafts even while traveling abroad. And Judy Gruber, who also served as my teaching mentor, shocked me at my oral examination by denouncing my original dependent variable (organizational strategy) and insisting that I make strategy secondary to the outcome that "we really care about," which was organizational success. She was right. During Judy's battle against cancer, her indomitable spirit helped us all cope with her illness. Her death in 2005 was a tremendous loss and she remains a source of inspiration.

Many scholars contributed to this project though comments on drafts and presentations related to the study. They include: Robert Adcock, Mauricio Benítez, Taylor Boas, Dexter Boniface, Chris Cardona, Ron Chilcote, Julio Cotler, Henry Dietz, Dwight Dyer, Zach Elkins, Sebastian Etchemendy, Tasha Fairfield, Natalia Ferretti, Claude Fischer, Candelaria Garay, Ben Goldfrank, Ken Greene, Sam Handlin, Bill Hurst, Maiah Jaskoski, Bert Johnson, Ollie Johnson, Diana Kapiszewski, Marcia Koth de Paredes, Eleanor Lahn, Nancy Lapp, Jonah Levy, Angelina Lopez, Olivia Maciuceanu, Sebastian Mazzuca, Verónica Montecinos, Al Montero, Gerardo Munck, Kathleen O'Neill, Jessica Rich, Sally Roever, Aaron Schneider, Jay Seawright, Kathryn Sikkink, Wendy Muse Sinek, William Smith, Richard Stahler-Sholk, Nicholas Taylor, Sandy Thatcher, Annie Virnig, and Deborah Yashar.

A Fulbright-Hays Doctoral Dissertation Research Abroad fellowship provided generous support while we worked in Peru and Ecuador in 2001–2. In 2005 and 2007, two grants from Macalester College supported follow-up research to expand the temporal scope of the case studies. While in Lima, I was an affiliated scholar at the Universidad del Pacífico Centro de Investigaciones. Thanks to Felipe Porto-Carrero for making this possible and for sharing with me his best student, César Flores. In Quito, I was an affiliated scholar at the Facultad Latinoamericana de Ciencias Sociales (FLACSO). Thanks to Fernando Carrión for his support, as the FLACSO name proved invaluable in opening doors throughout Quito. For logistical and technical support, I thank Ellen Borrowman, Brendan Dunn, Roxanne Fisher, Myriam Godfrey, Pat Hull, Kathy Sarconi, and Carol Zenouaki. For friendship and constant communication during our year in South America, I thank Zachary Drake, Shailja Patel, and Zachary Rothschild.

I am grateful for the support of my colleagues at Macalester College. The outstanding caliber of the Political Science and Latin American Studies departments fostered the success of this book, and I appreciate the patient mentorship of David Blaney, Adrienne Christiansen, and Raymond Robertson. Nicole Kligerman helped me revise the manuscript and discern which issues to resolve in this book and which to develop into a new research agenda focused on gender dynamics and popular movements in the Andes. It's been my great privilege to work and travel with Nicole, and our complementary collaboration has taken us to five countries in the Americas. And I am grateful to Emily Hedin, an extraordinary scholar and activist who not only sharpened the book's argument about mixed motives and collective action, but also insisted that our work in Peru mix the motives of scholarship, engagement, and action. In 2008, Emily and I founded Building Dignity, a development organization that supports popular movement leaders in Villa El Salvador through the Center for Development with Dignity.

Several hundred Peruvian and Ecuadorian friends have opened their homes and lives to us over the years. They shared with us their courage and humiliation, their generosity and desperation. After years of social activism among the poor, I thought I had experienced my last epiphany, but our friends showed us that there always remains room for further transformation. They pried our eyes a little wider, rescued us from hired bandits, and, when caught amid the water fights of Carnival laden with recording and photographic equipment, somehow kept us dry. It was exciting. Among these many friends, the especially heroic include Claudia Avelino, Milton Chamorro, Patricio Endara, María Hernández, Martha Huamán, Modesta Martinez, Jean Pierre Valencia, Karina Valencia, Rolando Valencia, and Celia Yabar. Proceeds and honoraria from book sales and speaking engagements go to support their work in Lima and Quito.

Thank you to my godparents, Clare Adams and Don Moncrieff; my rock star brother, Martin Dosh; and my delightful children, Araminta and Mateo, for their unconditional love and support. To my mother, Millie Dosh, an exemplar of selfless caring for the poor and marginalized, I would not have been motivated to study and work among the shantytowns without your example. And to my father, Terry Dosh, a scholar-activist who is far left and always right, thank you for teaching me to treasure history and humanity, art and action. It's good to know that if this book is censored or blacklisted, you will only grow prouder.

And for my beloved Andrea Galdames, an activist-educator, feminist-agitator, Latin Americanist–celebrator like no other. You are my irreplaceable partner and you have been at my side throughout this epic project. With love and profound appreciation, I dedicate this book to you.

Abbreviations

AP	Acción Popular (Popular Action, Peru)
APRA	Alianza Popular Revolucionaria Americana (American Popular Revolutionary Alliance, Peru)
CEBs	Comunidades Eclesiales de Base (base Christian communities)
COFOPRI	Comisión de Formalización de la Propiedad Informal (Commission for the Formalization of Informal Property, Peru)
CONAIE	Confederación de Nacionalidades Indígenas del Ecuador (Confederation of Indigenous Nationalities of Ecuador)
CPQ	Coordinadora Popular de Quito (People's Coordinating Committee of Quito)
CUAVES	Comunidad Urbana Autogestionaria de Villa El Salvador (Villa El Salvador Urban Self-Management Community, Peru)
DP	Democracia Popular (Popular Democracy, Ecuador)
FONAVI	Fondo Nacional de Vivienda (National Housing Fund, Peru)
FOVIDA	Fomento de la Vida (Promoting Quality of Life, Peru)
FREDEMO	Frente Democrático (Democratic Front, Peru)
FRN	Frente de Reconstrucción Nacional (National Reconstruction Front, Ecuador)
FUPP	Frente Unitario de los Pueblos de Perú (United Front of the Peoples of Peru)
IESS	Instituto Ecuatoriano de Seguridad Social (Ecuadorian Institute of Social Security)
INC	Instituto Nacional de Cultura (National Institute of Culture, Peru)
IU	Izquierda Unida (United Left, Peru)
MPD	Movimiento Popular Democrático (Popular Democratic Movement, Ecuador)
MST	Movimento dos Trabalhadores Rurais Sem Terra (Movement of Landless Rural Workers, Brazil)
PCE	Partido Comunista Ecuatoriano (Ecuadorian Communist Party)

SEDAPAL   Servicio de Agua Potable y Alcantarillado de Lima (Lima Potable Water and Sewer Drainage Service)

SINAMOS   Sistema Nacional de Apoyo a la Movilización Social (National System for the Support of Social Mobilization, Peru)

Introduction

Weak from hunger, sick from the stench of human and animal waste, and uncertain if tomorrow would bring a violent eviction by hired thugs, Jesús Valencia and Martha Huamán did not feel like cutting-edge innovators. It was 1996, and this destitute but determined Peruvian couple wondered if they had made a terrible mistake by casting their lot with a thousand other poor settlers who, days earlier, had seized a patch of barren desert—La Encantada (the Enchanted Place), the settlers now called it—and built an illegal shantytown in a single night.

Eight years earlier, Jesús Valencia had fled the poverty of Tablazo Norte, a farming village in the northern province of Piura, and migrated to the capital city of Lima. In Lima, he met Martha Huamán, a migrant from the mountain province of Cusco, and the young couple became involved in the urban popular movements of the district of Villa El Salvador. Ready to start a family, Jesús and Martha had joined the La Encantada land invasion, hoping to claim a tiny parcel of sand and build a home.

One week after La Encantada's founding, however, Jesús and Martha listened at a neighborhood meeting to reports of violent crime, cardboard shacks destroyed by arson, livestock-related pests and illness, and city hall's rejection of the fledgling community's pleas for water. On the brink of failure, there was little to suggest that in just a little over a decade, La Encantada would develop into a successful and resilient community, and that Jesús and Martha would become leaders not only of their own neighborhood, but also of a successful project to build water and sewer infrastructure for fifty-five thousand settlers in La Encantada and the surrounding land invasion neighborhoods.

The stories of poor settlers like Jesús Valencia and Martha Huamán and the struggles of ten land invasion neighborhoods, including La Encantada, anchor this book's exploration of urban popular movements in Peru and Ecuador and my own explanations for the strategy, success, and survival of popular movement organizations. Let me begin by posing a sharp three-way contrast in the outcomes I seek to explain.

In 1990, as Peru absorbed the initial shock of party system collapse and Alberto Fujimori's election as president, organized groups of poor people took advantage of the political turmoil to illegally seize vacant lands and found squatter communities. In Lima's northern district of Los Olivos, one such group founded "Rosales" and sought to bring electricity and piped water into their fledgling community through disruptive and militant protest actions. Yet while neighboring informal settlements encountered steady success in acquiring services, Rosales discovered that its own commitment to neighborhood-level elections resulted in volatile leadership shifts that debilitated the neighborhood organization. Led by veteran "Old Guard" land invaders who had seen radical and extralegal strategies work before, the group's stubborn determination to make militancy work for their community undermined the service initiatives of less rigid leaders. The resultant failure of service demands left the neighborhood leadership structure divided and weak.

By contrast, in the southern Lima district of Villa El Salvador (see Skinner 1983; Riofrío 1986, 47–100; Burga and Delpech 1989), a younger, "Next Generation" group of settlers founded the community of Oasis in 1994 and succeeded in acquiring important services for their neighborhood. Oasis was democratically organized but decision-making power was more diffuse, and the neighborhood did not experience the volatile shifts that characterized Rosales. The Oasis settlers had grown up in invasion neighborhoods founded by their parents, but unlike those ideologically committed parents, the strategically flexible younger generation employed a combination of legal and extralegal strategies. This blend of disruptive militancy and clientelist partnerships yielded electricity, piped water, and land titles. Ironically, however, with the acquisition of land titles, settlers felt secure and stopped participating in the neighborhood organization. With this decline in participation, the organization sank into a moribund state despite crucial unmet needs, such as sewer drainage.

Finally, the Villa El Salvador invasion of La Encantada—the community of Jesús Valencia and Martha Huamán—was founded in 1996 by a third type of settlement organization, which I call the "Innovators." This community managed both to acquire service infrastructure and land titles *and* to consolidate as an organization, meaning it continued to pursue community objectives. The Encantada settlers were similar to the Oasis group in that they had grown up in the invasion communities of their parents, had a democratic organization, and employed a flexible combination of legal and extralegal strategies. But unlike either Rosales or Oasis, the Encantada settlers employed an innovative mix of novel tactics. Further, when Encantada's acquisition of land titles precipitated a similar decline in participation, the organization rejuvenated participation by reorienting the neighborhood toward an activist mission of helping neighboring settlements. In this way, the Encantada organization was also able to continue acquiring services for its own membership.

Why did the Next Generation settlers of Oasis and the Innovator settlers of Encantada successfully acquire neighborhood services, while the Old Guard settlers of Rosales failed to do so? And since the demand-making methods of each group likely contributed to their success or failure, why did the experienced veterans of Rosales stubbornly refuse to modify their organizational strategy, while Oasis's and Encantada's squatter neophytes flexibly employed a savvy combination of strategies? Third, why did the Rosales and Oasis organizations falter precisely when settlers still needed an organizational vehicle to press their demands, while the Encantada group survived, consolidated its gains, and established a permanent local leadership role?

In the Latin American context, where illegal seizures of land and the development of informal housing settlements have become commonplace, understanding what factors contribute to both organizational success in demand-making and long-term organizational survival constitutes a crucial substantive goal. More broadly, understanding the major phenomenon of Latin American land invasions contributes to a critical theoretical goal: explaining the success or failure of social movements in general, both in terms of their objectives and in terms of movement survival.

Using a diverse set of conceptual and analytic tools, I examine squatter settlement development through ten neighborhood-level case studies of invasion organizations in Lima, Peru, and Quito, Ecuador. Although the founding dates of the organizations range from the 1980s to the early 2000s, the analysis focuses principally on the 1990–2005 period. The study sets forth a typology that identifies three types of invasion organizations, and the ten cases include one organization of each type from each city, as well as additional contrast cases from Lima that permit the study to control for some local factors.

In order to explain the key outcome of organizational success or failure in acquiring neighborhood services, I also explore the related questions of how invasions select their demand-making strategies and why such organizations survive or collapse. Hence, my three-part argument aims to explain three related outcomes: *organizational strategy*, *organizational success*, and *organizational survival*. To explain these outcomes, I develop dynamic conceptualizations of invasion organizations' identities and strategy repertoires in order to employ political process theory—not just at the point of initial mobilization, but also throughout the development of each invasion organization.

THE EVOLVING STRUGGLE FOR LAND AND URBAN SERVICES

Throughout the latter half of the twentieth century, tens of millions of Latin Americans participated in illegal land invasions (see, for example, Leeds and Leeds 1970; Cornelius 1975; Collier 1976; Gilbert and Ward 1978). Prior to the 1940s, self-help housing existed principally in isolated patches of a modest number of Latin American cities (Gilbert 1998, 79). Beginning in the late 1940s and early 1950s, however, the "explosion of the periphery" rapidly became a defining feature of urban Latin America. Describing the escalating growth of informal housing in cities such as Bogotá, Caracas, and Rio de Janeiro as "exponential," Alan Gilbert (1998, 80) cites the dramatic growth in Lima's number of settlements: 39 by 1955, 237 by 1970, and 782 by 1984. And this pattern was not limited to large cities like Santiago and Quito, but also manifested in medium-sized cities like Cochabamba, Concepción, and Maracaibo (Matos Mar 1968, 217–73).

Over the course of the 1970s and into the 1980s, informal settlement housing increasingly came to be viewed not as a problem, but as a solution to the region-wide migration to cities sparked by economic crisis (Driant 1991, 116). Though individual families often made quick decisions to join an imminent land invasion, the phenomenon was rarely spontaneous. To the contrary, such mobilizations typically required months of planning and preparation (Matos Mar 1966). Poor migrants leapt at the chance to claim land, even illegally, and state officials looked the other way or even actively helped settlers, since they had few other policy options for housing the thousands of rural migrants that poured into the cities (Collier 1976). As the trend grew, a second generation of settlers jumped on the bandwagon (Driant and Grey 1988), and the 1970s witnessed massive and now-legendary invasions such as Villa El Salvador in Lima (Riofrío 1978, 44–47; Burga and Delpech 1989) and Comité del Pueblo (Committee of the People) and Lucha de los Pobres (Struggle of the Poor) in Quito.

In addition to transforming the landscape of housing in urban Latin America, informal housing also changed the meaning and nature of local politics and grassroots participation (Riofrío 1991, 124–26). In cases like Peru, where the political crisis of 1968–75 was linked to a surge in land invasions, the politicization of informal settlements was obvious, as popular groups organized on behalf of national and local political leaders and then remained in a state of high mobilization (Tovar Samanez 1982b, 49; Ballón 1986, 17–25). More generally, however, a less visible but more enduring politicization occurred through the popular organizations spawned by the hundreds of new urban neighborhoods that had brought together marginalized families in coordinated acts of reclaiming both land and dignity (Matos Mar 1986).

Though these types of popular organizations were not new, their expanded scope and reach was breathtaking, including settler organizations (neighborhood, housing, owners, settlers), women's organizations (mothers' clubs, popular kitchens, child care groups, women's issues committees), cultural organizations (cultural groups, popular libraries, media groups), health organizations, religious organizations (base Christian communities), neighborhood markets, street vendors, provincial groups, sports groups, educational organizations, merchants' organizations, and social clubs (Tovar Samanez 1986, 146–47). The importance of this impact could be likened to the mid-twentieth-century process of labor incorporation (Collier and Collier 1991), which brought millions into the political arena, albeit in subordinate roles. Likewise, the 1980s surge in popular mobilization coincided with the rise of municipal- and neighborhood-level democratic elections, and though settlers remained on the margins, they increasingly felt entitled to a voice in politics (Tovar Samanez 1982a, 24–26).

By the 1980s, many observers anticipated that the pattern of settlement via illegal land invasions would wane as major cities became saturated with informal settlements, but the onset of neoliberalism, increases in economic vulnerability, and the expansion of informal labor sustained and reshaped land invasion patterns (Portes 1989; Eckstein 1990; Stokes 1991). Thus, invasions focused increasingly on land that was already in use, including private property (which created more conflict) or land that was precarious or barely habitable (Riofrío and Driant 1987, 126). During this period, the fundamental objectives of invasion organizations remained unchanged: reliable electricity, potable water, sewer drainage, and, often most important, legal title to illegally acquired land (Burgwal 1995; Dietz 1998b; Gilbert 1998). The context in which they demanded these services, however, changed in three ways.

First, the economic context changed as Peru, Ecuador, and other nations embraced neoliberalism (Stokes 2001, 69–70). Neoliberal reforms debilitated already weak social safety nets, sharply reduced the power of organized labor, and privatized some urban service monopolies, which reshaped the strategies available to settlers seeking service infrastructure and delivery (Gilbert and Gugler 1992).

Second, the national political context changed, as neoliberalism blurred party lines and many leftist parties moved toward the market (Roberts 1995, 100; Roberts and Arce 1998, 219–20). Despite important exceptions, such as Brazil's Partido dos Trabalhadores (Workers' Party), party identification became less important as party systems either faded in importance or collapsed out-right, making political parties less likely allies for settlers (Villalón 2007). Peru and Venezuela were the most dramatic cases of party system collapse and the rise of candidate-centered, personalist vehicles, but Ecuador and Bolivia also experienced major increases in political volatility (Corrales 2002, 252–77; Olivera 2004; Sawyer 2004, 15). For land invasion neighborhoods, these changes meant that clientelist partisan alliances became less reliable, leading some settlers to reevaluate their options (Burgwal 1993).

And third, the local political context changed, as Peru, Ecuador, and many other countries introduced democratic municipal elections in the 1980s (Dietz and Shidlo 1998). While struggles between democracy and authoritarianism continued to dominate Latin America, empowerment of municipal government took root and slowly grew, gradually transforming the local political context for invasion organizations (Myers and Dietz 2003). Although the budgetary power of local districts remained minimal, the introduction of democratically account-able local leaders provided settlers with fresh targets for their service demands.

Partly in response to these changes, new patterns of organization emerged at the neighborhood level. As decreased availability of convenient land led to seizures of distant and barely inhabitable terrain, new organizational types emerged from older patterns of settlement organization (see Holzner 2004). These newer organizational types represented a major shift in both ideology and strategy. In order to understand the causes and consequences of these shifts, this study examines these changes from the perspective of social move-ment theory.[1]

STRUCTURE OF THE STUDY

Given these changes in the political environment of invasion organizations, chapter 1 begins with a discussion of social movement theory, with special attention paid to the role of opportunity structures. Grounded in this litera-ture, chapter 1 lays out the conceptual and analytic foundations of the study. First, I conceptualize strategies in terms of their legality and autonomy. The resulting typology supports an analytic construct that I call the *strategy life cycle*. Second, I conceptualize external and internal factors that contribute to

All translations from Spanish are by the author.

1. Schönwälder (2002, 11) persuasively makes the case for treating urban popular movements as social movements, arguing that the former have a potential for social change, a proclivity for noninstitutional forms of action, and a unifying set of beliefs that movement participants share. See also Friedmann (1989) and Burgwal (1990).

the success or failure of demands for services by invasion organizations. These variables are presented in the *neighborhood service acquisition model,* which posits a series of causal claims to account for organizational success. Third, to explain varying outcomes in organizational survival, I introduce the concept of organizational stages of development and an analytic tool called the *security trap.* Building on this theoretical framework, the remainder of the study is arranged to examine the study's three-part argument at the metropolitan level (chapter 2), the neighborhood level (chapters 3–5), and the level of individual demands for services (chapter 6).

Chapter 2 compares land invasions in metropolitan Lima and Quito. In Lima, invasions have become routine and institutionalized, while in Quito they are considered aberrations. Controlling for population, Lima's invasion rate between 1990 and 2005 was double to triple that of Quito. In Lima, we often see vibrant neighborhood-level democracy, but in Quito local bosses dominate. In Peru, pro-settler legislation enacted by the progressive government of General Juan Velasco Alvarado (1968–75) makes public lands ripe targets for invasion organizations. Yet their Ecuadorian counterparts more often attempt to seize private land, partly because Quito's entrepreneurial city hall defends its own assets but leaves other landowners to fend for themselves.

Chapter 3 explores the argument in the context of four Old Guard land invasion organizations. Intra-city and cross-national comparison of three Old Guard case studies in Lima and one in Quito reveals variation in the success or failure or service demands, demonstrating that the Old Guard's fate depends on other internal and external factors.

Despite these contrasting outcomes across cases, the Old Guard organizations displayed several common traits. First, their pragmatic focus on material objectives made them likely victims of the security trap who would then struggle to consolidate their organizations. Second, the stubborn refusal of the Old Guard to adapt their strategy choices to an evolving political context meant that despite some victories, Old Guard organizations generally could not acquire 100 percent of basic services. And third, the Old Guard tendency toward power-concentrating neighborhood regimes meant that these groups were less able to take advantage of local avenues of participation.

Chapter 4 expands the scope of the argument to include four Next Generation case studies. Intra-district[2] comparison of three Next Generation case studies from Lima and cross-national comparison with one from Quito reveal wide variation in

---

2. Metropolitan Lima is divided into forty-three local districts, each with a democratically elected mayor and city (district) council. Metropolitan Quito is divided into sixteen local districts, each with an appointed administrator. Both cities have a democratically elected metropolitan mayor and council (Nickson 1995).

neighborhood regime type but a predictable pattern of strategy choices. Whereas Old Guard groups display rigid strategy preferences, the Next Generation follows the strategy life cycle. Consequently, Next Generation organizations are theoretically able to adapt to changing political contexts and select the most effective strategy. Empirically, however, the lack of experience of Next Generation leaders and their at times reckless faith in the lessons of their parents sometimes make their efforts at demand-making less successful.

As with the Old Guard cases, several broad findings emerge. First, Next Generation cases tend to use violence only in self-defense, or not at all. Second, although these groups use tactics similar to their Old Guard parents (such as defending land with a picket line), they are usually led by novice invaders and often eject veteran leaders as suspected "land traffickers" who might exploit the settlers. And third, although all four cases follow the strategy life cycle, only one case actually completed the cycle.

Chapter 5 presents the final two neighborhood-level case studies: the Innovators. Like the Next Generation, the strategy choices of Innovators also follow the strategy life cycle, but unlike the Next Generation's wide variation in neighborhood regime type, both Innovator case studies (one from Lima and one from Quito) are characterized by power-sharing methods of governance. Innovators sometimes appear to choose the "wrong" strategy, given existing political opportunities or lack thereof, but this is because Innovator objectives differ from those of conventional invasion organizations. Innovators exhibit mixed motives, meaning their material agenda is supplemented by a nonmaterial and often altruistic agenda, which sometimes leads to surprising choices that may not support their material demands.

Three traits unite the Innovator cases. First, their power-sharing leadership structures are similar and appear to be considered necessary by organization leaders to each group's broader democratic mission. Second, although not uniform, the Innovators' commitment to nonviolence is remarkable, particularly in the face of sometimes brutal attacks. And third, their use of technology and general creativity generates extraordinarily original tactics.

Chapter 6 analyzes all three major outcomes through comparison of 132 cases of demand-making across the ten neighborhoods. In order to analyze cases of demand-making by disparate organizations whose founding dates range from 1983 to 2001, I categorize each instance of demand-making in light of the group's organizational stage of development at the time of the demand. This classification scheme both helps standardize cases of demand-making and also generates additional insights into the strengths and weaknesses of the neighborhood service acquisition model, the study's typologies, and new analytic tools such as the strategy life cycle and the security trap.

Chapter 7 returns to the theoretical framework of chapter 1 and summarizes the study's implications in light of social movement theory. What determines movement success? External factors beyond the control of organizations do invite and curtail mobilization in a variety of ways, but this study shows that whatever the array of external variables, certain types of organizations, characterized by specific strategies, assets, and leadership structures, are better able than others to exploit those external factors. In short, organizations do in fact exert control over key aspects of their own process of acquiring resources.

And what shapes trajectories of movement survival? Selective incentives do play a key role in motivating high levels of participation; at later points in a movement's development, however, the interplay of mixed motives and collective action proves decisive, suggesting that mixed motives may be critical for the survival of any movement organization in the wake of diminishing selective incentives.

Although this analysis focuses on neighborhood-level cases in two Latin American cities, its empirical and theoretical findings raise important issues for social movements in nonurban contexts and in other world regions. Through a macro-longitudinal conceptualization of the evolution of invasion organizations, the study demonstrates that a historical dimension similar to Tarrow's "cycles of contention" (1998, 141–60) may be required to fully understand changes in opportunities for mobilization. More important, the main causal model for movement success relies critically on the study's micro-longitudinal framework for predicting organizational strategy selection. This indicates that the success or failure of social movements in general can only be understood through both an evolutionary conceptualization of invasion organizations and a dynamic deployment of political process theory.

1

The Strategy, Success, and Survival of Urban Popular Movements

Has the study of social movements as a unique political phenomenon already passed its zenith? In *Dynamics of Contention* (2001), Doug McAdam, Sidney Tarrow, and Charles Tilly argue that it has, and that it is time to move on. Critiquing an approach to social movement theory that they helped engineer, these scholars boldly argue that the time has come to set aside the "classic" social movement agenda and turn our collective scholarly attention to the search for recurrent causal mechanisms that span a variety of contentious politics, including social movements, revolutions, and democratization.

This chapter begins by framing the study with respect to several social movement theorists, including McAdam, Tarrow, and Tilly. This discussion identifies and debates specific contributions of these scholars and also describes how the study's analytic goals connect to related theoretical objectives. The chapter then presents three analytic tools that the study employs to explain outcomes in organizational strategy, organizational success, and organizational survival. With each analytic tool, I begin with the theoretical and conceptual foundations necessary to frame the outcome in question.

With respect to organizational strategy, I argue that understanding mobilization strategy selection requires both a macro- and micro-longitudinal (i.e., over time) perspective. At the macro level, changing patterns of mobilization only become clear when we examine the evolution of invasion organization types characteristic of the 1980s and 1990–2005. At the micro level, a new conceptualization of organizational strategy types helps reveal that the strategy choices of new types of organizations follow a predictable "life cycle" that is replicated in different political and geographic contexts.

I then turn to the key outcome: organizational success or failure in acquiring neighborhood services. Building on my explanation of organizational strategy, I introduce a new conceptualization of neighborhood regime types that helps me to specify causal hypotheses from the opportunity-structure side of political process theory, such that neighborhood service acquisition outcomes can be understood as the result of factors both external and internal to invasion organizations.

The theoretical framework concludes with a set of conceptual and analytic tools to explain variation in organizational survival. Drawing on a longitudinal approach to the development of invasion organizations, I argue that the key to their survival is found in agenda-setting practices that permit groups to achieve their central objectives without compromising their mobilizational momentum.

AN END TO THE SOCIAL MOVEMENT LITERATURE?

In their landmark synthesis of the resource mobilization approach to social movement theory, Doug McAdam, John McCarthy, and Mayer Zald (1988, 728–29) argue that the literature fails to capture "the dynamics of collective action past the emergence of a movement." They urge social movement scholars to: (1) "distinguish between the emergent and later developmental phases of collective action"; (2) "link processes at the macro and micro levels by means of the intervening organizational bridges crucial during each"; and (3) use systematic theoretical frameworks to study movements over time. Over a decade later, McAdam, Tarrow, and Tilly published *Dynamics of Contention* (2001), in which they forcefully argue that although the goals identified by McAdam, McCarthy, and Zald have been only partially fulfilled, it is now time to move on (see also McAdam, Tarrow, and Tilly 1997). Specifically, McAdam, Tarrow, and Tilly purport to arrest the classic social movement agenda that they helped engineer, and to redirect scholarship away from the task of specifying the best possible general model and toward the goal of identifying recurrent *partial* causal mechanisms and processes across many episodes of contentious politics, including social movements, revolutions, democratization, and nationalism. In introducing their "relational" approach to contentious politics, McAdam, Tarrow, and Tilly (2001, 42) echo the criticisms of McAdam, McCarthy, and Zald (1988) noted above—that scholarship has emphasized the origins of mobilization at the expense of later phases, has overemphasized individual movements, and has been static.

In some respects, this book conforms to the new agenda advanced by McAdam, Tarrow, and Tilly. The present study shies away from working toward a grand model for all social movements (and certainly a model for all contention). Additionally, my focus on movement change over time integrates dynamic change directly into the causal argument. This focus on change over time likewise responds to their call for attention to later phases beyond the origins of movement mobilization. Three aspects of this study, however, contrast with or challenge this new "relational" agenda.

First, McAdam, Tarrow, and Tilly divide contentious politics between "contained" contention and "transgressive" contention, and based on fifteen national-level case studies show that transgressive contention routinely (though not always) emerges from contained contention. "Most of our cases," they explain, "began with episodes of contained contention that eventually evolved into broader transgressive episodes." They define contained contention as cases in which "all parties are previously established actors employing well established means of claim making." By contrast, transgressive contention refers to instances in which "at least some of the parties are newly self-identified political actors," and these actors employ strategies that are "either unprecedented or forbidden" (2001, 7–8, 341).

Despite their attention to this dichotomy, McAdam, Tarrow, and Tilly examine only cases of transgressive contention that are sporadic and national in scope. They explicitly claim that although their case selection relies "overwhelmingly" on "*national* episodes of *transgressive* contention," they believe their claims have "far broader scope than even our cases suggest." In any event, they find the idea of a distinctly national scale of contention to be "illusory," pointing out that their own national-level cases, such as the 1989 Chinese student movement, were in fact concentrated in distinct locales, such as Beijing (340–41). By contrast, the present study focuses on local cases of either sporadic or continuous contention, many of which *begin* as transgressive, but eventually (and predictably, I will argue) become contained. Hence, I am interested in what O'Brien (2003, 52) calls "boundary-spanning contention"—the nexus of the contained and the transgressive. O'Brien criticizes McAdam, Tarrow, and Tilly for exaggerating the separation between contained and transgressive contention, and urges scholars to focus "on acts that sit near the fuzzy boundary between official, prescribed politics and politics by other means."

But are the legal and extralegal strategies of invasion organizations a fitting arena in which to examine the relationship between contained and transgressive contention? McAdam, Tarrow, and Tilly's cases—which include, among others, European revolutionary struggles, the U.S. civil rights movement, and Italian postwar conflicts—seem to be analytically distant from Latin American land invasions, perhaps pointing to the conclusion that these studies simply belong to different conceptual domains. Yet the core objective of their ambitious agenda is to transcend traditional analytic boundaries between "revolutions, social movements, industrial conflict, war, interest group politics, nationalism, [and] democratization." With such an incredibly broad scope, this study seems on safe ground in claiming to examine one small part of McAdam, Tarrow, and Tilly's large universe of potential cases, especially when land invasion conflicts fit well into those scholars' definitions of contained and transgressive contention (2001, 6–8).

Second, although Tarrow appears ready to move on to the new relational agenda, his important book *Power in Movement* (1998) remains one of the most persuasive articulations of the role of opportunity structures within political process theory. Of particular value is his identification of general "dimensions of opportunity," which include shifts in ruling alignments, repression and facilitation of collective action, the availability of influential allies, and increasing access to participation (76–80). One of the unfinished tasks of *Power in Movement*, however, was to specify how and when such opportunities result in success or failure, and it is here that this study aims to make another contribution: by operationalizing Tarrow's dimensions in order to solve the causal puzzle of movement success within the context of Latin American land invasion organizations.

And third, in order to explain organizational survival, I focus not on the origins of mobilization but instead on later stages of social movement development and the challenge of sustaining collective action in the face of diminishing selective incentives. My attempt to elucidate these later stages within what McAdam, Tarrow, and Tilly call the "classic" social movement framework points to the continued relevance and usefulness of the agenda they seem so ready to cast aside. This continued relevance is even more apparent when we consider that the scholarly attention devoted to contentious politics in the United States and Europe far exceeds that given to Latin America and other world regions. Hence, the readiness of these scholars to "move on" may in part reflect a more solidly filled-out body of knowledge in their regional specialties. But as this study illustrates, in regions like Latin America, whole subfields of knowledge have just begun to be explored (see, for example, Roberts 1998). Even the subject of land invasion communities, which received sustained scholarly attention in the 1960s and 1970s, has changed so significantly that the relatively straightforward task of discovering what is happening "on the ground" remains an important objective, and one that can be well served by many of the analytic tools McAdam, Tarrow, and Tilly now regard as outdated.

In this way, the present study seeks to answer McAdam, Tarrow, and Tilly's call for dynamic explanations of specific processes and mechanisms, but also advances: (1) a strategy typology grounded in a distinct conceptualization of contention; (2) a model for organizational success that relies on operationalized opportunity structures; and (3) a dynamic analysis of organizational survival that succeeds because of political process theory, not in spite of it. In these ways, I not only make use of the classic social movement agenda, but improve it through a fresh set of conceptual and analytic tools that can be tested in other contexts.

EXPLAINING ORGANIZATIONAL STRATEGY: TYPES OF INVASION ORGANIZATIONS AND THE STRATEGY LIFE CYCLE

In the introduction, the comparison of the Rosales, Oasis, and Encantada invasion neighborhoods exhibited a clear contrast in terms of the demand-making strategies of each group. In the Rosales case, veteran land invaders rigidly pursued disruptive and militant strategies even in the face of mounting failure, while the younger leaders of Oasis and Encantada displayed strategic fluidity and employed a successful blend of legal and extralegal strategies.

In *Power and Popular Protest*, Susan Eckstein (1989) offers a strong starting point for explaining such variation in strategy selection. Eckstein argues that responses to grievances are shaped by "local institutional arrangements, class alliances, popular cultures of resistance, and state structures" (7). Wildavsky (1987) echoes the cultural component of Eckstein's claim, positing that political culture offers a superior tool for understanding preferences in terms of both outcomes and the means of achieving them.

In the Peruvian case, this is the position staked out by Susan Stokes (1995, 61–84) in her explanation of settler strategy preferences in Lima. Stokes argues that the political culture of settlers prescribes an "enduring mental template" that results in strategic inflexibility. These rigid preferences lead Stokes to characterize individual settlers as either "clients," who prefer clientelist relationships and legal petitioning, or "radicals," who prefer extralegal "struggle methods."[1] Within the social movement literature, Stokes's "mental templates" concept emerges as a clear example of the collective process of interpretation, attribution, and social construction known as framing (Snow et al. 1986; Snow and Benford 1988; see also McAdam, Tarrow, and Tilly 2001, 41). In land invasion communities, settlement leaders use framing to build group solidarity and establish clear organizational identities and preferences for certain "repertoires of contention" (Tilly 1995, 41).

For Stokes (1995, 62), categorizing an individual settler as a client or a radical requires analysis of both how individuals "view the political and social world

---

1. Schönwälder (2002, 51) emphasizes the risks to movement autonomy posed by clientelism. In Auyero's (2001, 175–81) study of Peronist survival networks in the shantytowns of Buenos Aires, this pitfall is effectively illustrated from the perspective of poor settlers.

around them" (including ideology, political objectives, and class structure) and their "distinct strategic and behavioral patterns" (their views of the role of community leaders, efficacy, and the appropriateness of various tactics). Stokes does not see the world in black and white, but nonetheless convincingly argues that, by and large, most individual settlers can be fairly categorized as either a client or a radical. The causes of these "bifurcated patterns of political culture," argues Stokes, rest with the vibrant constellation of political actors that defined the context of settlement development, such as dominance of the Left in Lima politics in the mid-1980s and unions allied with popular movements, politically engaged base Christian communities working among informal settlements, and a profusion of grassroots popular organizations (Tovar Samanez 1986, 146; Levine 1992; Schönwälder 2002, 19, 113).

Although Stokes makes her argument at the level of the individual, I believe her claim also applies at the level of Old Guard organizations. Although the strategic inflexibility described by Stokes exhibits an excellent analytic fit with invasion organizations founded between 1980 and 1990, her perspective does not capture the impact of the emergent types of organizations particular to the 1990–2005 period. This makes sense, since several of the causal factors Stokes identifies in the 1980s period—the strength of unions, the electoral Left, and liberation theology—had diminished by the 1990s and early 2000s, though the scope and intensity of organization of grassroots popular groups remained robust.

Unlike the Old Guard organizations, which had clear preferences for either legal or extralegal methods of demand-making, I argue that the new types of invasion organizations follow a predictable "life cycle" of strategy choices and employ a diverse repertoire of legal *and* extralegal methods. Understanding this claim requires a historical dimension, as a cross-sectional "snapshot" of the invasion phenomenon at any given point in time cannot capture generational change.

Types of Invasion Organizations

The study's evolutionary perspective yields a three-part typology of invasion organizations that distinguishes between past generations of settlers and the two new types that have emerged.[2] Experienced settlers with rigid strategy preferences typically lead the first type of organization—the Old Guard (e.g., Rosales). These pragmatic veterans employ *either* legal strategies (such as clientelist partnerships; see Gilbert and Gugler 1992, 180) *or* extralegal strategies (such as disruptive

---

2. Portes and Walton (1976, 94) were the first to articulate the value of identifying the broad trends of the "evolution of organizations" in the context of Latin American informal settlements. See also Bennett (1992).

protests). For example, the leadership of Rosales insisted on a strategy of militant disruption. Old Guard organizations rely on the "same old playbook" of classic invasion strategies, often including willful violence, and they are led by pragmatic veteran leaders with a "win some, lose some" attitude. Once the dominant type in the 1980s, few Old Guard settlements have been founded since 1990.[3] Hundreds of Old Guard neighborhoods still exist, however, and many are still trying to acquire needed services, usually using the same unoriginal tactics.[4]

The strategically rigid Old Guard type has been largely replaced in the formation of new settlements by two strategically flexible organization types that I call the Next Generation and the Innovators. Next Generation organizations emerged in the 1990s as young men and women who had grown up in invasion communities went on to found their own squatter settlements (e.g., Oasis). These literal children of the Old Guard are inspired by the example of their parents, but are not bound by their parents' strong ideology or rigid strategy preferences. Having grown up learning the tactical lessons of their Old Guard parents, these novice settlers employ both legal *and* extralegal strategies, but otherwise exhibit little tactical innovation. Next Generation organizations generally eschew violence and often reject or expel veteran invasion leaders in favor of idealistic novice leaders whose "we will succeed" optimism can stoically (and sometimes blindly) endure even catastrophic failures.[5] This fear of veterans arises from the common presence of "land traffickers," real or suspected. Typically, land traffickers are predatory leaders who organize land invasions solely for the purpose of collecting dues from a vulnerable membership, only to later disappear with the organization's assets.[6]

---

3. This characterization of the Old Guard contrasts with the general claims about social movements made by Koopmans (2005, 28–29), whose interesting evolutionary approach emphasizes the capacity of movements to learn from their mistakes (or face "extinction" due to "natural selection"). From this perspective, movement decisions are made on a trial and error basis and, after each round of decisions, activists evaluate their options based on the successes of their movement and those of others. The Next Generation and Innovator types often do just this, so if the Old Guard continues its decline and eventually "dies out," it would offer strong evidence in support of Koopmans's argument.

4. Throughout this study, Old Guard strategy preferences are described as rigid, but always employing militant tactics may not automatically be a sign of rigidity. Norris, Walgrave, and Van Aelst (2005, 203) argue that the meaning of disruptive protests is dynamic and increasingly considered a core and legitimate channel of public voice. From this perspective, a group's seemingly static choice of militancy over many years may be seen in a more dynamic light.

5. Wolford (2003) also encountered this bold sense of entitlement in her study of the Movimento dos Trabalhadores Rurais Sem Terra (Movement of Landless Rural Workers, or MST) in southern Brazil. The MST settlers saw geographic mobility as a right because of historical resettlement and "an imaginary of unlimited land that rightfully belonged to anyone who worked it" (162).

6. *Traficante* is also an epithet directed at settlers judged to be invading lands for financial gain rather than a need for a home.

The Innovators, by contrast, are driven by a sense of mission and make a break from the uninspired tactics of their own Old Guard parents. The Innovators emerged in the mid-1990s in a fashion similar to that of the Next Generation, meaning that many had grown up in invasion communities and relied on a flexible combination of legal and extralegal strategies. Unlike the Next Generation, however, the Innovators reject violence entirely, employ creative and technology-oriented tactics, and seek to organize movements aimed at broader societal transformation (e.g., Encantada). Their goals include not only material gain—housing—but also a nonmaterial activist agenda and a sense of mission.[7] Prone to more consensus-oriented leadership structures, Innovators believe that "we must be different or we will fail," and often pursue even more ambitious goals than their Next Generation "cousins," though typically with more realistic assessments of political obstacles.[8]

Table 1.1 summarizes the key differences among the three organizational types. I divide the characteristics between *identity traits* (Mainwaring 1987; Melucci 1988; Dalton and Kuechler 1990; Schönwälder 2002, 17–19), crystallized through framing (Snow et al. 1986; Snow and Benford 1988), and *repertoire traits* (Tilly 1995; Tarrow 1998, 20), which summarize each group's preferences in terms of tactics (specific methods of demand-making) and strategies (broad categories of tactics).

Types of Strategies for Acquiring Neighborhood Services

In addition to identifying old and new types of organizations based in part on the rigidity or flexibility of their strategic preferences, a full explanation of organizational strategy requires additional work on concept formation in terms of the strategies themselves. In their review of resource mobilization theory, McAdam, McCarthy, and Zald (1988, 726–27) note that little systematic attention has been paid to social movement tactics despite the importance of strategy to the resource mobilization approach. In recent years, however, the subject has received increased scrutiny (Escobar and Alvarez 1992; Munck 1995; Ganz

---

7. In order to differentiate between the core objectives of each organizational type, I describe the Old Guard and the Next Generation as focused principally or exclusively on "material" objectives, while the Innovators seek to accomplish both "material and activist" objectives. This generalization usefully differentiates types of organizations on an important dimension, but may fail to capture nuances among different kinds of material objectives. For an alternative perspective on how settlers conceptualize their material needs, see Powers (2001, 87–109).

8. Innovators can be seen as part of the broader growth and maturation of Latin American social movements, which Vanden (2007) argues is generating new repertoires of action based on a nonauthoritarian and participatory political culture.

Table 1.1 Types of invasion organizations

		Type of organization		
		Old Guard	Next Generation	Innovator
Identity traits	Outlook	Pragmatic	Sense of entitlement	Sense of mission
	Objectives	Material	Material	Material and activist
	Leadership experience	Veteran	Novice	Novice
	"Motto"	"Win some, lose some."	"We will succeed."	"We must be different or we will fail."
Repertoire traits	Strategic flexibility	Rigid	Flexible	Flexible
	Tactics	Old	Old	New
	Violence use	Yes	Self-defense only	No
	Technology use	No	Rare	Yes

2000; Jasper 2004). William Gamson (1990, 41–49) was the first to explore these issues in depth and in relation to movement success.[9] Gamson identifies three key choices that confront all movements. Movements must choose between: (1) single issue demands and multiple demands; (2) antiestablishment demands and conformist demands; and (3) influencing elites and replacing elites. Gamson finds that groups that focus their efforts on a single demand are more likely to succeed than those with a complex agenda. Further, those who face entrenched antagonists are more likely to fail, especially those who refrain from using violence.

Gamson's framework appears to provide a reasonable starting point, given that the choice between antiestablishment and conformist demands confronts all Latin American invasion organizations. Examination of even a small number of these organizations, however, reveals that in this context, Gamson's dimensions provide little of the conceptual differentiation needed to identify causal mechanisms across cases with varying outcomes. In the first place, these organizations

9. Additionally, Hirschman's classic *Exit, Voice, and Loyalty* (1970) describes three major options that are relevant to the menu of strategic possibilities facing invasion organizations, but his framework only roughly fits the context of informal settlements. To begin with, nearly all squatter settlements *begin* with an "exit" strategy, meaning that the group has temporarily opted out of the existing rules of the game in their illegal seizure of land and (typically) their theft of electricity. Subsequent militant demands might be loosely described as "voice," and clientelism could often be fairly characterized as "loyalty," but taken as a whole, Hirschman's formulation does a poor job of capturing variation in organizational strategy.

automatically begin their existence with a decidedly antiestablishment act: an illegal invasion. Further, nearly all such organizations make multiple demands, even if they make them sequentially, and virtually no such organizations seek to replace elites. Invasion organizations do differ markedly in the conformity of their demands, but as we shall see, this difference is less of a dichotomy and more a question of how organizations move back and forth between antiestablishment (what I call "militant") and conformist demands. Thus, Gamson's pioneering work on the relationship between movement strategy and movement success offers a good example of an element of the classic social movement agenda that requires further development before we allow McAdam, Tarrow, and Tilly to "close the book" on this literature.

Additional unresolved questions emerge from Sidney Tarrow's (1998) argument that "opportunities and constraints" either invite or prohibit contentious politics. When the costs of organizing are high (e.g., the threat of repression), then the perceived consequences of inaction must be equally high to overcome a reluctance to act. Hence, resources *external* to the organization explain mobilization. Yet we see cases where settlers *not* facing high costs of inaction take big risks, *and* we see cases of settlers who face little threat of reprisal ignoring what seem to be golden opportunities to consolidate earlier gains. Either the settlers are irrational or misinformed, or some additional piece of the puzzle is missing. Articulation of the missing "analytic puzzle piece" requires a new set of labels to conceptualize organizational strategies of invasion organizations.

While previous work on Latin American squatter tactics (e.g., Stokes 1995) emphasizes the relevance of the legality of the strategies employed, empirical study of invasion neighborhoods in Lima and Quito reveals the importance of also identifying the autonomy of organizational strategies. Table 1.2 shows how organizational strategies can be classified in terms of their *legality* (legal vs. extralegal) and their *autonomy* (self-sufficient vs. externally dependent) to yield four distinct types: *rogue* strategies of seizing resources, *militant* strategies of demanding resources, *conformist* strategies of soliciting resources (often through clientelist relationships), and *bootstrap* strategies of buying resources.[10] While previous attention to the legality dimension underscored key differences among strategies, the introduction of the autonomy dimension not only reveals additional differences, but also highlights surprising commonalties among strategies. For example, the seemingly disparate rogue and bootstrap methods of service

10. Although this original conceptualization proved the most useful for the present study, there are many other ways to conceptualize strategy. For example, in his discussion of strategy analysis, Jasper (2004, 5–6) offers a conceptual vocabulary including player complexity, goals, arenas, resources and skills, official positions, and audience.

Table 1.2   Types of strategies for acquiring neighborhood services

| | | Legality of strategy | |
		Extralegal	Legal
Autonomy of strategy	Externally dependent	Militant (demanding resources)	Conformist (soliciting resources)
	Self-sufficient	Rogue (seizing resources)	Bootstrap (buying resources)

acquisition are both self-sufficient strategies—a key observation for under-standing the impact of privatization on available strategy choices, as a fully privatized service cannot typically be acquired through either militant demands or conformist solicitations directed at the government.

The Strategy Life Cycle

Based on ten case studies, qualitative analysis yields a *strategy life cycle* that synthesizes the strategy preferences of new types of invasion organiza-tions. Combined with paired-case comparisons and process tracing (George and McKeown 1985) of neighborhood-level cases, analysis of both invasion organi-zations and organizational strategies reveals how types of organizations share a common menu of strategies but differ in their preferences and methods of strategy selection.

Old Guard organizations have clear and consistent strategy preferences: while such organizations may sometimes "cross over" to use other methods, in general *either* legal methods (soliciting and buying) *or* extralegal methods (seizing and demanding) dominate their strategy choices. As noted above, these strong preferences led Stokes to characterize Old Guard individuals as either "clients" or "radicals."

By contrast, the Next Generation and the Innovators follow a dynamic strategy life cycle. These groups initiate their life cycle with rogue seizures of land and services. They soon begin using militant protest and pressure tactics to demand additional services and legal recognition. Organizations then fluctuate between militant strategies and conformist strategies, such as formally soliciting govern-ment agencies or establishing exchange-based relationships with politicians. Finally, a few invasion organizations give up on the government and manage to "pull themselves up by their bootstraps" by building the needed infrastruc-ture themselves and paying for service provision.

Figure 1.1 illustrates the archetypal trajectory of this strategy life cycle. The actual path of a Next Generation or Innovator organization is messier, and

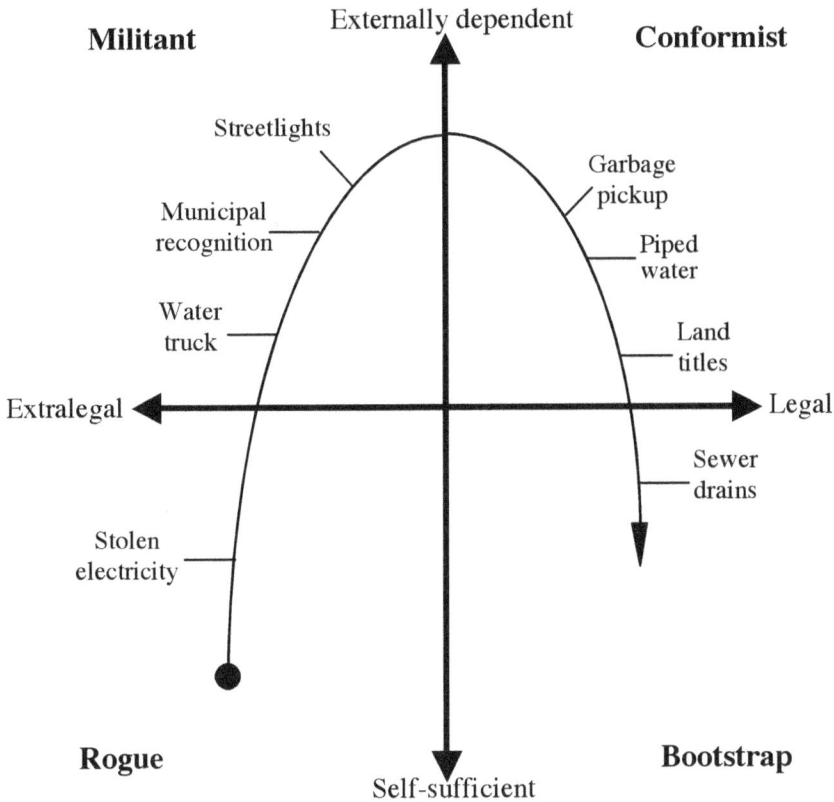

Fig. 1.1   Archetypal trajectory of an organization's strategy life cycle

involves changes in direction and sometimes-simultaneous activity in two or more quadrants of the figure. Nonetheless, figure 1.1 still usefully portrays the linear trend that typifies the general pattern of strategy choices.

The reasons for this pattern of strategy selection are threefold. First, changes in settler identity across organization types (see table 1.1) facilitate such changes. While Old Guard rigidity prohibits such strategic dynamism, the flexibility of newer organizational types makes variation in strategic preference possible.

Second, these changes in the framing of settler identity also make the life cycle of strategy selection more likely. While the pragmatic attitudes of veterans make them more likely to "stay with what they know," the bold sense of entitlement of novice Next Generation leaders makes them willing to indiscriminately employ all the tactics of the older generation, as they are convinced they will succeed; therefore, for example, they feel they need not fear alienating political allies with disruptive protests. The Innovators exhibit a different kind of boldness, and two traits make them even more likely to employ a dynamic combination of strategies: they *intend* to be different from the Old Guard and their creative innovation of new tactics yields highly diverse strategies.[11]

And third, since the 1990s the political opportunity structure (Tarrow 1998, 19–20) has changed in ways that make certain strategies better suited for certain demands than in the past. As noted above, the spread of neoliberalism altered the menu of strategic options available to settlers both through privatization and through transformation of the role of political parties. For example, in Peru, the 1997 privatization of electricity largely eliminated the option of employing militant demands to obtain electricity service.

This economic change occurred in the wake of the 1990 collapse of Peru's two previously dominant political parties—the center-left Alianza Popular Revolucionaria Americana (American Popular Revolutionary Alliance, or APRA) and the center-right Acción Popular (Popular Action, or AP)—which were replaced by Cambio 90, the personalist vehicle of President Alberto Fujimori. Whereas previous partisan alliances with either APRA or AP had provided Lima settlers with long-term, ideologically grounded guidance, the new clientelist bargains with Cambio 90 were unpredictable, often short lived, and owed allegiance not to an ideology or a political machine, but to an individual candidate prone to sometimes volatile policy shifts. Ecuador presents another case of growing volatility, with cumulative disruptions to the political order culminating in presidential overthrows in 1997, 2000, and 2005. Even prior to these momentous shifts, however, the once reliable position of establishment parties like the center-left Democracia Popular (Popular Democracy, or DP) had begun to erode, making partisan alliances less of a sure bet for fledgling invasion communities.

This new variability in relationships between neighborhood organization and politicians increased the importance of strategic flexibility. Further, the services needed by new settlements roughly follow the chronological order sketched in figure 1.1. Hence, there are theoretical reasons to believe that strategic diversity works better in the new political context, and that the strategy life cycle may work particularly well.

EXPLAINING ORGANIZATIONAL SUCCESS: NEIGHBORHOOD REGIME
TYPE AND THE NEIGHBORHOOD SERVICE ACQUISITION MODEL

The comparison of Rosales, Oasis, and Encantada also exhibited a contrast in the success or failure of their service demands. In the Rosales case, strategic

---

11. In his study of protest and politics in Italy, Tarrow (1989) argues that movement cycles are triggered by tactical innovation. The present study associates the evolution of organizational

rigidity failed to deliver services, but in the latter cases strategic fluidity fared much better. Oasis and Encantada acquired several needed services before their organizations declined, but only Encantada was able to extract itself from this moribund state and continue to win services. In all three cases, however, crucial factors external to the organizations also shaped opportunities for service demands to succeed.

Efforts to explain the success or failure of social movements to achieve their goals have tended to emphasize factors either external or internal to the movement. In the broadest sense, these two competing perspectives are captured by political opportunity structure theory and resource mobilization theory, which many scholars have merged into the more unified political process approach. Olson's (1965) classic work on collective action focuses on individuals—arguably "internal" factors within a movement—yet scholars disagree on whether internal or external factors dominate in helping individuals overcome, for example, the free-rider problem. Resource mobilization scholars, such as Lipsky (1968) and McCarthy and Zald (1977), attribute the potential of social movements to internal organizational features and resources. Piven and Cloward (1977) argue that this potential is highest in an informal movement, but they share the same emphasis on internal factors.

By contrast, opportunity structure theorists like Kitschelt (1986) and Tarrow (1998, 86–89) deemphasize internal factors and focus on external keys to mobilization, such as shifts in ruling alignment, influential allies, and access to participation. Tarrow's "cycles of contention" argument (141–60), for example, asserts that although a particular organization's resources may appear to play an important role in its success, a more holistic perspective recognizes that such success is in fact driven by national and international waves of collective action, whose decisive impact can only be viewed "from a distance." In this study, I argue that from a political process approach (McAdam 1982; Haber 1996), an emphasis on both external dimensions of opportunity and internal organizational factors can successfully explain why demands for neighborhood services either succeed or fail.[12]

---

type with this kind of innovation, but does not claim that such innovation actually triggers the change; rather, I hold that innovation constitutes a measurable change indicative of the new movement organizations.

12. McAdam's approach has appealed to an increasing number of scholars studying Latin America. Franceschet (2004), for example, argues that the successes of Chilean feminist movements were determined by both external opportunities and internal decisions about framing. For an overview of how the resource mobilization, political process, and cultural-cognitive schools of social movement theory diverge in their conceptualizations of social movement organizations, see Caniglia and Carmin (2005).

Types of Neighborhood Regimes

Just as the concept of regime type helps us understand political changes at the national (e.g., Linz and Stepan 1996, 38–65) or municipal (e.g., Pecorella 1987; DiGaetano 1989; Harrigan and Vogel 2000, 229–30) level, neighborhoods founded by organized land invasion routinely exhibit regime characteristics. In fact, understanding these neighborhood regimes can make a crucial contribution to understanding outcomes. In many urban neighborhoods, in both rich and poor countries, neighborhood leadership structures are irregular and are viewed as unimportant. In the context of Latin American squatter settlements, however, precarious living circumstances and an often hostile or even violent municipal regime combine to make the local invasion organization the sole neighborhood governance structure through which residents channel all administrative matters (Murakami 2000, 51–56). The term "neighborhood regime" thus refers to the invasion organization itself.

In *Regime Politics*, Clarence Stone (1989, 6) defines urban regimes as "the informal arrangements by which public bodies [local governments] and private interests function together in order to be able to make and carry out governing decisions," which include managing conflicts and responding to social changes in the community. In a separate study of major U.S. cities, Stone (1987, 272–74) describes three types of urban regimes: corporate, progressive, and caretaker. While theoretically useful in the U.S. context, these types provide little analytic insight into squatter settlements, but Stone's more general definition of regimes offers an excellent starting point for conceptualizing neighborhood regimes in Latin America. Stone's decision to leave conceptual room for variation in degree of power concentration, as well as the inclusion of nonelected actors, resonates with the limited exploration of such issues in Lima's informal housing settlements (Panfichi 1997).

Building on this limited body of relevant theory, table 1.3 demonstrates how regime type can be usefully conceptualized at the neighborhood level in terms of *organizational inclusiveness* (power-sharing vs. power-concentrating) and *organizational competitiveness* (competitive vs. noncompetitive).

Although most invasion neighborhoods have nominally democratic leadership structures, such as community elections, classifying neighborhood regimes as authoritarian, electoral, democratic, or consensual communicates critical differences in the actual governing practices of each organization. An *authoritarian* neighborhood regime may have regular elections, but in a fashion similar to Mexico under the Partido Revolucionario Institucional (Institutional Revolutionary Party, or PRI), the regime is fundamentally noncompetitive and decision-making power is highly concentrated. In an *electoral* neighborhood regime, however,

Table 1.3   Types of neighborhood regimes

		Organizational competitiveness	
		Competitive	Noncompetitive
Organizational inclusiveness	Power-sharing	Democratic	Consensual
	Power-concentrating	Electoral	Authoritarian

neighborhood elections offer settlers a genuine opportunity to install new leaders, though leadership shifts can be polarizing due to the tendency to hoard power and organizational assets. A national-level parallel here would be Chile between 1958 and 1973, during which time consecutive elected presidents polarized the country's politics (Power 2002, 249–53). In a *democratic* neighborhood regime, elections likewise allow for substantive shifts in leadership, but decision-making power is more diffuse, making power transfers less likely to divide the organization; this echoes the cordial shifts in power between Acción Democrática (Democratic Action) and the Partido Social Cristiano (Social Christian Party, or COPEI) in Venezuela between 1968 and 1988 (see Levine and Crisp 1999, 382–86). Finally, *consensual* neighborhood regimes, as one would expect, make decisions more often via consensus, but despite regular elections, power rarely or never changes hands; a national-level illustration of the latter phenomenon is Japan's Liberal Democratic Party, which ruled continuously from 1955 to 1993 despite free and fair elections.[13] Hence, my conceptualization focuses on dimensions quite distinct from those of Stone, while echoing his emphasis on the informal governing rules rather than the formally defined (and sometimes irrelevant) institutions.

The Neighborhood Service Acquisition Model

While substantive success varies depending on the objectives of each group, William Gamson (1990, 28–37) argues that we should measure success not "along the way," but rather at the "endpoint of a challenge." Such endpoints are marked when a challenging group ceases to exist or ceases mobilization, or when the group is accepted by its antagonist as a valid interest group representative and is dealt with as such. But although Gamson defines social movement success, he does not explain how it is achieved. Tarrow (1998, 76–80) goes further and identifies variables that contribute to organizational success, but does not theorize about specific patterns of how these variables interact to shape outcomes.

---

13. The Liberal Democratic Party continued to dominate until 2000 via a coalition government, but party hegemony had begun to decline.

As noted earlier, political opportunity structure theorists place great causal weight on external keys to mobilization, but despite the limited work done on organizational strategy, resource mobilization theorists widely accept the claim that—as an outgrowth of organizational resources and features—the methods used to demand objectives have a clear impact on whether the objective is achieved. Empirical evidence presented in later chapters underscores the claim that neighborhood regime type (another internal factor) also plays a role, but this claim finds less support in existing literature. Eckstein and Wickham-Crowley (2003, 9) argue that we should expect regime type to have some effect on movement success related to subsistence issues ("social consumption") because democratic regimes must be somewhat responsive to people's most basic needs. For example, Sen (1999) points out that only nondemocratic regimes permit famine. But subnational work on regimes, such as the U.S. urban politics literature, has focused much less on social movements.

In figure 1.2, I present the *neighborhood service acquisition model*, which shows how the political opportunity structure acts on three key internal factors to shape the success or failure of demands for services.[14] The left-hand column of external factors represents specifications of the dimensions of opportunity identified by Tarrow (1998, 76–80) and discussed above.

Beginning at the top of figure 1.2, we see that the *mayor's position* (hostile, neutral, or friendly) is an important determinant of *strategy type*. For example, a hostile mayor is more likely to repress the demands of the poor, making extralegal strategies less feasible.[15] Strategy type is also shaped by *organizational resources* (assets, practices, or skills) and whether the *service provider* is public or private. While groups with few assets will more likely depend on external actors, privatization of urban services can force neighborhoods to rely on self-sufficient strategies. In these respects, there are no automatic "winners" in terms of strategy choice. Rather, the success of a chosen strategy rests on how well it reflects existing constraints. For example, an asset-poor invasion group that elects a rogue strategy (extralegal, self-sufficient) of stealing resources in the face of a repressive right-wing government is likely to fail. Conversely, the same group might do well, materially speaking, to pursue a conformist strategy (legal, externally dependent) of selling their votes to the incumbent party.

---

14. Landowner resources and position do not appear in the model. While the landowner (if there is one) is a pivotal factor in the initial struggle for the land itself, the owner is typically not a central player in later struggles for services, except sometimes with respect to land titles. In the event that the owner accepts payment for title to the land, the owner is analytically represented as the (private) "service provider" in figure 1.2.

15. In his study of the MST, Ondetti (2006) argues that repression can sometimes engender even greater protest, which appears to have happened in the case of Pisulli (see chapter 3).

External factors   Internal factors   Dependent variable

Hostile/friendly
    mayor
                        Strategy type

Public/private
service provider
                        Organizational   Success/failure in
                        resources   service acquisition

Influential allies   Interaction

                        Neighborhood
                        regime type   Interaction
Local avenues
of participation

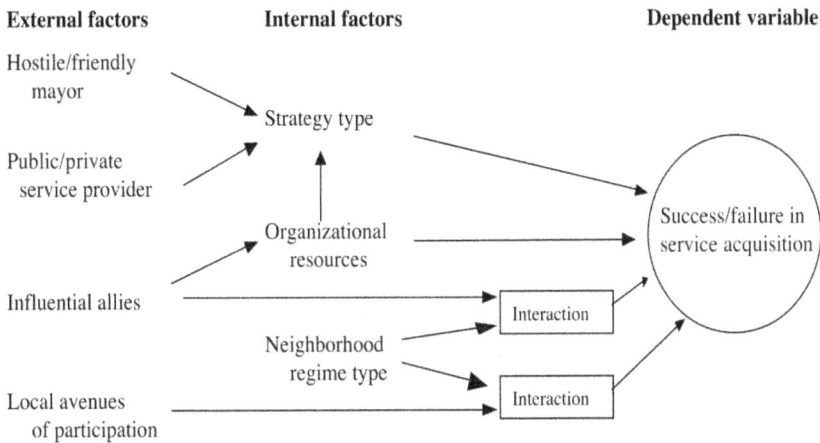

Fig. 1.2   The neighborhood service acquisition model

Looking at the bottom portion of figure 1.2, the causal effect of *influential allies* interacts with that of *neighborhood regime type*. The model predicts that the availability of influential allies is more likely to benefit noncompetitive organizations because they have more consistency in leadership. Predictable leadership makes groups better candidates for long-term partnerships with political parties and NGOs. Some NGOs prefer more democratic organizations, but I argue that noncompetitive groups (which are sometimes power-sharing groups) still have an overall advantage. Conversely, highly competitive organizations, whose leadership can experience 100 percent turnover as often as every two years, are less able to take advantage of the availability of allies.[16] Hence, in this respect, authoritarian and consensual organizations (see table 1.3) have the upper hand because they both generate predictable leadership. Similarly, the effect of *avenues of participation*—such as local elections, or a participatory institution for settlers to cooperate on infrastructure projects— also interacts with that of neighborhood regime type.[17] Opening up access to participation tends to help power-sharing groups who are well positioned to

16. Scholars of Latin America have long been interested in the advantages and pitfalls that popular movements encounter when forming alliances with more powerful actors, such as political parties. Attention has focused particularly on clientelist alliances (e.g., Holzner 2004; Wolff 2007), but in my model a variety of alliance types are considered.

17. In this study, *participation* generally refers to settler participation in neighborhood meetings, elections, and activities, such as protest marches or campaigning for political candidates. The study also discusses local *avenues of participation*, which refer to participatory opportunities external to the organization, such as district or metropolitan elections and participatory governance structures at the district level. For a discussion of different forms of participation among Lima settlement organizations, see Tanaka (1999, 108–13).

exploit this opening, but can hurt a power-concentrating group whose leader's grip on power is threatened by new avenues of participation and demand-making. In this regard, democratic and consensual organizations have an advantage.[18]

The model suggests that attention to the interaction of these external and internal factors will best explain the dependent variable of organizational success. Although the outcomes of individual demands are described and analyzed in fine-grained detail in chapters 3–5, the synthesis and analysis in chapter 6 relies on the necessarily imprecise dichotomy of the "success" or "failure" of demands. Although dichotomization importantly facilitates counting and comparison of a fairly large number of service demands (N = 132)—a process that generates valuable and unexpected insights—the significant drawbacks of a crude, all-or-nothing conceptualization necessitate careful use of qualitative inferences at every stage of the analysis. An important element not captured by the model is the impact of previous successful or unsuccessful demands. Thus, the model omits direct attention to how a group's past track record affects their current chance of success, which relates to the third outcome in question: *organizational survival*. For this part of the book's argument, we turn to a third set of conceptual and analytic tools.

EXPLAINING ORGANIZATIONAL SURVIVAL: ORGANIZATIONAL STAGES OF DEVELOPMENT AND THE SECURITY TRAP

By the early 2000s, the organizations of Rosales, Oasis, and Encantada were in very different conditions. While service demand failures had left the Rosales leadership bitterly divided, settler participation remained high, and the organization continued to seek services ineffectively. Oasis settlers, by contrast, had largely abandoned the organization because of its success (explained below). Only in Encantada had the neighborhood organization managed to succeed *and* consolidate. Why do many movement organizations promptly collapse after winning their most significant victory, while a smaller number of such groups endure, building on that victory to consolidate additional gains for the community?

I explain contrasting trajectories of community participation and organizational survival in order to shed light on a collective action puzzle: the interplay of selective incentives and mixed motives. I find that movement collapse is often

---

18. The complexity of the model suggests the detail with which data describing individual demands will be presented and analyzed. Ultimately, however, the model remains a simplification and generalization of complex processes that have vexed scholars of contentious politics. O'Brien and Li (2005), for example, grapple with the nuances of indirect and mediated consequences driven by both popular action and openings provided by sympathetic elites.

explained by a concept I call the "security trap," wherein settlers, after years of struggle, obtain their most important objective—property security, usually in the form of a legal land title or purchase agreement (similar to a mortgage)—thereby eliminating the key selective incentive that had motivated high levels of collective action. Despite the continued existence of less pressing incentives, such as infrastructure improvements, the fulfillment of the chief selective incentive leads to a precipitous decline in participation and a moribund organization incapable of achieving neighborhood objectives even under favorable circumstances.

Some land invasion neighborhoods, however, achieve property security and then continue to thrive, because—despite the disappearance of the key selective incentive—either authoritarian coercion or a combination of mixed motives sustains settler participation. In the latter scenario, settler participation is motivated both by an altruistic community mission and by remaining incentives, which, though important, are not as pressing as the need for property security. With respect to the collective action literature, this study thus not only engages the debate over selective incentives and mixed motives, but also, in the context of Latin American land invasion organizations, proposes an answer to the question of when mixed motives matter most: they matter immediately following the acquisition of property security, at which point some incentives remain, but none as powerful as the need to obtain a land title.

Straightforward coercion can sometimes motivate participation indefinitely, but analysis points to three principal factors that, in the absence of coercion, can lead to organizational consolidation in the face of the security trap: tactical innovation, democratic neighborhood governance, and mixed motives that combine material and nonmaterial goals. Innovator organizations thus appear ideally poised to exploit the intersection of mixed motives and the security trap, since they benefit from an identity grounded in these traits. Any movement can theoretically attempt to harness the power of mixed motives, but the Innovators seem especially good at it because of the synergy of tactical innovation and democratic governance, which enhances settlers' enthusiasm for their altruistic agenda. Innovators consider themselves activists with a greater mission, and this sense of higher purpose compensates for the fulfillment of their major selective incentive.

Collective Action, Popular Organizations, and Tactical Innovation

What starting points does social movement theory offer to the analysis of the organizational survival of Latin American popular movements? Scholars have paid considerable attention to movement emergence (e.g., Mainwaring 1987; Eckstein 1989; Foweraker 1990) and strategy selection as well as the success or failure of movement organizations to achieve their objectives (e.g., Assies, Burgwal, and Salman 1990; Escobar and Alvarez 1992; Roberts 1998). Fewer scholars have focused on movement trajectories over time (e.g., W. Gamson 1990; J. Gamson 1995; Klandermans 1997), though the need for analysis of "later developmental phases of collective action" has been articulated by McAdam, McCarthy, and Zald (1988, 728-29), McAdam, Tarrow, and Tilly (2001, 42), and Oliver and Myers (2003, 20-21). In this section, I draw on the work on collective action by Olson (1965), Elster (1989), and Udéhn (1993), literature on popular organizations by Levine (1992), and McAdam's (1983) claims about tactical innovation.

Understanding organizational survival requires that we examine how movements sustain collective action through the high and low points of their trajectories. Given the lasting impact of Olson's *The Logic of Collective Action* (1965), discussions of what sustains movements have often focused on self-interest. For example, in their recent analysis of collective action in six Latin American cities, Roberts and Portes (2006) describe twelve popular movements whose members participate in large part due to self-interest. Many such studies suggest the salience of Olson's finding that collective action hinges on whether participants can be selectively rewarded with divisible goods (material or otherwise), or at least punished for failure to contribute or participate.

Brian Barry (1970) and Jon Elster (1989), however, have argued that collective action could be best explained by *mixed motivations*, meaning that participants were motivated not only by self-interest but also by altruism, morality, and social norms. In his refutation of Olson's economic logic, Lars Udéhn (1993, 251-53) draws on Elster's work to argue convincingly that these alternate motives play a prominent role in explaining most collective action. For example, Guidry (2003, 196) found that movement success depended in part on a group's capacity to build a sense of citizenship, rather than an exclusive focus on material needs. A central trait of Innovator organizations is their commitment to mixed motives. In this way, the success of the Innovators will affirm the value of Elster's and Udéhn's work and also suggest that mixed motives may be increasingly important as a movement organization matures.

Scholars such as Levine and Mainwaring (1989) and Levine (1992) have explored the relevance of mixed motives to popular organization success in the context of Latin America's Comunidades Eclesiales de Base (base Christian communities, or CEBs). Although CEBs emerged in the context of the dictatorships of the 1970s (Bruneau and Hewitt 1989, 39), while the Innovators emerged in the context of neoliberalism and democratization in the 1990s, CEBs nonetheless offer a valuable point of comparison. For both types of popular organizations, "political" agendas are usually focused on basic needs, and the spark for the nonmaterial agenda comes from elites—either educated invasion leaders or priests, nuns, and church lay agents (Levine 1992, 48–49). Levine argues that religious motives, not material ones, best facilitate the emergence of enduring solidarities that sustain the organization in the long run: "Failure has been more likely when pastoral agents attempted to encourage the formation of highly politicized groups from the outset. Success has been more common in cases where religion and community were principal initial goals" (46). Unlike the Innovators, the non-material agenda of the CEBs *preceded* the material agenda that often followed (50), which Levine finds to be a powerfully effective sequence, concluding that "early decisions to give the groups a multiple character (simultaneously religious, social, and economic) made for more complex solidarities and greater resilience in the face of setbacks" (358). The experience of the CEBs will thus suggest that the sequence of mixed-motives development observed in this study's cases could be suboptimal with respect to movement resilience.

Doug McAdam (1983, 752) analyzes the U.S. civil rights movement as a "process of tactical interaction between insurgents and their opponents" and argues that movement participants overcome a lack of institutional power through tactical innovation; but as movement opponents adapt to the new tactics, he asserts, insurgents must continuously create new tactics. McAdam shows that tactical creativity helps explain the success of movement demands, but then might successful innovation actually hasten movement decline via the security trap? For many groups it does, but the Innovator case studies in chapter 5 not only confirm the value of McAdam's concepts, but also point to an additional benefit of tactical innovation: aside from augmenting the success of specific demands, the pattern of innovation actually helps sustain participation as enthusiasm for being part of an Innovator organization builds. The case studies will thus uphold McAdam's finding while also suggesting a new application of his argument to the issue of participation and movement survival.

Organizational Stages of Development

Explaining how invasion organizations acquire the services they need also helps us understand why invasion organizations either survive or gradually collapse. A key cause of organizational decline and failure can be summarized by what I call the *security trap*. As described above, when the primary goal of security seems achieved, many organizations wane despite other unmet needs. Yet some organizations obtain security and then endure, rather than collapse. How do they escape the trap?

A related quandary has been studied in the U.S. literature on identity politics. In his article "Must Identity Movements Self-Destruct? A Queer Dilemma," Joshua Gamson (1995) raises a similar dilemma. In the case of identity politics, Gamson shows that queer movements face a tension between their goal of breaking down discriminatory social boundaries and the fact that total success in eliminating such boundaries would make the organization irrelevant. Although instructive, Gamson's case applies only loosely to the invasion context, as invasion organizations often break down long before they are even close to acquiring needed neighborhood services.

Klandermans (1997) also examines internal factors, including the tension between moderate and militant activists within the organization. Yet in the cases I examine, such tensions typically arose early on, well before any objectives were accomplished, and internal tensions sometimes led to a more robust organization as the group learned to deal with problems internally before tackling external opponents. Still, many invasion organization leaders did cite internal problems as a major issue, so Klandermans's observation may have some relevance.

In his study of student social movements, Eric Hirsch (1990) argues that internal democracy in a movement organization increases member willingness to make a lengthy or risky commitment to the movement. Yet in the context of Peru and Ecuador, we see both democratic and nondemocratic organizations self-destruct. This may be part of the answer, but it does not offer a complete solution to the puzzle.

Instead, exploration of this important conundrum requires the use of a micro (at the level of the individual organization) longitudinal concept that I call the *organizational stages of development*. In the context of land invasion communities in Latin America, the organizational stages of development include:

1. *nascent* (invasion organization remains at risk of eviction, typically until recognized as a legal and representative entity by the district or metropolitan mayor);
2-A. *defeated* (organization evicted; may recover and try again);
2-B. *mature* (eviction no longer a threat; organization focused on acquiring services and property security);
3-A. *moribund* (property security leads to decline in participation and stagnation of service agenda; organization dying, but may never disappear completely);
3-B. *consolidated* (property security established without compromising organizational longevity; organization continues to pursue community objectives).

Beginning with its illegal founding, a *nascent* organization (see figure 1.3) remains at risk of eviction until recognized as a legal entity by the mayor. Groups steal electricity through illegal hookups and sometimes steal water by breaking open fire hydrants. While nascent organizations could be *defeated* by an eviction,

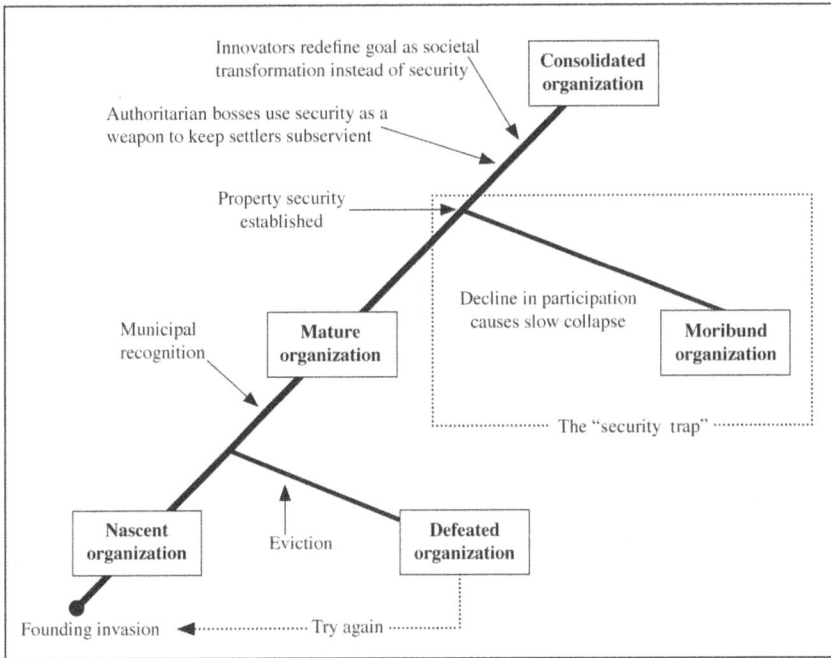

Fig. 1.3   Stages of development and the security trap

acquisition of some services is an important step toward demonstrating permanency, boosting settler confidence, and winning municipal recognition. Municipal recognition does not grant land ownership, but it establishes the organization's legal right to exist, which usually protects it from eviction, though pressure to leave often persists. Once an organization has acquired recognition, I characterize it as a *mature* organization; it is not likely to disappear. During this period, settlers are especially motivated to contribute to the process of seeking land titles, because the need for their participation is obvious; it is common to find titled homes adjacent to untitled homes, clear evidence that participation matters in determining who gains a title and who is left out. Mature organizations continue this struggle for services and most establish property security, but this can take anywhere from five to twenty-five years.

The Security Trap

And it is here that mature organizations confront the security trap. The achievement of security leads to a sharp decline in participation—now that settlers feel secure, they do not feel the need to contribute time or money. This leads to a *moribund* organization. With participation dropping steadily, the organization is dying, though it may never disappear completely. And so, ironically, when the primary goal of security seems achieved, the organization wanes despite unmet needs, such as clean water. Water and sewer benefits are less divisible than land titles, since street-by-street infrastructure does not automatically exclude free riders, but examples exist of whole streets left out due to a lack of organization, as well as individual families who never acquire service to their house because they fail to participate in collective efforts to finance connections from the main water line to individual houses (Valencia 2007, interview). Overall, however, the perception of water and sewers as collective goods contributes to the diminution of participation.

Yet some *consolidated* organizations obtain security but sustain participation and continue to pursue community objectives effectively. Figure 1.3 suggests the likelihood of linear development through the first two stages, at which point the "path" forks between two options: consolidated organizations that evade the security trap and moribund organizations that do not. The cases analyzed in this study conform to these stages, but alternate development patterns can occur. For example, consolidated organizations can become moribund, and moribund groups can become consolidated, though only the latter transformation is demonstrated empirically in this study (see chapter 5). What causes a mature organization to become consolidated rather than moribund?

Analysis of demands made by consolidated and moribund organizations helps solve the puzzle of the security trap. Two compatible explanations for this variation emerge. First, some (but not all) shrewd authoritarian bosses force settlers to stay involved in the organization. One way a boss can do this is by using the security trap as a weapon; he maintains a security monopoly in order to intentionally withhold security from individuals—all the land titles are "temporarily" held in the name of the organization. The local boss keeps everyone's title, always promising individuals their title if they work for the boss "just a few more months." Although such an organization is secure as a whole, client settlers remain trapped in a perpetual subservient role, thus preserving the organization.

Second, most (but not all) Innovators *evade* the trap by making security complementary to the group's mission of activism beyond its own community (i.e., they have mixed motives). This clever agenda setting means that rather than compromising the organization, security bolsters it because peer communities admire the Innovator as a successful role model whose tactics yield security, which then positively reinforces the Innovator's mission of helping other neighborhoods. Notably, leaders recognize the catch-22 they face if they actually deliver the goods. In interviews, Itchimbía and Encantada leaders acknowledged how winning the battle for property security can endanger their broader agenda

(Hernández 2002; Valencia 2005; Chamorro 2008). Thus, they work hard to inculcate a sense of mission in the membership, such that participation is not contingent on personal gain.

SUMMARY

This chapter presented related sets of conceptual foundations, analytic tools, and theoretical objectives. With respect to organizational strategy, a typology of approaches laid the foundation for qualitative analysis of the strategy life cycle. With respect to organizational success, a typology of neighborhood regimes as well as operationalization of dimensions of opportunity facilitated articulation of the neighborhood service acquisition model. With this model, analysis of individual service demands will rely on the synthesis of external and internal factors characteristic of political process theory. And with respect to organizational survival, the dynamic concept of organizational stages of development supported the analytic device of the security trap. Through examination of differing survival trajectories, this study will confirm both the value of longitudinal analysis and the importance of the classic social movement agenda to understanding substantive outcomes in the Latin American context.

2

Metropolitan Trends in Land Invasions:
Policy, Democratization, and Geography

The book began with a contrast among three Lima invasion organizations, intended to highlight differences in the study's major outcomes. My purpose here is to introduce the study's two metropolitan contexts, so I begin with a contrast between the now familiar case of Oasis (in Lima) and the new case of Camino (in Quito). In 1994, a bold and enterprising group of two thousand Peruvian families invaded a stretch of public land in southern Lima. Relying on cheap and flimsy construction materials, they founded the illegal settlement of Oasis. Although the Oasis settlers encountered a number of setbacks, they rather swiftly obtained legal title to their illegally seized land. As the settlement grew, it was governed by a democratic neighborhood organization—which succeeded in acquiring electricity service (paid for out of the residents' own pockets)—but ultimately collapsed before it could acquire other services, such as piped water.

A 1990 invasion settlement called Camino a la Libertad (Pathway to Freedom), founded by five hundred families in Quito, differed from Oasis in several respects. The Camino settlers invaded privately owned land, built sturdier homes, were largely unsuccessful in their struggle for land titles, and were governed by an authoritarian neighborhood organization that both delivered a wide array of important services and consolidated its control of local neighborhood governance.

What accounts for these differences? At a glance, the contrast appears to demonstrate little more than the great diversity of outcomes among land invasion organizations and other types of urban movements. The sheer variety of these outcomes seems to point to the need for examining individual settlement organizations to identify varying causes of success and failure. Considering scholarship focused specifically on Latin American settlement formation and development, the merit of this approach is borne out by a number of valuable studies of specific neighborhoods (Godard 1988; Stokes 1991; Burgwal 1995; Flores, Lingán, and Cayo 2002; Sosa and Flores 2002). Some of the most influential studies (Collier 1976; Stokes 1995) have complemented a neighborhood focus with careful consideration of the role of the state, but only a few (e.g., Dietz 1998b) have integrated neighborhood- and metropolitan-level analysis.

Neighborhood-level factors cannot, however, account for a series of striking similarities that emerge when analyzing the land invasion phenomenon within each individual metropolitan context. Therefore, on the basis of data collected from ten invasion settlements in Lima and Quito, I argue that the differences between Oasis and Camino are illustrative of differing citywide trends. Despite great variation among invasion organizations in both Lima and Quito, a key difference emerges: Lima's organizations are more likely to get off to a strong start and then falter, while the success of Quito settlements is typically more gradual and often leads to long-term organizational survival. Examining neighborhood-level trends in building materials, organizational competitiveness, and demands for land and electricity also reveals surprising consistency within each metropolitan context. Neighborhood-level factors account for part of this variation. What broader factors help explain these citywide trends?

To answer this question, I begin with a brief overview of the evolving phenomenon of urban land invasions in Latin America, with specific attention to the institutional settings of Lima and Quito. I then describe and analyze six contrasts between the invasions and invasion organizations of the two cities. Although neighborhood-level factors contribute to these differences, three national or citywide factors emerge as important explanations of metropolitan trends: public policy, local democratization, and geography and climate. While city-specific findings represent an important contribution, they are most notable for the questions they leave unanswered. Public policy may help us understand organizational strategy and success outcomes with respect to land and electricity, but what explains variation with respect to demands for other services such as piped water and sewer drainage? And if public policy is such a powerful determinant, what explains the existence of organizations whose success or failure "goes against the grain" of their cities' policies? Hence, the conclusion that national- and metropolitan-level analysis can explain only a handful of outcomes in this context confirms the sustained importance of neighborhood-level factors.

Thus, the final part of the chapter outlines my research design for exploring these issues through the ten neighborhood case studies. I identify the universe of cases, describe the logic of city and neighborhood case selection, and specify which urban service demands will receive sustained analytic attention. Finally, I provide a brief overview of the ten case studies, each of which initiated between eight and eighteen analytically separate (though not causally independent) service demands.

LIMA: CENTRALIZATION UNDER FUJIMORI

Located in coastal Peru, metropolitan Lima is Latin America's fifth-largest city. A polluted sprawl of over seven million people, it is divided into forty-three districts characterized by great economic inequality and often uncoordinated governance. Urban planning tends to be spread across multiple overlapping public and semipublic agencies, many of which are national (rather than regional or local) in scope. The metropolitan area of Lima includes the province of Lima (the downtown Cercado district and forty-two other district municipalities) and the province of Callao (six district municipalities). These forty-nine districts, each with its own elected mayor and city council, exhibit striking contrasts between wealthy, working-class, and poor zones of the city. District governments are fiscally autonomous, but with only 10 percent of Peru's revenues in their hands, their capabilities are severely limited (Pease 1989; Huamán, Cubas, and Mora 1999, 189).

All but one of these mayor/council governments is responsible solely for its specific district. The Cercado district mayor and council (called the Provincial Council), however, also serve as the metropolitan mayor and council, and these citywide responsibilities tend to prevail over concerns particular to the Cercado district. The metropolitan mayor and council are often overruled by national agencies and undercut by Lima's many district governments. Despite these problems, they directly govern about 12 percent of the metropolitan area and exert uneven influence throughout the city.

After the 1968–80 period of military rule in Peru, Lima's district and metropolitan leaders were directly elected, and political decentralization formally ceded some responsibilities to the metropolitan government (Arnillas 1999). The national government, however, maintained informal control of service-related revenues and decisions (Arnao Rondán and Meza Carey 1990; Araoz and Urrunaga 1996). Coordination difficulties over the few services that were decentralized, such as street paving, fueled reluctance to decentralize further, but many of the forty-two district mayors worked together in the 1980s, paving the way (at times literally) for further political decentralization in the provinces in 1989 (Pease 1994, 112). During this period, district leaders sustained old patterns of unofficially authorizing settlements as a cheap way of dealing with continuing immigration from rural Peru (see Collier 1976).

In the 1990s local service provision became increasingly politicized as Fujimori's re-centralization of some responsibilities provoked political conflict with opposition mayors, especially the metropolitan mayor of Lima. Following Fujimori's *autogolpe* (self-coup) in 1992 (see Kenney 2004, 199–207), his administration wrote the 1993 constitution, which recentralized some government powers (Pedraglio 1995).[1] This shift was marked by near-constant conflict because district governments resented the reduction of their already limited decision-making and fiscal powers.

Between 2000 and 2002, Lima's municipalities began to reassert themselves, but with respect to levels of service provision the situation remained unchanged. Two decades of robust democratic competition at the local level had consolidated democracy at the district level, but the impact of that consolidation remained limited by the paucity of resources entrusted to municipal authorities. Ecuador also remained highly centralized during this period, but with one important exception: the capital city of Quito.

QUITO: DECENTRALIZATION UNDER DURÁN BALLÉN

Like Lima, Quito is characterized by stark economic inequalities and an authoritarian past. Since 1979, elected presidents have governed, but a pendulum of ideological shifts has defined national politics. From 1979 to 1996, the office of the presidency regularly swung back and forth between the Left and the Right.[2] After 1996, however, these shifts gave way to outright volatility, and Presidents Abdala Bucarám (1996–97), Jamil Mahuad (1998–2000), and Lucio Gutiérrez (2003–5) were all forced from office by mass mobilizations led by Ecuador's indigenous movement (Selverston-Scher 2001, 1). Following the 1970–79 period of military rule in Ecuador, Quito's municipal mayor and council were directly elected, but the national government controlled provision of most services. In 1993, however, the government of Sixto Durán Ballén (1992–96) created Quito's

---

1. For example, the 1993 constitution formally codified previous executive decrees that centralized power in the national executive and eliminated the brief 1989 episode of political decentralization at the provincial level.

2. Following the end of military rule, Ecuador was governed by the leftist Jaime Roldós (1979–81), the rightist León Febres Cordero (1984–88), the leftist Rodrigo Borja (1988–92), and the rightist Sixto Durán Ballén (1992–96). See Gerlach (2003, 81).

metropolitan government, which assumed responsibility for electricity, water, sewers, and titling throughout the Quito metropolitan area. The 1993 shift represented an increase in decentralization and was remarkable for its smooth implementation (Gangotena 1994, 39–42; F. Carrión 1995, 146–50).[3]

Under the new metropolitan government, Quito's 1.8 million people remained divided among the city's sixteen administrative districts, but in contrast to Lima's elected district leaders, Quito's district officials remained appointed and not directly accountable to voters (F. Carrión 1987).[4] In 2002, despite some successes with metropolitan-level decentralization, Quito was in the process of further decentralizing some service delivery all the way to the district level, in an effort to foster greater responsiveness in policy areas where a citywide perspective was not deemed as important (D. Carrión 1996, 278). Hence, at a time when Lima was becoming more centralized, Quito became more decentralized but with a weaker commitment to local democratization, meaning that leaders at the sub-metropolitan level (either district or neighborhood level) continued to be either appointed or selected without competition (Gómez 1995). These contrasting institutional settings provide fertile analytic ground for comparative analysis.

DIFFERENCES BETWEEN ORGANIZATIONS IN LIMA AND QUITO: QUICK SUCCESS AND GRADUAL DECLINE VERSUS GRADUAL SUCCESS AND LONG-TERM SURVIVAL

Although the similarities of urban land invasions in both Lima and Quito outnumber the differences, comparison of invasions and invasion organizations across metropolitan contexts reveals fairly consistent contrasts. Specifically, Lima's settlement organizations rely on cheaper building materials, which makes it easier to initiate an invasion attempt. Second, Lima groups find it relatively easy to invade public lands, while Quiteño settlers often find public lands difficult to seize. Lima invasion organizations also have an easier time acquiring

---

3. As late as 1994, the Ecuadorian government was continuing to centralize in most respects. Quito is the only city in the country whose spending exceeds its revenue. Thus, although Quito is decentralizing internally, it is also the hub of a larger centralization process (i.e., centralization in Ecuador fuels decentralization within Quito). The final 1993 version of the Metropolitan District Law decentralized most services, but also centralized management of urban transport and the preservation of the environment (Gangotena 1994). For a discussion of the broader context of decentralization in Latin America during this period, see Campbell (2003, 14–18).

4. In addition to these sixteen urban districts, Quito's metropolitan area also includes thirty-three outlying rural districts.

title to seized lands, but this makes these neighborhoods more susceptible to organizational decline precipitated by a drop in levels of participation by those who no longer fear losing their homes. Further, Lima settlements are more likely to employ self-sufficient strategies to acquire formal electricity service. Finally, neighborhood regimes in Lima are more likely to be competitive than their counterparts in Quito.[5]

Although individual cases often exhibit exceptions to citywide trends, two of the neighborhood-level cases examined in this study—Oasis de Villa (in Lima) and Camino a la Libertad (in Quito)—analytically capture all six key differences. Although my analysis is based on all ten of the study's neighborhood case studies, I refer to these cases because they illustrate the above contrasts most clearly. In the southern Lima district of Villa El Salvador, the neighborhood of Oasis was characterized by: (1) cheap and flimsy construction materials; (2) successful seizure of public land; (3) relatively easy acquisition of land titles; (4) subsequent organizational decline; (5) a self-sufficient, bootstrap strategy for acquiring electricity; and (6) a competitive democratic neighborhood regime. By contrast, in the northern Quito district of Cotocollao, the neighborhood of Camino was characterized by: (1) a quick shift from flimsy to durable building materials; (2) successful seizure of private land; (3) a difficult and largely unsuccessful struggle for land titles; (4) organizational consolidation; (5) externally dependent conformist strategies for acquiring electricity; and (6) a noncompetitive, authoritarian neighborhood regime. Although no other case studies so perfectly conform to these six cross-city contrasts, Oasis and Camino are nonetheless emblematic of common differences between the two metropolitan contexts, which are summarized in table 2.1.

The case studies examined in chapters 3–5 provide neighborhood-level insights into traits and outcomes like those of Oasis and Camino, and also describe various exceptions to these generalizations, but what country- and city-specific factors help explain these broad contrasts across metropolitan contexts? First, and most important, the public policies of Peru and Ecuador regarding land invasions, land titling, and electricity privatization account for trends in land ownership and titling outcomes, organizational survival, and strategies for acquiring electricity. Second, significant differences in each city's degree of local democratization have influenced neighborhood regime formation. And third, dramatic

---

5. These six metropolitan-level claims are an analytically and empirically more limited attempt at assessing causation than the study's claims at the neighborhood level. This study focuses principally on a systematic neighborhood-level analysis, where most of the variation with respect to organizational strategy, success, and survival occurs. Nonetheless, these findings at the metropolitan level provide a crucial backdrop for understanding causal relationships at the neighborhood level.

Table 2.1   General differences in invasion organizations by city

Outcome or trait	Lima	Quito
Relative quality of initial building materials	Flimsy	Sturdy
Relative ease of invading public land	Easy	Difficult
Relative ease of acquiring land titles	Easy	Difficult
Common organizational survival outcome	Moribund	Consolidated
Autonomy of strategy for acquiring electricity*	Self-sufficient	Externally dependent
Competitiveness of typical neighborhood regime	Competitive	Noncompetitive

*This refers to formal electricity provision. Settlement organizations in both cities usually rely on rogue strategies for initial acquisition of informal electrical hookups.

differences in geography and climate between Lima and Quito account for some of the physical challenges encountered by settlers as well as their responses.

Explaining Differences in Building Materials:
Arid Desert Versus Rainy Mountains

In Lima, the lack of rain permits settlers to build flimsy homes in precarious locations with relative safety, while in Quito mountain rainstorms force settlers to invest in sturdier and more expensive building materials. This simple difference has significant consequences in terms of the ease with which settlers establish a more or less permanent foothold on seized lands. Although settlers in both cities often employ the same flimsy plastic shelters in the early days of an invasion, Limeños and Quiteños differ when they build their first makeshift homes. In Lima, settlers can get away with using virtually any material that will stay in place, and some shantyhomes made with cardboard last for years. In Villa El Salvador's Lomo de Corvina region, for example, a 2002 physical comparison of neighborhoods founded in 1996 and 2001 discovered many homes that exhibited only minimal differences in terms of the building materials used despite a five-year difference in neighborhood age.

In Quito, however, such cheap construction is often soon destroyed by the mountain weather. In the 1995 Quito settlement of Itchimbía, for example, a fierce downpour during the neighborhood's first week of existence forced a one-day abandonment of the neighborhood, as the settlers' plastic shelters were wrecked. Geographic and climatic pressures thus force Quito settlers to invest in sturdier building materials as soon as possible. Since more durable homes better communicate a sense of permanence, one might infer that Lima's ramshackle homes would put them at a disadvantage in terms of avoiding eviction. The legacy of Peruvian dictator Juan Velasco Alvarado, however, creates just the opposite effect: Lima settlers have a relatively easy time claiming vacant lands, regardless of the durability or permanence of their initial homes.

Explaining Differences in Previous Land Ownership:
Pro-settler Policies Versus Metropolitan Decentralization

As mentioned above, the unique legacy of Peru's General Velasco (1968–75) makes it unusually easy for settlers to seize vacant—and especially public—lands, while in Quito a 1993 law decentralizing control of land zoning and titling to a new metropolitan government created incentives for the mayor to defend public land more vigorously than private land. Peru is notable for its history of dictatorships, but Velasco left a particularly significant legacy for invasion communities in the form of pro-squatter legislation that laid out the "rules of the game" for land invasions (Collier 1976, 113–16). The initial impetus for these laws was a tremendous influx of in-migration from rural Peru to urban Lima, which put continual pressure on consecutive governments to house, employ, and provide services to this burgeoning population. After more than three decades, these laws continue to afford protections to Peruvian settlers that their counterparts in Ecuador and the rest of Latin America lack.[6] For example, in Peru, mayors and landowners have only one day to forcibly evict settlers. After twenty-four hours, the settlers do not gain ownership of the land, but they do earn a critical legal shield against a forced eviction. Instead, the conflict becomes a judicial process of arbitration and negotiation. Unsurprisingly, the rules are not always respected, and many landowners hire thugs to intimidate or attack settlers well beyond the first twenty-four hours. Yet the importance of this legal protection persists.

While Velasco's legislation makes public lands in Lima ripe targets for invasion organizations, Quito organizations often attempt to occupy private land, in part because of an entrepreneurial city hall that vigorously defends its own (public) property while leaving landowners who lack political connections to fend for themselves. Putting aside the entrepreneurial dispositions of particular mayors (e.g., Quito's Jamil Mahuad, mayor from 1992 to 1998), Ecuador's 1993 creation of the Metropolitan District of Quito presents a major policy explanation for this trend. Prior to 1993, the authority of the Municipality of Quito was limited and its initiatives largely confined to the downtown district. With the 1993 experiment in decentralization, however, the national government

6. An exception may be Brazil, where President Lula da Silva has enacted pro-settler legislation, but this change remains too recent to permit assessment of its impact on Brazilian settlers.

decentralized political authority and functional responsibility (see Willis, Garman, and Haggard, 1999) for most major services, including land titling, to the new metropolitan government.[7] This was a major change, as the outlying areas of Quito had previously been governed by provincial administrators whose authority included pieces of the capital city as well as large rural areas outside Quito. These areas were now governed by an executive (the metropolitan mayor) and the new Metropolitan Council, which included fifteen at-large council members who exhibited a sustained interest in exercising their authority throughout the metropolitan area.

Public policies of settler protection in Peru and decentralization of zoning and titling authority in Quito played an important role in creating a situation in Lima where invasions have become routine and institutionalized, while in Quito they are considered aberrations. For example, most settlers in Lima are aware of the Velasco legislation and cite it as both justification and protection for their extralegal actions, while in Quito irate landowners blame the metropolitan government for failing to protect their assets (López 2002, interview; Pazmiño Navas 2002, interview). The commonplace nature of invasions in Lima also points to the lasting impact of the Velasco laws. Controlling for population, Lima's invasion rate between 1990 and 2005 was double to triple that of Quito.[8]

Two counterpoints deserve mention. First, in the case of Quito, the breadth and enthusiasm of opposition to land invasions exhibited by the first metropolitan mayor, Jamil Mahuad (1992–98), may lead to an exaggeration of the importance of decentralization policies. At the same time, efforts by three consecutive mayors (Mahuad, Roque Sevilla from 1998 to 2000, and Paco Moncayo from 2000 to 2008) to evict or relocate from public land a settlement known as Itchimbía support the claim that public lands in Quito are often vigorously defended. Second, in the case of Lima, a sustained effort by Villa El Salvador mayor Michel Azcueta to drive the settlement of Encantada off public land in 1996 (see chapter 5) appears to weaken the claim that public land is more easily invaded in Lima. Although the land was ultimately deemed public, it was being used by Agrosilves, a private agribusiness supported by the mayor. Azcueta also opposed the Oasis de Villa invasion of land zoned for future construction of a university (see chapter 4), but the point remains that public lands in Lima are easier to invade than private lands.[9]

7. This experiment was limited to the capital city.

8. This estimate is derived from the synthesis of government census data, news articles, and consultation with government officials and academics in Lima and Quito.

9. For example, in 2001–2, several invasions of public land in southern Lima attracted little media attention, while a pair of invasions of private land in northern Lima drew extended news coverage and opinion pieces defending private property.

Although Peru's settler-friendly laws clearly invite more frequent invasions, comparison across cities reveals remarkable similarities in the obstacles encountered despite contrasting institutional contexts. This surprising finding points to an important observation: while Peru's laws significantly ease the process of seizing land, they exert considerably less impact on subsequent struggles for services. The major exception, unsurprisingly, is the related struggle for land titles.

Explaining Differences in Acquiring Land Titles:
Pro-settler Policies Versus Metropolitan Decentralization

In Peru, President Fujimori implemented a plan to formalize two million informal homes, making it much easier for settlers to gain legal title to seized land than in Ecuador; in Quito, this trend was sometimes magnified by the metropolitan-level decentralization discussed above. Beginning with Velasco's creation of the Sistema Nacional de Apoyo a la Movilización Social (National System for the Support of Social Mobilization, or SINAMOS) in 1971, Peruvian settlement policy aimed both to promote development based on self-help and to create and sustain political support (Collier 1976, 106–11). Since then, four major policy changes have marked the evolution of regulations for settlements seeking land titles: the 1979 constitution's law guiding the expropriation of land, the 1993 constitution's amendment of those rules, the 1996 creation of the Comisión de Formalización de la Propiedad Informal (Commission on Formalization of Informal Property, or COFOPRI), and the 1999 Law of Prescriptions, which altered the rights of both settlers and owners of invaded lands.

Under the 1979 constitution, expropriation of land was permissible for public necessity, national security, and "social interest," which included formalization of informal property. The constitution also gave the Municipality of Lima responsibility for land titling in the capital city, and about thirty thousand titles were granted to informal landholders in the 1980s (Romero 2002, interview). The titling process remained politicized, however, and many titles were not well done in technical terms (e.g., measurement), which led to subsequent disputes over ownership of lands located in archaeological zones, privately owned parcels, and high-risk zones (e.g., steep hillsides).

The 1993 constitution retracted some of the power that had been given to the municipalities, especially the Municipality of Lima, which was controlled by opposition mayors throughout Fujimori's decade in office. It also eliminated social interest as a legitimate reason for expropriating land. This element was not replaced with a concrete alternative until 1996, with the creation of COFOPRI. Founded on the work of the Peruvian economist Hernando de Soto, COFOPRI was created with the ambitious goal of granting two million land titles to informal landholders in Peru. De Soto (1989) believed that these two million homes represented "sleeping capital" that could not be accessed because the homes existed outside the domain of formal property. With the granting of titles, de Soto (2000) hoped that settlers would, for example, use their homes as collateral to take out loans for various initiatives and thus stimulate the economy.

Although conceived as a nonpartisan effort, supporters and detractors agree that the Fujimori administration often employed COFOPRI for political ends. Said one COFOPRI official of Fujimori's political tampering in the district of Villa El Salvador, "[Villa El Salvador] was unusual because they had a [zoning] plan. They are right that we have messed up their plan. We really tried not to, we are a young organization and a political one and have made mistakes" (Romero 2002, interview).[10] Despite the intrusion of political favoritism into some of COFOPRI's work, the sheer scale of its operations meant that most titling occurred independently of the political process. Under COFOPRI, settlers suddenly found it much easier to acquire land titles. Although titling still required a detailed bureaucratic procedure, the fact that the process was run by an office deeply committed to de Soto's vision meant that settlers often had the state government in their corner. While some Lima invasion organizations complained that COFOPRI was unwilling to expropriate private land on behalf of settlers, the granting of over one million titles in five years suggests that most settlers had a quite easy time with the process.[11]

While the creation of COFOPRI was the most significant event in Peruvian settlement policy since Velasco, the 1999 Law of Prescriptions modified the rules to favor land invaders even more. Under the law, COFOPRI could declare previous ownership claims "extinct" after ten years under certain conditions. For example, if settlers could demonstrate a prior good-faith belief that they were invading public lands and if the landowner had not contested the settlers' occupancy at the time of invasion, then after ten years of occupation the settlers gained a right to the land. The settler would still have to pay the owner, but the owner would now be obliged to accept a price determined by the COFOPRI arbitration process. Further, although this new law technically applied only to certain settlements, it lent an air of legitimacy to all settlements over ten years old, helping them with their various legal struggles (Romero 2002, interview). By 2002 COFOPRI had already granted over one million titles—nearly half its goal—

---

10. For more details, see the Encantada case study in chapter 5.

11. Although titles are granted on a lot-by-lot basis, COFOPRI generally works on whole neighborhoods, so that settlers can be taken through the process as a group. Although some settlers fail to convince COFOPRI of the legitimacy of their claims, the organization gives settlers opportunities to improve their claims or to try again in the future.

and after a brief political scuffle between the provinces and the state under interim President Valentín Paniagua (2000–2001), it was back in business under President Alejandro Toledo (2001–6).[12]

In Ecuador, the 1993 creation of the metropolitan government of Quito decentralized land titling authority from the state to the city, but throughout the 1990s the situation on the ground remained unchanged, and informal property holders often waited fifteen years to establish legal ownership (Unidad de Suelo y Vivienda 2002). Many communities simply gave up, unwilling to persist in their efforts for such a minimal gain because they were already de facto home owners; without a title, however, it was difficult (and illegal) to sell land.[13] In November 2001, the metropolitan government created the Unidad de Suelo y Vivienda (Office of Land and Housing), which centralized the titling process in Quito and, in several important ways, emulated the mission of COFOPRI in Lima. In its first year, Suelo y Vivienda formalized thirty-three informal neighborhoods (not all of them founded by invasion), or about 8 percent of Quito's four hundred informal settlements; by 2003, it had begun the process of titling twenty-eight thousand informal houses (Unidad de Suelo y Vivienda 2002; *El Comercio*, 1/6/03). Suelo y Vivienda lacked the zeal of COFOPRI and often rejected settler petitions on the basis of lands being located on dangerous terrain or in ecological zones, but the office's creation in 2001 and subsequent work nonetheless marked a major change in Quito settlement policy. While it is too early to assess the impact of this recent policy change, the more general difference in ease of land titling has already had an effect on the survival of neighborhood regimes.

Explaining Differences in Organizational Survival:
Security Trap Versus Trap Evasion

Ironically, Peru's eagerness to formalize informal settlements through state-granted land titles often undermined the very organizations best positioned to pursue settler needs. Many Lima organizations found that once land titles had been acquired, attendance at community meetings and protest marches plummeted, as settlers no longer felt insecure, despite a continued lack of basic

12. After Fujimori's exile in November 2000, Peru's provinces demanded that the state return power (including titling authority) that had been centralized by Fujimori. To prevent COFOPRI from being disbanded, Paniagua created the Provincial Commission on Formalization, which in some ways gave the provinces what they wanted. Under Toledo, COFOPRI reopened its doors and continued to control the process of titling informal lands throughout Lima (Romero 2002, interview).

13. In the Next Generation case of Camino, four settlement leaders were imprisoned for the crime of selling land that did not legally belong to them. Although such prosecutions are rare, recognition of the sale of untitled land as a crime is commonplace.

services like piped water. This phenomenon is better explained at the neighborhood level in chapters 3–5, but because a key determinant of property security—land titles—varies by metropolitan context, it is important to comment briefly on the citywide trends.

After 1996 it became much easier to acquire land titles in Lima than in Quito. Unfortunately, this also made it easier for Lima organizations to lose momentum and even collapse, as acquisition of titles often led to a drop in rates of neighborhood participation. In Lima, for example, both the Oasis and Encantada invasion organizations invaded public land, acquired land titles, experienced a drop in participation, and became moribund, unable to pursue the remainder of their agendas, such as acquisition of piped water or a *comedor popular* (communal soup kitchen). In Quito, by contrast, both the Pisulli and Itchimbía organizations invaded public land, failed to acquire individual land titles, maintained high participation, and consolidated their control of neighborhood governance.[14]

Two additional factors also eroded some of Lima's invasion organizations: political violence and the paternalism and centralism of the Fujimori era. In the 1970s and 1980s, neighborhood "base" organizations in Lima were vibrant and productive (Dietz 1998b, 112–13), but terrorist attacks by Sendero Luminoso (Shining Path) often targeted local organizations not aligned with the guerrillas (Zapata 1996, 243–46). Sendero killed neighborhood leaders and destroyed community organizations through both attacks and fear. Said one settler whose organization was targeted, "We were caught between Sendero and the state forces, which also targeted us" (J. Valencia 2002, interview). Fujimori further weakened local organizations through centralization (Azcueta 2002, interview), and relationships between state officials and base organizations became more paternalistic (Dietz and Tanaka 2002, 216–18). The causal link between demands for titles and organizational survival outcomes requires a neighborhood-level analysis, but the fact remains that citywide trends play an important role in this causal process. In addition to provision of land titles, however, Lima and Quito also differ in their provision of electricity.

Differences in Electricity Service Demands: Private Versus Public Provision

Although settlers must often pay some or all the costs of publicly provided electricity, privatization both forecloses the possibility of successful externally dependent strategies (e.g., demanding or petitioning the government for

14. In the case of Pisulli (chapter 3), the organization acquired titles but individuals did not, while in the case of Itchimbía (chapter 5), the settlers eventually built self-help condominiums on new land but never acquired title to their original invasion site.

services) and also makes self-sufficient methods less feasible because of price hikes. Of the principal services sought by invasion organizations—electricity, water, sewer drainage, and land titles—only electricity was privatized in Peru, and none of these services was privatized in Ecuador (though in both countries titles to indisputably private lands are, in effect, "privately provided" by the legal owners, often through a judicial process).[15] Between 1999 and 2002, Ecuadorian presidents Mahuad and Noboa attempted to privatize electricity provision in Ecuador, but both efforts were foiled by political opposition from indigenous organizations, unions, and local governments (Gerlach 2003, 135, 215).[16]

In Lima, electricity provision was fully privatized in 1997, changing the menu of feasible strategy types available for demanding service.[17] Martín Pumar, Villa El Salvador mayor, complained in a 2002 interview, "Privatization of electricity hasn't improved anything. Now it's harder than before to get electricity." Prior to 1997, settlers could employ both externally dependent strategies (i.e., militant and conformist) and self-sufficient strategies (i.e., rogue and bootstrap), but with privatization only the latter could succeed, as private companies like Electro Lima and Luz del Sur could not normally be pressured into providing free or subsidized service. Given this contrast, we would expect to see no difference in the strategies for demanding electricity between Quito and pre-1997 Lima; after 1997, however, we would expect Quito settlers to continue using both self-sufficient and externally dependent strategies, while Lima settlers should begin to rely exclusively on rogue and bootstrap methods (or they should at least fail if they attempt a militant or conformist strategy). Further, we would expect even bootstrap strategies to become less feasible in post-1997 Lima because of privatization-driven price hikes, which make service unaffordable for many settlers (Inter-American Development Bank 2004). As the chapter 6 synthesis will make clear, with respect to demands for electricity these theoretical expectations were met by the ten neighborhood case studies. In short, out of nineteen efforts to acquire privately provided service, seven of nine self-sufficient attempts succeeded, but all the externally dependent attempts failed. This does not demonstrate that privatization constitutes the whole causal story, but it does suggest the importance of including this kind of national-level

15. Fujimori did move to privatize Lima's water and sewer drainage provision in the early 1990s, but the effort failed (Alcázar, Xu, and Zuluaga 2002), though he was successful in privatizing a large number of state-owned enterprises (Kay 1996, 61–69).

16. In November 2003, President Lucio Gutiérrez initiated partial privatization of the electricity sector through three-year management contracts for thirteen of the country's state-owned electricity distributors, but this did not include Quito (Energy Information Administration 2004).

17. The law initiating privatization was passed in 1992, and sale of state-owned electric companies began in 1994, but in the Lima districts examined in this study, full private control was not achieved until early 1997 (Inter-American Development Bank 2004). For a recent summary of the imposition of neoliberal privatization in Latin America, see Hershberg and Rosen (2006, 6–8).

factor in any analysis.[18] In addition to differences in service demands in Lima and Quito, the organizations themselves also differed with respect to the competitiveness of their neighborhood regimes.

Explaining Differences in Neighborhood Regimes: Local Democratization Versus Caciquismo

In Lima, the introduction of district-level democratic elections supported neighborhood-level democracy, but in Quito the rule of local bosses persisted in a context of appointed district administrators whose actions were often circumscribed by provincial—and later metropolitan—authorities. With respect to neighborhood regimes, this meant that Lima invasion organizations were more likely to have a competitive regime type (i.e., democratic or electoral), while their Quito counterparts were more likely to have noncompetitive regimes (i.e., consensual or authoritarian).

While district municipalities were granted significant responsibilities in the 1980s, Fujimori recentralized some of this authority, especially that of the metropolitan government of Lima, in the 1990s. By one count, Fujimori created as many as forty laws regarding taxes, licenses, and other minutiae that, cumulatively, reduced the power of the metropolitan government (Azcueta 2002, interview). Local-level democratization thrived, however, and all of Lima's districts maintained a two-decade string of fair and competitive local elections (Dietz and Tanaka 2002, 194). Further, with Fujimori's exit from Peruvian politics in 2000, Lima's districts slowly began to reverse some of the centralization of the 1990s as national-municipal government relations recovered.[19]

At the same time, there is reason to consider the possibility that municipal empowerment actually weakened neighborhood-level democratization. With the introduction of district-level municipal elections in 1980 (Dietz 1998b, 209–10), local politics focused principally on party interests. Neighborhood leaders began to dialogue with candidates, but this sometimes weakened their community relationships. The new political elite sometimes did not see the importance of

---

18. Privatization of electricity in Lima is described as a national-level factor because in 1997 it was initiated by the national government (i.e., the Fujimori administration), but in many provinces outside Lima public provision of electricity continued. In 2002, President Toledo attempted to privatize two electric companies in southern Peru, but major protests forced him to abort the plan. The November 2002 electoral defeat of many Toledo-endorsed municipal candidates was seen as a rebuke of his neoliberal economic policies, especially privatization.

19. For example, in the early 2000s President Toledo's "Programa a Trabajar" job training program successfully relied on cooperation between the state and municipal governments (Azcueta 2002, interview).

local base organizations, and this made them seem like a mere extension of the broader political structure (Azcueta 2002, interview).

While both perspectives are important, the cases examined in this study better support the contention that district-level democratization in Lima fostered neighborhood-level competition, while a lack of district-level democratization in Quito left the rule of neighborhood caciques, or bosses, generally unchallenged. Of the Quito organizations studied, all had noncompetitive neighborhood regimes, and of the Lima organizations studied, only one was noncompetitive. Of the six contrasts presented in this chapter, however, this finding is perhaps the most tentative. Although the project's ten principal case studies, as well as cursory examination of eighteen other invasion organizations, appear to confirm it, detailed study of a larger sample of cases could weaken the conclusion that noncompetitive regimes are more prevalent in Quito. This difference in neighborhood regimes, as well as the other five differences identified between Lima and Quito, helps provide a richer contextual understanding of neighborhood-level struggles. But these generalizations leave the key questions about organizational strategy, success, and survival unanswered, as well as the study's central theoretical agenda unresolved.

FROM METROPOLITAN CONTEXT TO LOCAL POLITICS: A NEIGHBORHOOD-LEVEL APPROACH TO URBAN POPULAR MOVEMENTS

Although metropolitan-level analysis has provided a crucial backdrop, testing the study's analytic tools and accomplishing its theoretical goals requires a neighborhood-level study of urban popular movements and local politics. Understanding the role of private and public electricity provision in Lima and Quito is important, but service provision relates primarily to the autonomy dimension of the strategy typology and strategy life cycle, and does not yet help us understand the relationship between contained and transgressive contention (i.e., the legality dimension). Likewise, analysis of citywide differences in both settlement policies external to invasion organizations and neighborhood regime competitiveness internal to these organizations has advanced our understanding of aspects of the neighborhood service acquisition model, but has neither analyzed the model nor operationalized key parts of the hypothesized opportunity structure. Finally, cross-city examination of land seizures and consequences of title acquisition hints at the analytic promise of the security trap, but does not provide a dynamic deployment of political process theory aimed at explaining organization survival outcomes. In short, much remains to be done. To accomplish this analytic and theoretical agenda, we turn now to a research design focused on a neighborhood-level universe of organizational cases.

Universe of Cases

The relevant universe of cases for this study includes all land invasion organizations that have reached at least the *mature* stage of organizational development (i.e., they are no longer at risk of being evicted) and are located in major Latin American cities (population over one million).[20] By focusing only on organizations that have reached a mature state, I exclude two groups of organizations: *defeated* organizations that no longer exist, and *nascent* organizations that in 2005 still faced a threat of eviction. This approach makes sense practically because little information exists about defeated groups that disbanded, and analytically because all mature organizations went through the nascent stage of development, and most such organizations went through one or more defeats before finally retaining possession of their land. In this way, a case like Oasis—which was defeated eight times through repeated evictions—offers an opportunity to understand both these earlier stages and also the later stages when most service demands occur, which are the principal focus of the study.

    Note that the unit of analysis is invasion *organizations*, rather than invasion neighborhoods.[21] In most cases, the two are analytically coterminous, but in some instances a single organization serves two or more neighborhoods, often of different ages. Hence, in the Old Guard case of Sector C, the neighborhood's early demand for water truck service is excluded from the case study because, as part of the larger Olivos de Pro umbrella organization, Sector C did not yet have its own organization and neighborhood regime. Conversely, in the Innovator case of Encantada, the organization's decision to absorb an adjacent invasion that cropped up during Encantada's sixth year created the unusual situation of a consolidated organization pressing quite basic demands, such as municipal recognition and informal electrical hookups (both immediately succeeded). These demands by the expanded Encantada organization are included in the study.

Logic of City and Service Demand Selection

In seeking to understand settler demands for services provided both by different levels of government and occasionally by private companies, Lima and Quito

<hr>

20. In 1995, Latin America was 74 percent urban, and nearly half of all urban dwellers lived in major cities of this size (Gilbert 1998, 34).
21. For a related discussion of the analytic differences—or lack thereof—between urban movements and urban organizations, see Burgwal (1995, 17).

proved to be the best analytic laboratory in which to observe the evolving struggles of land invasion organizations. Lima and Quito provide variation in service provision both across and within cities. Peru decentralized provision of land titles in 1979, and recentralized this responsibility in 1993, while Ecuador decentralized provision of nearly all Quito services in 1993. Peru privatized electricity provision in 1997, but Ecuador's initiatives to privatize electricity largely failed until 2005. In Lima, the task of granting recognition to new neighborhood organizations fell to the district government, while state or provincial authorities often guided recognition by the Municipality of Quito until 1993.[22] Hence, study of organizations in these cities permits analytically useful examination of settler demands for five services: electricity, water, sewer drainage, land titles, and municipal recognition.[23] Provision of these services is summarized in table 2.2.

Other services could be examined, but each poses analytic problems. Schools, health clinics, parks, and police service, for example, were pursued by a few of the groups chosen for this study, but unlike the more basic services pursued by all invasion organizations, demands for these secondary services were too sporadic across cases to permit systematic analysis. Street paving and trash collection constituted feasible alternatives to the services chosen for analysis, but neither was central to the agendas of invasion organizations, and so they were excluded.

Logic of Neighborhood Organization Selection

Exploration of the study's theoretical framework required the selection of neighborhood-level cases that exhibited variation with respect to the three key outcomes of organizational strategy, success, and survival. While this variation was crucial to drawing inferences from a sample of ten neighborhood cases, the specific outcomes and types of organizations represented were unknown when the cases were selected. Casual observation yielded estimates of each neighborhood's level of infrastructure development, but it could not be ascertained in advance how long an organization had struggled for services, what strategies were used, or how many times it had failed. In this sense, it is fair to say that while cases were selected with careful thought relative to the dependent variable, they were not selected on the basis of these outcomes.

22. District populations in Lima range from under 1,000 to about 600,000. In Quito, districts include 20,000 to 250,000 inhabitants. Note that even if a service is provided by a metropolitan or national agency, it is often administered by a district office. This office is not usually subject to political pressure, since its appointed bureaucrats are accountable to the central agency office, not local voters.

23. "Municipal recognition" is the legal legitimation of a neighborhood regime's existence. While this never grants land to a settlement organization, it does permit the struggle for land titles to begin, as the organization is now recognized as the legal representative of its members.

Table 2.2 Service provision by city and time period

| | | City and time period | | | |
		Lima 1980–1993	Lima 1993–2005	Quito 1979–1993	Quito 1993–2005
Level of service provision	State (public)	Water Sewers Electricity	Water Sewers Land titles	Water Sewers Electricity Land titles	
	Metropolitan (public)	Land titles			Water Sewers Electricity Land titles Municipal recognition
	District (public)	Municipal recognition	Municipal recognition	Municipal recognition*	
	Private		Electricity (1997–)		

*Prior to 1993, the task of granting municipal recognition to new organizations fell to the Municipality of Quito, but for organizations in peripheral parts of the city, the decision to grant recognition was driven by the state government or provincial authorities.

It was also desirable for some of the organizations to be located in the same local political context, in order to examine neighborhood-level factors unfettered by their district context. Hence, I included additional cases from the same districts, though this was not always feasible. The Quito case of Itchimbía, for example, emerged as a crucial case to include in the study, but it was the only invasion settlement in the downtown district. Finally, the sample needed to include cases whose founding dates varied, in order to examine more "basic" and more "advanced" service demands during different periods.

After narrowing the focus of the study through archival research and field interviews with twenty-one possible neighborhood organizations, ten case studies were selected. Subsequent analysis allowed me to group the cases into five analytically useful pairs, including two Old Guard "clients," two Old Guard "radicals," two large, older Next Generation cases, two small, newer Next Generation cases, and two Innovators. This sample achieved the desired case selection criteria and also provided an opportunity to study five different districts: Los Olivos and San Martín de Porres in northern Lima, Villa El Salvador in southern Lima, Cotocollao in northern Quito, and San Blas in downtown Quito. Inclusion of multiple cases in the same district permits the analysis to control for district-level factors in two of the paired-case comparisons. Founding dates ranged from 1983 to 2001, but seven of the ten neighborhoods were founded in the 1990–96 period. The study also managed to include the cases that local political observers judged to be the most analytically important, such as Pisulli and Itchimbía in Quito, and Oasis in Lima. Further, the sample included at least two of each of the four types of neighborhood regimes and also involved parcels of land with a mix of types of previous land ownership. Table 2.3 provides an overview of the ten case studies.

SUMMARY

The chapter began with the claim that three factors—public policy, local democratization, and geography and climate—best explain a series of six surprising differences between land invasions in Lima and those in Quito, yet it is apparent that of the three factors, public policy is by far the most important. Although geography and climate explain differences in building materials, and local democratization helps explain contrasting trends in neighborhood governance, it is national and metropolitan public policy that serves as the chief explanation for most of the citywide trends analyzed above. Specifically, public policies regarding decentralization in general and informal housing in particular explain trends in previous land ownership, ease of acquiring land titles, and methods of acquiring electricity. Public policy also constitutes part of the explanation for differences in the long-term survival of invasion organizations, but a full explanation of survival outcomes requires a neighborhood-level analysis.

Collectively, these differences have resulted in an important contrast between land invasions in the two cities. In Lima, a continuing history of permissive settlement policy allows fledgling invasion organizations to score early victories more quickly than their Quito counterparts with respect to land occupation and land titles. This easier attainment of property security, however, means that Lima organizations are also quicker to reach the point where participation drops. The fate of individual invasion settlements also rests on neighborhood-level factors, but this citywide trend speaks to the complementary influence of national- and metropolitan-level factors.

Returning to the broader theoretical question of neighborhood- and metropolitan-level analysis, it is important to underscore two earlier points: (1) these are citywide trends observed in a small number of cases, not deterministic predictions; and (2) although national and metropolitan factors appear pivotal in explaining them, neighborhood factors prove critical in explaining most other outcomes. With respect to the first point, many exceptions occur. Some Lima organizations promptly turn to the use of sturdier construction material, some Quito organizations have an easier time invading public land,

Table 2.3 Overview of invasion organization case studies

Organization type	Invasion organization	Neighborhood regime	Year founded	City	Land ownership	# Houses in 2005	# Service demands
Old Guard (clients)	Pro	Authoritarian/Electoral	1990	Lima	Private	2,800	13
	Sector C	Electoral	1991	Lima	Private	580	13
Old Guard (radicals)	Rosales	Electoral	1990	Lima	Private	955	18
	Pisulli	Authoritarian	1983	Quito	Public	1,800	12
Next Generation (large, older)	Camino	Authoritarian	1990	Quito	Private	1,224	14
	Oasis	Democratic	1994	Lima	Mixed	2,166	13
Next Generation (small, younger)	Villa Mar	Consensual	1999	Lima	Unresolved	240	12
	Paraíso	Democratic	2001	Lima	Mixed	350	8
Innovators	Encantada	Democratic	1996	Lima	Public*	1,320	14
	Itchimbía	Consensual	1995	Quito	Public	220	15

*Public land leased to a private company.

some Lima organizations fail to ever obtain land titles, and so on. With respect to the second point, it is important to keep in mind the many outcomes that do *not* vary by city, among them strategy selection for services other than electricity (e.g., piped water), the success of attempts to acquire services other than land titles (e.g., sewer drainage), and dimensions of neighborhood governance other than competitiveness (e.g., degree of inclusiveness or power sharing).

Scholarship focused on neighborhood-level processes remains at the core of understanding the emergence and development of land invasion communities and the neighborhood regimes that govern them, but this focus, though always necessary, is only sometimes sufficient. In a number of outcomes—here I have identified six in particular—the neighborhood-level approach must be complemented or even superseded by a national- or metropolitan-level analysis in order to understand the sometimes surprising differences that characterize urban land invasion organizations in Lima, Quito, and likely other Latin American cities as well.

3

The Old Guard:
Pragmatism and Strategic Rigidity

Up until about 1990, invasion organizations in Peru and Ecuador tended to be characterized by veteran leadership, a pragmatic outlook, a focus on material goals, and strategic rigidity. This rigidity meant that these "Old Guard" organizations exhibited a strong (and occasionally absolute) preference for either legal petitioning or radical struggle methods. In her study of Lima invasion communities in the 1980s, Susan Stokes (1995) usefully identified these two types of settlers as "clients" and "radicals." This chapter compares the organizational strategy, success, and survival of four Old Guard organizations. I begin with two Old Guard *client* organizations (both in Lima, separated by a district boundary) and then examine two Old Guard *radical* organizations (one in Lima and one in Quito).

In northern Lima, the adjacent invasion neighborhoods of Pro and Sector C pursued similar clientelist strategies, but while Pro was successful, Sector C largely failed. Pro and Sector C had been subgroups of the same organization for one month, but when the umbrella "Olivos de Pro" group split into three separate organizations, the now-independent Sector C found itself in a different city district than Pro. Separated by a municipal boundary, the trajectories of Pro and Sector C diverged dramatically, permitting observation of the effects of local political context across largely homogeneous cases. In the district of Los Olivos, Pro employed legal strategies to great effect, while in the district of San Martín de Porres, Sector C's legal petitioning failed. By 2005, Pro had successfully built a functional neighborhood, while Sector C languished with unreliable infrastructure and internal disputes.

Eschewing clientelism, the second pair of Old Guard organizations—Rosales and Pisulli—instead relied on radical extralegal strategies, but while the electoral regime of Rosales failed miserably, the noncompetitive authoritarian regime of Pisulli succeeded and consolidated its organization. Rosales was the third organization to split off from the Olivos de Pro umbrella group in Lima, but while its client "siblings," Pro and Sector C, relied on legal petitioning, the radical Rosales settlers heavily favored extralegal pressure tactics. Rosales's militancy might have succeeded, but its highly competitive neighborhood regime produced such a destructive pendulum of polarized leadership that the community's efforts were waylaid by internal disputes. In 2005, Rosales had finally made some important gains, but remained the laggard of the entire Los Olivos district, ranking ninety-third out of ninety-three neighborhoods in terms of service provision.

In Quito, however, the archetypal Old Guard radical case of Pisulli demonstrated that a purely extralegal strategy of disruption and political pressure can succeed. Unlike the competitive neighborhood regime of Rosales, however, the Pisulli organization was founded, matured, and consolidated all under the iron fist of a single neighborhood leader, Edgar Coral. Coral concentrated power in his own hands, and his authoritarian leadership resulted in nonstop (if unwilling) mobilization by the entire neighborhood. Coral's harsh leadership punished dissent, but rewarded loyalty and obedience with a well-developed neighborhood infrastructure—though never with freedom from the organization. He delivered infrastructure, schools, recreation, stability, and more, but the settlers of Pisulli never owned their own homes and were permanently dependent on Coral.

Comparison of these four case studies reveals the strengths and weaknesses of the Old Guard organizational type. Despite the failures of the Sector C clients and the Rosales radicals, the success of the Pro clients and the Pisulli radicals demonstrates that either form of Old Guard rigidity can succeed. In terms of organizational survival, however, Pro, Sector C, and most of Rosales all failed to acquire land titles and to consolidate organizationally. Pisulli managed to consolidate, but only through the authoritarian maneuvering of Edgar Coral, who *prevented* settlers from acquiring individual land titles in order to maintain his personal control of the neighborhood. While Old Guard cases not included in this study did acquire titles, the cases studies here nonetheless point to a general weakness of the Old Guard type, in that its strategic rigidity makes it less able to navigate the changing political and economic terrain of Latin America in the 1990s and early 2000s.

Each neighborhood organization case study is presented in chronological periods that correspond to its *nascent*, *mature*, *moribund*, or *consolidated* stages of organizational development. Within each period, service demands and their outcomes are identified and analyzed with respect to the neighborhood service acquisition model. Based on these paired-case comparisons of two Old Guard clients and two Old Guard radicals, I then identify the *identity traits*, *repertoire traits*, and *neighborhood regimes* common to the Old Guard type. The chapter concludes with a synthesis of the implications for other Old Guard organizations.

THE OLIVOS DE PRO CASE STUDIES: PRO, SECTOR C, AND ROSALES

The invasion neighborhoods of Pro, Sector C, and Rosales began as the unified Olivos de Pro organization, but quickly split into three separate organizations. Although each group followed a unique trajectory that yielded different outcomes, the three cases emerged from a common starting point. Hence, for analytic clarity, it is most useful to begin with a single description of the political context that surrounded the founding moments of these neighborhoods before presenting each separate case study in detail.

National and Local Context of the Olivos de Pro Invasions

By 1989, President Alán García (1985–90, 2006–present) and the APRA party had become immensely unpopular in Peru due to economic stagnation (Kenney 2004, 35) and the rise of terrorist violence. Ironically, APRA's support was especially weak in Lima, a traditional stronghold of the Left. In the November 1989 municipal elections, the once-powerful APRA garnered only 20 percent of votes nationwide and a feeble 12 percent of votes in metropolitan Lima (Tuesta 2001, 515, 518). At the metropolitan level, the APRA candidate lost to independent Ricardo Belmont, and at the district level, the Left was defeated by the rightist Frente Democrático (Democratic Front, or FREDEMO) coalition, which won twenty-nine of forty district races, including those in San Martín de Porres and the newly created district of Los Olivos (Dietz 1998a, 211–16).[1] Notably, the new San Martín–Los Olivos district boundary cut through a parcel of agricultural land owned by Pro Developers, which would soon become an invasion target.

Newly elected mayors Marcelino Morales (San Martín, 1990–92) and Carmen Lezama (Los Olivos, 1990–92) were confronted with the problem of continuing political violence. The northern parts of San Martín de Porres and Los Olivos were

---

1. The older district of San Martín was incorporated in 1950 and occupied about fifty-five square kilometers. In 1989, however, San Martín had become the largest district in northern Lima, and one-third of San Martín broke off and was incorporated as the new district of Los Olivos (Hidalgo 1999, 15).

a flash point for the conflict between Sendero Luminoso militants and the APRA-controlled Peruvian Army. The area was the scene of gun battles, with one zone controlled by APRA and the other dominated by a covert Sendero presence. But with the elections of Mayors Morales and Lezama, both members of the center-right AP, APRA's local influence was aborted, and Sendero aggravated these two transitions—the transfer of local power from the Left to the Right, and the creation of a new district—with violent attacks and material efforts to recruit settlers to their side of the conflict (Burt 1997, 291). Amid this tumult, a group of settlers made its first invasion attempt.

The First Invasion Attempt

In December 1989, sixty settlers invaded the rugged Pro Hill, which stood amid agricultural flatlands owned by Pro Developers in Los Olivos. The settlers expected that their allegiance to APRA and their opposition both to the local FREDEMO mayor and to Sendero would be rewarded with government support, especially as the presidential election of April 1990 approached. They were mistaken. Although the remaining APRA party forces took advantage of the settlers' presence and enlisted them in their war with Sendero, no services ever arrived, and the settlers went for months with neither electrical hookups nor water truck service (Yicate 2002, interview). Loyalty to APRA may have protected the settlers from eviction by Mayor Lezama, but their nascent settlement's location was so physically precarious that it seemed doomed to fail on its own. And it probably would have, had they remained on the hillside.

The sixty original settlers were gradually joined by others, however, and their numbers grew to four hundred. In January 1990, the settlers announced that they had "suffered enough," and moved off the hillside and invaded the flatlands of Pro Developers (Bustamente 2002, interview). Pro Developers and Mayor Lezama immediately requested an eviction, and the settlers were dispersed by soldiers from the nearby Santa Ana army post. The invasion attempt failed, and the defeated settlers retreated back to the hillside.

Enter Fujimori

On June 10, 1990, economic crisis and political violence contributed to Fujimori's landslide election by 56 percent of second-round voters (or a whopping 62 percent, if blank and spoiled ballots are excluded).[2] Under Fujimori, neoliberal

2. His opponent, Mario Vargas Llosa, received only 34 percent (38 percent of valid votes), with the remaining 10 percent either blank or spoiled (Tuesta 2001, 497).

"Fujishock" economic policies would soon reshape the political and economic landscape (McClintock 1999, 330), but his policies toward informal housing and terrorism had more immediate impacts on land invasions in Lima. With respect to housing, Fujimori's appointment of Hernando de Soto as his "personal representative and principal adviser" sent a strong signal of encouragement to prospective land invaders.[3] And with respect to terrorism, Fujimori's popular mandate translated into broad support for his aggressive and violent approach to fighting Sendero, despite media attention to government-sponsored human rights violations (Schönwälder 2002, 192). The Fujimori administration's anti-Sendero strategy involved paramilitary forces (Kenney 2004, 165), and some of these clandestine soldiers would soon be enmeshed in the leadership circle of Olivos de Pro.

The Three Founding Invasions

The defeated settlers had contemplated abandoning their steep perch and attempting a second invasion of the agricultural flatlands, but this plan was not acted on until the arrival of Luis "Chito" Rios. Chito Rios was an infamous land trafficker, a veteran Old Guard invasion ringleader, and a paramilitary captain who killed suspected Sendero members and sympathizers (Bustamente 2002, interview; la Madrid 2002, interview; Rojas 2002, interview). In public, Rios spoke the language of democratic cooperation and social justice, but his authoritarian leadership brooked no dissent, and his henchmen enforced his rule with violence (Yicate 2002, interview).[4]

Following Fujimori's inauguration on July 28, 1990, Rios moved in and seized control of the fledgling Olivos de Pro organization. Rios planned to attract several thousand settlers, charge each of them fifty dollars in membership dues, invade all the Pro Developers' land, and trade the political support of Olivos de Pro—as well as the paramilitary support of his inner circle—for government favors (Montesinos 2002, interview; Yicate 2002, interview). And he would succeed.

By October 1990, Rios had attracted 3,500 prospective settlers, and they invaded two-thirds of the Pro Developers' land.[5] The developers and Mayor Lezama

3. Frustrated with Fujimori's leadership and economic policy, de Soto resigned after the coup in April 1992 (de Soto 2002, interview).
4. Rios's thugs were known as "Los Verdes" for the dark green that some of them wore. A founding settler who later became an elected neighborhood leader commented on the prevalence of death threats and violence: "[They] were almost always armed and in conflict with people. They pressured settlers. There were seven [deaths], one in [the victim's] own house" (Tapia 2002, interview).
5. Rios and his agents recruited prospective settlers not only in Los Olivos and San Martín de Porres, but also in the districts of Comas, Independencia, and Surquillo (la Madrid 2002, interview).

again requested an eviction by the army, but curiously, the eviction attempt failed. Popular wisdom pointed to the size of the invasion as its source of resilience (Tapia 2002, interview), but although size makes evictions more difficult, a determined military can evict even very large groups.[6] An alternative explanation, however, was that it was not a serious eviction attempt. Chito Rios had already made a conformist deal with Fujimori's military, and Rios's pledge of political and paramilitary support in the battle against Sendero protected his invasion from eviction (Montesinos 2002, interview; Vasquez 2002, interview). This neighborhood would eventually stabilize at 2,800 families and be called "Pro."

On December 16, 1990, Rios initiated a second successful invasion, and more than 1,000 settlers seized a nearby (but separate) parcel of Pro Developers' land, which they named "Rosales." Mayor Lezama attempted another eviction, but failed again. Rosales would eventually have 955 families.

The next month, Rios organized a third successful invasion and, with 700 settlers, seized the remaining Pro Developers' land. Local residents often referred to Pro as "Sector A," and to Rosales as "Sector B," so they named this third neighborhood "Sector C." Sector C would eventually stabilize at 580 families. Although Sector C had been part of the same parcel of land as Pro, Sector C was located in the district of San Martín de Porres. Predictably, San Martín mayor Marcelino Morales requested an eviction, but had no better luck than Mayor Lezama.

The Split

Combined, the three neighborhoods of the Olivos de Pro organization now included close to five thousand families spread across two parcels of land, one of which spanned two city districts. Settlers in Sector C and Rosales began quietly agitating for organizational independence, and Rios was willing to oblige. He had already extracted dues from the settlers, so in February 1991 he cut them loose, and Rios's fief was split into three separate organizations. Pro remained under the authoritarian control of Rios, while Sector C and Rosales each elected their own neighborhood councils. Rios's fearful influence could still be felt a year later, however, as leaders would meet in darkened rooms and go by code names to avoid being blacklisted by Rios as Sendero sympathizers (Rojas 2002, interview).

Despite some differences (such as size), these three neighborhoods looked largely the same in February 1991. Hence, they provide a good laboratory in

6. For example, on January 20, 2002, during a political era in Peru that was much less tolerant of government-sponsored violence, the army evicted five thousand invading families with relative ease in the district of Carabayllo (Pérez 2002, interview). See also Flores, Lingán, and Cayo (2002).

which to observe their respective fifteen-year trajectories. Operating in the district of Los Olivos, the Old Guard "clients" of Pro successfully employed conformist strategies to acquire all major services except land titles. By contrast, the Old Guard clients of Sector C employed conformist strategies similar to those of Pro, but in the district of San Martín this strategy largely failed. Finally, the settlers of Rosales elected a slate of Old Guard "radicals" to lead their neighborhood, but their militant strategies would fail for nearly fifteen years, making Rosales the least developed of Los Olivos's ninety-three neighborhoods. Grounded in this description of the common history shared by Pro, Sector C, and Rosales, we turn now to the developmental trajectory and service demands of each separate neighborhood organization.

OLD GUARD CLIENTS GET THE GOODS: THE CASE OF PRO

The Old Guard organization of Pro began as a classic *client* focused on legal conformist strategies to acquire services. At one point, frustrated Pro leaders experimented briefly with extralegal militant demands, but this soon dissipated and Pro's clientelist identity reasserted itself. Pro began with an authoritarian neighborhood regime, but with the departure of Chito Rios in 1992 this gave way to an electoral regime that democratically elected its neighborhood council and secretary general throughout the 1992–2005 period.

The First Three Years: Caught in the Crossfire

From its founding in October 1990 until Los Olivos mayor Jesús Martínez (1993–95) recognized Pro on June 18, 1993, this *nascent* invasion organization relied principally on conformist strategies, but also dabbled in militant protest marches when deal making failed at the local level. During this period, the Pro organization made six attempts to acquire services: (1) *conformist* solicitation of provisional electricity hookups for all settlers in Pro—a success; (2) *conformist* acquisition of low-quality water truck service for all settlers—a success; (3) a *conformist* attempt at municipal recognition by the district mayor—a failure; (4) a *conformist* request for de facto recognition by the metropolitan mayor—a success; (5) *militant* marches on Congress demanding recognition—a failure; and (6) a combination *militant/conformist* demand for official municipal recognition from the new district mayor—a success. The details of all of Pro's demands, including these six, are summarized as a data matrix in table 3.1, which serves as a useful reference while reading the Pro case study. Subsequent case studies each include a similar data matrix.

Table 3.1 Pro data matrix

Stage of development	Neighborhood leader	Service demand	District mayor	Service provider	Allies	Avenue of participation	Strategy type	Key resources	Neighborhood regime type	Outcome
				External factors			Internal factors			
		Electricity	Hostile	State	Cambio 90		Conformist	Medium participation	Authoritarian	Success
	Rios (90–92)	Water truck	Hostile	State	Cambio 90		Conformist	Medium participation	Authoritarian	Success
Nascent (90–93)		Recognition	Hostile	District	Cambio 90		Conformist	Medium participation	Authoritarian	Failure
		Recognition	Hostile	District	Metro myr.		Conformist	Leadership	Electoral	Success
		Recognition	Hostile	District	Cambio 90	93 Election	Militant	High participation	Electoral	Failure
	Flores (92–95)	Recognition	Friendly	District			Militant/Conformist	High participation	Electoral	Success
		Electricity	Friendly	State	FONAVI	95 Election	Conformist	High participation	Electoral	Success
Mature (93–97)		Piped water	Friendly	State	Cambio 90	Fraternidad	Conformist	High participation	Electoral	Success
	Rurush (95–99)	Sewers	Friendly	State	Cambio 90	Fraternidad	Conformist	High participation	Electoral	Success
		Land titles	Neutral	Private		98 Election	Conformist	Low participation	Electoral	Failure
	Silva (99–01)	Land titles	Neutral	Private			Militant	Low participation	Electoral	Failure
Moribund (97–05)	Bustamente (01–03)	Land titles	Neutral	Private		02 Election	Bootstrap	Low participation	Electoral	Failure
	Remuzgo (03–05)	Land titles	Neutral	Private		Fraternidad	Militant/Bootstrap	Low participation	Electoral	Failure

Although these first six service demands occurred during Pro's nascent stage of development, the three years are best thought of as two separate periods. During the first period (1990–92), Chito Rios ruled Pro with an authoritarian fist and relied exclusively on conformist partnerships with Cambio 90 allies.[7] This period ended when Rios left Pro. During the second period (1992–93), Pro experienced its first elected leadership, and founding secretary general Donato Flores pursued municipal recognition through both conformist and militant strategies.

The Rios Administration: Classic Clientelism

During the first period, Rios demanded that settlers participate in meetings and political actions on behalf of Cambio 90 patrons, but the constant danger of political violence dampened participation. The line between political violence and criminal violence was blurred, and settlers lived in fear of Sendero, the army, and their own boss, Rios. Over twenty Pro residents disappeared in 1990–91, though it is unknown how many were killed and how many simply fled. One execution by the army is well remembered by founding settlers (speech at a Pro assembly, 3/10/02).

Despite the violence, Rios's partnership with Absalón Vásquez yielded both protection from eviction and immediate electricity and water provision.[8] Nearly all nascent invasion organizations steal electricity through illegal hookups, but isolated or large invasion neighborhoods sometimes have difficulty stealing electricity. Pro was such a community, but within weeks the patronage of Cambio 90 delivered provisional electrical hookups as well as water truck service, primarily through government agents, but also with help from local businesses loyal to Cambio 90. Rios also made a conformist bid for prompt recognition by the Municipality of Los Olivos, but his Cambio 90 allies were of little use in persuading the opposition mayor to recognize Pro, and the attempt failed.

Despite these early conformist successes, by 1992 Rios's relationship with Vásquez had soured, and the military turned on Rios. With Fujimori's dissolution of Congress in April 1992, the army was free to act without oversight

7. Cambio 90 was the first of four different "parties" that Fujimori created. These included Cambio 90 in 1990, Cambio 90–Nueva Mayoría (New Majority) in 1993, Vamos Vecino in 1998 (for the municipal elections), and Peru 2000 (Roberts 2006, 137–39). Although the overarching Cambio 90 label persisted, none of these parties lasted longer than one electoral cycle, and none of them resulted in an institutionalized party.

8. Absalón Vásquez Villanueva was a member of the Fujimori administration and was later appointed minister of agriculture (1992–96). Although not a major figure in the Fujimori administration overall, he was one of the administration's two key players in the Olivos de Pro region. The other was the infamous spy chief Vladimir Montesinos, whose relationship to the paramilitaries of Olivos de Pro remains unclear.

(Kenney 2004, 238–40). The army raided Pro, killing members of Rios's inner circle, but Rios had vanished, along with the assets of the Pro organization (Yicate 2002, interview).

The dangerous atmosphere in Pro persisted until at least the November 1992 constituent assembly elections, but with Rios gone, a new neighborhood regime quickly took shape. Donato Flores, a previously quiet critic of Rios, was elected as Pro's first secretary general (1992–95) and leader of the Pro neighborhood council.

The Flores Administration: A Brief Deviation from Clientelism

Flores resuscitated Pro's conformist relationship with Cambio 90, but also turned to militancy to pursue municipal recognition. Since district mayor Carmen Lezama remained hostile toward Pro, Flores turned to metropolitan mayor Ricardo Belmont. Belmont agreed to recognize Pro in exchange for votes in the January 1993 metropolitan election (Belmont was reelected). Recognition by Belmont was helpful, but only the district of Los Olivos had the legal authority to grant municipal recognition, so Flores organized six major protest marches. The first four marches blocked the Pan-American Highway and aimed to pressure Congress (i.e., the constituent assembly, since Fujimori had dissolved the legislature) into granting recognition (again, this was technically not within their purview, but power was extremely centralized during this authoritarian period in Peru). This failed, but following the 1993 elections Mayor Lezama was replaced by Obras ("Works") candidate Jesús Martinez, so Flores redirected his pressure tactics to the district level. Following two marches on the Municipality of Los Olivos, Mayor Martínez (1993–95) agreed both to recognize Pro and to work with them to deliver services, in exchange for political support. With this partnership, Flores abandoned his experiment with militancy and returned Pro to clientelism.

The Return to Clientelism: Steady Acquisition of Most Services

Between 1993 and 1997, the *mature* Pro organization abandoned its brief flirtation with militancy and embraced clientelism. Pro formed political partnerships at the district, metropolitan, and state level, and was rewarded with steady acquisition of almost all key services. The three major service demands (summarized in table 3.1) were: (1) *conformist* solicitation of the Fondo Nacional de Vivienda (National Housing Fund, or FONAVI) for formal electricity service—a success; (2) a *conformist* deal with Cambio 90 to install piped water—a success; and (3) a *conformist* deal with Cambio 90 to install sewer drainage—a success. In addition, Belmont authorized road paving in Pro, and district mayor Jesús Martínez initiated garbage collection and a health clinic.

The Flores and Rurush Administrations:
High Participation Sustains Conformist Deals

This successful string of service demands began with Secretary General Flores (1992–95) and continued with his replacement, Fermín Rurush (1995–99). Acquisition of formal electricity hookups, road paving, garbage collection, and the health clinic were the easiest, because these services were initiated prior to the November 1995 municipal elections. Thus, in 1995 the state (Cambio 90), metropolitan (Obras), and district (Obras) governments all supported Pro.[9] In November, however, Belmont was replaced by metropolitan mayor Alberto Andrade (1995–2002), and Martínez was replaced by district mayor Felipe Castillo (1995–2002). Andrade assumed a neutral stance toward Pro, but Castillo was a member of Cambio 90–Nueva Mayoría. Pro had lost its ally at the metropolitan level, but gained an even friendlier ally at the district level, which was arguably more important for the implementation of service projects.

Complemented by support from Mayor Castillo, Rurush's conformist partnerships at the state level paid off rapidly, with both piped water and sewer drainage installed within two years. In exchange, Pro settlers cast votes in support of allied candidates, turned out relatives to the polls, and attended rallies and public events in support of Cambio 90. By 1997, Pro had acquired high-quality electricity, water, and drainage entirely with conformist strategies that yielded patronage from Cambio 90 allies. Key to their success were high levels of participation in planning meetings and political gatherings, which assured Cambio 90 patrons like Castillo that Pro would deliver needed support at election time.

Also critical to Pro's success was a local participatory institution called the Fraternidad Municipal Housing Program. "Fraternidad" was a pan-settlement association that included Pro and six other informal neighborhoods.[10] Under the aegis of the Municipality of Los Olivos, Fraternidad provided a participatory framework for settlers to cooperate for common objectives. The power-concentrating Rios administration had shown no interest in such a framework, but under Pro's subsequent electoral regime, power had become less concentrated and the organization joined Fraternidad. Through Fraternidad, Pro was able to

---

9. As a presidential candidate, Mayor Belmont did run against Fujimori in the 1995 general elections, but leaders in Pro nonetheless had relationships with members of both Cambio 90 and Obras, though they supported Fujimori in the presidential election. Fujimori won reelection with 53 percent of the ballots (which represented 64 percent of the valid votes). Javier Pérez de Cuéllar garnered 17.7 percent for second place, but 17.9 percent of ballots were blank or spoiled (Tuesta 2001, 444).

10. In addition to Pro, "Fraternidad" included the informal neighborhoods of Los Norteños, Juan Pablo II, Caller, Milla Ochoa, Olivos, and San Martín, all located in the district of Los Olivos.

coordinate its water and sewer projects with similar initiatives in nearby informal neighborhoods (Bustamante 2002, interview).

Material Success Dampens Participation: Pro Becomes Moribund

With all major services acquired except land titles—that is, recognition, electricity, water, and sewers—the Pro organization had achieved de facto property security, which led to a decline in participation and a *moribund* state of the neighborhood regime from 1997 to 2005. By 2002 participation had dropped to less than 20 percent (Bustamante 2002, interview), and by 2005 some meetings garnered only 10 percent attendance (Remuzgo 2005, interview). Although most settlers still lacked legal title to their home, the relatively high quality of urban infrastructure (including trash collection and paved streets) and the steady development of the neighborhood (e.g., construction of three-story buildings) contributed to a sense that the community was secure, even if official titles might not arrive for some time. During this eight-year period, Pro made three attempts to acquire titles: (1) a *conformist* attempt at land titles—a failure; (2) *militant* demands for land titles—a failure; and (3) a *bootstrap* attempt to buy land titles—another failure. All three attempts failed principally because of the organization's moribund state and low rates of participation, as well as a lack of money.[11]

Unlike some landowners who aggressively fight invaders, Pro Developers was relatively passive in its response. The organization had always planned to sell the land, so despite some efforts to the contrary, their basic attitude was that Chito Rios had provided them 4,335 customers who would eventually (they hoped) pay. Although each of the three settlements—Pro, Sector C, and Rosales—challenged Pro Developers' legal claim to the land at one point or another, the developer's claim was basically secure, and no matter how high the buildings grew or how many services were installed, it seemed unlikely that the COFOPRI informal housing agency would grant titles to settlers occupying private land.

The Rurush and Silva Administrations: Private Service Provision Blocks Externally Dependent Strategies

In this context, it is unsurprising that the conformist approach of Secretary General Rurush, as well as the militant strategy of his successor, Ruperto Silva (1999–2001), failed. These failures were largely explained by the fact that Pro Developers' claim to the land was valid. When services are privately provided,

---

11. In 2001, Pro managed to pave several additional roads, but this was a minor service improvement.

externally dependent strategies are rarely successful. Short of passing a new law, Rurush's Cambio 90 allies' only option would have been to buy the land outright. By 2002, Pro Developers was asking for five thousand dollars per lot, which would have amounted to fourteen million dollars. The price in 1998 was lower, but still far in excess of Cambio 90's generosity, especially since the moribund organization had little to offer Cambio 90 now that participation had declined.

Silva organized several protest marches aimed at pressuring Pro Developers to lower its price and COFOPRI to declare the land public, but even with a massive mobilization, it is unclear that this would have occurred. In any case, the marches were poorly attended. Now in a moribund state, Silva could not even rally half the numbers that his predecessor, Donato Flores, had managed when demanding municipal recognition. The marches failed. What is more surprising, however, is that the bootstrap strategy of Silva's successor, Victoriano Bustamente, *also* failed.

The Bustamente and Remuzgo Administrations: Low Participation Cripples Bootstrap Strategies

Finally, Secretary General Victoriano Bustamente (2001–3) and Secretary General Elvis Remuzgo (2003–5) both bowed to the inevitable and pursued a purchase agreement with Pro Developers, but neither could close the deal. Although many Pro settlers had the money to begin monthly payments toward the purchase of land titles, even these efforts collapsed due to internal conflict and low participation. Said Bustamente in a 2002 interview: "The latest price is $14 million for all of [Pro], which is $40–45/m². So each 120m² lot is $5,000. And the price keeps going up! We're still struggling for a contract. We are fighting a wealthy capitalist opponent. Our only defense is organization. Thus our principal focus now is not just fighting Pro Developers, but raising participation and organization."

Bustamente's and Remuzgo's attempts to negotiate with Pro Developers were similar in most respects. Both leaders struggled to attract settler participation in a stalled process and both had their bargaining power undercut by settlers who negotiated individual purchase agreements with Pro Developers, diminishing the settlers' capacity to demand an affordable price. Under Remuzgo, however, the group's unsuccessful bootstrap strategy was briefly augmented by an unsuccessful militant strategy.

In August 2004, Pro Developers and other realty companies lobbied Mitchell Martínez and other legislators of Perú Posible—the party of incumbent president Alejandro Toledo (2001–6)—to annul Article 4 of Law 24-5-13, which forced companies like Pro Developers to assess many invaded lands as "rustic," which meant a substantially lower price. In response, the leaders of Fraternidad (including Pro and six other informal settlements) organized a march to Congress to protest the proposed annulment of Article 4. Several thousand Fraternidad settlers participated in the October march, but Remuzgo struggled to turn out Pro settlers (Remuzgo 2005, interview). The protest may have helped undermine the legislation, which Congress rejected, but this victory did not translate to success in Pro's fourth failed attempt to acquire land titles.

As of July 2005, Remuzgo faced an uphill battle to reunite the settlement. Mistrust among settlers of both Remuzgo and the Pro council had aggravated neighborhood dissatisfaction with the cooperative, Pro Developers seemed in no hurry to lower its price, and there were no new ideas on the table (Remuzgo 2005, interview). The settlers had developed a functional neighborhood, but they still were not owners of their homes.

Summary of Pro's Organizational Successes and Failures

Reviewing the case of Pro, seven of its thirteen attempts at services succeeded. Of these seven successful demands, all but one relied exclusively on conformist strategies. Not only did Pro exhibit a clear clientelist identity, but this approach worked well for them. Pro's success hinged almost entirely on conformist partnerships supported by medium to high rates of participation and leaders who knew how to exploit clientelism to their benefit. Further, although Pro initially had to contend with a hostile district mayor, during its mature stage it benefited from the support of Mayor Castillo, who facilitated the patronage of the ruling Cambio 90 party.

In the end Pro failed to acquire land titles because of private service provision and falling rates of participation, but it can be argued that the organization had served its purpose, and it made sense for settlers to abandon a regime that had outgrown its usefulness. This is an important claim to keep in mind, but it should be tempered with a reminder that the descriptions of service provision quality in this study are all relative. Despite the services acquired, Pro remained an impoverished community that would benefit from a robust neighborhood regime pursuing services like parks and emergency services, in addition to the more basic services that are the focus of this study.

In this context, the moribund state of the Pro organization is unfortunate. In 2005, Secretary General Remuzgo had plans for more street paving and parks in Pro, but with participation low, even these modest objectives were in doubt, to say nothing of loftier goals, like a good-quality neighborhood school.

OLD GUARD CLIENTS IN SEARCH OF A PATRON: THE CASE OF SECTOR C

Sector C was founded as part of the clientelist Olivos de Pro invasion, but when Olivos de Pro split into three organizations, Pro and Rosales developed in the new district of Los Olivos while Sector C was in the old district of San Martín de Porres. Like Pro, Sector C attempted a conformist strategy of clientelism, but failed to find influential allies either in the San Martín district or at higher levels of government. Subsequent Sector C leaders attempted to steer the neighborhood toward extralegal strategies that might succeed in this different local political context, but the Old Guard clients could not be induced to give up their ways and adapt to a more established district with no interest in a new political player on the block.

Although the Sector C lands were invaded in January 1991, the Sector C organization was not created for another month. Sector C (as well as Rosales) was unusual in that the neighborhood regime was created when the neighborhood already existed, rather than the two being created simultaneously or, as is often the case, the organization being created in anticipation of a land invasion. Additionally, water truck service (but not electrical hookups) already existed, thanks to the deal making of Chito Rios.

The First Two Years: External Factors Shape Opportunities

From its creation in February 1991 until San Martín mayor José Rubio (1993–95) granted municipal recognition in 1993, the *nascent* Sector C organization relied primarily on conformist strategies, but also experimented with some extralegal strategies. The four main demands during this period included: (1) *rogue* theft of electricity through informal hookups—a success; (2) *conformist* solicitation of municipal recognition—a failure; (3) a token *militant* demand for recognition at election time—a failure; and (4) *conformist* solicitation of recognition from the new district mayor—a success. Table 3.2 summarizes these and other demands by Sector C.

The La Madrid Administration: Client Settlers Uninterested in Militant Experiment

The success or failure of these demands hinged principally on external factors. Unlike the original Pro organization that was unable to steal electricity, as is typical, Sector C was able to tap into existing power sources in San Martín to informally provide electricity to its smaller neighborhood. If not for this opportunity, it likely would have failed as well. Similarly, the failure of Secretary General Diego la Madrid's (1991–94) first two attempts at municipal

Table 3.2 Sector C data matrix

| Stage of development | Neighborhood leader | External factors | | | | | | Internal Factors | | |
		Service demand	District mayor	Service provider	Allies	Avenue of participation	Strategy type	Key resources	Neighborhood regime type	Outcome
Nascent (91–93)		Electricity	Hostile	State			Rogue	High participation	Electoral	Success
		Recognition	Hostile	District			Conformist		Electoral	Failure
	La Madrid (91–94)	Recognition	Hostile	District		93 Election	Militant	Low participation	Electoral	Failure
		Recognition	Friendly	District			Conformist		Electoral	Success
		Electricity	Friendly	State			Conformist		Electoral	Failure
		Electricity	Friendly	State			Bootstrap	Money	Electoral	Success
		Land titles	Friendly	Private		95 Election	Conformist		Electoral	Failure
Mature (93–01)	Ostros (94–98)	Piped water	Neutral	State		98 Election	Militant	Medium participation	Electoral	Failure
		Piped water	Neutral	State	FONAVI		Conformist	Leadership	Electoral	Success
	Vega (00–03)	Sewers	Neutral	State	FONAVI		Conformist	Leadership	Electoral	Failure**
		Land titles	Neutral	Private			Bootstrap	No money	Electoral	Failure**
Moribund (01–05)		Sewers	Neutral	State		02 Election	Militant	Low participation	Electoral	Failure
	Hilario (05)	Sewers	Neutral	State	Metro government		Conformist	Low participation	Electoral	Success

*No neighborhood leader is listed for 1998–2000 or 2003–5. Between 1998 and 2000, Secretary General María Chávez initiated no new service demands. Between 2003 and 2005, there were no neighborhood leader, and consequently there were no demands for services.

**I characterize these two demands as failures. Sector C's conformist appeal for sewers resulted in installation of a drainage system, but it was never connected due to local leaders' poor handling of irate neighbors, who blocked the sewer system's activation. Similarly, Sector C's bootstrap purchase agreement with Pro Developers did result in 40–50 land titles (out of 580), but since so few settlers could actually afford the title, I characterize the attempt as a failure.

recognition had less to do with poor negotiating skills or low turnout (a mere 50–70 people joined the march for recognition), and more to do with the hostile FREDEMO mayor Marcelino Morales (in neighboring Los Olivos, for example, FREDEMO mayor Carmen Lezama similarly refused to recognize Rosales during the same period, despite a disruptive march by 1,500 people). In 1993, la Madrid's third attempt—via legal petitioning—succeeded principally because of the friendly position of the new Obras mayor, José Rubio (1993–95), rather than any change in the Sector C organization (la Madrid 2002, interview).[12]

Eight Years of Limited Progress: External and Internal Factors Shape a Pattern of Failure

From 1993 until 2001, the *mature* Sector C organization continued to seek out conformist partnerships, but was largely unsuccessful. Frustrated at the lack of progress, two different neighborhood leaders attempted to switch gears to a more militant approach, but the clientelist settlers were not interested, preferring patience (i.e., stagnation) over mobilization. The seven service demands during this period were: (1) *conformist* solicitation of formal electricity provision from the state government—a failure; (2) *bootstrap* purchase of medium-quality electricity service for all settlers—a success; (3) *conformist* solicitation of land titles from the state titling agency—a failure; (4) *militant* demands for piped water at election time—a failure; (5) *conformist* solicitation of piped water—a success; (6) *conformist* solicitation of sewer drainage—a qualified failure; and (7) a *bootstrap* attempt to buy land titles from Pro Developers—a success of such limited scope that, analytically, it was a failure.

During this eight-year period, a combination of external and internal factors shaped the success and failure of Sector C's conformist and bootstrap strategies, as well as a brief experiment with militant demands. The key external factors were a lack of influential allies, the position of the San Martín mayor, and in the case of land titles, private service provision (see table 3.2). Internally, strategy choices and mismatches played an important role, as did organizational resources.

Under la Madrid, Sector C's first attempt at formal electricity hookups failed due to a lack of allies, and its second attempt succeeded due to organizational resources and a friendly mayor. La Madrid shopped around for a political ally to take Sector C under his or her wing, but the community was either too small

---

12. One cause of the Sector C settlers' (misplaced, in this case) faith in elected officials was that between 1984 and 1986, some of the same settlers had benefited from the Izquierda Unida (United Left, or IU) administration of Mayor Alfonso Barrantes, which left a lasting impression regarding the capacity of city leaders to improve the lives of the poor. See Schönwälder (2002, 130–48) for a detailed discussion of this period of IU dominance in Lima.

or la Madrid was too ineffective, and this approach failed (la Madrid 2002, interview). In 1994, la Madrid finally gave up, and worked with Mayor Rubio to purchase electrical hookups at a cost of sixty dollars per home.[13]

The Ostros Administration: Poor Strategy and a Lack of Allies

Under the leadership of Secretary General Florian Ostros (1994–98), Sector C failed to acquire either land titles or piped water due to poor strategy choices and a lack of allies. As the November 1995 municipal elections approached, Ostros attempted to exchange Sector C's political support for intervention in the organization's land dispute with Pro Developers, but the clear private ownership of the land kept any politicians from taking up Sector C's cause. Hence, this externally dependent strategy failed to acquire a privately provided service.

Three years later, as the October 1998 municipal elections approached, Ostros again tried to capitalize on the timing of the election to pressure officials into providing water service to Sector C.[14] Ostros's militant strategy might have worked with a different organization, but the settlers of Sector C had already proven themselves uninterested in protest methods, and the four lukewarm marches barely drew three hundred people (Vega 2002, interview).[15] Their militant demands failed.

The Chávez Administration: Internal Problems Stall Service Acquisition

Under the leadership of Secretary General María Chávez (1998–2000), Sector C's attempts at service acquisition stagnated due to internal division, and no service demands were made. Chávez was elected by settlers who had grown mistrustful of Ostros and believed he was making side deals with Pro Developers (Vega 2002, interview). Chávez accused Ostros of embezzlement, as eight thousand dollars in payments to Pro Developers had disappeared (and Ostros was the middleman). The hostility between Ostros and Chávez meant that Ostros withheld all documents and organization assets from Chávez when she began her tenure (Chávez 2002, interview). With Sector C's electoral regime temporarily crippled by this polarization, Chávez turned away from infrastructure projects and focused instead on social projects, such as the Glass of Milk nutrition program for poor children. By the end of her two-year term, however, many settlers had

13. Note that electricity had not yet been privatized in Peru, but Sector C settlers were forced to pay the cost themselves as they could not get the state government to provide service.
14. If the Fraternidad Municipal Housing Program had extended to the district of San Martín de Porres, it seems possible that Ostros would have pursued a conformist strategy to acquire water, but Fraternidad was limited to informal neighborhoods in the district of Los Olivos.
15. Two marches targeted the northern Lima office of the Servicio de Agua Potable y Alcantarillado de Lima (Lima Potable Water and Sewer Drainage Service, or SEDAPAL), and the other two marches targeted the FONAVI housing agency.

turned against her as well, blaming her for Sector C's stagnation. Said Chávez in a 2002 interview: "[In 1999] people broke down my door. I'm the black sheep of Sector C. It's 'my fault' we don't advance. Now [in 2002] we have water, but not drainage. People blame me for this too! It's me against all the other ex-secretaries general." With many settlers hostile to either Ostros or Chávez (or both), they elected a newcomer to replace Chávez, a former teacher named Miguel Arturo Vega who had arrived in 1998. Vega promised to rise above the factionalism that divided Sector C and organize to build a water and sewer system.

The Vega Administration: Legal Strategies Achieve Empty Success

Under the leadership of Secretary General Vega (2000–2002), Sector C acquired water and sewer infrastructure, but it did not function, making the project an overall failure driven by mayoral indifference and poor neighborhood leadership. Where Ostros had attempted to pressure the SEDAPAL water agency and the FONAVI housing agency, Vega chose the route of legal petitioning. Fujimori had just forced his way into a third term, and following his fraud-tainted inauguration in July 2000, state agencies seemed eager to dole out services in hopes of quelling growing accusations of scandal and corruption (Vega 2002, interview).[16] Thanks to Vega's leadership, FONAVI agreed to finance both the water and drainage infrastructure, though each family would incur an eight-hundred-dollar debt, payable over ten years.[17] The project began in September 2000 and ended in October 2001, when water began to flow. The sewer network, however, was to empty into the neighboring community of San Diego, but San Diego blocked the system's activation due to health concerns. Vega requested arbitration by San Martín mayor Gladys Ugaz (Somos Perú, 1998–2002), but Ugaz was indifferent to Sector C's plight, and Vega was unable to negotiate a solution with San Diego (la Madrid 2002, interview; Vega 2002, interview). Without a drainage system, Sector C had to severely curtail its use of water, since there was nowhere for the water to go, except holes in the ground. Unable to take full advantage of water service, the project was a very limited success.

Vega also brokered a land title purchase agreement with Pro Developers, but this effort failed due to a lack of organizational resources. First of all, only 230 of the 580 families (40 percent) participated in the purchase agreement. Of those 230, however, only 40–50 (about 8 percent of Sector C) actually had the money to buy a title. Since this bootstrap effort yielded such an incremental

16. Fujimori's efforts to stay in power failed, and in November 2000 his presidency was terminated while he was abroad in Japan, where he remained in exile (Brooke 2004).

17. This amount included three hundred dollars for water and five hundred dollars for sewer drainage.

gain, I characterize it as a failure. It seems possible that with other factors in play, such as a friendly mayor, an influential ally, or better participation, Vega might have been able to negotiate better terms or a lower price, but absent these factors, a general lack of money meant that very few settlers received a title.

Low Participation Derails Infrastructure Agenda: Sector C Becomes Moribund

From November 2001 until May 2005, the Sector C organization sank into a *moribund* state that compromised its major service demand during this period: a *militant* demand for completion of the drainage project—a failure. In May 2005, an unremarkable *conformist* petition for activation of the sewer system was granted—a success—but this long-overdue victory did not signal a change in Sector's C's moribund condition.

As Miguel Arturo Vega's term in office drew to a close, Sector C's hamstrung purchase agreement and barely functioning water system did nothing to reverse intra-neighborhood divisions and the steady decline of community participation. "I'm for participation in the community," said Vega in a 2002 interview. "We need to create pressure." But even as the elected leader of Sector C, Vega could not force the settlers to pursue a militant strategy. Vega coordinated with other San Martín neighborhoods to organize a district-wide march in 2002, but the Sector C clients were not interested, and few attended. Vega also organized a march on the San Martin de Porres municipality to demand street paving, but fewer than one hundred people showed up, about the same number that still participated in neighborhood meetings. Without a change in this key internal factor, it looked unlikely that Sector C would make further progress.

Between 2003 and 2005, Sector C's internal conflicts and accusations of vote fraud resulted in a two-year period in which the community did not have any elected leadership. During these years, periodic assemblies attempted to resolve the group's divisions, but it was not until April 2005 that a new neighborhood council was elected and allowed to take power. During this period, water service was irregular and sometimes absent entirely, but Sector C lacked the organizational coherence to even attempt to do anything about it.

In April 2005, Secretary General María Ariza Hilario de Peña began a two-year term, and much-improved water service arrived just a month after she took office. Hilario de Peña claims that it was her (conformist) petition to metropolitan mayor Luis Castañeda that finally brought water to Sector C (Hilario de Peña 2005, interview), but the striking weakness of the Sector C organization casts doubt on her claim. An ally of former secretary general María Chávez, Hilario de Peña had no previous leadership or organizing experience and no contacts outside

Sector C; she was elected for her honesty, not her political skills or knowledge.[18] Further, municipal bureaucrats had made sporadic efforts to get Sector C's water and drainage systems running during the neighborhood's leaderless period of 2003–5, so it seems equally plausible that one of these efforts happened to succeed shortly after Hilario de Peña was elected.

Summary of Sector C's Organizational Successes and Failures

Reviewing the case of Sector C, only five of its thirteen service demands were unqualified successes. Although all three of Sector C's attempts at militancy failed both to mobilize the membership and to achieve gains in services, Sector C also had difficulty with its preferred legal approach of conformist and bootstrap strategies. Although Sector C's organizational identity had been shaped by the clientelism of Chito Rios, Sector C's elected leaders were rarely able to deliver the goods with the tactics that worked so well for Pro. This was due to several factors, including a different district-level political context,[19] a population only one-fifth that of Pro, and elected leaders who lacked the contacts and leadership skills necessary to make clientelism work for their organization. This was aggravated by Sector C's electoral regime, which resulted in two sudden changes of power between enemy factions (Ostros to Chávez in 1998, and Chávez to Vega in 2000), which further destabilized the neighborhood. This did not stop the group from trying, but its limited successes were due more to persistence and by-the-book legal petitioning than to any real partnerships with influential allies. Secretary General Vega, for example, worked with the FONAVI housing agency to acquire water and sewer infrastructure, but this was straightforward petitioning rather than a clientelist partnership. In 2005, Sector C still did not appear on official maps of Lima, and other services like trash collection and schools had not arrived. After fourteen years, Sector C remained a client in search of a patron.

STUBBORN OLD GUARD RADICALS DESPITE REPEATED FAILURE: THE CASE OF ROSALES

Despite over a decade of repeated failures that made Rosales the laggard neighborhood of the entire Los Olivos district, the Rosales settlers rarely diverged from

---

18. In a 2005 interview, Hilario de Peña suggested that she would pursue title to the (privately owned) land via a strategy of petitioning, but she did not indicate any concrete plan or knowledge regarding the titling process.

19. The shift from the friendly Mayor Rubio between 1993 and 1995 to two consecutive neutral mayors—Javier Kanashiro (Cambio 90) from 1995 to 1998 and Gladys Ugaz (Somos Perú) from 1998

their militant strategies of demanding services through disruption and political pressure. Like Sector C, Rosales had acquired water truck service through a conformist deal soon after its founding (in December 1990) while still a part of the Olivos de Pro organization of Chito Rios. When the Rosales organization was created in February 1991, however, the new elected leaders of Rosales took the neighborhood in a direction very different from the clientelism of Pro.

The First Three Years: The Importance of the Local Mayor

From its creation in 1991 until it won recognition from Mayor Martínez in 1994, the *nascent* Rosales organization relied exclusively on extralegal strategies. The four service demands during this period were: (1) a *rogue* attempt to steal electricity under Mayor Lezama—a failure; (2) *militant* demands for recognition by Lezama—a failure; (3) a *rogue* attempt to steal electricity under Mayor Martínez—a success; and (4) *militant* demands for recognition by Martínez—a success. The varying outcomes of these early demands hinged on an external factor: the position of the district mayor. Other factors were also important, such as organizational resources, but since this did not vary significantly during these three years (see table 3.3), the antagonism of Mayor Lezama and the friendliness of Mayor Martínez explain most of the variation.

The Sauñe Administration: Militant Failure

Under its first secretary general, Nestor Sauñe (1991–93), Rosales failed to steal electricity and failed to earn recognition due to mayoral hostility. The settlers did establish informal electrical hookups, but these were disrupted and sometimes destroyed by municipal police, leaving Rosales without reliable electrical power for its first two years. Sauñe also organized two major marches on the Los Olivos city hall demanding municipal recognition, but despite high attendance and disruption of traffic, Mayor Lezama would not budge (Montesinos 2002, interview; Rojas 2002, interview).

The Rojas Administration: The Glory Days of Militancy

Under Sauñe's successor, Willy Rojas (1993–95), Rosales repeated its earlier efforts and was rewarded by Mayor Martínez. During this period, the Rosales settlers marched on city hall and other targets so often that Rojas remarked in a 2002 interview, "When I was secretary general, the municipality was practically our house." Rojas was a former union organizer, and with eight highway-blocking

---

to 2002—hurt Sector C's efforts to acquire services. While Rubio facilitated installation of formal electricity hookups, Kanashiro did nothing for Sector C, and Ugaz was not even willing to broker an agreement between Sector C and San Diego to allow the activation of the already built sewer system.

Table 3.3 Rosales data matrix

| | | | External factors | | | | Internal factors | | | |
Stage of development	Neighborhood leader	Service demand	District mayor	Service provider	Allies	Avenue of participation	Strategy type	Key resources	Neighborhood regime type	Outcome
Nascent (91–94)	Sauñe (91–93)	Electricity	Hostile	State			Rogue		Electoral	Failure
		Recognition	Hostile	District		93 Election	Militant	High participation	Electoral	Failure
	Rojas (93–95)	Electricity	Friendly	State			Rogue		Electoral	Success
		Recognition	Friendly	District			Militant	High participation	Electoral	Success
Mature (94–05)		Land titles	Friendly	Private		95 Election	Militant	High participation	Electoral	Failure
		Piped water	Neutral	State			Militant	High participation	Electoral	Failure
	Encarnación (95–98)	Sewers	Neutral	State			Militant	High participation	Electoral	Failure
		Electricity	Neutral	Private			Bootstrap	Money	Electoral	Success
		Land titles	Neutral	Private			Conformist	Low unity	Electoral	Failure
	López (98–00)	Land titles	Neutral	Private		98 Election	Militant	Low unity	Electoral	Failure
		Piped water	Neutral	State			Militant	Low unity	Electoral	Failure
	Tapia (00–02)	Piped water	Friendly	State	Local NGO		Conformist	Low unity	Electoral	Failure*
		Sewers	Friendly	State	Local NGO		Conformist	Low unity	Electoral	Failure*
		Land titles	Neutral	Private			Conformist	Low unity	Electoral	Failure
	Peña (02)	Land titles	Neutral	Private		02 Election	Militant	Low unity	Electoral	Failure
	Montesinos (03–05)	Piped water	Friendly	State	NGO		Militant/ Conformist	Low unity	Electoral	Success
		Sewers	Friendly	State	NGO		Militant/ Conformist	Low unity	Electoral	Success
		Land titles	Neutral	Private			Bootstrap	Money	Electoral	Success

*Tapia's petitioning for both piped water and sewer drainage was approved by state agencies, but the projects were not funded and construction never began.

marches to the municipality, Congress, the metropolitan mayor's office, and the Ministry of the Presidency, Rosales became a visible and militant presence.[20] In 1993, Martínez reversed the policy of his predecessor and looked the other way while Rosales stole electricity. Settlers were occasionally forced to pay token fees, but the service was largely free. Militant demands also yielded help in building a small community center, and in 1994 Mayor Martínez ignored the objections of Pro Developers and granted recognition to Rosales, which also helped settlers enroll their children in school (Rojas 2002, interview; Tapia 2002, interview). These militant successes relied on high participation and service provision by a local district government that they could effectively target, but the key factor was the position of the district mayor.

Nine Years of Failure: Internal Problems and Little External Help

From 1994 until 2005, the *mature* Rosales organization continued to rely primarily on militant strategies of demand-making. Two neighborhood leaders diverged from this pattern and employed conformist and bootstrap methods, but the Rosales settlers quickly replaced these "deviant" leaders with more militant candidates. These abrupt shifts in leadership meant that during this eleven-year period the neighborhood council and secretary general changed hands five times, further undermining efforts to develop the neighborhood. The fourteen service demands during this period were: (1) *militant* demands for land titles—a failure; (2) *militant* demands for piped water—a failure; (3) *militant* demands for sewer drainage—a failure; (4) *bootstrap* purchase of privatized electricity service—a success; (5) a *conformist* attempt at land titles— a failure; (6) another *militant* demand for land titles—a failure; (7) another *militant* demand for piped water—a failure; (8) a *conformist* petition for water that was approved, but not implemented—a failure; (9) a *conformist* petition for drainage that was approved but not implemented—a failure; (10) another *conformist* attempt at land titles—a failure; (11) yet another *militant* demand for land titles—a failure; (12) a combination *militant/conformist* campaign for water, backed by an Italian NGO—a success; (13) a combination *militant/conformist* campaign for drainage backed by the same NGO—a success; and (14) a *bootstrap* purchase contract for land titles at a negotiated price—a success, albeit one that benefits only families able to pay the negotiated price.

20. The most militant settlers of Rosales offer a good illustration of the "revolutionary approach" described by Schönwälder (2002, 100), in which settlers often rejected institutionalized democracy because of its failure to overturn societal inequalities. Even when opportunities appeared, Rosales settlers remained skeptical of what the democratic process could deliver, and they were particularly skeptical given the 1990s dissolution of the Peruvian Left (Roberts 1997, 321–27).

Amazingly, despite years of organizing and marching, Rosales netted only a single success in the first nine years of this period, and that success relied not on mobilization but on the settlers' pocketbooks: their bootstrap purchase of electricity. How could they fail so completely, making Rosales the least developed neighborhood in the entire district? And why, between 2003 and 2005, did three important demands at last succeed?

Two external and two internal factors largely explain these outcomes. Externally, a general lack of allies as well as unresponsive service providers affected their demands, and internally, poor strategy choices and intraorganization squabbles often killed any remaining chance of success (see table 3.3). Since the services sought were provided either by the state government (water and drainage) or private companies (the land itself and, after 1997, electricity), mobilization of even all 955 Rosales families was unlikely to win services without allied neighborhoods or innovative leadership. Rosales had neither. Internal disputes further weakened the Rosales organization and hurt individual leaders' attempts to mobilize the membership, as many settlers took sides in the disputes and then refused to support protest actions organized by a rival leader.

The Rojas Administration: Stubbornly Militant

In addition to municipal recognition, Secretary General Rojas also made Rosales's first of five unsuccessful attempts to acquire land titles. Pro Developers held a relatively clear private claim to the land, but Rojas and most of the Rosales membership believed that the land could be won politically, if they could just mount sufficient pressure on COFOPRI to challenge Pro Developers. They were wrong. With the 1995 elections approaching, both Fujimori and Jaime Yoshiyama visited Rosales,[21] but the candidates offered only empty promises, and the demands for land titles went nowhere. Rojas felt that the settlers were not militant enough: "Two years was not enough [time] to develop a worker's consciousness" (2002, interview). Given the success of militant demands for titles elsewhere in Lima, however, the resilience of the Pro Developers' claim on the land is a better explanation (Romero 2002, interview). At the end of Rojas's tenure, his failure to procure titles provoked an internal dispute over dues, and settlers accused him of stealing from the organization. Despite this dispute, Rojas's service victories (electricity and municipal recognition, as well as trash

21. The former minister of transportation and communication (1991) and of energy and mines (1991–92), Jaime Yoshiyama had become the leader of Peru's constituent assembly (1992–95) and at this time was Fujimori's candidate for metropolitan mayor of Lima. In November 1995, Yoshiyama narrowly (52 percent to 48 percent) lost the mayoral race to Alberto Andrade (1995–2002), but Fujimori rewarded Yoshiyama's loyalty by appointing him as the new minister of the presidency (1995–97) just three days after losing the mayoral election (Tuesta 2001, 53, 59, 65, 79, 426).

collection) sustained his popularity, and he was able to anoint his successor, Jorge Encarnación Sandoval.[22]

The Encarnación Administration: Settlers Punish Conformist Experiment

Under the leadership of Secretary General Encarnación (1995–98), Rosales initially continued the Rojas approach of militant protest, but when these tactics failed to deliver water or drainage service, Encarnación shifted gears and sought formal electricity service and land titles through bootstrap and conformist strategies. As the protégé of Rojas, Encarnación was happy to organize marches in support of the neighborhood demands, but he was never the Old Guard radical that Rojas was. He attempted to bolster the group's demands for water and sewer infrastructure with more conventional legal petitioning. He formed a committee to work on the project, but committee members felt that direct action was the best route to take, and so their only accomplishment was a feasibility study of the water project. Although not hostile, district mayor Felipe Castillo refused to work with Encarnación, which further stalled the process (Encarnación 2002, interview).[23]

Frustrated, Encarnación refocused on electricity. With electricity now privatized, he had an easier time coaxing the militant settlers into his bootstrap plan—even the more radical settlers conceded that the Electro Lima corporation would not bow to political pressure. The effort more than tripled the settlers' electricity bills, but the project went through smoothly due to methodical leadership and the settlers' ability to pay.

Encarnación's legal approach faltered, however, when he tried to apply it to the land itself. In 1997, Encarnación orchestrated a meeting between the COFOPRI housing agency, Pro Developers, and the Rosales neighborhood council. At the meeting, Encarnación conceded that the land was private, and he worked on a tentative purchase agreement. Most settlers, however, still believed the land was public, so they were furious at their leader's "betrayal" (Montesinos 2002, interview). Encarnación described the conflict in a 2002 interview: "I was accused of stealing. There were formal complaints, but the investigation discovered nothing. I was under suspicion. We had a general assembly. People asked: 'Why do we have to pay?' Accused me of all kinds of stuff." The investigation cleared Encarnación, but his administration was hobbled and undertook no new initiatives. His successor, Francisco López, was elected in early 1998 by a flurry of anti-Encarnación votes.

22. Prior to his election as secretary general of Rosales, Encarnación served as the chair of the Rosales Culture and Sports Committee under Rojas.

23. Mayor Felipe Castillo (Cambio 90, 1995–98; Vamos Vecino, 1998–2006) worked with the neighboring Pro organization, but the disruptive struggle methods of Rosales apparently wrecked Encarnación's chances of working with the mayor, who initially dismissed Rosales as a group of troublemakers. By 2000, however, Castillo would assume a more friendly stance toward Rosales.

The López Administration: Internal Division Cripples Renewed Militancy

Under the leadership of Secretary General López (1998–2000), Rosales returned to its radical approach, but the internal disputes of the previous years hampered López's efforts. To differentiate himself from his failed predecessor, López immediately organized a pressure campaign for land titles; while popular in the neighborhood, it was entirely ineffective, especially since the faction that still supported Encarnación refused to participate. An official at COFOPRI explained the situation: "In Rosales, there was no majority ratification of the required arbitration process. They were one of the first, so they were still getting things straightened out. They are taking the route of political pressure, rather than legal process" (Romero 2002, interview).

With neither COFOPRI nor Pro Developers willing to budge, López attempted to organize once again on the issue of piped water, but internal conflicts led to postponements and the effort never got off the ground. Rosales had an opportunity to join the Fraternidad Municipal Housing Program during this period, which might have helped its aspirations for piped water, but power was too concentrated in the hands of López for Rosales to consider a nonmilitant strategy. López ended his two-year term having attempted little and accomplished nothing.

The Tapia Administration: Settlers Punish
Second Conformist Experiment

Under López's successor, Secretary General Claudio Tapia (2000–2002), Rosales again experimented with conformist strategies, and the settlers again rejected the experiment. Tapia was savvy enough to publicly invoke the heyday of militancy under Sauñe and Rojas, but his actual tactics were akin to those of Encarnación. Initially setting aside the divisive issue of land, Tapia instead focused on petitioning for water and sewer service, theoretically "supported by marches." But the talk of marches was window dressing, as Tapia's chair of the Rosales Public Works Committee, Harold Vásquez Solano, explained: "We considered [marches], but they don't generate results" (2002, interview). This was a straightforward conformist bid with the conventional assistance of a local NGO, the Asociación Latinoamericana para Desarrollo Regional (Latin American Association for Regional Development, or ALADER).

Founded in 1993, ALADER was eager to help Rosales catch up with the rest of the Los Olivos district, but persistent internal divisions within both the community and the neighborhood regime ruined this effort. ALADER's aid was technical, not financial, so the success of the project hinged on Rosales's borrowing $1.7 million ($1,800 per family) from the Bank of Materials to pay for the infrastructure. People were eager to attend meetings for the water and drainage project, but for families surviving on as little as $3 per day, borrowing $1,000 for water pipes and $800 for sewer pipes was not realistic (Santos 2002, interview).

Tapia's conformist approach also yielded a friendly response from the previously indifferent Mayor Castillo. The deplorable conditions in Rosales had become something of a district embarrassment, leading Castillo to pledge modest funds for technical support (but not actual construction). Castillo announced his support in person at a 2001 neighborhood meeting (Jaimes 2002, interview). By the end of 2001, both the water and drainage projects had been approved by SEDAPAL, but the project still lacked funding.

In late 2001, Secretary General Tapia dared to pick up the land issue once again, and was punished for it. When running for neighborhood office, Tapia had argued that the land was public, but like Encarnación before him, Tapia now attempted to work with Pro Developers and COFOPRI to create a purchase agreement at a price of $1,100 per lot.[24] Led by neighborhood council member Elvira Peña, the settlers revolted against Tapia (Peña 2002, interview). "I was denounced as a traitor while I was secretary general," said Tapia in a 2002 interview. "I had a general assembly to clear up everything, but [it didn't work]." Tapia blamed Peña and another council member for the disappearance of some related funds, but blaming them did not rekindle support among the membership, and the secretary general made no further progress on any significant front.

The Tapia scandal led to a contested neighborhood election between Tapia's opponent, Elvira Peña, and an old stalwart of the Rojas administration, Lino Montesinos. Montesinos also objected to Tapia's rule, but he still lost to Peña, 71 percent to 29 percent (Montesinos 2002, interview).[25]

The Peña Administration: Rosales Swings Back to Ineffective Militancy

Under the leadership of Secretary General Elvira Peña (elected in 2002 and impeached the same year), Rosales made its third unsuccessful demand for land titles through protest marches and disruption (and its fifth attempt overall), but failed yet again. Peña generated renewed support for the rather tired militant demand with a 1995 document she claimed proved public ownership of the land. COFOPRI rejected her claim and ignored the several hundred protesters

24. The $1,100 figure was considerably less than the $5,000-per-lot price quoted to Pro in 2002. Most likely, the lower figure represented Pro Developers' effort to get Rosales to come to the bargaining table. As noted in the Pro case study, once negotiations had begun, the price steadily rose each year as Pro Developers repeatedly declared that the assessed value of the land had risen (which was probably true).

25. Montesinos blamed his defeat on residual resentment toward his coordination of the Rosales lot plan, designed in 1991 under Secretary General Saùñe. As chair of the Lot Plan Committee, Montesinos had overseen the assignment of lots based on need and contributions to the community, and many had accused him of favoritism (Montesinos 2002, interview).

assembled at the downtown COFOPRI office in early 2002 (Peña 2002, interview; Romero 2002, interview). COFOPRI was particularly indisposed to help Peña since the agency had already offered to help Rosales pay for all the community land in the settlement (e.g., open spaces, streets, the plaza), but Peña was dead set on winning 100 percent of the land at no cost. The demand suffered from low neighborhood unity and a once again indifferent Mayor Castillo, but the core cause of failure was the private ownership of the land, which made externally dependent strategies ineffective. In 2002, Elvira Peña received threats of violence from what she presumed was the Tapia faction, and several families left Rosales, citing health problems caused by living with outhouses for almost twelve years (Peña 2002, interview). Some settlers continued to support Peña, but the majority viewed her as an obstacle to Rosales's development, and she was impeached and removed from office in late 2002.

The Montesinos Administration: Conformist Success Sugarcoated with Militancy

Elected to replace his opponent, Elvira Peña, Secretary General Lino Montesinos (2003–5) employed a mix of militant, conformist, and bootstrap strategies to win Rosales's most significant services victories yet, but he skillfully played up the militant dimension of these demands, keeping settlers satisfied that they were not "selling out." Montesinos scored two major victories in 2003, bringing permanent water and drainage infrastructure to the entire neighborhood, and one partial victory in 2004–5, bringing the issue of land titles to closure for a portion of the settlement.

Montesinos employed a combination of protest marches and legal petitioning to finally bring piped water and sewer drainage to Rosales. Montesinos initially worked behind the scenes, utilizing his role as *gobernador* (unofficial local party leader) for Perú Posible to solicit funds from Los Olivos mayor Felipe Castillo and from the Fondo Italo-Peruano de la Deuda (Italian-Peruvian Debt Reduction Fund).[26] These meetings went well, and Montesinos warned both groups that he would soon organize symbolic marches to galvanize community participation in the initiatives. Returning to Rosales, Montesinos gave the settlers a different story, claiming that political pressure was required to get city hall and the Italian NGO to act. Always ready for a protest march, the Rosales settlers protested at both Los Olivos city hall and at the Italian-Peruvian Fund headquarters. Montesinos's scheme worked, and in early 2003 Mayor Castillo laid the symbolic "first

---

26. The Italian-Peruvian Debt Reduction Fund is a foreign NGO that negotiates funding for infrastructure projects in poor neighborhoods in Lima. In exchange for funding such projects, the Peruvian government receives credit toward its external debt owed to Italy.

pipe" of the new water and drainage system.[27] But internal divisions marred Rosales's most significant victory in fourteen years, as Elvira Peña and her faction bombarded the opening ceremony with garbage and rotten fruit, provoking fistfights and recriminations (Montesinos 2005, interview). The spectacle was carried on local television and radio, reminding the district that Rosales was the neighborhood where things just never seemed to work.

Montesinos also managed to mend the relationships with COFOPRI and the municipality, resulting in partial resolution of the long-standing struggle over land titles. Montesinos accepted that the land was private, and focused his efforts on negotiating an affordable price. In 2004–5, Pro Developers offered a price of $41/m^2$ for the land; Montesinos countered with an offer of $12/m^2$, and Pro Developers, which viewed Montesinos as a credible negotiator, countered with a final offer of $25/m^2$. About 40 percent of the settlers rejected this deal, clinging to Elvira Peña's promise that they could get the land for free, but nearly 60 percent accepted it and moved to sign contracts. By the end of 2005, about 175 families (18 percent) owned their homes, 150 (16 percent) had equity but still carried debt, and 250 (26 percent) were in the process of signing contracts. The remaining 380 (40 percent) continued to occupy their homes but would not deal with Pro Developers (Montesinos 2005, interview).

Summary of Rosales's Organizational Successes and Failures

Reviewing the case of Rosales, only six of eighteen demands succeeded. A key source of failure for Rosales was the frequency with which its electoral regime produced polarizing leaders. Internal competition meant that about every two years there was a new set of leaders in charge, and each hoarded power from the incumbents they had displaced. Rosales faced such daunting external challenges that this internal leadership pendulum undermined most service demands, including not only the more conformist attempts but also the militant tactics these Old Guard radicals preferred. While Old Guard radicals tend to avoid clientelist partnerships, they can benefit from alliances, but Rosales had few chances to find such allies since it was consumed by internal disputes. This organizational volatility also compromised Rosales's ability to work with allies and governments. It took over a decade of failure and miserable living conditions before Lino Montesinos was able to deftly manage both his radical settlers and the bureaucratic terrain of municipal and state politics.

27. About 90 percent of the project cost was paid by the state via the Italian-Peruvian Debt Reduction Fund. The remaining 10 percent of funds were loaned to the settlers by the Los Olivos municipality (Montesinos 2005, interview).

With full water and drainage service completed and the land title situation partially resolved, Rosales had, after fourteen years, finally achieved property security. Yet in 2005, Rosales remained the least developed of the ninety-three neighborhoods in the Los Olivos district. This study ended just as Rosales concluded its *mature* stage of development, and it was not clear what would happen next. Given the "security trap" argument articulated in chapter 1 (and the analysis of organizational survival outcomes in chapter 6), it seemed likely that Rosales would enter a moribund period of low participation, especially given its tumultuous internal problems. Not all Old Guard radicals are destined to encounter so many failures, however, as we see in the contrasting Quito case of Pisulli.

CAN'T TEACH THIS OLD GUARD RADICAL NEW TRICKS: THE ARCHETYPAL CASE OF PISULLI

From its 1983 founding until 2005, the Old Guard organization of Pisulli maintained an almost exclusive commitment to militant strategies and succeeded in acquiring all major services. Although the organization acquired title to the land from the Quito government, however, Pisulli's authoritarian neighborhood leader withheld the titles from individual settlers in order to enforce their indefinite loyalty to the organization. Ironically, this entrapment of individual settlers permitted the settlement organization as a whole to evade the security trap and consolidate.

National and Local Context

Following the death of Ecuadorian president Jaime Roldós Aguilera (1979–91, DP) in a plane crash, the administration of former vice president Osvaldo Hurtado Larrea (1981–84, Movimiento Popular Democrático) took a turn to the right, but full-fledged structural adjustment would not begin until León Febres Cordero took office (1984–88, Frente de Reconstrucción Nacional, or FRN). But although Pisulli was founded on Hurtado's watch, it was the four years of the Febres Cordero administration that most shaped Pisulli's permanently combative stance.

In 1983, the simultaneous invasions of Pisulli and Roldós settled adjacent parcels of land, but the two became bitter enemies. While Pisulli was a maverick outsider oriented toward the ideology of the Partido Comunista Ecuatoriano (Ecuadorian Communist Party), Roldós was a creature of the political establishment, paying nominal fealty to the Hurtado administration, but actually loyal to the rising rightist ideology of Febres Cordero. For Pisulli, this meant that its hostile neighbor had the willing support of political elites, while Pisulli had to fight for everything.

The politics of the local Cotocollao district played little role in Pisulli's struggles during this period. Prior to the creation of the Quito metropolitan government in 1993, the scope of the Municipality of Quito was more limited, extending to Cotocollao mainly on paper. Local Cotocollao administrations were appointed rather than elected, putting local control of the capital city's periphery in the hands of the national government.

Both nationally and locally, land invasions had not yet gone out of style. The rightist FRN had found invasion communities in Guayaquil to be fertile ground for sowing political support, and some politicians now set their sights on Quito, which had experienced several large-scale invasions in the 1970s (Godard 1988).

Origins of the Pisulli Invasion

The Pisulli invasion was the brainchild of Edgar Coral, an engineering student at Quito's Universidad Central in the early 1980s. At Universidad Central, Coral became a member of the student council and president of a federation of students from Quito's various universities. Under Coral's leadership, the federation's main project was to extend education to the popular sectors. To this end, a team of activist-minded students and professors began working in Cangahua, an old neighborhood on Quito's northern periphery (Cangahua was not an invasion community). Founded in the 1930s, Cangahua still did not have running water (and did not get it until 2002), and the students sought to preserve Cangahua's historical buildings while enhancing the local residents' quality of life through workshops on architecture and urban development.

While working in Cangahua, Coral studied the adjacent Condado hacienda, a large stretch (over six square kilometers) of abandoned land owned by the Ministry of Public Health, and began planning an invasion. Coral was familiar with the history of invasions in Quito and Guayaquil, but in his mind, this community would be different, as it would be founded on socialist ideals and led exclusively by him; Pisulli would not be an invasion at all, but simply "an extension of the university project" (Coral 2002, interview). Coral would emerge not as an innovative leader, however, but as an almost archetypal Old Guard radical.[28]

Another organizer had a competing plan, however, and was preparing to invade the same land. Segundo Aguilar was a classic Old Guard client. He had led invasions before Roldós (e.g., Atucucho in 1983) and would organize others in the

---

28. Coral was only "almost" an archetypal Old Guard radical because he was not a veteran invasion leader; his circle of advisers, however, included invasion "experts."

future (e.g., San Carlos and Tumbaco between 1988 and 1990). Aguilar had the backing of the right-wing establishment that would elect Febres Cordero to the presidency in 1984, but he planned to name the settlement "Roldós" after the dead president Jaime Roldós in order to curry favor with the current Hurtado administration (Andrade 2005).[29]

Since the two fledgling invasion organizations were both recruiting members in the same neighborhoods, Coral and Aguilar quickly learned about each other and accelerated their respective efforts in order to beat the other to the punch. Leaders and founders on both sides of the conflict claim that their group made the first move, but it seems more likely that Roldós moved first, since it ended up with the more desirable 450 hectares of lower land, while Pisulli was stuck with 180 hectares of higher and less accessible land. Regardless, on November 11, 1983, *both* groups invaded.

Simultaneous Invasions: Belligerent Siblings from Day One

On November 11, 1983, Coral led one thousand families to the upper end of the abandoned Condado hacienda, approaching from the west, while Aguilar led nearly two thousand families to the lower land, approaching from the east. Although the area was vast (sufficient for perhaps ten thousand or more families), the two groups met in the middle and conflict erupted. Gunshots were fired, sparking a five-year period of inter-neighborhood violence. The police arrived and attempted to evict the Pisulli settlers but left the Roldós group alone, as Aguilar had already made deals with several politicians. Within two days, the violence escalated. Hired thugs tore through Pisulli, firing guns and burning shantyhomes. One firebomb killed nine-month-old Jaime Vargas, and the infant's name became an instant rallying cry for the Pisulli settlers, who responded in kind. Within a year, more than twenty funerals would be held in both Pisulli and Roldós, but neither Coral nor Aguilar would back down (Ramírez 2002, interview; Silva 2002, interview).

A Bloody First Year: Aggressive Demands Yield Quick Success

From November 1983 until April 1984, the Pisulli settlers fought for their neighborhood and sometimes for their lives. Despite the violence that permeated community life, the settlers made three demands for services during the organization's *nascent* stage of development: (1) *rogue* theft of electricity through

---

29. See also Swyngedouw (1995), who looks at the contradictions of urban water provision in Guayaquil, where networks of patron-client relations complicate service provision among invasion neighborhoods, many of them with connections to the political right.

informal hookups—a success; (2) *militant* demands for water truck service—a success; and (3) *militant* demands for municipal recognition—a success. These demands succeeded because of three main factors, noted in table 3.4. First, participation rates approached 100 percent. Coral demanded maximum participation, and in an atmosphere of guerrilla warfare, he got it. Second, Coral's continued connection with Universidad Central resulted in enhanced legitimacy for their many protest marches, as students and some professors sided with the leftist side of what became one of Quito's most famous Left-Right conflicts of the day. And third, although Aguilar already had a web of political support established, the violence of his minions was fast becoming infamous. President Hurtado did not wish to appear to be endorsing right-wing thugs, so he acquiesced to some of Pisulli's demands as well.

During the first month, university students helped Pisulli's settlers establish informal electricity hookups. Their main obstacle was not the state electric company, but saboteurs from Roldós. Given the warlike atmosphere that was quickly developing, however, there was already a rigorous schedule for guard duty, so safeguarding the community's electricity connection simply became one more area that required security.

In the first weeks of 1984, university-assisted protest marches yielded rapid water truck service. The isolated Pisulli had no chance of survival without a regular water source, and so the protest actions were overwhelmingly attended by settlers not posted on guard duty. Participants were also highly militant, going so far as to break down the doors of the state water agency and demand a face-to-face meeting with the water company officials (Coral 2002, interview).

On April 12, 1984, just four months after its founding, Pisulli gained official status as a legal organization recognized by the Municipality of Quito. Again, university support and highly confrontational demands were key to their success, as the settlers again occupied a building, this time belonging to the municipality. Notably, the tenor of the protests was not just that of poor people needing homes, but also that of indignant Quiteños demanding protection from the predations of thugs and paramilitaries. The scene of grieving widows and the memory of the murdered infant Jaime Vargas also helped their cause.

Navigating Through Bad Times and Good: Invariably Militant

From 1984 to 1995, Pisulli was a *mature* organization that had been recognized legally but had not yet achieved property security. Within this stage of development, however, two distinct periods are evident. First, the violence of the 1984–88 period kept Pisulli's rates of participation very high, but the hostile administration of President Febres Cordero effectively quashed all service demands from

Table 3.4 Pisulli data matrix

Stage of development	Neighborhood leader	External factors						Internal factors		Outcome
		Service demand	District mayor	Service provider	Allies	Avenue of participation	Strategy type	Key resources	Neighborhood regime type	
Consolidated (95–05)		Electricity	Neutral*	State	University		Rogue	Minga***	Authoritarian	Success
		Water truck	Neutral*	State	University		Militant	High participation	Authoritarian	Success
		Recognition	Neutral*	Municipal	University	84 Election	Militant	High participation	Authoritarian	Success
		Land titles	Hostile*	State			Militant	High participation	Authoritarian	Failure
		Electricity	Hostile*	State			Militant	High participation	Authoritarian	Failure
Mature (84–95)	Coral (83–05)	Piped water	Hostile*	State			Militant	High participation	Authoritarian	Failure
		Piped water	Neutral	Metro			Militant	High participation	Authoritarian	Success
		Sewers	Neutral	Metro			Militant	High participation	Authoritarian	Success
		Land titles**	Neutral	Metro/Private		96 Election	Militant/ Bootstrap	Money	Authoritarian	Failure**
Nascent (83–84)		Electricity	Neutral	Metro			Militant	High participation	Authoritarian	Success
		Piped water	Neutral	Metro	Roldós	00 Election	Militant	High participation	Authoritarian	Success
		Sewers	Neutral	Metro	Roldós		Militant	High participation	Authoritarian	Success

*Prior to the 1993 creation of Quito's metropolitan mayoralty, the national government dominated municipal governance of peripheral parts of Quito, like Pisulli's district of Cotocollao. Hence, these six scorings reflect the position of the national government, not the mayor of Quito.

**Pisulli's second attempt at land titles succeeded in acquiring title to all 1,800 lots, but the titles remained in the name of the Pisulli cooperative, controlled by Edgar Coral, who refused to distribute them to individual settlers. Coral held the titles for at least ten years, keeping settlers insecure and trapped in the organization.

*** A minga is an obligatory community work project; nonparticipants are fined.

Pisulli. Second, with the removal of Febres Cordero from the presidency, the 1988–95 period witnessed the cessation of most violence, and several demands for services encountered modest success. Throughout the entire period, however, Pisulli relied almost exclusively on militant strategies of demand-making. Six demands, summarized in table 3.4, can be identified: (1) *militant* demands for land titles—an abysmal failure; (2) *militant* demands for electricity—a failure; (3) *militant* demands for piped water—a failure; (4) renewed *militant* demands for piped water in some parts of Pisulli—a success; (5) renewed *militant* demands for sewers in some parts of Pisulli—a success; and (6) a combination *militant/bootstrap* demand for land titles—a highly unusual outcome that requires explanation (discussed below).

Four Years of Failed Demands: Sustained Participation and Mobilization

Pisulli's first attempt at land titles was an abysmal failure because not only did they fail to acquire the titles, but Febres Cordero actually granted the titles to their enemies in Roldós! With this aggressive move, Febres Cordero made the Roldós cooperative the legal owner of Roldós *and* Pisulli. Pisulli's subsequent demands for formal electricity and piped water (both from state agencies) also failed (Ramírez 2002, interview).

The first three demands failed for one major reason: President Febres Cordero wished to destroy Pisulli, and he expended considerable resources foiling its every move. Analytically, one could argue that Coral made the wrong strategy choice, and that conformist negotiations would have yielded better results. To Coral and his followers, however, such an option was anathema, especially since the president's followers were trying to kill them. Despite his own invariably authoritarian leadership, Coral felt that Pisulli was on the side of democracy and therefore could not compromise. As Coral modestly explained in a 2002 interview: "It wasn't a conflict between cooperatives. It was a conflict between the forward-thinking democratic part of society—led by me—and how the Right wanted to co-opt the social groups to form repressive paramilitaries." A more interesting question might be: how did Pisulli manage to survive this four-year period of violent hostility?

Two likely explanations include strong internal organization and perpetual mobilization. With the next violent raid always just around the corner (with some initiated by Pisulli), Coral kept the entire population of Pisulli in a constant cycle of meetings, marches, and other actions. And as the 1988 elections drew near, Febres Cordero and other politicians became more sensitive to negative media attention.

As the conflict wore on, it became evident that some Roldós settlers were unhappy with Aguilar and felt that his drive to destroy Pisulli was also damaging their own community. In 1987, when Aguilar's men bombed an unoccupied school in Pisulli, the Roldós settlers considered getting rid of their leader.

Ten Years of Incremental Progress: The Mobilization Continues

A turning point arrived in 1988 with the election of President Rodrigo Borja (1988–92, Izquierda Democrática), who swung the political establishment away from the extremes of Febres Cordero. Although they lost the presidency, the Right was hardly eliminated from Quito politics, but it was enough to weaken Aguilar's support network. Unhappy Roldós settlers seized the moment and expelled him, also ending their relationship with the FRN.[30]

At the same time, the 1988 construction of a Catholic church at the epicenter of the conflict also proved to be a moderating force between Pisulli and Roldós. A team of Boston priests had been working in northern Quito since the 1970s, and Father Robert Thomas hoped that the new church might help bring peace. With the violence winding down, the church became a symbol of this moderating trend, leading some settlers to view the church as a "peace barrier" between the two neighborhoods (Silva 2002, interview). The church's many infrastructure- and service-oriented projects also helped soothe the wounds of the past and even move the two communities toward cooperation, though that would take another decade to actually occur.

With the abatement of inter-neighborhood violence (though occasional intra-neighborhood violence by Coral's enforcers persisted), Pisulli resumed its militant strategies of demand-making or, as Coral called it, "permanent mobilization." With neutral officials now in government, various services would often be nominally authorized through routine petitioning, but no service was ever delivered to Pisulli without militant pressure to force the issue. Whether it was piped water or sewers from the Metropolitan Council (newly created in 1993), or other services like roads and a medical clinic, Pisulli's approach was invariably militant and disruptive.

Coral also rejected partisan alliances. As Coral said in a 2002 interview: "We don't maintain any relationship with any political party. Once we turn over our affiliation, we turn over our personal freedom and lose our bargaining power." Coral spoke of autonomy, but what he clearly wanted was personal control. From 1983 to 2005, Coral never let any voice in Pisulli challenge him, and he even rejected free infrastructure projects from Father Robert Thomas because he would not be able to control the project funds (Thomas 2002, interview).

---

30. This would not be the last time Aguilar was expelled from an invasion he helped organize. In the early 1990s, the infamous Aguilar headed up an invasion in Tumbaco, until the Tumbaco settlers likewise expelled him for his violent excesses (Chamorro 2002, interview; Coral 2002, interview).

Coral's militant approach worked to a considerable degree. With nearly a decade of experience under their belts, the Pisulli settlers knew how to mobilize, and although the threat of violence had largely vanished, Coral was a tireless taskmaster. And so, even with installation of medium-quality water pipes and sewer drainage in some parts of Pisulli, Coral kept up the pressure on the most important issue: land titles.

Technically, the Pisulli land was now private and owned by the Roldós cooperative, whose president, Angel Rodríguez, requested a steep price. The militant Pisulli settlers, however, rejected Roldós's ownership claim (with fairly good justification, since granting the land to Roldós had been an obvious political move by Febres Cordero), and continued targeting the newly created metropolitan government, headed by Mayor Jamil Mahuad (1992–98). In the end, Pisulli's militant pressure led to a metropolitan government–brokered deal between Coral and Rodríguez. Coral paid an undisclosed sum for title to all 1,800 Pisulli lots—and then Coral kept the titles to himself.

Although the Pisulli cooperative successfully bought its own land from Roldós in 1995, Coral remained the sole legal authority of the cooperative, and he maintained a legal monopoly on all land in Pisulli. Ostensibly, Coral was willing to grant a title to any settler who reimbursed "the cooperative," but by 2005 fewer than fifty titles had actually been distributed. Coral claimed he would release any lot title for the proper $250 fee, but some settlers claimed that they had paid more than $250, and that Coral kept raising the price (Ramírez 2002, interview). Further, Coral used the titles as a form of blackmail to coerce settlers into working on his political campaigns (Tamaca 2002, interview). In 2002, Coral made his third unsuccessful bid for a seat in Congress, but despite these repeated failures, he continued to have a base whose loyalty was strictly enforced.[31]

Secure Organization, Insecure Individuals: High Participation Sustained

From 1995 until 2005, the authoritarian Pisulli organization acquired high-quality delivery of all major services—except land titles. During its *consolidated* stage, three major service initiatives occurred: (1) *militant* demands for formal electrical hookups in most of Pisulli—a success; (2) *militant* demands for piped water in most of Pisulli—a success; and (3) *militant* demands for sewer drainage

---

31. Among the invasion organizations examined in this study, relatively few leaders used their neighborhood leadership position as base from which to seek higher elected office. The two clearest examples of such a trajectory were Edgar Coral in Pisulli and María Hernández in Itchimbía (see chapter 5). For a full discussion of the transformation of urban popular movement leaders into electoral players, see Haber (2006).

in most of Pisulli—a success. These successes were largely an extension of the later portion of Pisulli's *mature* stage.

Although the Pisulli organization now had property security, individual settlers remained insecure, and so the same formula of authoritarian leadership and high participation in militant demands led to victories over a neutral metropolitan mayor and council. This formula proved sufficient to extract electricity provision from Mayor Mahuad, but subsequent demands of Mayor Sevilla (1998–2000) and Mayor Moncayo (2000–2008) also relied on additional external factors: the pressure of the 2000 and 2002 elections and modest cooperation with Pisulli's former enemy, Roldós (noted in table 3.4). This cooperation should not be overstated, as tension still existed between the communities, but over a decade after the violent Febres Cordero period, at least two joint Pisulli-Roldos marches delivered high-quality piped water and sewer drainage to most of Pisulli (as well as an expansion of the Roldós neighborhood), though its upper reaches (30 percent of the neighborhood) still lacked these services. Additionally, the metropolitan government began providing resources for street paving, telephone service, and garbage collection.

Settlers were genuinely pleased with these infrastructure improvements, but many of them questioned the ultimate value of these gains if they were never able to become owners of their homes. Aside from Coral's aides and loyalists who worked directly for the Pisulli organization, settler interviews yielded a stark picture of a community living in fear of its own leader. This was especially evident when speaking with indigenous and black residents, who described a three-race neighborhood hierarchy of "mestizos," "indios," and "negros," with blacks occupying the lowest rung. In 1995, a black block captain dared to challenge Coral's "recommended" slate of candidates for the neighborhood elections, and his family received threats of violence.[32] Heads of household of six black families complained and tried to organize the other two hundred black families in Pisulli, but in 2002 those six families were run out of town (Ramírez 2002, interview; Villavicencio 2005, interview). Said one community leader of the residents of Pisulli: "They live under fear. We can't do anything with this man" (Thomas 2002, interview).

Others were not so lucky and were killed by lynch mobs. In 1993, Father Robert Thomas intervened in the lynching of an indigenous "thief," who had been tied to a lamppost and doused with gasoline. In 1999, no one was around to stop the killing of a black "thief," who was burned at the stake. No evidence

---

32. Coral himself was never a candidate for neighborhood elections. Between 1983 and 2005 he was the unelected "manager" of Pisulli, but in truth, elected leaders served at his pleasure.

(or even a victim, in the latter incident) was ever produced in either case, but Coral considered both victims troublemakers (Thomas 2002, interview). Whatever the motivations behind these lynchings, they contributed to an atmosphere where internal dissent was not permitted.

The Frente Cívico: An Emerging Challenge to Coral's Power

After twenty years of successfully repressing or expelling any dissent, Edgar Coral finally encountered local opposition that he could not easily dislodge. Emerging in 2003, the Frente Cívico Democrático para la Dignidad de Pisulli (Democratic Civic Front for the Dignity of Pisulli) became the first sustained alternative to Coral's authoritarian leadership, and by 2005 had drawn the support of two hundred families, or about 11 percent of the settlement (Andrade 2005, interview). The Frente Cívico was founded by Juvenal Andrade Rodríguez, a former neighborhood leader who was elected (i.e., anointed by Coral) president of the Pisulli cooperative in 1996. Coral chose Andrade because he viewed him as a model resident who had worked for Coral since the community's 1983 founding, but when Andrade dared to request access to the settlement's financial records, Coral quickly replaced him as president with a loyalist. Expelled from the cooperative leadership, Andrade slowly and quietly began telling his story to Pisulli residents, explaining how Coral's lack of transparency shielded his spending of member dues on his political campaigns, rather than on neighborhood services (Andrade 2005, interview).

By 2003, Andrade felt he had enough support to openly challenge Coral, and he announced the formation of the Frente Cívico. For over a year, Coral did little to stop Andrade's organizing, but on December 10, 2004, when the Frente publicly denounced Coral at the Ministerio de Bienestar Social (Ministry of Social Welfare) and the Dirección Nacional de Cooperativas (National Directorate of Cooperatives, an umbrella organization of 170 informal settlements), the atmosphere of fear that had characterized Pisulli's early years began to reemerge. The National Directorate ordered an investigation of the Frente's allegations of corruption and intimidation, but an unrelated reshuffling of government appointees within the Ministry of Social Welfare apparently caused the planned investigation to be forgotten.

Even with the investigation cancelled, settlers did not have to wait long for Coral's response: just two weeks later, the night before Christmas Eve, the families of Andrade and three other Frente leaders awoke to find their houses on fire. Fleeing the burning buildings with their few valuables, they were met by thugs with clubs, who robbed them and then allowed the houses to burn to the ground

(Villavicencio 2005, interview). According to Andrade (2005, interview), the per-petrators were promptly arrested but spent only nine days in jail before their early release was purchased with bribes.

Despite these attacks, the Frente Cívico continued to organize, and community members helped rebuild some of the burned homes, but the intimidation had its desired effect as many Frente members stopped attending opposition meetings. In 2005, the Frente continued to advocate for three related goals: (1) to open up the cooperative accounting books; (2) to distribute the land titles to individual settlers; and (3) to dissolve the Pisulli cooperative, which Frente members con-sidered too corrupt to be reformed (Andrade 2005, interview). But despite these ambitious goals and plans to meet with Mayor Paco Moncayo and the Ministry of Social Welfare (again), the Frente Cívico's position looked precarious in 2005, with few resources, no significant allies, and an uncertain membership.[33]

Summary of Pisulli's Organizational Successes and Failures

Reviewing the case of Pisulli, three service demands failed, eight succeeded, and one (for land titles) yielded a special result. Such an aggregate view is less useful, however, than identifying the clearly demarcated periods of success and failure. Three clear periods stand out. During the first year (the *nascent* stage), all three service attempts succeeded. During the four years of the Febres Cordero administration (i.e., the first four years of the *mature* stage), all three service attempts failed. And during the 1988–2005 period (the end of the *mature* stage and the first ten years of the *consolidated* stage), nearly all service demands succeeded, although they tended to deliver only incremental gains.

In 2005, the once clear boundaries between Roldós and Pisulli were fading, and although the upper reaches with new lots still lacked most basic services, the lower two-thirds of Pisulli had not only electricity, water, and drainage, but also schools and a health clinic (albeit without staff or medicine). According to one settler, this was "all thanks to Edgar Coral" (Silva 2002, interview).

But land titles remained elusive, provoking bitter resentment. Said one settler, "I still owe eighty dollars, but even if I pay all of it, [Coral] will just raise the price" (Ramírez 2002, interview). Similarly, a single mother who arrived in 1999 explained that she did not have time to take care of her seven-year-old daughter because "Edgar Coral demands that we work on his campaign" (Tamaca 2002, interview). In 2002, Coral ran for Congress with the socialist Unión Patriótica

---

33. The Frente Cívico considered the Federación de Barrios Populares del Nororiente de Quito (Federation of Popular Neighborhoods of Northeastern Quito) an ally, but this alliance had not yet provided any significant advantages or resources to the Pisulli group (Andrade 2005, interview).

del Pueblo (Patriotic Union of the People) party, and in 2004 he ran for a seat on the Metropolitan Council. These were his third and fourth failed bids for elected office. His campaign slogan was "Contra la corrupción y la pobreza!" (Fighting corruption and poverty!).

THE OLD GUARD TYPE

Synthesis of the cases of Pro, Sector C, Rosales, and Pisulli provides a composite picture of the *identity traits*, *repertoire traits*, and *neighborhood regimes* characteristic of the Old Guard type. With respect to identity, Old Guard organizations tend to have pragmatic veteran leadership that pursues material objectives. With respect to strategic repertoire, the Old Guard exhibits strong and sometimes rigid strategy preferences, which are analytically captured by the labels *client* and *radical*. Both the clients and the radicals, however, rely on unoriginal tactics, sometimes including the use of violence, and rarely make use of technology. Finally, with respect to neighborhood regime type, Old Guard regimes vary in their competitiveness, but tend to be power-concentrating, meaning that they are usually *electoral* or *authoritarian*.

Old Guard Identity Traits: Pragmatic, Materialist, and Experienced

Old Guard organizations are characterized by a pragmatic outlook, material objectives, and leaders with experience in founding or organizing invasion communities. The pragmatic "win some, lose some" attitude of the Old Guard is perhaps most obvious in the cold-blooded calculations of authoritarian leaders like Chito Rios in Pro and Edgar Coral in Pisulli. This pragmatism is also evident, however, in the patient attitudes of leaders like Willy Rojas in Rosales. Rojas relied exclusively on disruptive militant strategies, but when demands aimed at a particular agency failed, he was ready to redirect mobilizations against a variety of other government targets.

All four Old Guard organizations operated almost exclusively for the pursuit of material needs, such as infrastructure and security. In Pro, Chito Rios professed to be an antiterrorism warrior dedicated to defeating Sendero Luminoso, but like his talk of social justice, this was a cover for the more mundane calculus of clientelism. In 1996, Jorge Encarnación Sandoval organized a Rosales march "in defense of the ecology," but he was simply putting an environmental face on demands for sewer drainage and sanitation; this did not represent any broader eco-friendly agenda by the settlers. Perhaps the most significant challenge to this generalization was Edgar Coral in Pisulli. Coral saw Pisulli not just as a vehicle for his own political aspirations, but also as a neighborhood-level socialist experiment, with himself as the leader. Still, the Pisulli organization, however dominated by Coral, clearly expended its resources on material-oriented projects rather than social transformation.

With few exceptions, the four organizations all exhibited a preference for veteran leaders who had participated in or even organized successful invasions in the past. Chito Rios and Donato Flores in Pro, Nestor Sauñe and Lino Montesinos in Rosales, and Diego la Madrid and Florian Ostros in Sector C fit this generalization especially well. Even Willy Rojas of Rosales, though he was a novice settler, had years of union experience to draw on in his organizing. The two principal exceptions were Coral in Pisulli and Miguel Arturo Vega in Sector C. Coral had no prior experience with invasions, but his circle of advisers did. Only Vega was a true neophyte (he had not even participated in Sector C's founding, but rather joined the community years later).

Old Guard Repertoire Traits: Rigid, Unoriginal, and Sometimes Violent

The repertoire of Old Guard methods of demand-making is characterized by strategic rigidity, unoriginal tactics, the use of violence, and the nonuse of technology. The typology of invasion organizations claimed that Old Guard groups have a strong preference for either legal or extralegal strategies, and that they are resistant to crossing the line. All four case studies bear this out, though to varying degrees. The archetypal radical case of Pisulli was clearly the most rigid, but the clients of Pro took a close second place. Perhaps more significant, this rigidity worked well for both organizations. With one exception (Pro's partly militant demand for recognition), no strategically "deviant" demand resulted in an unqualified success. On the contrary, of the fifteen successful demands made by Pisulli and Pro, fourteen of them relied on the respective organization's preferred strategy type.

Sector C and Rosales were considerably less rigid, but deviations by some leaders in these cases actually demonstrate the resilience of each group's strategy preference. In Sector C, la Madrid, Ostros, and Vega all attempted to organize militant demands, but none could muster the participation of their client settlers. Even more dramatically, Rosales leaders Encarnación and Tapia dared to cross the line into conformist strategies, and the radical settlers punished them in neighborhood elections. While Pisulli and Pro relied on strategic rigidity to build successful neighborhoods, the struggling cases of Sector C and Rosales point to the dangers of inflexibility: both missed possible opportunities to gain services because of their resistance to new types of strategies. Rosales, for example, could have followed Pro's conformist example of taking advantage of Cambio 90 allies at the national and district level, especially during the mayoral administration of Felipe Castillo. And Sector C's militant attempt to pressure its San Diego neighbors into permitting activation of its sewer system could well have succeeded with a more committed membership. Between 2003 and 2005, the radicals of Rosales appeared to belatedly learn their lesson, allowing Lino Montesinos to blend militant and conformist strategies to good effect, but Montesinos still had to publicly emphasize the militant dimension of these demands.

Within the framework of strategic rigidity, Old Guard organizations rely on unoriginal tactics, such as stealing electricity (but not other services), protest marches to the same old locations, and conventional petitioning for land titles and other services. Some actions are more dramatic than others (e.g., Pisulli's breaking down the doors of the water agency), but few are original. When these tactics work, as in Pisulli and Pro, it makes sense for organizations to use them. In Rosales, however, it is remarkable that after over a decade of failure, Secretary General Elvira Peña decided to embark on a third militant demand for land titles, with yet another march on Congress.

Finally, Old Guard organizations often employ violence and rarely use new technologies. Here the case studies examined in this chapter are perhaps an unrepresentative sample. On the one hand, Pro and Pisulli were rife with violence, both against external "enemies" and within their own organizations. On the other hand, neither Sector C nor Rosales had any major violent episodes, except residual problems related to the founding of Olivos de Pro and the 2003 incident, when Peña's followers provoked a brawl by pelting the mayor with garbage at the ceremonial opening of construction.[34] Based on familiarity with other Old Guard cases not included in this study, I estimate the typical Old Guard level of violence to be somewhere between the killing in Pro and Pisulli and the general pacifism of Rosales's disruptive marches.[35]

Old Guard Neighborhood Regimes: Electoral or Authoritarian

Old Guard regimes vary in their competitiveness, but tend to be power-concentrating, meaning they are usually *electoral* or *authoritarian*. Ranking these case studies in terms of their competitiveness, the electoral Rosales regime was clearly

34. Though in 2002, Elvira Peña may have been threatened by Rosales settlers supporting Claudio Tapia.
35. Examples include Fraternidad and Caller in Lima, and Tumbaco and Roldos in Quito.

the most competitive, followed by the electoral regimes of Pro (1992–2005) and Sector C. Least competitive were the authoritarian regimes of Pro (1990–92) and Pisulli. In terms of organizational inclusiveness, the cases are remarkably similar in their high degree of power concentration. Only the post-Rios electoral regime of Pro was somewhat moderate in its degree of power-concentration, though it remained an *electoral*, rather than a *democratic*, neighborhood regime.

The theoretical framework introduced in chapter 1 argued that noncompetitive regimes have a relative advantage over competitive regimes in their ability to maintain alliances, because they have a predictable and often unchanging leadership. These Old Guard cases generally support this claim. The difficulty competitive regimes encounter in this regard is apparent in the cases of Sector C and Rosales, both neighborhoods notable for their general lack of allies. Pisulli avoided alliances for ideological reasons, but Coral's uncontested leadership provided a stable anchor when Pisulli chose to ally with Universidad Central during its nascent stage and with Roldós during its consolidated stage. Similarly, the noncompetitive Pro under Chito Rios built solid clientelist partnerships. Under the subsequent electoral regime, however, Pro continued to rely successfully on allies, demonstrating that competitive regimes need not go it alone.

The theoretical framework also proposed that power-sharing regimes have a relative advantage over power-concentrating regimes in their ability to take advantage of local avenues of participation, because power-sharing groups are not threatened by new openings in the political process. Since all four Old Guard cases had power-concentrating regimes, it is difficult to evaluate this claim without comparison to the cases examined in chapters 4 and 5, but the varying experiences with the Fraternidad housing association provide some evidence in support of this claim. Located in the San Martín de Porres district, Sector C was not eligible to join Fraternidad, but while both Rosales and Pro were eligible, only Pro worked with the association. Rosales might have joined, but its potential participation was blocked by the power-concentrating leadership of the López administration.

Given that the Rosales case clearly fits the theoretical expectation (i.e., being a power-concentrator hurt its chances of joining Fraternidad), it is tempting to also portray Pro as a supporting case, since it was less power-concentrating than Rosales and more able to take advantage of Fraternidad. But although Rosales had a more power-concentrating regime than did Pro (1992–2005), the difference was not great, and both were electoral in nature. Hence, within the framework of the entire neighborhood regime typology, Pro actually contradicts the theoretical claim: it was a power-concentrating regime that still managed to benefit from a local participatory institution. This deviation will be considered in chapter 6, which compares neighborhood regimes across all types of invasion organizations.

Implications for the Old Guard Type

The identity traits, repertoire traits, and neighborhood regimes common to Old Guard organizations have implications for similar invasion organizations not included in this study. With respect to identity, the Old Guard's pragmatic focus on material improvement and property security makes such organizations likely victims of the security trap. Both Pro and Sector C fell prey to the security trap, and declining rates of participation led each to a moribund state. After more than a decade, Rosales still had not attained property security, but such security looked imminent in 2005 and may pitch Rosales into a similarly moribund state. Only Pisulli escaped the trap and consolidated, but that community hardly seems like a desirable model given that its organizational security hinged on the perpetual insecurity of individual settlers. In short, the Old Guard identity seems best suited to deliver short- and medium-term gains, but may be of considerably more limited use for individuals' long-term benefits.[36]

With respect to repertoire, strategic rigidity and unoriginal tactics mean lost opportunities and little chance for Old Guard organizations to acquire 100 percent of services (unless the unusual case of Pisulli is considered 100 percent). Of the approximately 6,135 families living in these four Old Guard neighborhoods in 2005, fewer than 300 could claim unfettered electricity, water, and drainage service, as well as ownership of their home. Still, if land titles are excluded, this figure jumps to almost 5,000 with good-quality electricity, water, and drainage. These figures point to the pattern of Old Guard regimes delivering rapid and meaningful short- and medium-term gains, but rarely meeting the full needs of their membership.

Finally, the electoral and authoritarian regimes that typify Old Guard organizations raise important questions about such regimes' ability to build and maintain alliances and to take advantage of local participatory institutions. The cases in this study hint at a trade-off between regime openness and the capacity to work with allies, but a complete understanding of these trade-offs requires examination of all types of neighborhood regimes. To continue building this composite, we now turn to the children of the Old Guard: the Next Generation.

---

36. Old Guard clients may be especially unable to achieve long-term benefits, as they can find themselves trapped in exploitative patron-client relationships that prove difficult to exit. For a discussion of the challenging pathway from "clientelism to citizenship," see Fox (1997, 414–20).

4

The Next Generation:
Strategic Flexibility and a Sense of Entitlement

In the 1990s, a new type of invasion organization emerged that was characterized by novice leadership, a sense of entitlement, a focus on material goals, and strategic flexibility. The leaders of these "Next Generation" organizations had grown up in the invasion communities of their Old Guard parents and now founded their own neighborhoods. Unlike their parents, however, Next Generation settlers do not exhibit strong strategic preferences. Instead, they "mix and match," using both legal and extralegal tactics in a predictable pattern I call the *strategy life cycle*. This chapter compares the organizational strategy, success, and survival of four Next Generation case studies. I begin with two large-scale Next Generation organizations founded in the early 1990s—one in Quito and one in Lima—and then examine a second pair of Next Generation organizations founded in the same Lima district in 1999 and 2001.

The Next Generation invasion organizations of Camino a la Libertad (in Quito) and Oasis de Villa (in Lima) both relied on strategic flexibility, settler participation, and selective allies to acquire services. But while Camino sustained settler participation for fifteen years and consolidated, participation in Oasis faltered after just six years, and the organization sank into a moribund state. Why?

In the case of Camino, bold settlers shrugged off the threat of hired gunmen and displaced the inhabitants of a working ranch. The settlers then employed a series of rogue, militant, conformist, and bootstrap strategies to acquire services, but despite an authoritarian neighborhood regime, the entire community was involved in all projects. This community investment helped sustain the organization past the point when settlers had attained de facto property security. In this way, Camino evaded the security trap, consolidated organizationally, and continued to pursue community objectives.

In the case of Oasis, equally bold settlers endured *eight* consecutive evictions before finally seizing and holding prized lands reserved for a university. Oasis also employed a combination of rogue, militant, conformist, and bootstrap strategies, but community involvement was low, despite strong attendance at a few high-profile events. Further, while Camino benefited from influential allies and patrons, Oasis often relied entirely on allies for some of its key victories, meaning that services were sometimes simply handed to the community. For example, when the European Union built the entire Oasis water system, the settlers played almost no role. Hence, when settlers acquired land titles, many promptly abandoned the organization and it sank into a moribund state, embarrassingly incapable of acquiring new services even under incredibly favorable conditions (e.g., the district mayor allocated funds for sewer drainage, but Oasis failed to spend the money).

The second pair of Next Generation cases—Villa Mar and Paraíso—also relied on strategic flexibility, but settler participation suffered from internal disputes, and neither organization had any allies, other than a generally amicable mayor. But while Villa Mar was nearly destroyed by its internal problems and failed to acquire services, Paraíso managed to overcome its divisions and win three quick service victories in its first year. Why?

In the case of Villa Mar, extremely limited resources, a precarious location, and poor timing led to service demand failure. Frustrated with failure, some settlers agitated for change, but the consensual neighborhood regime could not resolve the polarized dispute and the organization broke apart. Villa Mar did eventually move from rogue and militant strategies to a conformist approach, but it was too late to preserve internal unity. Only a surprising revelation in 2002 saved Villa Mar from a slow organizational death.

By contrast, the Paraíso organization possessed slightly greater resources, a slightly less undesirable location, and excellent timing, which led to quick service victories despite fierce internal problems. Where Villa Mar's consensual regime had fallen into a deadlock, Paraíso's democratic regime proved better able to accommodate differences, with authority divided territorially among several leaders. While this created a community environment of perpetual tension, it also permitted the Paraíso settlers to repeatedly set aside their differences to work toward common goals. As Paraíso moved through the strategy life cycle and began demanding more "advanced" services (land titles and piped water), however, these modest advantages proved insufficient and it entered a period of repeated failures.

Comparison of these four case studies illuminates the strengths and weak-nesses of the Next Generation type. For example, the success of Camino and Paraíso relative to Oasis and Villa Mar demonstrates that strategic flexibility can either succeed or fail in organizations large and small, competitive and noncompetitive. In terms of organizational survival, however, the case of Oasis demonstrates that the Next Generation shares the Old Guard's vulnerability to the security trap. Camino, however, evaded the trap and consolidated, though close inspection shows that the Camino case may actually reinforce the claim that property security poses a threat to organizational survival. Camino did consolidate, but it did so on the basis of de facto property security, without actually obtaining land titles for two-thirds of its settlers. Further, Camino's authoritarian regime obligated settlers to participate in community projects or face steep fines. Although the explanation is different, this is reminiscent of how another authoritarian neighborhood regime—that of Pisulli—evaded the security trap, in part, through the sustained *insecurity* of individual settlers. Titles aside, however, the widely varied successes of Next Generation organiza-tions employing all four types of strategies point to the major strength of the Next Generation type: its strategic flexibility better equips it to exploit the often limited opportunities for Latin American invasion communities in the 1990s and early 2000s.

As in chapter 3, each neighborhood organization is presented in chronological periods that identify and analyze specific service demands. Based on these two paired-case comparisons of two large, "middle-aged" Next Generation cases and two small, "young" Next Generation organizations, I then identify their pre-dictable identity and repertoire traits and their unpredictable regime types. The chapter concludes with a discussion of implications for other Next Genera-tion organizations.

AUTHORITARIAN LEADERSHIP AND COMMUNITY INVOLVEMENT FACILITATE CONSOLIDATION: THE CASE OF CAMINO A LA LIBERTAD

National and Local Context

The year 1990 was not a promising time for a new land invasion in Quito. Although many Quiteños spoke of the famous Comité del Pueblo and Lucha de los Pobres invasions of the 1970s (Godard 1988) with a certain pride in the resourcefulness of their fellow Ecuadorians, there was a broad consensus in many sectors that the time for invasions had passed. And although President Rodrigo

Borja (1988–92) was a populist and a social democrat (Gerlach 2003, 81), various invasion attempts in the capital city region had met with violent failure in 1988 and 1989, either at the hands of the militarized National Police or the municipal police of Mayor Rodrigo Paz (1988–92). President Borja seemed caught halfway between the harsh neoliberal policies of his predecessor and his own round of halfhearted neoliberal reforms (Gerlach 2003, 45). Economically caught in between, tens of thousands of poor Quiteños were in need of homes (Glasser 1988, 153–55), and Celso Meza decided that he was just the man to provide them.

Origins of the Camino Invasion: An Ambitious Son of Comité del Pueblo

Born in the coastal province of Manabi in 1956, Celso Meza moved to Quito with his family as a teenager. There his family joined the massive 1974 founding of Comité del Pueblo, which would become two hundred city blocks of houses. Inspired by the successful Comité invasion, a twenty-two-year-old Celso Meza set out in 1978 to found his own settlement. As the first neighborhood president of the new community, named "Comité del Pueblo #2," Meza was an active and ambitious leader, but he was soon demoted to a lesser role as Comité #2 expanded.[1] Although he remained active in Comité #2, Meza was dissatisfied with the rigidity of its Old Guard leaders even in the face of poor results.

Inspired by the militant demands of the original Comité settlement, the Comité #2 leaders were dead set on what Susan Stokes (1995) calls "radical struggle methods," even when such strategies repeatedly failed. Beginning in 1983, Meza also observed the brutal competition between the Pisulli and Roldós invasions (see chapter 3), and he decided that while sometimes appropriate in self-defense, the tit-for-tat escalation of violence that consumed Pisulli and Roldós was in no one's interest. Taken together, these lessons taught Meza that violence was a tool to be used sparingly, and that while disruptive protests could be effective (as they were in the original Comité del Pueblo), a leader needed to also avail himself of other opportunities, such as the clientelist deals that seemed to be working well for Roldós (Meza 2002, interview).

By the late 1980s, Meza was ready to give up on Comité #2. After more than a decade, levels of service provision and quality of living were still very low, and, most frustrating, he was not in charge. Deciding to start fresh, Meza assembled his team: Sergio Bravo (the architect), Oscar Verdugo (the lawyer), Nelson Castro (the bookkeeper), Roberto Oña (the charisma), and Meza himself (the boss). Their target: the Pazmiño Navas family ranch.

1. Comité del Pueblo #2 was far removed from the original Comité del Pueblo, but confusion over their names would lead to Comité #2 being renamed "Colinas del Norte."

Cucho Hacienda: The Pazmiño Navas Family Ranch

Originally a rugged plot of forested land on Quito's unpopulated northern periphery, by 1990 the Pazmiño Navas family ranch was sandwiched between two major land invasion communities: Comité #2 to the west and Roldós to the northeast. Two enormous ravines provided natural barriers that had kept both Comité #2 and Roldós from creeping onto Pazmiño Navas land, but pedestrian traffic often passed across it, as the ranch occupied only a fraction of the lands held by the three Pazmiño Navas brothers.

Part of Quito's wealthy Pazmiño Navas clan, brothers Jorge (a priest and a lawyer), Guillermo (a businessman), and Ricardo (a lawyer) decided to acquire a country home where they would maintain only a minimal complement of servants. In 1972, Quito's Metropolitan Curia was auctioning off church assets deemed financial liabilities, including the land in question. As a church lawyer, the eldest brother, Jorge, used his position to "remove" the thirty-two hectares of land from the auction process and buy it at the bargain price of sixteen thousand dollars (or as Father Jorge put it, "about the price of a Mercedes"; Pazmiño Navas 2002, interview). The youngest brother, Ricardo, the lay lawyer, then transformed the thirty-two hectares of church land into a forty-six-hectare parcel, at least on paper. This illegal maneuver would later pave the way for Celso Meza's successful conformist bid for legal title to those extra fourteen hectares in 2002 (Pazmiño Navas 2002).

The Pazmiño Navas brothers cleared some of the land and built a ranch named "Cucho Hacienda," but they spent most of their time at their houses in the city, and increasingly left the care of the ranch house to their nephew Rommel López and the in-residence family of servants, including the groundskeeper, Arnoldo Muñoz. This three-story house would later prove sufficiently vast to house a kindergarten, a community center, office space, recreational space, and storage for large machinery.

Prelude to Invasion: Pretending to Buy the Land

Arnoldo Muñoz was unhappy with his employers, whom he felt looked down on "blacks and Indians," but it was no easy choice to betray the Pazmiño Navas family (Pazmiño Navas 2002, interview).[2] Aside from his misgivings about the

---

2. In addition to newspaper accounts and other primary documents, this case study draws heavily on extended interviews with the principal players: Celso Meza and the Pazmiño Navas family. Despite the enmity between these antagonists, the accounts given by the two sides are remarkable for their near-complete agreement on the facts of what occurred at each stage of Camino's history. They disagree vehemently, however, in their evaluations of whose actions were justified.

project Celso Meza proposed to Muñoz in the first of many secret meetings at the local Roldós elementary school, Muñoz had reason to fear the Pazmiño Navas brothers: they were wealthy, they were influential, and they had guns. But betray them he did, providing the information Meza needed to plan the invasion (López 2002, interview).

As a preliminary step, in November 1989 Meza daringly brought his team to one of Father Jorge's houses in the city, ostensibly to initiate negotiations for the purchase of Cucho Hacienda. Meza had no intention of buying the land, but based on his experience in Comité #2, he gambled that his proposed "Camino a la Libertad" cooperative would benefit politically if they could claim to have invaded only as a last resort, when the Pazmiño Navas family "backed out" of an imaginary agreement.

Father Jorge was not home, but the nephew Rommel López met with Meza, Castro, Oña, Verdugo, Bravo, and five others (but not Muñoz). Meza offered $250,000 for Cucho Hacienda.[3] The ranch was worth much more, and the settlers did not actually have any money, but Meza got what he wanted: López did not reject them outright. Meza would be able to claim that they had "begun negotiations," but he paid a price. Before admitting them to his house, López had demanded identification and contact information for each man. This price would not be worth the gain: Meza's later 1992 conformist expropriation bid, based on his "broken contract" story, would fail, and the detailed contact information would help the Pazmiño Navas family imprison Meza and Castro and send Oña into hiding.

Suspicious of Meza's intentions, López spied on the settlers and was shocked to observe his groundskeeper, Muñoz, meeting with Meza. But the family patriarch, Father Jorge, assured his nephew that Ecuador's constitution would protect their private property. Nevertheless, Guillermo Pazmiño Navas complained to Minister of Government Andrés Vallejo about a rumored invasion, and Vallejo agreed to provide twenty-four-hour ranch security at government expense, beginning in June 1990. But Vallejo was due to be replaced by a new minister of government, César Verduga, on August 10, Independence Day, when the new Congress would be sworn in (*Últimas Noticias*, 9/5/91). Hence, Vallejo's patronage would end on August 9, the eve of a major holiday, leaving Cucho Hacienda undefended at a time when the nation's security forces were on vacation or attending parades. And the coup de grace: a disgruntled Pazmiño Navas in-law had joined the settlers and informed them that the entire Pazmiño Navas clan would spend Independence Day weekend vacationing in Ambato (López 2002, interview). Celso Meza was ready.

---

3. In adjusted dollars, this was about four times the price the Pazmiño Navas family had paid for the land, or, as Father Pazmiño Navas would put it, about the price of four luxury cars.

The Invasion: Smoothly Executed

The initial invasion could not have been easier: no residents, no guards—only Arnoldo Muñoz and his family, waiting with the keys to the ranch house. Meza arrived with two thousand eager settlers (about five hundred families) armed with axes and machetes to chop down the eucalyptus trees that blanketed the land.[4] The duplicitous Muñoz proved invaluable, as he knew the ranch well, including the location of the Pazmiño Navas gun collection, which Meza delegated to a security team assigned to guard the access bridge (over one of the bordering ravines). But while some aspects of the invasion were smoothly executed, Meza admitted in a 2002 interview that it was largely a chaotic affair, "with no plan or real organization, since we planned on having a lottery for lots later on, once things were settled down. It was pretty crazy. We didn't have a good sense of the topography, and it was all covered with trees." The settlers constructed makeshift homes out of tree trunks, cardboard, and plastic sheets, with tree branches for roofs (*Hoy*, 4/26/91).

Four police cars arrived and the officers made a brief inspection late that night, but they had little appetite for confronting two thousand people. By sunrise, however, the Pazmiño Navas brothers had rushed back to Quito and arrived with fifty municipal police. When confronted with armed guards at the bridge making claims about a "broken contract," however, these police also backed down. Serious eviction attempts would follow, but the settlers had gained a critical foothold.

The First Four Years: Uncertainty in the Face of Violence

From its founding in August 1990 until the settlers outmaneuvered the final serious eviction attempt in 1994, Camino grew steadily as a *nascent* invasion organization whose chances of survival fluctuated from excellent to slim. During this unpredictable period, Camino made six attempts to acquire services: (1) *rogue* theft of electricity through informal hookups—a success; (2) *militant* demands for recognition from Mayor Paz—a failure; (3) *militant* demands for water truck service—a success; (4) a *conformist* deal with legislators for legal recognition—a limited success; (5) a *conformist* lawsuit for land titles—a failure; and (6) a *conformist* deal to avoid eviction and gain full recognition—a success. Why did Camino's rogue, militant, and conformist strategies succeed or fail during its nascent stage of development?

---

4. Within a year, Quito newspapers would report that the settlers had chopped down four hundred thousand trees (*Últimas Noticias*, 9/5/91).

Organizational success in this period hinged on five key factors: strategy choice, a lack of allies, organizational resources, public service provision, and mayor neutrality, all scored in the "nascent" portion of table 4.1. In the wake of the settlers' first victory of seizing the land, Meza continued his offensive. The settlers immediately began stealing electricity and water through the ranch's limited infrastructure as well as additional informal hookups. Initial theft of electricity succeeded because of the settlers' rogue strategy; had they attempted any other type of strategy so early on, they likely would have failed.

Although Mayor Paz refused to recognize them, they successfully demanded that the Cotocollao district provide water truck service. This first attempt at municipal recognition had been premature, as Camino had neither the allies nor the organizational resources to push their demands through over the objections of the Pazmiño Navas brothers. Obtaining publicly provided water truck service proved feasible for their level of resources, however, as no group actively opposed them in this effort.

Although Camino would soon encounter a string of conformist successes, their first conformist attempts at legitimacy and services largely failed. Just three weeks into the invasion, Meza invited Catholic and Episcopal leaders to build churches in Camino in order to increase the settlement's legitimacy, but this was initially unsuccessful. In October, Meza hired a topographical cartographer to map the site in order to plan a network of roads and divide the land into lots, but pressure for an eviction continued to grow.

Meza also allied with Congressman Víctor Granda of the Partido Socialista Ecuatoriano (Ecuadorian Socialist Party, or PSE) to acquire recognition, but the value of this recognition was compromised by a neutral mayor not ready to reject the Pazmiño Navas family's demands for an eviction. Two days before Christmas, Granda visited Camino a la Libertad and gave a speech in which he promised to provide services, so long as the settlers supported him politically (*Últimas Noticias*, 9/5/91). Hence, when Meza's petition for legal recognition reached Minister of Social Welfare Raúl Baca, the ministry bowed to congressional pressure and recognized Camino.

De Jure Recognition: Still at Risk

Despite this de jure recognition, eviction attempts would persist, and so Camino's nascent stage of development continued, with the organization still at risk of outright defeat. With Granda's blessing, Camino officially formed its cooperative, assigned lots, and elected its first slate of leaders, including Meza as manager, Oña as president, and two dozen other officers. Meza and Oña would be reelected to their posts in 1992, 1994, 1996, 1998, 2000, 2002, *and* 2004, with only three challenges from other neighborhood candidates during all this time. Like the

Table 4.1 Camino data matrix

Stage of development	Neighborhood leader	External factors					Internal factors			
		Service demand	District mayor	Service provider	Allies	Avenue of participation	Strategy type	Key resources	Neighborhood regime type	Outcome
Nascent (90–94)		Electricity	Neutral	State			Rogue	*Minga*	Authoritarian	Success
		Recognition	Neutral	Municipal			Militant	High participation	Authoritarian	Failure
		Water truck	Neutral	State			Militant	High participation	Authoritarian	Success
		Recognition	Neutral	Municipal	Granda		Conformist	Leadership	Authoritarian	Success
		Land titles	Neutral	Private			Conformist	Lawyer	Authoritarian	Failure
Mature (94–00)	Meza (90–05)	Recognition	Friendly	Metro	Mahuad	96 Election	Conformist	High participation	Authoritarian	Success
		Electricity	Friendly	Metro	Rivera		Conformist	High participation	Authoritarian	Success
		Sewers	Friendly	Metro	Granda		Conformist/Bootstrap	*Minga*	Authoritarian	Success
		Electricity	Friendly	Metro	Rivera		Conformist	High participation	Authoritarian	Success
		Piped water	Friendly	Metro	Mahuad		Conformist/Bootstrap	*Minga*	Authoritarian	Success
		Sewers	Friendly	Metro	Sevilla	00 Election	Conformist/Bootstrap	*Minga*	Authoritarian	Success
		Sewers	Hostile	Metro			Bootstrap	Money/*Minga*	Authoritarian	Success
Consolidated (00–05)		Land titles	Neutral	Metro/Private	Metro		Conformist/Bootstrap	Lawyer/Money	Authoritarian	Success
		Sewers	Friendly	Metro	Moncayo	04 Election	Conformist/Bootstrap	Money/*Minga*	Authoritarian	Success

old PRI in Mexico, however, Meza never permitted his challengers any chance of dethroning his anointed leaders. As the all-powerful incumbent, Meza used his ostensibly nonpartisan position as manager to ensure that only those loyal to him were elected to neighborhood posts. The charismatic Oña was Camino's nominal leader, but in a 2002 interview Meza explained who was really in charge:

> I'm more or less the real power in Camino. Roberto Oña is the president, but he usually defers to me. After all, this is my full-time, salaried job, as the only paid neighborhood representative. The rest are all volunteer. I do have a small brick business on the side, but this is my main career. Like Oña, I have been uninterrupted in my tenure as manager, well, except for the thirty-two months I spent in jail for [supposedly] being a land trafficker, a guerrilla, a member of the FARC [Revolutionary Armed Forces of Colombia], a human rights violator, and, of course, a leader of an illegal land invasion.

Although the Pazmiño Navas family's faith in Quito's criminal justice system had bought Meza time to win several victories through an aggressive and eclectic mix of strategies, the settlement leaders were in fact guilty of property destruction, theft, carrying illegal firearms, and selling land that did not belong to them (National Police arrest warrant, 2/8/91). So in February 1991, Meza, Castro, and two other Camino leaders went to jail (for thirty-two, twenty-four, eighteen, and two months, respectively). President Oña, however, escaped arrest by going into hiding, and continued to lead the neighborhood (López 2002, interview; Meza 2002, interview).

With Meza's arrest bolstering Father Pazmiño Navas's legal claims and generating media attention favorable to Pazmiño Navas, Mayor Paz agreed to order an eviction. Reported details of the incident vary, but the eviction attempt failed. October 1991 newspaper articles report that Meza, Castro, Oña, Bravo, and Verdugo fought off the police with "guns, tear gas bombs, molotov cocktails, and machetes," going so far as to "wound a police captain" and "break the rear windshield of Guillermo Pazmiño Navas's blue BMW." Meza and Castro were in jail at the time, however, and could not have participated in the battle, which casts doubt on these journalistic accounts ("Invasores impiden desalojo," *La Hora,* 10/11/91).

Whatever the truth of the failed eviction attempt, things had taken a turn for the worse for the settlers, so Meza decided to reassert his leadership. Dozens of Camino residents visited him each week in jail, and he developed their legal case and resumed running the community, giving daily orders from behind bars. Working from jail, Meza's first conformist attempt at land titles was rejected due to inadequate juridical resources, and failed to move the settlers closer to ownership of their homes. In 1992, Meza filed an expropriation lawsuit alleging that Pazmiño Navas had "broken their agreement." The expropriations proposal was denied as an unconstitutional threat against private property, but the maneuver elicited admiration from Camino settlers, who reelected their incarcerated boss to his second of eight terms.

The Pazmiño Navas legal strategy was gaining ground, but after the 1991 eviction debacle, no politician wanted to authorize another attempt as the 1992 presidential and mayoral elections drew near. But the inauguration of President Sixto Durán Ballén (1992–96) and Mayor Jamil Mahuad (1992–98) did not improve the Pazmiño Navas family's situation, as the new politicians did not want to sully their own reputations with the leftover problems from previous administrations. Finally out of patience, an indignant Rommel López decided to take matters into his own hands.

In early 1993, López stormed into a Camino meeting and emptied his gun into several buildings, demanding that the settlers leave. Out of bullets, López fled (leaving yet another luxury car to be vandalized by irate settlers), but a warrant for his arrest (for attempted murder) was soon issued, forcing López into hiding as well. López was soon caught and jailed for three days until a preliminary hearing. In August he began serving time for a lesser charge, but after twenty-one days in a high-security facility, he paid a two-hundred-dollar bribe for his early release. In a 2002 interview López explained that he just could not accept his detention, which he considered unethical: "I was in prison with the worst of society: killers, drug dealers, even Colombians."

In 1994, Meza's clientelist partnerships finally bore fruit: Mayor Mahuad protected them from being evicted. The final serious eviction attempt would have been a bloodbath if Meza had not convinced Mahuad to call it off in exchange for political support in his 1996 reelection campaign. López explained how the eviction was supposed to work:

> In 1994, the municipality gave the order to evict them. We rented four tractors. We bought two hundred guns and hired two hundred men from Manabí. We had an order for demolition for their not having a building permit, plus it was not their land, but the police decided not to do the operation. There's no justice. Our men never came. We never actually followed through with the plan. In Calderón, there were violent evictions. If land is owned by the municipality, they defend it with police. But when land is private, they make excuses. It was supposed to be just police, but we decided to help with two hundred men. You have to pay a lot because some will die. One month's pay for one night's work. But orders from high up gave a red light on the operation. . . . This is typical: the

owner organizes with police and "men of confidence." First the men come through to soften things up for the police. In Guayaquil they have violent evictions [all the time], why not us? (2002, interview)

And so, despite the Pazmiño Navas family's plans, Camino finally achieved full municipal recognition. Although they had legal recognition as early as 1990, it was not until 1994 that Mahuad's support put an end to any possibility of forceful eviction. With its tenure stabilized until at least the next mayoral election, the Camino organization could pursue more sustained efforts at acquiring services.

Camino Embraces Clientelism: Steady Acquisition of Services

Following Mahuad's refusal to help the Pazmiño Navas family evict the settlers in 1994, the *mature* Camino organization embarked on a successful period of steady service acquisition until 2000. These efforts included: (1) a *conformist* exchange of political support for electricity service through legal but provisional hookups—a success; (2) a similar *conformist* deal for sewer drainage installation in parts of Camino—a success; (3) a third *conformist* partnership that yielded full and permanent electricity service—a success; (4) a combination *conformist/bootstrap* effort to install piped water in most of Camino—a success; and (5) a *conformist/bootstrap* expansion of sewer drainage—a success. Why did the mature Camino organization's predominantly conformist strategy deliver such great success?

Camino succeeded because of three key factors: congressional allies, clientelism, and Camino's noncompetitive regime, which maintained an unchanging leadership throughout this period. In the years since Meza got out of jail, Camino made great progress, principally through clientelist partnerships with DP politicians like Jamil Mahuad, his mayoral successor, Roque Sevilla, and Congressman Ramiro Rivera, but also with PSE congressman Víctor Granda. Each process was slightly different, but during this stage, all strategies were conformist and none relied on militant protest or direct pressure (see table 4.1). "[It was always] friendship," explained Meza in a 2002 interview, "and of course, we helped our friends in return."

Such friendships delivered a steady stream of good-quality services. In late 1994, Congressman Rivera authorized provisional electricity for most of Camino. That same month, Granda steered ten thousand dollars in funding toward sewer drainage in one-third of Camino. And in 1996, Rivera finished the job by leaning on the Ecuadorian Housing Bank to finance permanent electricity in nearly all of Camino. Meza's mayoral allies were equally responsive to Camino's political support. In 1998, shortly after Camino helped elect Mahuad to the presidency, he authorized a major piped water project. And in 1999, Mayor Sevilla followed suit with funds for additional sewers, though the project still left many parts of Camino without drainage. Both the latter projects also relied on many months of nightly community work projects, known as *mingas*, as the settlers provided the labor for installation. Meza required all settlers to participate, and those who disobeyed were fined. Repeated delinquency could result in expulsion on Meza's word alone.

In addition to allies, clientelism, and an authoritarian neighborhood regime, mayoral support, public service provision, and organizational resources also played a regular contributing role, though they were decisive in only two instances: settler economic investment in their own water pipe system, and Mayor Sevilla's financial support of sewer drainage expansion. But despite these two cases, the broader picture is clear: a noncompetitive neighborhood regime facilitated clientelist partnerships with congressional allies who delivered material goods in exchange for political support. This picture is even clearer if additional service demands (e.g., roads, schools, transit) are considered (though they are beyond the scope of the services examined for this study). Camino made enormous progress during this period, and the ten-year-old settlement would soon surpass even its twenty-two-year-old "older sibling," Comité del Pueblo #2, whose service provision had stagnated, leaving it without sewer drainage.

Camino Consolidated: Continued Progress Despite Less Favorable Conditions

After eight years under the friendly leadership of Mayors Mahuad and Sevilla, the election of Mayor Paco Moncayo (2000–2008, Izquierda Democrática, or ID) ended Camino's heady days of mayoral and congressional giveaways.[5] Yet despite Moncayo's initial hostility toward continued "illegal" infrastructure development in Camino, the settlement overcame this opposition and proved itself a consolidated organization that could survive and grow, even in the absence of a mayoral ally. Despite new and initially more adverse conditions, the *consolidated* Camino organization made three of its most significant service victories yet: (1) a *bootstrap* extension of sewer drainage to encompass nearly all of Camino—a success; (2) a *conformist/bootstrap* legal process that delivered land titles to one-third of Camino settlers for a substantial fee—a success; and (3) a *conformist/bootstrap*

5. Although leaders of Camino (as well as Itchimbía, described in chapter 5) initially viewed Mayor Moncayo as an unfriendly obstacle to settlement development, he eventually proved to be a respectful and often helpful mayor to these and many other informal settlements. A retired military officer, Moncayo participated in the 2000 and 2005 popular coups, and made it a goal of his administration to formalize forty thousand informal lots in metropolitan Quito (*El Comercio*, 1/6/03). Moncayo's landslide victory in May 2000 helped cement the ID as the second strongest political party in Ecuador.

effort to build sewer drainage for all remaining homes without service—a success. How did the consolidated Camino organization succeed with both conformist and bootstrap methods despite an initially unfriendly mayor?

During this stage, Camino succeeded chiefly because of internal factors, including well-developed organizational resources and good strategy choices. Moncayo was more neutral than hostile toward Camino, but after the staunch support of previous mayors, it seemed like hostility to the settlers. Intent on balancing the metropolitan budget and pursuing downtown development, in August 2002 Moncayo withdrew municipal support of Camino's ongoing infrastructure projects on the grounds that they were illegal. As a flexible Next Generation organization, however, Camino adapted to the changing political environment by employing a bootstrap approach to its sewer drainage project (see table 4.1). Heavy support during the organization's mature stage of development had permitted some families to save enough money to begin paying for sewer pipes themselves, and they had been providing the labor all along (though not always by choice). By the end of 2005, 100 percent of Camino had drainage—an immense success, but one that would have been impossible if not for the 1994 and 1999 drainage projects during the neighborhood's mature stage.

Although Moncayo's withdrawal of economic support had forced the settlers to "reach for their bootstraps," Meza and Oña continued to employ the conformist approach in the legal arena. City hall proved receptive, as Meza showed them how they could profit from cooperation with the settlers. Meza explained to the Metropolitan Council that back in 1972, the youngest Pazmiño Navas brother had illegally claimed an extra fourteen hectares that the Metropolitan Curia had never owned. Hence, argued Meza, the four hundred families on this land should pay the city, not the Pazmiño Navas family. The council found this to be a grand solution to at least part of "the Camino problem," and in December 2002 granted land titles to these families in exchange for an agreement that families would pay the city $818 per lot—a bargain considering the infrastructure that now existed. Said Father Jorge of the decision, "The worse betrayal was the betrayal by the municipality" (Pazmiño Navas 2002, interview). Indeed, the city was now collecting fees, while the Pazmiño Navas brothers never received a centavo. Although the family condemned the Metropolitan Council's decision, they concentrated their continuing legal efforts on winning compensation for the other eight hundred lots, which they argued were worth $3,000 each (for a total of $2.4 million).

This agreement with city hall contributed to a gradual thawing of relations with Mayor Moncayo, and Meza cultivated this relationship in the hopes that Camino's ongoing bootstrap efforts might be augmented by a fresh clientelist partnership with the metropolitan government. In 2004, with Moncayo preparing a reelection campaign, Meza's efforts bore fruit, and Camino's final bootstrap push to complete the neighborhood's drainage system greatly benefited from Moncayo's patronage. In addition to $100,000 from Camino settlers, Moncayo steered $260,000 in metropolitan government funds toward the project in exchange for support on his political campaign. By election time, the sewers were complete, and Moncayo was reelected. Pleased with this success, Moncayo facilitated other Camino service initiatives not examined in this study, such as street paving and a new grade school for 280 children. Camino also built a modest sports facility in 2004–5, with help from the administration of President Lucio Gutiérrez. Although Gutiérrez was ousted from power in April 2005, the sports facility was already complete and thus not affected by the national political tumult (Meza 2005, interview).

In 2005, it was clear that despite the lingering land battle, Camino's 1,224 families were a permanent presence. They had achieved an impressive level of services, and participation levels remained high due both to the unresolved status of the land and to Meza's authoritarian leadership: he levied steep ten-to-twenty-five-dollar fines on settlers who skipped required activities, like *minga* work projects. Although 95 percent of the families were poor, most settlers remained optimistic. Said one Camino resident: "Now we have services. Everyone is working to make things better. I'm from the north of the province. I came seeking opportunity that doesn't exist in the north. I have two children. There are better schools here" (de Riobamba 2002, interview). This was a far cry from the bitter resentment stoked by Edgar Coral's authoritarian leadership in Pisulli. Said Meza in a 2005 interview: "Coral is my friend, but I can't believe he still holds the land titles. I don't support this."

Although Meza's authoritarian leadership was accepted—even celebrated—by most in Camino, a March 2004 incident in which a lynch mob burned and killed a black man suggested that the contrast between Meza and Coral should not be exaggerated. The killing followed a Camino assembly in which Meza declared, "We have to put a stop to delinquency." Though Meza was out of town when the lynching occurred, the Comisión de Derechos Humanos (Human Rights Commission) investigated, alleged that Meza was responsible, and concluded that racism was prevalent in Camino.[6] Community leaders, including a scholar from FLACSO and prominent Catholic priest, argued that the victim was no thief, just a drug addict with a criminal record (Meza 2005, interview).

Where the mature Camino organization clearly relied on mayoral and congressional allies, the consolidated Camino had the resources to succeed through self-sufficient methods, both in the courtroom and in communal construction projects that required full settler participation. It is interesting to note the

6. Approximately 5 percent of Camino's population is black. In 2003, black youth in the neighborhood formed a cultural and dance group called Afro-Ecuatoriana.

uneven presence of clientelist partnerships in Camino's consolidated phase. Where some Old Guard organizations like Pro in Lima were "born, grew, and grew old" as subordinate clients, this Next Generation organization seems to draw on such partnerships when convenient, but does not rely on them exclusively, instead moving ahead with bootstrap efforts when necessary. Although chapter 3 argued that clientelism could be a fruitful trap, but a trap nonetheless, Camino seems to extract what it needs from political allies and then move on unscathed.

In 2005, Meza was on the verge of launching his third serious bid to acquire land titles, calling for a meeting between himself, Pazmiño Navas, and a judge. He planned to first make a bootstrap attempt at titles, and failing that, a conformist attempt. First, he planned to use the fact that Pazmiño Navas had not paid taxes on the land since 1990 as leverage to negotiate a reasonable price for the land ("we want to pay, but at a just price"), since his failure to pay taxes had weakened his claim to the land. If buying the land failed, Meza would turn to Moncayo, offering further political support in the next election in exchange for political pressure on the land negotiating process.

Asked about other plans for the future, Meza indicated that in 2006 he would probably replace Oña as cooperative president, installing another loyal follower. Asked in a 2005 interview if he would pursue a political career, like his neighbor Edgar Coral, Meza replied: "I used to aspire to a political career, but no more. I see myself as caretaker of 1,200 families. I can't leave them."

Summary of Camino's Organizational Successes and Failures

Overall, Camino a la Libertad made fourteen service attempts between 1990 and 2005. Whereas many organizations either succeed or fail outright, Camino had a number of incremental successes, with ever-improving service provision that eventually reached all settlers. In total, Camino had only two outright failures, but scored four partial victories that left work unfinished for another day. The remaining eight demands succeeded, but despite these victories, in 2005 Camino still had not acquired land titles for two-thirds of its families.

PROPERTY SECURITY LEADS TO ORGANIZATIONAL DECLINE: THE CASE OF OASIS DE VILLA

National and Local Context

The Oasis de Villa invasion occurred shortly after Fujimori's peak of authoritarian power in Peru. Following his *autogolpe* in April 1992 (Kenney 2004, 203–10),

Fujimori replaced the bicameral legislature with an eighty-member Democratic Constituent Congress (1992–95), 55 percent of whose members belonged to Fujimori's Cambio 90–Nueva Mayoría party (Tuesta 2001, 79–80). Although Fujimori continued to dominate Peru after his 1995 reelection, during this post-coup/pre-election period he enjoyed unprecedented political freedom, which allowed him to draft and pass a new constitution in 1993 (McClintock 1999, 333–35). Authoritarian rule also had an impact locally, as Fujimori undermined traditional local power in matters of zoning, planning, and titling by creating COFOPRI (see chapter 2). The ambitious COFOPRI office would soon be charged with partisan meddling by Fujimori's district and metropolitan opponents, though in truth, many district mayors loyal to Fujimori were also frustrated with what they saw as COFOPRI's overzealous crusade to carry out Hernando de Soto's vision of granting two million titles to informal landholders.

Locally, Villa El Salvador was in an uproar. District mayor Jorge Vásquez (1992–94) was now a fugitive, on the run with eighteen thousand dollars of public money, and though he would soon be caught and imprisoned, his emergency replacement, César Soplín, was also under investigation for corruption (*Reto*, 6/95). Amid this political tumult, six small land invasions had recently stretched Villa El Salvador's southern boundary in unpredictable directions, and Máximo Caroas thought that one more would hardly be noticed.

A Sense of Entitlement: Persistent Invasion Attempts Despite Eight Defeats

Máximo Caroas decided to start small. Some land invasions start big, but with each eviction, the number of settlers dwindles, as more and more participants grow discouraged and give up.[7] In the case of Oasis, however, the reverse occurred. The first invasion attempt involved a small number of people, and failed. A series of additional failed attempts followed, but with each failure, the group's numbers grew, until they reached a critical mass that could not be evicted without a commitment to violence that the district mayor was unwilling to make.

Like his one hundred fellow settlers, Caroas was part of the Next Generation, having grown up in the Villa El Salvador invasion neighborhood founded by his parents in the 1970s. Caroas did not really know what he was doing, but having observed a half dozen equally novice invasions succeed in the past two years, he anticipated that his group would succeed as well.

---

7. In the "20 de Enero" invasion of 2002, for example, five consecutive invasion attempts inside of three days consisted of approximately five thousand, one thousand, five hundred, three hundred, and finally only two hundred people (*El Comercio*, 1/21/02; Pérez 2002). See also Flores, Lingán, and Cayo (2002).

Caroas targeted vacant land that Mayor Azcueta (1984–89) had reserved for a university in the mid-1980s. By 1994, residential blocks had extended around this land, making it more attractive as it gradually became central to the expanding district. Caroas doubted the university would materialize in his lifetime, and reasoned that one hundred homes would occupy only a fraction of the space (Geronimo 2002, interview; Varas 2002, interview).

The first invasion attempt was a routine failure. On September 9, 1994, the one hundred settlers made camp, thirty police forcefully evicted them, and ten of the settlers gave up and went home. The other ninety settlers remained in the area and were spontaneously joined by one hundred more would-be settlers. On September 11, the group of about two hundred chose a different spot, but the next day, the police forcefully ejected this second attempt as well. So they moved to another nearby site alongside the invasion-founded Pachacamac neighborhood. This third attempt lasted fifteen days, during which time the group grew to five hundred members. But still they were forcefully thrown out, with some injuries.

So it went for all of October, during which time Mayor Soplín authorized five more forceful evictions of the settlers as they shuffled from site to site, all within the same general area. The eighth and final eviction was the most violent, and involved gunshots, tear gas, injuries, and many burned shacks (Morales 2002, interview). By November the settlers numbered 1,000, and for their ninth attempt they occupied a street for a full month. While desperation and confusion had led them to this location, Caroas realized that they could not remain in the middle of what was destined to be a major avenue as the district grew. He proposed that the group, which numbered 1,500 by early December, return to the original site of land reserved for the university (*Reto*, 6/95).

The Founding Invasion: Well Timed and Well Organized

On December 8, 1994, the settlers reinvaded desert lands reserved for a future university and named their community "Oasis de Villa." December 8 was the Feast of the Immaculate Conception, a national holiday, but the police nonetheless responded with a force of 200 officers. But the 1,500 settlers had brought their families, so over 5,000 people blanketed the hillside, including every woman and child they could muster (Campos 2002, interview). And Caroas was right: even Mayor Soplín would not order the police to attack families on one of Peru's major religious holidays.

But though Caroas's timing was critical, his organizational skills were likely more pivotal. Although the Oasis founding spawned the typical internal conflicts over lot size and location, the invasion was, in relative terms, quite methodically done, as evidenced by the precise symmetrical layout of the ninety city blocks and 2,166 houses that would eventually make up Oasis.

The First Seventeen Months: High Participation Scores Early Gains

From its founding in December 1994, until Mayor Azcueta agreed to municipal recognition in May 1996, Oasis grew as a *nascent* invasion organization whose early service demands generally succeeded because of high neighborhood partici- pation, congressional allies, and the pressure of upcoming elections in November 1995. During this period, Oasis made five attempts to acquire services: (1) *rogue* theft of low-quality electrical hookups for all settlers—a success; (2) *militant* demands for low-quality water truck service for most settlers—a success; (3) *con- formist* acquisition of high-quality electricity service for all settlers—a success; (4) repeated *militant* demands for recognition by a hostile mayor—a failure; and (5) renewed *militant* demands for recognition by a neutral mayor—a success. Table 4.2 summarizes these demands.

High neighborhood participation proved to be a necessary but often insuffi- cient condition for successful service demands during Oasis's nascent stage. This internal resource did prove sufficient for stealing low-quality electrical hookups for all houses, but the settlers' acquisition of water truck service in January 1995 also relied on election-year pressures, which made the Fujimori-controlled state water agency more responsive to Oasis's vigorous protest marches.

The lure of thousands of votes provoked sustained interest from Cambio 90–Nueva Mayoría. Congressmen Jorge Figueroa (1992–2000) and Andrés Reg- giardo (1992–2001) had been swept into office on the coattails of Fujimori's pop- ular *autogolpe*, and the two of them approached Oasis with offers of assistance. Even before the invasion had stabilized, commented Oasis leader Efraín Huamán in a 2002 interview, "we were already coordinating with the Fujimoristas." Hence, just four months after their founding, high-quality electricity hookups arrived through a conformist partnership grounded in clientelism.[8] The adjacent Ramos neighborhood, however, did not support Cambio 90 and thus did not receive electricity, a point driven home by President Fujimori's campaign stop in Oasis in September 1995. In November, Fujimori won 70 percent of the general vote in Villa El Salvador, and he sent a clear message of his gratitude: one month

---

8. Surveyors announced that the settlement's hillside location would complicate electricity installation, so on March 8, 1994, the settlers literally picked up their entire community and moved it two hundred meters to flatter terrain. They maintained a near-identical block and lot layout, and moved all 1,700 makeshift homes in five hours (Campos 2002, interview). To the surprise of the settlers, posts for streetlights arrived the next day.

Table 4.2 Oasis data matrix

			External factors				Internal Factors			
Stage of development	Neighborhood leader	Service demand	District mayor	Service provider	Allies	Avenue of participation	Strategy type	Key resources	Neighborhood regime type	Outcome
Nascent (94–96)	Caroas (94–95)	Electricity	Hostile	State			Rogue	High participation	Democratic	Success
		Water truck	Hostile	State		95 Election	Militant	High participation	Democratic	Success
		Electricity	Hostile	State	Cambio 90	95 Election	Conformist	Organized	Democratic	Success*
	Campos (95–97)	Recognition	Hostile	District		95 Election	Militant	High participation	Democratic	Failure
		Recognition	Neutral	District			Militant	High participation	Democratic	Success
		Land titles	Neutral	State			Militant	High participation	Democratic	Failure
Mature (96–00)		Electricity	Neutral	Private	Sector IX	Multisector	Bootstrap	Money	Democratic	Success*
	Goñe (97–05)	Piped water	Friendly	State	Election/ EU NGO	Multisector	Conformist	Leadership	Democratic	Success
		Land titles	Friendly	State	Cambio 90	Multisector	Conformist	Low participation	Democratic	Success
		Sewers	Friendly	State	Sector IX	Multisector	Conformist	Low participation	Democratic	Failure
Moribund (00–05)		Sewers	Friendly	State	Sector IX	Multisector	Militant	Low participation	Democratic	Failure
		Land titles	Friendly	State	Sector IX	Multisector	Conformist	Low participation	Democratic	Failure
		Sewers	Friendly	State	Sector IX	Multisector	Conformist	Leadership	Democratic	Success

*In 1995, Oasis acquired good-quality electricity service for all settlers. The subsequent arrival of new settlers, however, necessitated a third demand for electricity (now privatized) in 1997. This additional service was purchased from the Luz del Sur company.

later the Peruvian Army arrived in Oasis and built several good-quality streets (Campos 2002, interview).

But while the pressure of the upcoming election favored settler demands for state-provided services like water and electricity, it hurt their militant demands for municipal recognition, as the embattled Mayor Soplín was not seeking reelection and did not think "appeasing invaders" would help him fight off corruption charges. Despite seven five-hundred-person marches, Mayor Soplín would not budge. In their most extreme attempt, on May 10, 1995 (the twenty-fourth anniversary of Villa's founding), thousands of settlers seized control of the Comunidad Urbana Autogestionaria de Villa El Salvador (Villa El Salvador Urban Self-Management Community, or CUAVES) office and surrounded the mayor in his car, demanding recognition, but to no avail (Reto, 6/95).

In January 1996, however, Villa's founding mayor, Michel Azcueta, returned for a third term (1996–98) with a strong local mandate to "save the district" from the scandals that had consumed it.[9] Azcueta had opposed the Oasis invasion because it threatened his vision of a future Villa university, but once back in office, he acknowledged that Oasis was here to stay. He visited Oasis in March 1996, and in May responded to its continued high-participation marches with official municipal recognition (Azcueta 2002, interview).

Four Years of Modest Progress: Internal Resources Bolstered by Allies

From May 1996 until most settlers received land titles in August 2000, the *mature* Oasis organization relied on district, state, and international allies as well as its own resources, including leadership, money, and continued high participation. During this four-year period, Oasis made four service attempts: (1) large-scale *militant* demands for land titles—a failure; (2) *bootstrap* purchase of high-quality electricity for new settlers in the neighborhood—a success; (3) *conformist* acquisition of medium-quality piped water for most settlers—a success; and (4) *conformist* acquisition of land titles for most settlers—a success.

Bolstered by continued strong participation, Oasis attempted to parlay its successful district-level demands for recognition into state-level demands for land titles. Oasis's secretary general, a teacher named Victor Campos (1995–97), saw the Instituto Nacional de Cultura (National Institute of Culture, or INC) and COFOPRI as the main two obstacles, so he organized two major marches that began with blocking the Pan-American Highway and ended at the offices

---

9. In the November 1995 district election, Azcueta received 59 percent of the vote, compared to 40 percent for his Fujimori-backed opponent. Villa El Salvador voters may have supported Fujimori as president, but they remained loyal to their local hero (Tuesta 2001, 443).

of each agency. The settlers demanded that the INC accelerate the process of investigating whether the land held any archaeological ruins, a concern that was obstructing the titling process (*La República*, 10/19/96). They also demanded that COFOPRI reject a recently surfaced claim that the land belonged to the wealthy Fernández Concha family. Neither state agency was responsive to these militant demands (Campos 2002, interview).

High rates of participation also permitted Oasis to take advantage of alliances. In 1997, Macario Goñe (1997–2005) became the new leader of Oasis,[10] and he steered the settlers away from militant strategies and toward conformist partnerships with both influential allies and other nearby invasion neighborhoods (see table 4.2). Goñe cofounded the grassroots Multisectoral Commission, which included leaders from neighboring invasion communities like "Sector IX," which had been founded in 1992 and had similar needs (Multisectoral propaganda, 4/22/97). Together Oasis and Sector IX represented a formidable 3,090 families, whose pooled resources achieved three major service victories (Goñe 2002, interview).

First, Goñe led a bootstrap approach to purchase electricity installation—now privately provided by Luz del Sur—for the new houses that had been built since the 1996 electricity project (INC 1997a, letter). It worked, and this earned credibility for Goñe's Multisectoral Commission. Second, in 1999 the combined community was sufficiently large to forge a conformist partnership with the European Union's Project Ala. Through Project Ala, the EU financed water tanks and pipes in most of Oasis and Sector IX.[11] Third, the Multisectoral hired lawyers to resolve the land ownership issue. Prodded by the Multisectoral and their Cambio 90 ally Jorge Figueroa, the INC concluded that the land was not archaeologically significant and therefore could be rezoned for residential use (Azcueta 1997, letter; INC 1997b, letter; Figueroa 1999, letter). COFOPRI, however, concluded that one-third of the land was indeed owned by the Fernández Concha family, who had paid the Velasco government for a mining concession on the land in 1970, before the founding of Villa El Salvador. The Multisectoral's lawyer negotiated a bargain price for the fraction that was privately owned, which

10. Officially there is no single leader of the entire Oasis settlement, as each of the four main quadrants (Groups 1–4) of the neighborhood elects its own slate of leaders. In practice, however, there is one leader who speaks for Oasis in matters of service provision, and following Caroas and Campos, that leader was Goñe.

11. Oasis was divided into Groups 1–4, but due to a failure of organization within Group 1, it did not belong to the Multisectoral Commission and was left out of Project Ala. "Group 1 was generally patient, not agitating," explained a community leader. "But if we just wait, no one hears our needs. This patient strategy has not served us well" (Geronimo 2002, interview). This failure provoked bitterness among Group 1 residents, who were then forced to buy or steal water from Group 2.

amounted to about $200 per lot. Families would struggle to pay this sum, but it was a good price, since the settlers could (and many did) then sell their homes for $750–$900. With a contract signed, land titles reached most Oasis residents in August 2000 (COFOPRI 2000). And that was the beginning of the end.

The Security Trap: Low Participation Derails Service Demands

After acquiring land titles for most Oasis settlers, what seemed like a thriving neighborhood organization rapidly sunk into a *moribund* state in which low rates of participation compromised highly achievable service initiatives that had municipal support. The four attempts between 2000 and 2005 included: (1) a *conformist* attempt to install sewers—a failure; (2) a *militant* attempt to revive the sewer installation plan—a failure; (3) a *conformist* attempt to establish legal ownership for the remaining settlers without a title—a failure; and (4) a *conformist* attempt to build drainage in about 12 percent of Oasis—a modest success.

A lack of a key organizational resource—neighborhood participation—weakened all four service demands, despite favorable conditions, as noted in table 4.2. After struggling with neutral or hostile mayors for most of its existence, Oasis now encountered a friendly mayor, Martín Pumar, who in 2001 authorized seventy thousand dollars in municipal funds for the Multisectoral's conformist sewer installation project (Velásquez 2002, interview). Further, the Multisectoral now had a proven track record and could arguably be expected to provide an even better framework for effective cooperation than during Oasis's mature stage.

Yet with the acquisition of land titles, the Oasis organization broke down surprisingly quickly. Within two years, nearly half the original settlers had sold or were trying to sell their lots. Either they had grown weary of the years-long struggle, or they had intended to sell their lots all along. This crippling drop in participation meant that even the simple bureaucratic side of the sewer project failed, such as getting each family to fill out the right paperwork to receive the municipal funds (Campos 2002, interview). City Councilman Jorge Varas commented in a 2002 interview on the trajectory of participation in Oasis: "It was very participatory early on, but now not much. There are scars of bad leaders that have hurt participation. Now people won't pay one centavo due to lack of trust, so we have no money to do anything."

In 2002, the window for using the earmarked money closed, and the funds were spent on other projects in Villa El Salvador. Pumar's representatives attempted to explain to Goñe and the other Oasis leaders how they had lost this opportunity, but the latter were hardly satisfied (meeting between Multisectoral and Pumar administration representative, 2/8/02). Instead, they decided to rejuvenate the militant approach that had won them early gains, and they organized a march to demand the money. Turnout exceeded one thousand people, but it was a one-shot effort and did not reverse the organization's moribund slide.

In late 2002, the more remote residents of Oasis, who still did not have land titles, tried to organize another conformist agreement with COFOPRI and the Fernández Concha family of landowners, but Goñe felt he had his hands full trying to get back the lost municipal money, and told the settlers that their claim was too specific to rally the entire Multisectoral Commission (Muñoz 2002, interview).[12] Without broad backing, however, the settlers had no leverage to force a reasonable settlement with Fernández Concha, and the attempt failed.

In 2004, the moribund Oasis managed to pull off a single modest victory, bringing sewer drainage to about 12 percent of the settlement. As the first such infrastructure project in Oasis, this was an important success, but in 2005 there was no evidence that similar infrastructure would reach the other 88 percent of settlers. The settlers who benefited from this project were all in the quadrant of Oasis known as "Group 3," and Group 3's leader, Efraín Huamán, attributed their success to a decision to go it alone, forgoing cooperation with Groups 1, 2, and 4. Huamán agreed that participation in these other groups had become "moribund," but argued that Group 3 had rejuvenated its levels of participation because of his leadership and dedication to sustained organizing and "consciousness-raising" (Huamán 2005, interview). This was supported by Goñe's description of Group 3 as the best-organized segment of Oasis (Goñe 2002, interview), and this difference appears to have allowed Group 3 to succeed where the rest of Oasis failed. Notably, about 30 percent of Group 3 settlers were still without land titles in 2005 (compared to only 5–10 percent of settlers without titles in the other groups), which likely contributed to their continued active participation in the organization.

Summary of Oasis's Organizational Successes and Failures

Reviewing the case of Oasis, this Next Generation organization made thirteen attempts to acquire services, eight of which succeeded. But these victories were mostly confined to the 1994–2000 period, when only 12 percent of service demands failed, compared to 75 percent failure between 2000 and 2005. The service demands examined in this study (e.g., electricity, water, land titles) tend to highlight the success of the Multisectoral Commission, but the commission's failures between 2000 and 2005 fit a larger pattern described by former mayor Michel Azcueta in a 2002 interview:

12. See the Paraíso case study later in this chapter for details on the Fernández Concha family and their role in the land disputes of the Lomo de Corvina region.

Oasis has not integrated completely with Villa El Salvador and the Villa El Salvador vision and has always had a slightly different dynamic. Oasis hasn't really bought into the idea of creating a dynamic of participation and progress, rather than simply trying to get a service or something concrete. Oasis was not created in accordance with the Villa El Salvador development plan. It didn't leave space for parks, schools, and markets. A good question to ask is how many founders still live in a community. In Oasis, many of the original invaders have sold off their lots and left. So there isn't a strong sense of identity or community. Oasis has been a very divided community, because of internal conflicts. It has been difficult to successfully get services. Projects are generally done piece by piece, and somewhat haphazardly.

In mid-2005, Goñe was attempting to jumpstart the Multisectoral project for sewer drainage in all of Oasis and the neighboring Sector IX, but construction had not yet begun, and each step of the process was proving painfully difficult, as the decline in participation had not abated. Oasis may eventually succeed in acquiring this key service, but the organization showed no signs of shrugging off its moribund state and rejuvenating the vigorous participation that had earned its early victories.

INTERNAL DISPUTE RUPTURES A CONSENSUAL REGIME: THE CASE OF VILLA MAR

National and Local Context

By the time the small Villa Mar invasion occurred on the periphery of Villa El Salvador in 1999, invasion communities like Oasis, Encantada (see chapter 5), and eight others had already occupied a large portion of the sandy dune known as "Lomo de Corvina."[13] Compared to the intense conflict these earlier invasions had caused, the founding of Villa Mar created hardly any stir at all. In fact, given its precarious location on the backside of the hill, the invaders' arrival was practically invisible for several days, until a district representative finally made a perfunctory visit to inform the settlers that they could not stay. Yet it was clear that Mayor Pumar would do nothing about this collection of 180 fragile shacks. Pumar was at the beginning of what would become a

---

13. The other eight invasion neighborhoods were Sector IX, Edilberto Ramos, Laureles de Villa Mar, Jardines de Pachacamac, Valle de Jesús, Jaime Yoshiyama, Palmeras, and Héroes de Cenepa.

four-year term (1998–2002) due to the disruption caused by President Fujimori's exile in November 2000, and had little incentive to take either positive or negative action. The land was nominally controlled by the INC on the grounds that it might contain archaeological ruins. Nationally, interest in the Lomo de Corvina region had also evaporated, and though the usual election-year visits could be expected, there were no congressional factions that cared one way or another about one more tiny settlement in a region already inundated with invasion communities.

The Invasion: The Villa Mar Cooperative

On August 20, 1999, 180 families founded Villa Mar on a small stretch of steep desert terrain with a beautiful view of the Pan-American Highway and the Pacific Ocean. The settlers observed standard invasion protocol and arrived at night, but in hindsight it's likely that they could have arrived by day and would have had an easier time navigating the treacherous terrain. One district official observed that the land was so steep and the soil so unstable that the land was useless. His main objection to the settlement was that the municipality would end up having to protect the settlers from their own foolishness in choosing such a dangerous site (Velásquez 2002, interview).

Like the settlers of Oasis, the founders of Villa Mar had grown up in Villa El Salvador and other invasion-dominated districts like Villa María del Triunfo and El Agustino. Some of them had participated in failed invasion attempts during the 1990s. Their leader was Modesta Martínez, a stubborn and strong-willed human rights activist with no prior experience organizing an invasion. In 2002, Martínez would be reelected as secretary general of Villa Mar, but power was dispersed in the small neighborhood organization, and most decisions were made by consensus rather than voting. This consensus style, however, would eventually rupture the organization when no agreement could be reached on what strategy to pursue in order to acquire legal ownership of the land.

A Strong Start Quickly Falters: Few Resources, No Allies

Between its founding in August 1999 and municipal recognition in March 2002, Villa Mar began as a fairly robust *nascent* organization, but deteriorated as its attempts to acquire services failed (two attempts nominally succeeded, but delivered very low-quality services). Six attempts can be identified during this thirty-one-month period: (1) *rogue* theft of electricity through low-quality informal hookups—a success; (2) *militant* demands for water truck service—a failure; (3) *rogue* theft of low-quality water provision—a success; (4) *militant* protest marches demanding municipal recognition—a failure; (5) a *conformist* plea for municipal recognition—a failure; and (6) a *conformist* negotiation for municipal recognition during an election year—a success. Table 4.3 summarizes the demands.

Although the dogged leadership of Secretary General Martínez would eventually win them recognition from Mayor Pumar, leadership and settler enthusiasm could not overcome the weaknesses of low numbers and almost no money, a lack of resources that would be crucial if Villa Mar was to overcome the difficulties of its remote and precarious geography. Electricity had been privatized in 1997, forcing Villa Mar to adopt a self-sufficient strategy. With no money to speak of, a bootstrap approach was impossible, so Villa Mar had to illegally tap into the local power lines. Even this barely worked, as they lacked the money for decent-quality power cables, resulting in weak, incomplete, and interrupted service (Domínguez 2001, interview).

The settlers used militant marches to demand water truck service from the local SEDAPAL office, but Villa Mar's location was too inconvenient (no roads) and not worth their trouble, as many of the settlers could not even afford the thirty-cent fee for filling a plastic trash can with water. "We live like animals," declared one settler (Cabana 2001, interview). The settlers did break into a nearby water line to connect a cheap hose, but this proved so unreliable that most settlers were forced to buy water elsewhere and haul it in by foot. Even the organization's recognition marches failed, as they were too small a group to attract notice from the basically friendly municipality.

Changing to a conformist strategy, Martínez conducted research on the land in the downtown Lima archives and then, armed with a sheaf of documents, staked out the mayor's office for days on end. She was there in the hallway when the mayor arrived in the morning; she was at his door asking for an appointment all day long; and she was following him to his car when he left. After a week of this, Pumar finally agreed to meet with her. He explained to her that just as Ernesto Fernández Concha had laid claim to a portion of the Oasis settlement, he also claimed to own the Villa Mar land. Although the mayor lacked proof, Pumar felt that Fernández Concha was just a high-class land trafficker who was exploiting poor settlers in need of a home. He strongly urged Martínez not to sign any "reconciliation" agreement with Fernández Concha (as Oasis had done through the Multisectoral), as that would be acknowledging the private ownership of the land. But he would not grant recognition, explaining that the INC had to first make a determination about whether the land had any archaeological value (Pumar 2002, interview).

By March 2001, it was clear to many Villa Mar settlers that Martínez's extralegal strategy had not succeeded. Their militant demands for water truck service and recognition had failed completely due to low numbers and poor strategy

Table 4.3 Villa Mar data matrix

		External factors					Internal factors			
Stage of development	Neighborhood leader	Service demand	District mayor	Service provider	Allies	Avenue of participation	Strategy type	Key resources	Neighborhood regime type	Outcome
		Electricity	Friendly	Private			Rogue	No money	Consensual	Success
		Water truck	Friendly	State			Militant	Small group	Consensual	Failure
Nascent (99–02)		Water hose	Friendly	State			Rogue	No money	Consensual	Success
		Recognition	Friendly	District			Militant	Small group	Consensual	Failure
		Recognition	Friendly	District			Conformist	Leadership	Consensual	Failure
	Martínez (99–05)	Recognition	Friendly	District	Neighbors	02 Election	Militant	Small group	Consensual	Success
		Water truck	Friendly	State			Militant	Small group	Consensual	Failure
		Land titles	Friendly	State			Militant	Small group	Consensual	Failure
		Land titles	Friendly	State			Conformist	Lawyer	Consensual	Failure
Mature (02–05)		Water hose	Neutral	State			Bootstrap	Money	Consensual	Success
		Piped water	Neutral	State	Neighbors		Militant	Small group	Consensual	Failure
		Land titles	Neutral	State	Neighbors		Militant	Small group	Consensual	Failure

choices, and their rogue theft of electricity and water were delivering very low-quality service. In the face of these failures, the Villa Mar organization imploded.

Domitila Macurí and Sixto Rodríguez were two block captains within Villa Mar who were already unhappy with Martínez's leadership, and they took advantage of this low point to push for her ouster. Macurí argued that the settlers should sign an agreement with Fernández Concha, as the Oasis settlers had, and this would lead to better services. Martínez believed in Mayor Pumar's advice, however, and insisted that the settlers hold out for free land, rather than pay the supposed owner a price they could not afford.

The consensus-oriented group could not reach an agreement, so Macurí and Rodríguez took their loyal followers and left the organization. Some settlers went so far as to relocate their makeshift homes to be near Macurí and away from Martínez. Many other settlers left Villa Mar altogether, as they judged the invasion a failure and were unwilling to invest further in what they saw as a dead-end project. Most of those who left had families they could stay with, while those who stayed had nowhere else to go (Martínez 2002, interview).

Steady Organizational Disintegration: Service Agenda Stagnates

Between March 2001 and February 2002, the Villa Mar organization lost 140 of its 180 families. During this period, no serious service demands were made, as the community was preoccupied with survival and containing an escalating conflict that included threats, arson, and a destructive raid (Villa Mar assembly, 2/1/02).

Although unwilling to make a deal with the Fernández Concha family, Villa Mar did shift to a conformist strategy. "They have all the money and guns," noted Villa Mar leader Máximo Cabana in a 2001 interview, "but we hired a professional lawyer." The settlers hired an attorney, Isaías Casas, and began to fight Fernández Concha legally. It was an uphill battle, both figuratively and literally. In the figurative sense, they were severely outmatched: the Villa Mar settlers could barely pay the photocopy expenses of their pro bono lawyer, and Fernández Concha had a professional team of attorneys at work on a pan–Lomo de Corvina legal strategy (Casas 2001, interview). And in the literal sense, a violent conflict broke out with their uphill enemies, Macurí and Rodríguez. Since Macurí and Rodríguez controlled the higher terrain, adjacent to more developed invasion communities, they could and did tamper with the electricity and water supply of Villa Mar. Macurí filed legal complaints about Villa Mar and, in early 2002, continued harassing the community, through written threats of violence, homemade firebombs in the two shantyhomes adjacent to Martínez's, and the destruction and looting of Villa Mar's meager communal kitchen (Avendaño 2002, interview; formal written complaint, 1/15/02).

Although the source of this string of attacks and intimidation was clear, its motivation was not. Villa Mar discovered that Macurí's faction had signed an agreement with Fernández Concha, and so Fernández Concha seemed to be behind the attacks, but why would this wealthy and ambitious businessman care about a few dozen poor families tucked away in a remote corner of Villa El Salvador?

With this puzzle unsolved, Villa Mar made its sixth and final service demand as a nascent organization: the settlers again demanded that Pumar grant them municipal recognition—but this time it was during an election year. Further, Martínez cleverly staged the Villa Mar recognition march in conjunction with a larger march for services by Lomo de Corvina neighborhoods. With the help of these allies and the pressure of the election, this militant strategy worked, and on March 15, Pumar recognized Villa Mar (Municipality of Villa El Salvador 2002).

Solving the Riddle: Discovery of Land's Value Rejuvenates Organization

From March 2002 until the November 2002 elections, the *mature* Villa Mar organization attempted unsuccessfully to capitalize on its recognition by Mayor Pumar to achieve better services, but did solve the riddle of Fernández Concha's irrational hostility toward their small group. Villa Mar's militancy continued under the newly elected mayor, Jaime Zea (2002–present), with equally poor results. The six service initiatives during this period were: (1) renewed *militant* demands for water truck service—a failure; (2) *militant* demands for land titles—a failure; (3) *conformist* negotiations for land titles—a failure; (4) a *bootstrap* agreement to continue low-quality water provision—a success; (5) a militant march demanding piped water—a failure; and (6) a *militant* march demanding land titles—a failure (see table 4.3).

Martínez hoped that Villa Mar's new status as a legal entity would bolster its demands for water truck service, but local SEDAPAL officials were unimpressed and ignored the settlers' protests at the district SEDAPAL office.[14] Undeterred, the settlers took their cardboard protest signs to the INC office and demanded that the land be rezoned as residential, but this also went nowhere. In both cases, the Villa Mar group was simply too small to have an impact, especially in the case of zoning and titling of land, a lengthy bureaucratic process that consistently proves difficult to complete except via a conformist strategy (INC 2002, letter).

The Fernández Concha puzzle was finally solved in September 2002 when it was revealed that Lima's metropolitan government had proposed building a road

14. In an interview at the SEDAPAL office, local officials did not even remember the recent protest (Toche Lara 2002).

to connect the Pan-American Highway with Villa El Salvador—and the only practical place to build it was up the steep bottleneck that Villa Mar occupied. Although the proposed access road might never be built, it became clear that this land might actually be quite valuable, and that Fernández Concha could perhaps extract a high price from the government.

More determined than ever, the Villa Mar settlers dug in their heels and planned for the long haul. They lowered the fee required of new members in order to attract thirty new families, they hired a daytime guard to protect the settlement while the residents were out working their informal jobs, and Casas continued his legal work on the titling claim, now in the vague hope that he might actually get paid for his service to the Villa Mar cooperative (Martínez 2002, interview).

The effort to attract new families proved quite successful, and the boundary of Villa Mar steadily stretched downhill toward the Pan-American Highway, eventually stabilizing at 240 lots and families, which was about 60 more than they had started with in 1999. All told, about 700 people now called Villa Mar home. Tensions with Villa Mar's uphill neighbors continued sporadically, peaking in 2003 with another arson, this time at the house of Secretary General Martínez. Martínez was also assaulted while walking home alone, but she continued to lead the community despite these challenges (Martínez 2005, interview).

Learning from the ineffectiveness of Villa Mar's earlier protest marches, Martínez resolved to only attempt direct action when backed up by allied neighborhoods. The *bootstrap* purchase of water (via a low-quality hose) did not improve the quality of water service, but it did mend relations with the neighborhood from which Villa Mar had been stealing water.[15] The modest growth of the settlement's population also afforded two new community buildings, one of which served as a chapel and one as a *wawa wasi*, or day care. Both buildings were extremely basic and cost less than forty dollars each for materials.

In 2004–5, Villa Mar participated in six marches aimed at two demands—piped water and land titles—but none of these actions had any effect, despite the participation of neighborhoods including Valle de Jesús, Héroes de Cenepa, Palmeras, and Paraíso. The most dramatic of these ineffective marches took place in September 2004, when a few hundred settlers blocked the Pan-American Highway, stalling thousands of cars and drawing swift retaliation from riot police with tear gas. A less disruptive but well-attended march in April 2005 pressured Mayor Zea to intervene in the ongoing land title dispute with the Fernández Concha family, but this too was ignored.

15. Settlers paid about six dollars per person each month for water. For most settlers, this figure easily exceeded 10 percent of their irregular income.

Summary of Villa Mar's Organizational Successes and Failures

The Next Generation organization of Villa Mar initiated twelve attempts to acquire services, and nearly all of them failed. Its two rogue thefts and one boot-strap purchase were nominally successful, but the quality of service was unusually low. Villa Mar's only unqualified success was its third (militant) bid for municipal recognition, prior to the 2002 district elections, which was supported by neigh-boring settlements. Excluding this one success, the key causal factors explaining Villa Mar's overall failure were internal—chiefly a lack of resources, or a poor strategy choice given those limited resources (e.g., trying to use militant pressure tactics with a very small group). Villa Mar had a friendly mayor between 1999 and 2002, but this did little to help it acquire services other than recognition, a service whose main value is in bolstering demands for tangible needs like water. The most significant external factor was likely Villa Mar's lack of influential allies. Most of the organizations examined in chapters 3–5 had allies at some point in their growth, but Villa Mar had only the occasional solidarity of similar settlements in the region.

By 2005, Villa Mar's renewed efforts to stake its claim to land that might prove valuable was still not secure. Eviction looked unlikely, and the number of families had risen to 240, but with most families earning less than four dollars per day, the settlement remained precarious both physically and economically (Martínez 2005, interview). Still, despite Villa Mar's small numbers, rates of participation in the weekly meetings were high, and the threats of violence had ended. But any optimistic appraisal falters in the face of their gains up to that point: after six years of struggle, the only nearby source of water for these 240 families was three leaky garden hoses connected to a distant water line with tape.

QUICK PROGRESS DESPITE INTERNAL DIVISIONS: THE CASE OF PARAÍSO

National and Local Context

By the time Paraíso was founded in September 2001, Peru's national political context had changed dramatically from that of the other Lima cases examined in this study. While the other six case study communities were founded during the rule of Fujimori (1990–2000), the Paraíso invasion occurred just six weeks into the tenure of President Alejandro Toledo (2001–6). Prior to Toledo's inauguration in July 2001, interim president Valentín Paniagua (2000–2001) had governed over an uncertain period that left many issues related to land invasion commu-nities in limbo. The COFOPRI office, for example, largely closed its doors to new claims during this eight-month interim, preferring to wait for signals about the policy direction of Paniagua's successor. With the start of Toledo's presidential term and his promises of food, housing, and employment for the nation's poor, COFOPRI resumed its frenzied pace of land titling, and the briefly dormant land invasion phenomenon surged back to life (Romero 2002, interview).

By this point, many of the land invasions in Villa El Salvador's Lomo de Corvina region had something in common: a legal and sometimes extralegal conflict with the wealthy Fernández Concha family. During the 1990s, confusion had surrounded settlers' dealings with agents and lawyers representing the secretive Fernández Concha clan, and all manner of rumors had circulated, but by 2001 the facts were well known by most major players in the region.

The original Ernesto Fernández Concha had, prior to 1971, paid the Velasco government for a mining concession (but not ownership) in the region. With the founding of Villa El Salvador, however, General Velasco had declared that all the land in the Villa region was public and "for the people." By the 1990s, the senior Fernández Concha had died, but his son (of the same name) and various relatives observed that Villa El Salvador had finally extended itself to the region of the family's old mining concession. Seeing an opportunity, the younger Fernández Concha made a series of claims, backed by dubious legal documents, to coerce groups of settlers into paying him for what was not his land to begin with. Once some settlers in a given community had paid Fernández Concha, they became his implicit allies, since upholding his (false) ownership meant upholding their own claim to the land. By 2001, Mayor Pumar had taken a public stand against Fernández Concha's exploitation, which cost him nothing, and likely won him settler votes for his 2002 reelection bid (which he lost).

Preparing to Invade

By 1999, settlers were wising up, so Fernández Concha experimented with a new strategy. Rather than waiting for "his" lands to be invaded, he had his agents initiated a new community in order to sell lots in an orderly fashion. To this end, he fenced off four adjacent parcels of land, built a guardhouse on each, and put four men in charge of overseeing the land and selling deeds for lots. The four men—Sr. Gutiérrez, Sr. Torres, Sr. Lara, and Sr. Huamán—followed their orders, but few people were interested in paying for lots of empty desert with no community and no services other than a concrete playground for basketball and soccer.[16]

---

16. Although I interviewed José Lara, I never met Sr. Gutiérrez, Sr. Torres, or Sr. Huamán, and settlers I interviewed referred to them only by their last names.

In May 2001, however, Abrahím Ruíz secretly approached Torres and Huamán and proposed that they betray Fernández Concha and help Ruíz organize an invasion of the land. Like many of the Next Generation leaders discussed in this chapter, Ruíz was the son of parents who had participated in the 1971 founding of Villa El Salvador. Ruíz knew about Fernández Concha and saw him as a symbol of exploitation. He thought it fitting justice that Fernández Concha would lose the land to an invasion. Seeing an opportunity to make more money than their security guard salaries provided, Torres and Huamán agreed. Although Torres and Huamán would be the "men inside" who would open the gates, Ruíz did not trust them, so he excluded them from the four months of preparatory organizing, which resulted in Ruíz's election as the secretary general of the "pre-cooperative." By September 2001, Ruíz and one hundred other settlers were ready to invade (Ruíz 2001, interview).

The Invasion: Homes Arise as Towers Fall

Ruíz meant to invade when Torres and Huamán were on duty, with Gutiérrez and Lara absent, but invasion plans are difficult to keep secret, and when the settlers arrived, all four guards were there and conflict erupted, aggravated by several hundred additional settlers who spontaneously arrived on the scene. All five men (and other founders) disagree on what exactly happened that night, but by morning, the land was split into five camps of settlers, each led by one of the five (see table 4.4). Gutiérrez, Lara, and Huamán each controlled three blocks of houses that corresponded to the area under the nominal protection of their guardhouses (Blocks A–C, J–L, and M–O, respectively). The terrain that had been Torres's responsibility was split between three small blocks controlled by Ruíz (Blocks D–F) and three small blocks controlled by Torres (Blocks G–I). Within these fifteen blocks there was sufficient space for 288 lots (at the standard ninety square meters each), but instead 400 lots were haphazardly created, ranging from twenty-eight to ninety square meters. Adding to the confusion, some settlers claimed more than one lot, often in two different blocks or zones of control (Yabar 2001, interview).[17]

17. The crowding of 400 shantyhomes into a space sufficient for only 288 lots raises an interesting question: why was the playground left untouched? Unlike the rest of the land, which was sand, the playground was a smooth and level concrete surface, identical to the concrete floors that would soon be poured to create foundations for the few settlers who could afford it. The answer seems fairly simple: the playground was used for soccer. I am sure cases of soccer field invasions occur, but I am not aware of any. Consider the case of the Oasis invasion, which occupied land reserved for a future university. An enormous parcel of far better land sits in the middle of Villa El Salvador, ostensibly reserved for a future soccer stadium. Even the most optimistic politician does

Table 4.4   Land division of Paraíso by leader

Gutiérrez	Ruíz	Torres	Lara	Huamán
A	D	G	J	M
B	E	H	K	N
	F			
C	Playground	I	L	O

Note: Dimensions of land: approximately 90 meters by 360 meters.
Total area: approximately 3 hectares (excluding playground).

Recriminations flew in every direction. Ruíz was the undisputed leader of the Paraíso organization, but the other men contested his authority over "their" respective fiefs. Table 4.4 suggests clearly defined boundaries for the sake of simplicity, but border disagreements persisted for days. As the morning progressed, Gutiérrez and Lara expressed surprise and frustration that the police had not arrived, as is typical the morning after an invasion. But it was the morning of September 11, 2001, and all eyes were glued to television reports of the attacks in the United States. For the time being, the settlers were on their own to sort out their differences (Lara 2001, interview).

The First Year: Strategy and Resources Shape Organizational Success

From its founding in September 2001 until Mayor Pumar recognized the settlers in July 2002, the *nascent* Paraíso organization made considerable progress despite internal conflicts and some intra-settlement violence. The four major service attempts during this period were: (1) *rogue* installation of illegal electricity connections—a success; (2) *militant* demands for water truck service—a success; (3) *militant* demands for municipal recognition—a failure; and (4) *conformist* solicitation of municipal recognition during an election year—a success.

During this period, the internal factors of resources, strategy, and tactics proved pivotal (see table 4.5). In October, Paraíso was able to rig illegal connections to the electricity lines of an adjacent neighborhood, but since these

---

not foresee the stadium being built within the next twenty years, but in the meantime it provides space for many soccer fields. When I inquired about the stadium land as a possible site, an Oasis settler looked incredulous and said, "There would be blood in the streets!" (Morales 2002, interview). The stadium dream was considered sacred. Presumably the cramped Paraíso feared a similar social sanction if it attempted to encroach on land that clearly had a communal use. Further, settlers recognize the value of recreation space for a healthy community. But when I asked settlers, a different explanation was repeated several times: it had never occurred to them.

neighbors would be charged by Luz del Sur for the extra power, the settlers were forced to pay their neighbors about seven dollars per month per family. This arrangement was illegal (and a fire hazard), but it served the nascent Paraíso organization well, since they could not afford to pay for formal electricity service.

The ability to pay also yielded reasonably quick water truck service in response to their militant demands at the local SEDAPAL office. Paraíso was in an inconvenient location, but it had enough paying families to merit the water truck's daily trip up the hill. Militant demands failed, however, when it came to municipal recognition. This was partly due to timing—without the pressure of district elections, Mayor Pumar was in no hurry to deal with yet another land invasion—but also due to poor targeting by the novice settlers. Their downtown marches at the Supreme Court were loud and well attended, but the Supreme Court has no role in the process of municipal recognition. The settlers also protested at the Municipality of Villa El Salvador, but the local march drew fewer participants than the more exciting downtown event.

When election time came, however, Mayor Pumar hit the campaign trail and quickly agreed to municipal recognition of Paraíso in July 2002, as part of his broader opposition to what he called the "exploitation" of the Fernández Concha clan. In one stump speech, he urged settlers to denounce anyone attempting to sell land and circumvent the legal process (Lomo de Corvina campaign stop by Pumar, 2/17/02). In the meantime, however, Fernández Concha had not been idle. Torres and Huamán had crawled back to their former master (probably with some economic incentive) and now all four of the land's original guardians were united in their backing of Fernández Concha's claim of ownership. Of Paraíso's five power brokers, only Secretary General Ruíz insisted that—at a minimum—the blocks under his direct control (D–F) were public land. With the issue of recognition settled in a short eleven months, the factions were now divided over how best to pursue land titles for their rapidly developing settlement. It was not an amicable discussion. Lara forced his blocks of settlers to boycott meetings led by Ruíz, and in February 2002 the Gutiérrez faction tried to violently expand into Ruíz's Block D, resulting in destroyed houses and police intervention (Solar 2002, interview).

A Mature but Weak Organization: Early Successes Evaporate

Following recognition in July 2002, the *mature* Paraíso organization employed a mix of strategies to seek land titles and piped water, but none of their efforts succeeded. The four attempts between 2002 and 2005 included: (1) a *bootstrap*

Table 4.5 Paraíso data matrix

| Stage of development | Neighborhood leader | External factors | | | | | | Internal factors | | | Outcome |
		Service demand	District mayor	Service provider	Allies	Avenue of participation	Strategy type	Key resources	Neighborhood regime type	
Nascent (01–02)	Ruíz (01–05)	Electricity	Friendly	Private			Rogue	Money	Democratic	Success
		Water truck	Friendly	State			Militant	Money	Democratic	Success
		Recognition	Friendly	District			Militant	Low participation	Democratic	Failure
		Recognition	Friendly	District		02 Election	Conformist		Democratic	Success
		Land titles	Friendly	State			Bootstrap	No money	Democratic	Failure
Mature (02–05)		Land titles	Friendly	State			Conformist	Lawyer	Democratic	Failure
		Piped water	Neutral	State	Neighbors		Militant	Small group	Democratic	Failure
	Fierro (05)	Land titles	Neutral	State	Neighbors		Militant	Small group	Democratic	Failure

attempt by 85 percent of Paraíso to buy land titles; (2) a *conformist* attempt by the other 15 percent of Paraíso to receive land titles for free—a failure, at least for now; (3) a militant march demanding piped water—a failure; and (4) a *militant* march demanding land titles—a failure.

In late 2002, settlers in the 85 percent of lots controlled by Gutiérrez, Torres, Lara, and Huamán began negotiating a contract with Fernández Concha to pay three dollars per square meter of land (i.e., $270 for a 90m² lot). Even this modest sum proved too much for the penniless settlers, however, and the deal fell through. At the same time, Abrahím Ruíz's lawyer had successfully demonstrated that Fernández Concha's claims—whatever their legal merit—did not encompass an east-west strip of land that included the playground, Ruíz's Blocks D–F, and a narrow strip of lots on the southern end of Torres's Blocks H and I. Apparently the playground had been there back when Fernández Concha filed his claim, and his lawyers had inadvertently failed to claim the vacant land west of the playground. As of 2005, this legal advantage had not yet translated into land titles, since the process of titling public land still costs something and the settlers could not afford even these modest fees, but Ruíz's strong legal position suggested that in due time the settlers in his portion of Paraíso would gain title at only a nominal cost.

In my 2001 interview with Ruíz, he had mentioned his archival research on the land prior to the invasion, so it seemed rather suspicious that his zone of control just happened to wind up entirely on land that was indisputably public. But when I asked him about this, he simply replied: "We're not professionals, but we know our rights. The professionals live in rich neighborhoods with cars. We should not have to pay anything for [a land title]." And he smiled.

Under Ruíz, the Paraíso settlers participated in the 2004 blocking of the Pan-American Highway described in the Villa Mar case study, but like Villa Mar, Paraíso received no benefits for their trouble. Although Ruíz continued to serve as a block captain for his fief, Edgar Fierro was elected secretary general in his stead in 2005 and led the Paraíso settlers to participate in the ineffective 2005 march for land titles (also described above in the Villa Mar case study).

Summary of Paraíso's Organizational Successes and Failures

The Next Generation Paraíso organization made eight attempts to acquire services, three of which succeeded and five of which failed. Why did Paraíso encounter greater initial success than Villa Mar but end up in a similarly stalled position? Both communities suffered severe internal conflicts, but Villa Mar's developed over time, while Paraíso's were congenital. Further, although Villa Mar had a more serious peak of conflict (e.g., arson), Villa Mar managed to get past these difficulties as an organization, but this persistence did not deliver services.

Comparison of individual demands reveals that although the results were sometimes different, the causal explanations were nearly always identical. In both cases, organizational resources were the key determinant of rogue and militant attempts at electricity and water. Paraíso had some money and scored a couple of early successes; Villa Mar did not have any money and failed. When it came to municipal recognition, both groups initially failed due to their mutual lack of political leverage. When district elections approached, however, both groups earned quick recognition. Although their strategies diverged—a militant march by Villa Mar and a conformist deal by Paraíso—it was the timing of the election that yielded success in each case. In the Villa Mar case, I argued that a lack of influential allies hampered their service demands—and it did— but Paraíso shows that given only slightly more favorable conditions, a similar settlement could at least initially succeed.

In 2005, Paraíso showed signs of moving beyond the virulent conflicts that had characterized its first years. Some settlers had given up on Paraíso and left, freeing up space for holders of smaller lots to expand their homes, which relieved some of the tension. But bitterness remained between the settlers lucky enough to have chosen public lots in Ruíz's zone (and a few in Torres's zone) and the rest, who would likely have to eventually pay as much as $270 to the Fernández Concha family.

THE NEXT GENERATION TYPE

Synthesis of the cases of Camino a la Libertad, Oasis de Villa, Villa Mar, and Paraíso provides a composite picture of the identity traits, repertoire traits, and neighborhood regimes characteristic of the Next Generation type. With respect to identity, Next Generation organizations tend to have idealistic and novice leaders whose pursuit of material objectives is driven by a bold sense of entitlement. With respect to repertoire, the Next Generation exhibits strategic flexibility and follows the strategy life cycle. While each Next Generation organization's strategy type varies over time, the specific tactics employed resemble those of the Old Guard, except perhaps for a greater reluctance to use violence. Finally, the Next Generation exhibits no clear pattern with respect to neighborhood regime. While Next Generation organizations tend to be more inclusive than the Old Guard, variation in both organizational inclusiveness and competitiveness makes all four regime types a possibility (though among these four cases, the electoral regime type is not represented).

Next Generation Identity Traits: Sense of
Entitlement, Materialist, and Inexperienced

Next Generation organizations are characterized by a sense of entitlement, material objectives, and novice leaders with little experience organizing land invasions. The Next Generation's sense of "we will succeed" is clearest in the bold seizure of occupied lands by Camino (a ranch) and Paraíso (fenced and guarded land), but is also evident in the case of Oasis (university land). Only Villa Mar invaded land that (to their knowledge) was of no interest to anyone, though it turned out that the land was destined for a possible highway access road.

All four Next Generation organizations operated solely for the pursuit of material needs, and are perhaps notable for their *lack* of any effort to cloak their demands with loftier goals. These settlers believe that they deserve a decent neighborhood and that they are going to get one. This sometimes reckless pursuit of material needs can lead to shameless theft, such as Camino's floor-to-ceiling looting of the Pazmiño Navas ranchhouse. Among these four cases, there were no exceptions to the Next Generation's focus on material gain.

Next Generation neighborhoods also tend to be led by inexperienced settlers, especially at their founding. This was true of Caroas in Oasis, Martínez in Villa Mar, and Ruíz in Paraíso; the major exception was clearly Meza in Camino. Although Meza was a novice when he co-founded Comité #2 in 1978, Camino was the second organization he had organized and his experience showed. On the other hand, this experience should not be overstated or overvalued: he was still reckless enough to land himself in jail due to his too-clever scheme of pretending to attempt purchase of the land.

Next Generation Repertoire Traits: Flexible, Unoriginal, and Rarely Violent

Next Generation organizations employ a flexible repertoire of strategies, use unoriginal tactics, and use violence only in self-defense. As will be demonstrated in chapter 6, all four Next Generation organizations followed the broad contours of the strategy life cycle. They began with rogue strategies, moved on to militant demands, and then shifted to conformist soliciting after some movement back and forth between strategy types. Of the four cases, only Camino "graduated" to bootstrap methods, completing the cycle. Oasis "stalled out" at conformist strategies and never made it to the bootstrap stage (although Oasis did make one early bootstrap demand for privately provided electricity). Villa Mar and Paraíso were too young in 2005 for us to gauge whether they would complete the strategy life cycle, but their early years demonstrated a fairly good fit with the life cycle's expectations, and both organizations clearly exhibited strategic flexibility. Although none of the Next Generation cases exhibited Old Guard–style rigidity in their strategy choices, Camino did employ conformist and largely clientelist strategies for eight years before moving on to bootstrap methods. Still, it seems clear from the Camino case study that Meza's lasting— but ultimately not permanent—reliance on clientelism had little to do with rigidity, but rather a willingness to exhaust a successful strategy until a new approach was required.

Like the Old Guard, the Next Generation employs unoriginal tactics. Although the incendiary internal disputes of Villa Mar and Paraíso and the explosive antagonism between Camino and the Pazmiño Navas family made these cases memorable, the specific tactics used differed little from those of the Old Guard: stealing electricity (but not other services, unless the Villa Mar garden hose is counted), protest marches to the same old locations, conventional petitions for titles and other services, and clientelist deals. Perhaps the most original tactic was Meza turning the Quito Metropolitan Council against the Pazmiño Navas by suggesting that the settlers ought to instead pay the council for the land (at a lower price). But overall, the Next Generation preferred to use the "playbook" of their parents.

Finally, Next Generation organizations use violence only in self-defense and rarely use new technologies. Oasis and Camino did engage and even injure the police while resisting evictions, but this was a far cry from the preemptive violence of some Old Guard organizations. Intra-neighborhood antagonism in Villa Mar did escalate to include arson and threats, but Villa Mar's leader was a target of violence, not an instigator.[18]

With respect to technology use, its absence would probably go unnoticed if not for comparison with the Innovator organizations examined in chapter 5. None of these Next Generation communities made significant use of Internet or mobile technology, but other Next Generation organizations, not included in this study, did use cell phones to coordinate protest marches.[19]

Next Generation Neighborhood Regimes: Moderately Inclusive

Next Generation neighborhood regimes vary both in their competitiveness and their inclusiveness, meaning that they can be of any type, though they are often moderate examples of their respective regime types. Ranking these case studies

18. This shift away from the intentional use of violent tactics does not imply that such poor neighborhoods are necessarily much safer. Although Peru and Ecuador's *pueblos jóvenes* are a far cry from the notoriously violent favelas of Rio de Janeiro and other Brazilian cities (Arias 2004), these remain impoverished communities with relatively high levels of crime.

19. The Frente Unitario de los Pueblos de Perú (United Front of the Peoples of Peru), for example, made use of cell phone coordination in their marches on the Bank of Materials and Ministry of the Presidency (field observations, 12/29/01 and 3/19/02).

in terms of their organizational competitiveness, the democratic regimes of Oasis and Paraíso were the most competitive, followed by the consensual regime of Villa Mar and the authoritarian regime of Camino. This sample included no electoral Next Generation organizations, but such groups do exist.[20] In terms of organizational inclusiveness, the power-sharing regimes of Villa Mar, Oasis, and Paraíso were roughly comparable, followed by the power-concentrating regime of Camino.

Given this study's theoretical claims regarding neighborhood regimes, we would expect a sample of Next Generation cases to vary in their capacity both to maintain alliances and to take advantage of local participatory institutions. This sample of four cases varies on both dimensions, but observations of specific cases are perhaps more worthwhile.

With respect to allies, the noncompetitive Camino proved to be a stable alliance partner, but so did the competitive Oasis regime. In the case of Oasis, however, six of the seven alliance-backed service demands occurred under the same leader, Macario Goñe (1997–2005), whose long tenure provided a stable leadership platform.

With respect to local avenues of participation, other than local elections that affected all four cases, only Oasis had an opportunity to participate in a participatory institution (the Multisectoral), of which its power-sharing regime made good use. This seems a poor test, however, since the Multisectoral founder was also the spokesman for Oasis! A better test will be whether Villa Mar and Paraíso (both power-sharing) join the Multisectoral once they begin seeking piped water and drainage.

Implications for the Next Generation Type

The identity traits, repertoire traits, and neighborhood regimes common to Next Generation organizations have implications for similar organizations. With respect to identity, the Next Generation's focus on material gains and property security makes them—like their Old Guard parents—likely victims of the security trap. In 2005, Villa Mar and Paraíso had not yet achieved property security, but when Oasis acquired land titles, its regime experienced a sharp and damaging drop not only in participation but also in membership, as many settlers sold their land and abandoned Oasis. From an organizational perspective, Camino should perhaps consider itself lucky that its battle with the Pazmiño Navas family delayed the arrival of land titles. In the absence of legal ownership, Camino had time to build a deeper level of community commitment

---

20. In the Next Generation neighborhood of Jaime Yoshiyama, for example, elections are competitive but power is concentrated.

and consolidate the organization. Although the achievement of all other services resulted in de facto property security, it remains to be seen if the consolidated Camino organization can survive the eventual delivery of land titles (assuming they ever arrive).

With respect to repertoire, strategic flexibility seems to be a boon to Next Generation organizations. Camino and Oasis each scored at least one major success with each of the four strategy types, and Villa Mar and Paraíso both scored a success with each of three different types. Note, however, that Oasis used a bootstrap strategy only for the purchase of privatized electricity. This one bootstrap demand did not usher in a new phase of the strategy life cycle for Oasis; instead, the community "stalled out" at conformist methods.

A possible downside of the strategy life cycle, however, may be a loss of tactical specialization. Recall the predictable strength of Pisulli's militant demands or the reliable partnerships of Pro's clientelism. While specialization is no guarantee of success (e.g., the stubbornly militant and ineffective Rosales), an organization like Villa Mar might benefit from focusing on using one type of strategy effectively, rather than using several types poorly.

Despite their strategic flexibility, however, the specific tactics of the Next Generation remain, for the most part, carbon copies of their clientelist or radical parents, which may mean lost opportunities. It is not fruitful to draw up counterfactual scenarios of wildly innovative tactics that might have fared better, but it is worth noting that of the approximately 3,400 families living in Camino and Oasis in 2005, only about 1,500 homes had indoor plumbing.[21] There is no "right" number that should have services by a certain point, but with over two-thirds of these settlers still lacking this basic necessity, it is worth asking what could be done differently. To observe some examples of such alternative tactics, we turn now to a different type of invasion organization that grew up alongside the Next Generation: the Innovators.

---

21. I exclude Villa Mar and Paraíso's roughly six hundred families because these organizations are arguably too young to have acquired piped water and drainage.

5

The Innovators:
Strategic Creativity and a Sense of Mission

In the mid-1990s, a third type of invasion organization emerged. It was characterized by novice leadership, a sense of mission, strategic flexibility and innovation, and a focus on organizational activism. Like the Next Generation, the
leaders of these "Innovator" organizations had grown up in the invasion communities of their Old Guard parents, then founded their own neighborhoods, and
relied on a flexible combination of strategies. These groups, however, exhibited
innovative tactics and organizational activism. This chapter compares the organizational strategy, success, and survival of two Innovator organizations. The first
case, in Lima, quickly developed the trademark creativity of the Innovator
type but did not develop an organizational sense of mission until later. The
second case, in Quito, was a "born Innovator" whose tactical creativity and goal
of helping peer organizations defined the invasion community from the start.

The invasion neighborhoods of La Encantada (in Lima) and San Juan Bosco
de Itchimbía (in Quito) both relied on strategic flexibility and innovative tactics
to acquire services. In the case of Encantada, however, successful acquisition of
services initially led the neighborhood organization into a moribund state,
while in Itchimbía success resulted in organizational consolidation. Why did
success hurt Encantada but help Itchimbía? And even more curious, how was
Encantada then able to overcome its moribund status and consolidate?

In the case of Encantada, property security led the organization to a moribund
state, but an organizational reorientation from material objectives to activism

saved the neighborhood regime and permitted it to consolidate. In 1996, Encantada invaded lands that were being used for raising pigs and other livestock. Further, the powerful and popular district mayor strongly opposed the Encantada settlers. Yet through Encantada's innovative use of the media, the settlers succeeded in winning over public opinion by portraying the struggle as a public health crisis, since their children were getting sick from livestock-related diseases. In the end, the settlers received permanent title to the land and rapidly acquired most basic services, but these victories led to a sharp drop in rates of participation. Spurred by the surprise arrival of an adjacent land invasion, however, Encantada leaders resuscitated their regime through a new focus on helping their peer community, which resulted in a resurgence of participation and organizational consolidation.

In the case of Itchimbía, the community's founding activist principles permitted its organizational success to facilitate consolidation rather than leading the neighborhood into the security trap. Led by a cadre of career activists involved in Ecuador's national indigenous movement, Itchimbía fended off militarized eviction attempts with headline-grabbing nonviolence, obtained high-quality services through audacious thefts, and forced the city to cofinance self-help condominiums for the settlers. These Innovators went to bed hungry but found the resources to produce professional educational videos, make heavy use of the Internet, and present organizing workshops throughout Quito. The Itchimbía organization was founded on an activist premise, and it was this sense of mission that helped it become one of the most successful invasion communities in Quito.

Although both of these organizations had their share of obstacles and organizational failures, their overall success points to the potential strength of the Innovator type. As these two case studies will make clear, the Innovators replicate the strategic flexibility of the Next Generation type while enhancing it with unusual creativity and a broader organizational mission based on mixed motives that can galvanize their membership.

The case of Itchimbía offers a clear illustration of the strength of the Innovator type, but perhaps the more persuasive case is that of the tactically creative Encantada, whose regime sank into a moribund state only to be "rescued" by the emergence of an activist impulse. While the former cases show how innovative tactics and a sense of mission can help an organization succeed and consolidate, the latter case shows how an organization can succeed in acquiring services but still fail to consolidate without *both* of these factors. For Innovators, tactical creativity is insufficient to deliver long-term organization survival without the second key ingredient of organizational activism.

NEW ACTIVIST MISSION REJUVENATES MORIBUND INNOVATOR:
THE CASE OF ENCANTADA

National and Local Context

The early 1990s was a terrible period for Lima's district of Villa El Salvador. Between 1990 and 1995, six different men claimed the mantle of district mayor for brief periods, each worse than the last, with Mayor Jorge Vásquez (1993-94) convicted of corruption and sent to prison. Terrorist attacks by Sendero Luminoso continued during this period as well, and although violence in Villa steadily declined from its peak around 1990 (see Dietz 1998b, 199), it fueled general dissatisfaction with the municipal government and distrust of elected leaders (Zapata 1996, 265-77).

Looking for a savior, voters in late 1995 brought back Villa's legendary first mayor, Michel Azcueta, for yet another term (1984-86, 1987-89, 1996-98). But as a political opponent of President Fujimori, Azcueta's leadership put Villa El Salvador at odds with the national government (Zapata 1996, 79-85). Fujimori sought to undermine opposition mayors through highly targeted antipoverty programs that often contradicted their plans (Arce 2006, 43-44). For example, after Villa's many minor land invasions between 1993 and 1996, Azcueta declared that the time for unplanned invasions had ended, and proceeded to develop a land use plan for the district. Fujimori responded by bankrolling an invasion in Azcueta's political backyard, going so far as to name the community "Jaime Yoshiyama," after the dominant Fujimorista politician who had just lost the metropolitan mayoral race in 1995 (Dietz 1998a, 216). The Yoshiyama settlement directly contradicted Azcueta's zoning plan, and Fujimori supplied ample funds for household electricity and streetlights in Yoshiyama, highlighting Azcueta's inability to do the same for other settlements not loyal to Fujimori.

Despite this hostility from the national government, as well as other obstacles, Azcueta sustained his broad political support and even earned the respect of his local opponents. By the time he concluded his final mayoral term in 1998, he was sufficiently popular to anoint his successor, Martín Pumar, who was elected mayor in Azcueta's stead.

Preparing to Invade: What Better Way to Celebrate an Anniversary?

The story of Encantada began in 1996, at the beginning of Azcueta's final term in office, when a group of men and women in their twenties formed "the Sons and

Daughters of Villa El Salvador."[1] These young people, many recently married and with infants and children, had grown up in Villa El Salvador, Lima's most famous invasion-founded district. Many of the parents of Encantada's founders had themselves participated in the historic 1971 founding of Villa El Salvador under the Velasco administration (1968–75). General Velasco was a dictator and had seized power from elected president Fernando Belaúnde Terry (1963–68), but in Villa El Salvador the general became an instant hero due to his support of the twenty-five thousand founding settlers, who were delivered to the desert site on a combination of military vehicles and the historic blue-and-yellow buses that in 2005 were still used for district transit (see Collier 1976, 109–10). Villa's main boulevard was soon named in Velasco's honor.

Although the Sons and Daughters organization emerged from a number of grassroots discussions and meetings, two members—Angélica Salas and Arturo Laynes—were the first to formalize the group by placing themselves in charge of collecting membership dues to cover the anticipated costs of the invasion, such as the purchase of building materials. Fearing exploitative land traffickers, the prospective settlers were suspicious of anyone who asked them for money, and Salas and Laynes aggravated their suspicions by refusing to disclose the invasion site to the general membership (ostensibly to protect its secret location from becoming public knowledge). Hence, in their February 1996 founding election, Sons and Daughters members elected neither Salas nor Laynes, instead choosing Máximo Quispe as their first secretary general (1996–97). Salas and Laynes found Quispe an acceptable choice because he did not share the growing suspicions regarding land traffickers, leading them to anticipate that they would be able to maintain control of the organization while Quispe led in name only.

The Sons and Daughters planned their invasion for May 10, 1996, the silver anniversary of Villa's founding invasion. They anticipated that the timing of their land seizure would provide political cover, since Mayor Azcueta could less easily evict them if he was busy toasting the district's founding invasion. Further, Azcueta had just reassumed the mayoral office in December after several years of corrupt governance by other mayors, so the settlers hoped he would move cautiously.

Led by Quispe, the Sons and Daughters began their three-month preinvasion preparations, but it was a haphazard affair. Internal conflict plagued the group at each step as the idealism of leaders like Quispe collided with the pragmatism

---

1. This section draws on four interviews with founding Encantada settlers, all of whom served as elected neighborhood leaders at multiple points between 1996 and 2005 (J. Valencia 2001; Montenegro 2002; P. Valencia 2002; Yataco 2002).

of Salas and Laynes. Meanwhile, Salas and Laynes took advantage of the organizational tumult to work an exploitative scheme.

In the district of Villa El Salvador, land invasions had become routinized in that they regularly replicated the land use pattern of the district's original 1971 invasion. In this framework, each sector of the city was divided into a number of square zones called "groups." Each group consisted of a symmetrical arrangement of sixteen blocks (*manzanas*) and a central recreation area. Each block was then subdivided into twenty-four roughly equal lots for houses. This land use pattern had been applied with remarkable regularity throughout Villa's history, though as the district spread into rougher terrain, geography forced settlers to adjust the precise number of blocks in each group. But whatever this number, each block predictably consisted of twenty-four lots that were about the same size as lots all over the district. It was this ironclad predictability that was exploited by Salas and Laynes.

In the months prior to the invasion, Salas and Laynes sold tickets to prospective settlers. A ticket cost about fifteen dollars and supposedly entitled the holder to one lot, but Salas and Laynes double-sold each lot. While the original plan called for five hundred families on five hundred lots, Salas and Laynes initially sold about one thousand tickets.

The night of May 10 arrived and the settlers were ready, but Salas and Laynes had rented only three buses to carry the huge group of more than one thousand settlers, so most had to walk alongside the vehicles. Despite the problems they had already encountered, spirits were high and the group buoyantly set out for the site that they had already dubbed La Encantada (the Enchanted Place). As the column of obvious land invaders wound its way through the district, it drew hundreds of additional settlers who eagerly bought yet more tickets from Salas and Laynes, who accepted whatever price they could extract, effectively triple-selling each lot. And then there was the problem that the land was already occupied. Clearly, the settlers had some obstacles before them.

The Invasion: A Violent and Bitter Founding

The land chosen by Salas and Laynes was a stretch of desert measuring a little less than a square kilometer and largely occupied by a commercial pig-raising operation run by Agrosilves, an agribusiness firm. Mayor Azcueta had leased the land to Agrosilves, and the company considered itself the proper owner of the land (Azcueta 2002, interview).

The Sons and Daughters were hardly subtle in their approach, and by the time they reached the farm around midnight, Agrosilves had stationed nearly one hundred guards armed with clubs and guns. Violence erupted, but it was not a pitched battle. Although the Agrosilves guards had guns, they were out-numbered almost fifteen to one and they did not want to kill anybody. Some settlers were hurt and one was shot, but no one was killed. In the end, the guards contented themselves with keeping the settlers out of the offices and barns, and the settlers occupied all the land used to raise the pigs (P. Valencia 2002, interview).

With an uneasy truce established, at least for the night, internal conflict consumed the Sons and Daughters. Salas and Laynes had vanished, and although the land use blueprints they had provided the group corresponded to the Agrosilves land, their double- and triple-selling of lots was soon apparent, and people began planting their construction materials and aggressively marking their territory. In hindsight, there is general agreement among observers that some of these individuals were provocateurs sent by Agrosilves to foment chaos, but this is impossible to confirm. Regardless, internal conflicts ensued, especially between the original group and those who had joined that same night, but Secretary General Quispe managed to hold the group together, declaring that they would find a way to accommodate everyone.

The next morning, the National Police arrived to evict the settlers. Journalists also arrived and photographed the standoff between the police and a wall of invaders armed with sticks, ready to defend "their land." The Agrosilves guards urged the police to eject "the terrorists," but the police instead waited for instruc-tions from Mayor Azcueta, a progressive politician whom few believed would use force against the poor. With reporters on the scene from Channels 2 and 4, as well as from Lima's major paper, *El Comercio*, Azcueta was indeed loath to authorize violence and instead tried diplomacy, arguing that the invaders were wrecking the district's efforts at city planning. This went nowhere, and by the end of the day the police retired, eliciting a wave of celebration and cheering among the settlers.

The First Two Years: A Prolonged Struggle for Organizational Survival

From its founding invasion in May 1996 until it acquired tacit municipal recog-nition in September 1998, Encantada struggled as a *nascent* organization whose survival remained in question. During this difficult period, six attempts to acquire services can be identified: (1) *rogue* theft of electricity through infor-mal hookups—a success; (2) *militant* demands for municipal recognition from Azcueta—a failure; (3) disruptive *militant* pressure for water truck service—a failure; (4) media-oriented *conformist* pressure for water truck service—a suc-cess; (5) mixed *militant* and *conformist* demands for streetlights and household electricity—a limited success; and (6) *militant* demands for recognition—a de facto success. Why did Encantada's various strategies succeed or fail during its nascent stage of development?

Variation in the success or failure of service demands hinged on four causal factors: persistent mayoral hostility, strategy type, organizational resources, and, in one instance, allies in the Fujimori administration. Each of these variables is scored in table 5.1.

Before Encantada could demand services, however, it would have to survive its difficult first months. In the aftermath of the founding invasion, the settlers were furious with Salas and Laynes, who had fled with their money, but Secretary General Quispe still had the settlers' trust and used the momentum of having "defeated" the police to decree that each of the original blocks in Group 1 would be divided into 28 to 36 lots, rather than the standard 24, and that they would establish a second group of additional blocks to accommodate everyone else. With many adjustments, Quispe's plan would eventually result in 920 lots split between Encantada's Groups 1 and 2.[2]

In the meantime, the conflict with Agrosilves was literally on their doorstep, as the settlers' makeshift homes occupied the land that Agrosilves continued to use to raise pigs. Agrosilves president Augusto Béjar Jara gambled that the sheer misery the settlers were sure to experience would overcome their determination. Many settlers did give up during the frightening and unstable first months, but the number of families stabilized between nine hundred and one thousand.[3] Houses were frequently robbed, reports of assaults and rapes circulated, and families were practically living with the pigs and the consequent fleas, flies, and cockroaches (*El Comercio*, 8/15/97). In a matter of days, the settlers began to steal electricity through illegal and unreliable hookups to existing power lines, but despite this small victory, families remained hungry and overwhelmed. The odor of human and animal waste, pest-related skin diseases, and Azcueta's refusal of militant demands for water truck service—which provided daily water in many parts of Villa—all combined to make life unbearable (*Ajá*, 2/17/97).

By early 1997, both sides had realized that their opponents would not give up, and tensions escalated. But while Agrosilves turned to violence—hiring thugs and an arsonist to intimidate the settlers—the Encantada leaders concluded that the violence of the initial invasion had been a mistake, as it turned public opinion against the settlers (Montenegro 2002, interview). Instead, they would eschew all

2. As in many informal settlements, the *manzana*, or block, is the primary form of organization. In Villa El Salvador, there are usually twenty-four lots per block, and each block has a five-person committee (secretary general, treasurer, and secretaries of health, sports, and social events).

3. Many Encantada documents, however, would claim membership of as many as 1,600 hundred families in order to bolster the organization's claims of legitimacy (Encantada Cooperative 1996).

Table 5.1 Encantada data matrix

Stage of development	Neighborhood leader	Service demand	External factors					Internal Factors		
			District mayor	Service provider	Allies	Avenue of participation	Strategy type	Key resources	Neighborhood regime type	Outcome
Nascent (96–98)		Electricity	Hostile	State			Rogue	High participation	Democratic	Success
	Quispe (96–97)	Recognition	Hostile	District			Militant	High participation	Democratic	Failure
		Water truck	Hostile	State			Militant	High participation	Democratic	Failure
		Water truck	Hostile	State			Conformist	TV/Lawyer	Democratic	Success
		Electricity	Hostile	State	Cambio 90		Milit/Conf	High participation	Democratic	Success
		Recognition	Neutral	District		98 Election	Militant	TV/Lawyer	Democratic	Success
	Condori (97–01)	Recognition	Friendly	District		98 Election	Conformist	TV/Lawyer	Democratic	Success
Mature (98–00)		Electricity	Friendly	Private	City Hall		Bootstrap	Money	Democratic	Success
		Land titles	Friendly	State	COFOPRI		Conformist	Lawyer	Democratic	Success
		Piped water	Friendly	State	EU NGO		Conformist	Leadership	Democratic	Success**
Moribund (00–02)	Garces (01–02)	Piped water*	Friendly	State	FONAVI	Multisector	Bootstrap	Low participation	Democratic	Failure
Consolidated (02–05)	Ipanaque (02–03)	Recognition	Friendly	District		00 Election	Militant	High participation	Democratic	Success***
		Electricity	Friendly	Private			Rogue	Cooperation	Democratic	Success***
	Valencia (03–05)	Piped water*	Friendly	State	FONAVI	Multisector	Bootstrap	High participation	Democratic	In progress

*These piped-water demands were part of the Multisectoral Commission's water and sewer project, but I treat them as only water demands because Encantada did not make enough progress on the project to demand sewers.

**Piped water was installed but shut off after four months due to poor water quality.

***Demands made by the entire Encantada organization on behalf of the new Groups 3 and 4.

violence and pursue a media-oriented pressure strategy aimed at winning over public opinion in Villa El Salvador and in Lima. To this end, Quispe hired Oscar Zuñiga, a lawyer who specialized in land invasions.

Zuñiga was from the neighboring district of Villa María del Triunfo, which was originally made up of informal settlements. Zuñiga also had relatives who lived near La Encantada and had several years experience defending informal land claims, so Quispe trusted him (Zuñiga 2002, interview). At the invitation of Quispe and Zuñiga, Dirección General de Salud Ambiental (Department of Environmental Health, or DIGESA) inspectors visited Encantada in April 1997, and their report concluded that the Agrosilves farm was in flagrant violation of virtually all applicable regulations, that these violations posed serious health risks to the Encantada children, including risk of an epidemic of typhoid and stomach viruses, and that the farm should be immediately moved to a more appropriate location (DIGESA 1997).

While the DIGESA report had no power behind it to force Agrosilves to relocate, the report represented the first major salvo of Quispe and Zuñiga's media-oriented, conformist strategy. While media coverage of early court rulings against Encantada had consistently favored Agrosilves, the photographs and gripping anecdotes of suffering children spurred by the DIGESA report rapidly turned public opinion against Agrosilves and Azcueta.[4] While Azcueta was adamant in his refusal to grant municipal recognition, outraged letters and phone calls yielded much-needed water truck service (whereas disruptive protest marches had failed). Although Quispe and Zuñiga's goals were much broader than water truck service, this was the first gain of their innovative approach, and it infused the settlers with confidence and a willingness to pay for Zuñiga's legal work.[5]

Although the public health strategy did yield water truck service, its primary result was staving off eviction rather than acquiring services. Likewise, although Zuñiga's legal maneuvering would win the settlers land titles in later stages of the organization's development, during this period the primary benefit of contesting Agrosilves's "ownership" was to foil two court-ordered evictions and buy the settlers more time (El Tío, n.d.). While this was a crucial victory for the invasion organization's survival, it would not deliver either official municipal recognition or state land titles until the administration of Martín Pumar (1998–2002).

4. For example, two typical post-inspection news articles referred to "environmental damage" and "subhuman conditions" caused by "clandestine pig farms," and also to "asphyxiating and toxic gases" that posed "extreme risk" to "helpless children" (El Comercio, 8/15/97; La República, 9/26/98).

5. All told, Encantada paid Zuñiga eight thousand dollars for legal services between 1997 and 2000 (Zuñiga 2002, interview).

Even Encantada's acquisition of electricity was only a partial success. In 1997, Peru was in the process of privatizing electricity provision to—in the case of Villa El Salvador—a company named Luz del Sur. The move to privatize sparked opposition throughout Lima; in an effort to quell fears that privatization would hurt the poor, some communities were able to extract electricity installation at state expense during the transition. Unsurprisingly, beneficiaries tended to be either Fujimori supporters or, in the case of Máximo Quispe and Encantada, at least opponents of Fujimori's enemies (i.e., Azcueta). Azcueta obstructed the electrical installation (which some observers joke may have actually helped!), and so only four blocks (about 130 families) received street-lights and household hookups—a limited success for considerable militant and conformist effort (Azcueta 2002, interview).

Toward the end of his term, Azcueta did tacitly authorize recognition of the Encantada neighborhood council, but rather than representing a fundamental shift in Azcueta's position, this indicated Azcueta's acquiescence to the new policies of his protégé, Martín Pumar, who was expected to succeed him following the 1998 mayoral elections. Hence, I characterize Encantada's attempt to pressure Azcueta for recognition as a de facto success, while its negotiations with Pumar (described below) were an unconditional success.

Under Azcueta, the Municipality of Villa El Salvador initially constituted an insurmountable obstacle that stalled Encantada's efforts at every turn, even foiling the Fujimori-sponsored attempt at electricity. The limited victories the settlers scored in terms of minimal electricity and water provision were primarily due to internal factors, including innovative leadership and a small reserve of money used to hire a committed and skilled lawyer. Public provision of all services also played a contributing role—in that it permitted externally dependent strategies a chance at success (though in this case they largely failed due to entrenched municipal opposition)—but with respect to electricity, this would soon change with privatization.

Encantada's Brief Golden Age: Rapid Acquisition of Most Services

Following Azcueta's tacit recognition in September 1998, the *mature* Encantada organization entered a two-year period of rapid service acquisition. These initiatives included: (1) *conformist* negotiation for official recognition from Mayor Pumar—a success; (2) *bootstrap* methods of installing full electricity service—a success; (3) a *conformist* legal victory in the battle for land titles—a success; and (4) a *conformist* NGO partnership to install piped water—a short-lived success. During its nascent organizational stage, Encantada had pursued a largely unsuccessful mix of rogue and militant strategies, but in this period, the settlers progressed to a mix of conformist and bootstrap strategies and encountered great success. Why did these conformist methods fare better than Encantada's earlier efforts?

These conformist successes relied on a blend of external and internal factors (see table 5.1). Externally, Encantada benefited from municipal and state allies, a friendly mayor eager to attract support, and a generous international NGO. Internally, Encantada relied on good strategy choices, innovative media and legal tactics, and a democratic neighborhood regime. These victories were all achieved under the leadership of Nestor Condori, the popular secretary general who succeeded Quispe and would serve two consecutive terms as the leader of Encantada (1997–2001).

In early 1999, Condori's conformist demand for official recognition came to fruition because of the settlers' recent support of Pumar's campaign and because of Encantada's continuing public relations push in the media. Condori's negotiations for recognition took the shape of a standard votes-for-favors transaction (Condori 2002, interview). Although Pumar had been expected to inherit the mayoralty in the 1998 district elections, he could not take for granted a victory over his Fujimori-backed opponent. Taking a different stance on Encantada also helped quell criticism that he was merely an Azcueta puppet.[6]

In mid-1999, with Azcueta out of office, Condori convinced Villa El Salvador city councilman Alfredo Vivanco to help Encantada secure full electricity service from Luz del Sur (Vivanco 2002, interview). Privatization of electricity meant that neither militant *nor* conformist strategies could succeed, forcing Encantada to rely on a bootstrap approach. The bootstrap strategy succeeded due to modest economic resources and the influence of Encantada's ally Vivanco. The settler would have to pay out of their own pockets, but with Vivanco's help, Encantada persuaded Luz del Sur to let it finance the installation and pay the cost over a period of months. Not long thereafter, Luz del Sur raised its prices by 600 percent, eliciting a sigh of relief from the Encantada settlers—they had gotten electricity just in time (Azcueta 2002, interview).

In 2000, Condori won his third major service victory: permanent state-issued land titles for almost all settlers. With this demand, strategy choice and (hired) legal resources were key, but Encantada may have also benefited from a powerful state ally. Encantada's conformist negotiations with COFOPRI—the state agency for informal land titling—dated back to late 1996, when then secretary general Máximo Quispe sent a letter dated November 6 to COFOPRI, requesting that the agency initiate the titling process. COFOPRI had just been created by Fujimori

---

6. At the ballot box, it appeared that Pumar had made the right choice, as he only beat the Vamos Vecino nominee 35.0 percent to 32.6 percent (Tuesta 2001, 404).

and was clearly enthusiastic about fulfilling its Hernando de Soto–inspired mission of granting two million titles to informal landholders. There is no concrete evidence that COFOPRI's support of Encantada was politically motivated, but the mildly incredible fact that COFOPRI's affirmative reply was dated November 7—*the very next day*—points to an uncharacteristic eagerness coming from a bureaucratic office (COFOPRI 1996, letter; Zuñiga 1996, letter).

But despite COFOPRI's early support of the settlers, there had been little the state agency could do until Villa El Salvador granted recognition to the Encantada neighborhood council as a legitimate and representative entity. Once de facto recognition occurred under Azcueta, however, the titling process began to move quickly. In 1998, Condori and Zuñiga succeeded in changing Encantada's zoning from agricultural to residential (Zuñiga 2002, interview). An INC inspection concluded that although the region was officially an archaeological zone, its lack of any substantial ruins (they found only trivial ceramics) meant that the land could be developed (which, of course, it already was).

In 1999, COFOPRI began the bureaucratic process of collecting documentation proving each settler's constancy of occupation and other details, and this progress secured Condori's reelection as secretary general. On May 6, 2000, titles arrived for 834 of 920 families (90 percent)—a major victory (Zuñiga 2002, interview). Zuñiga then used the settlement's new stature to strike the killing blow against Agrosilves resistance: he filed an August 2000 letter with the courts announcing the community's intention to file a lawsuit against Agrosilves president Augusto Béjar. It alleged that he was running a clandestine livestock operation on the settlers' legally owned land, resulting in infectious disease and some deaths (Zuñiga 2000, letter). After four bitter and violent years, Agrosilves gave up and left town.

Finally, in 2000, Condori also initiated and completed an ambitious water project that succeeded because of international aid, his own leadership, and Encantada's neighborhood regime type. Condori formed partnerships with the local Fomento de la Vida (Promoting Quality of Life, or FOVIDA) agency and the EU's Project Ala (see Oasis case study in chapter 4), and the project moved quickly, with only token funding from the settlers. City Councilman Vivanco noted how lucky the settlers were to receive FOVIDA's help, as Villa's last state-funded water project was in 1995; according to Vivanco, although water remained a publicly provided service, the financially strapped SEDAPAL left settlements little better off than if water were privatized.[7]

---

7. Many neighborhood and local leaders echoed the view of Julio Cotler, at the Instituto de Estudios Peruanos, who argues that after Peru's experience with electricity privatization and consequent price hikes, the country will never privatize water service, no matter how little SEDAPAL really does for Peruvians (Cotler 2001, interview).

Photographing *Demanding the Land*

From this project's inception, we considered photographic documentation to be an integral component of our research. Through photographs we hoped to visually share our research with academic and community audiences, and prints would serve as a reciprocal gift to our interview subjects.

The two months of photography—undertaken in Lima in March 2002 and in Quito in September 2002—had an additional impact on the field research. While our research was in progress, we developed exposed rolls of film and made contact sheets. We observed visual patterns of information in these contact sheets, providing new insights into people and communities, and prompting unexpected and productive avenues of inquiry.

We have shared the photographs through prints, presentations, an online photo essay, and exhibitions. Distributing hundreds of prints to the individuals we interviewed, we built trust and were invited to document community meetings, elections, and protests. Slideshows have accompanied presentations of our findings in academic and community venues in several countries in the Americas. In 2007, we published an online photo essay with 120 images accompanied by text (www.webphotoessay.com). Finally, photographs have been exhibited in galleries and museums in the United States and Latin America, and an exhibition is now permanently mounted in the Center for Development with Dignity—a community center in La Encantada that is an outgrowth of this project.

—*James Lerager and Paul Dosh*

In 2002, the Frente Unitario de los Pueblos de Perú (United Front of the Peoples of Peru, or FUPP) protested at the Ministry of the Presidency in Lima, demanding cancellation of debts to public banks accrued in developing their self-help housing neighborhoods.

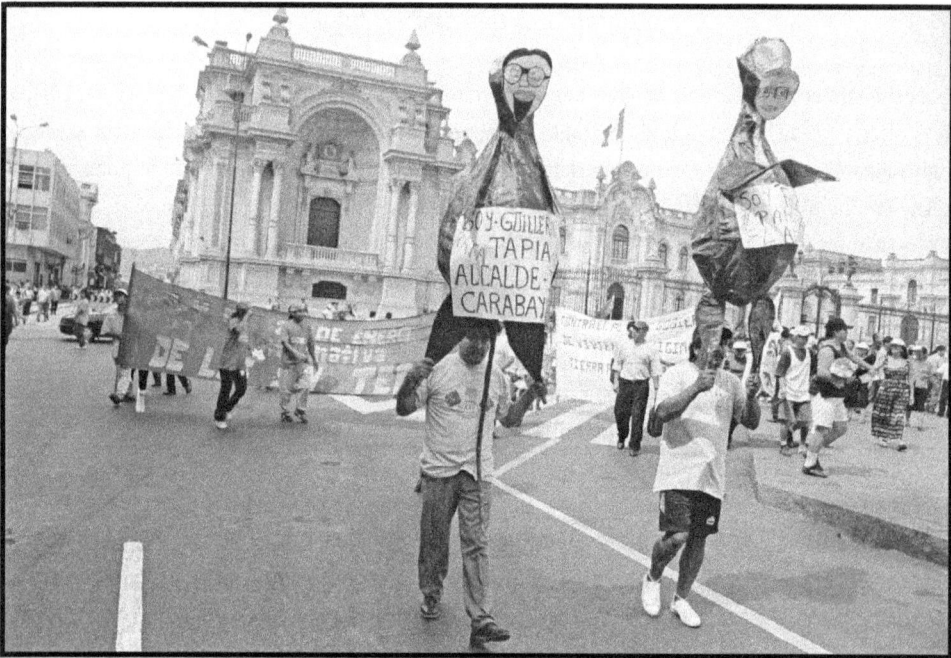

In downtown Lima, large mobilizations became so common in the early 2000s that land invasion organizations, unions, and other groups with grievances would sometimes have to wait their turn at popular protest sites like the Congress and the Ministry of the Presidency.

Lima's decades of land invasions have left little terrain untouched, forcing new settlers to occupy increasingly rugged and inaccessible land, such as the side of this steep river gorge.

Looking down from the surrounding mountains, it is clear that Quito's urban growth has consumed almost all available land not set aside for parks or the airport.

Every week thousands of Quiteños take advantage of recreation opportunities in La Carolina Park, including soccer fields, basketball and volleyball courts, a BMX bike race track, a skate park, and other family diversions.

After fifteen years, the Lima settlement of Pro is still poorly developed, with most buildings only a single story tall.

In Pro, settlers gather each month to debate the future of their community. Continued uncertainty over the legal status of their land sparks debate between those wishing to pay off the landowners and those agitating for a political solution.

In Rosales, former secretary general Claudio Tapia and his wife express frustration over the neighborhood's lack of progress. They worked for two years to initiate water and drainage service but could not unite the settlement around a common project.

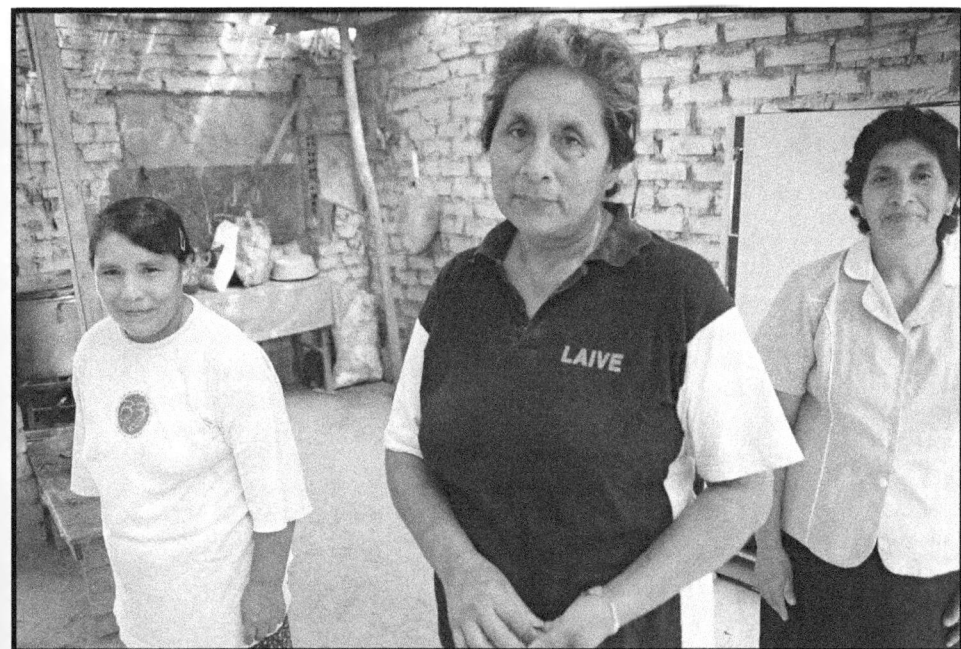

In Sector C, former secretary general María Chávez (*center*) laments the factionalism that plagued her administration in 1998–2000. The previous leader was so hostile to her election that he refused to hand over the group's files and assets, crippling her ability to initiate new projects.

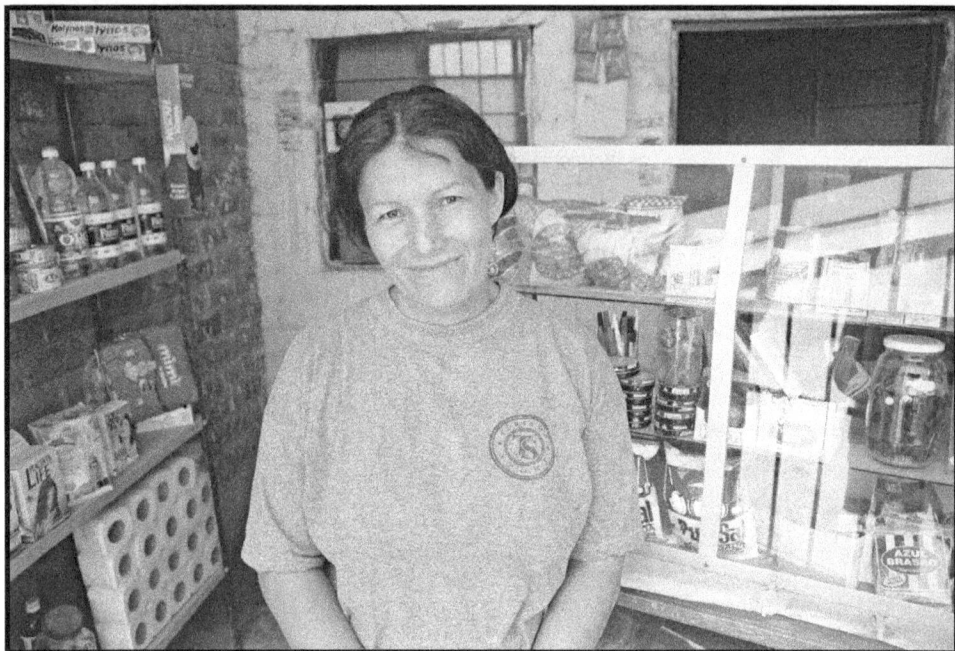

In Rosales, former secretary general Elvira Peña's commitment to winning land titles at state expense cost the settlement several potential allies, who were alienated by her uncompromising position.

In the northern Quito neighborhood of Pisulli, Edgar Coral's brass-knuckled leadership remained uninterrupted for over two decades, with opposition candidates intimidated or run out of town.

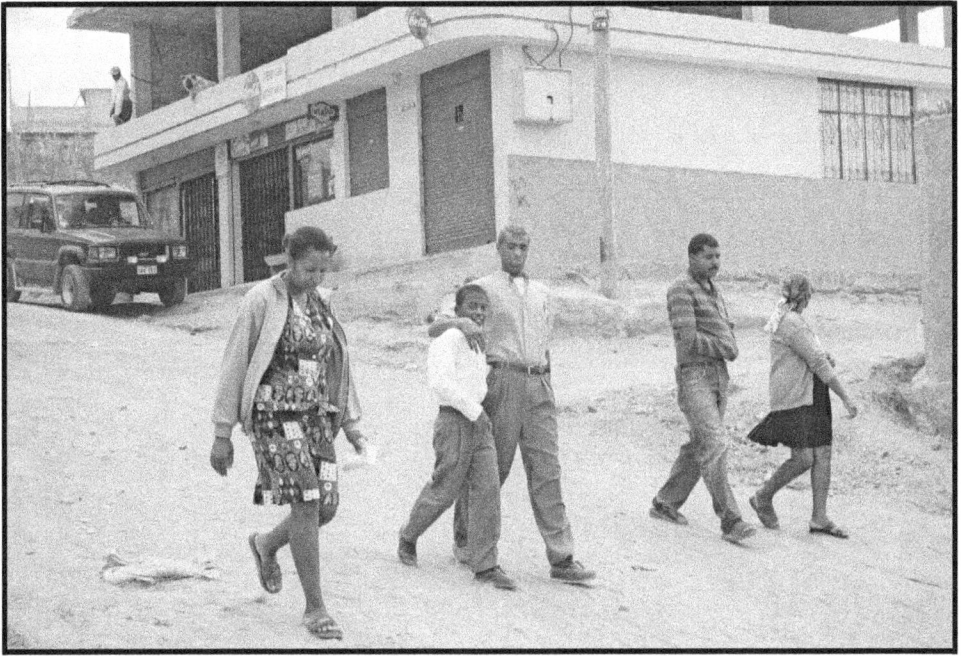

On Sunday afternoon, a Pisulli family strolls through the adjacent neighborhood of Roldos. Recent lynchings demonstrate that racial hostility toward blacks remains a dangerous undercurrent in community conflicts.

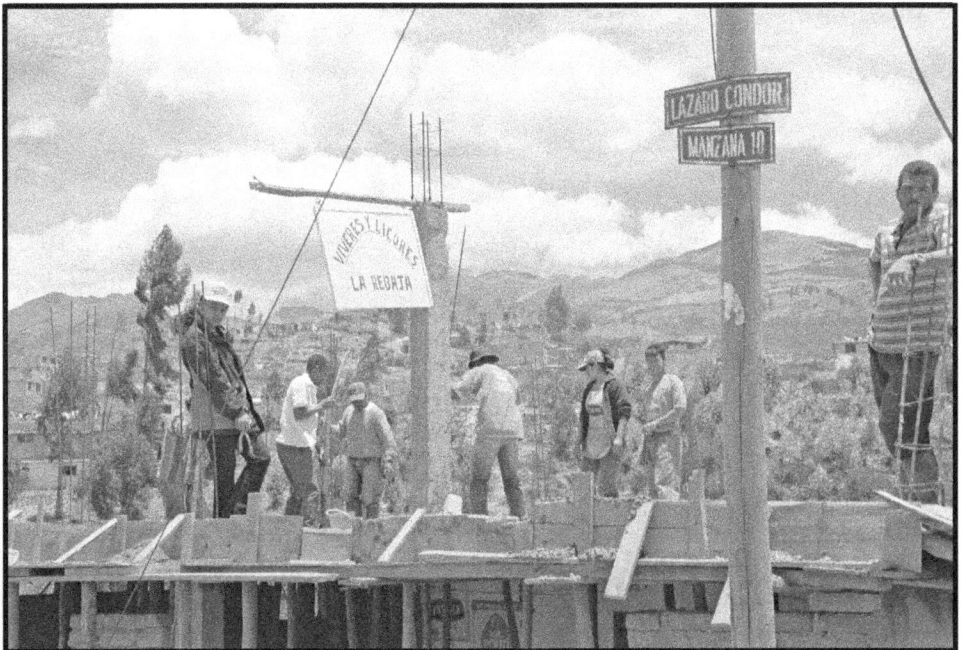

As in many invasion neighborhoods, Pisulli settlers are fined by the cooperative if they fail to contribute free labor to community work projects known as *mingas*.

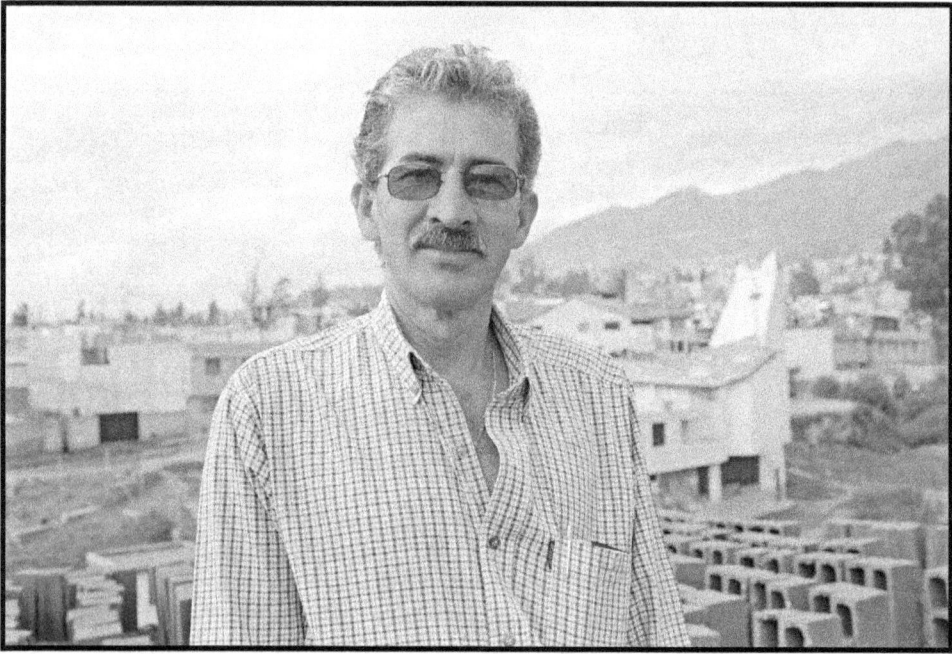

Adored by many Camino settlers, neighborhood boss Celso Meza continued to manage the settlement and his own brick-making business even when jailed for his leadership of an illegal invasion.

Begun in 1990 with five hundred families, the Camino settlement grew to cover not only the Cucho Hacienda ranch but also the hillside above it.

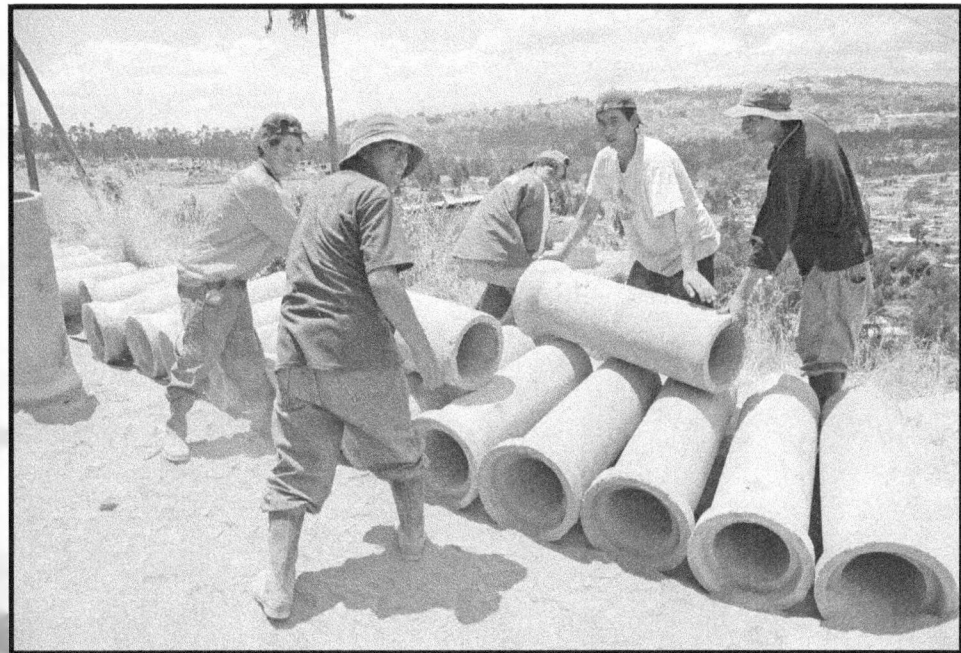

Camino's steady acquisition of urban services, such as sewer drainage, depended both on patronage and on free labor by the settlers.

Before the Camino invasion, the Cucho Hacienda ranch belonged to the family of Father Jorge Pazmiño Navas and his nephew Rommel López. A collector of old religious books, Father Pazmiño and his brothers had acquired the land from the Catholic Church.

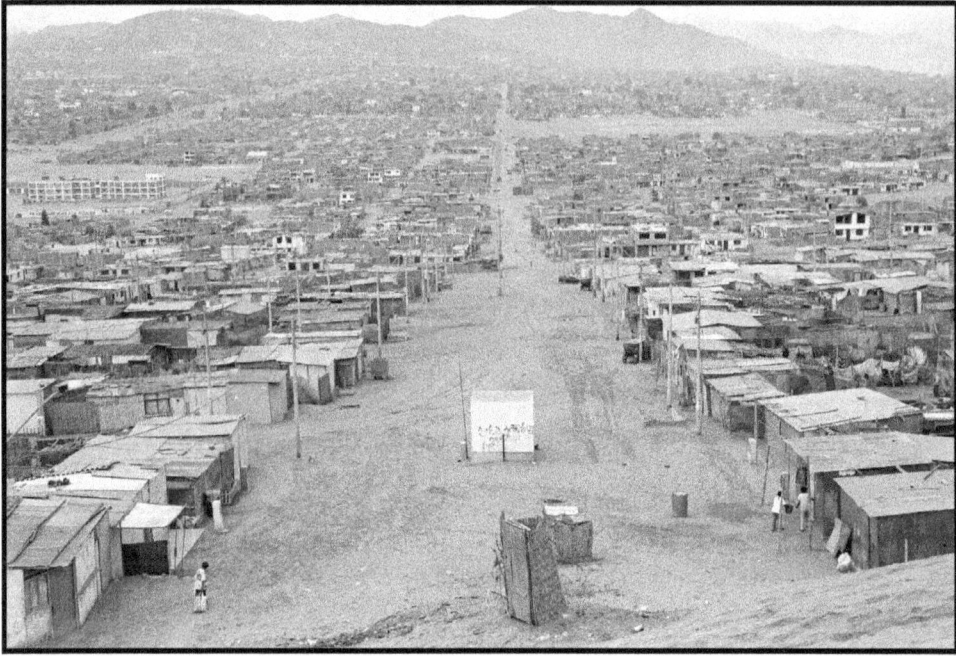

Located in the famous land invasion district of Villa El Salvador, the streets of Oasis follow the same orderly grid that characterizes much of this Lima district.

The precarious location of Villa Mar, founded in 1999, has contributed to the neighborhood's decline. Settlers must frequently shore up their homes to keep them from tumbling down the steep slope.

As the elected leader of Villa Mar, Modesta Martínez splits her time between administrative duties, human rights activism, and survival. Too poor to buy clothes, she is forced to wear whatever shirt she can find, even if it promotes a political party she does not support.

Founded on September 10, 2001, Paraíso took shape as a ramshackle collection of 400 shantyhomes crammed into an area meant for only 288 lots.

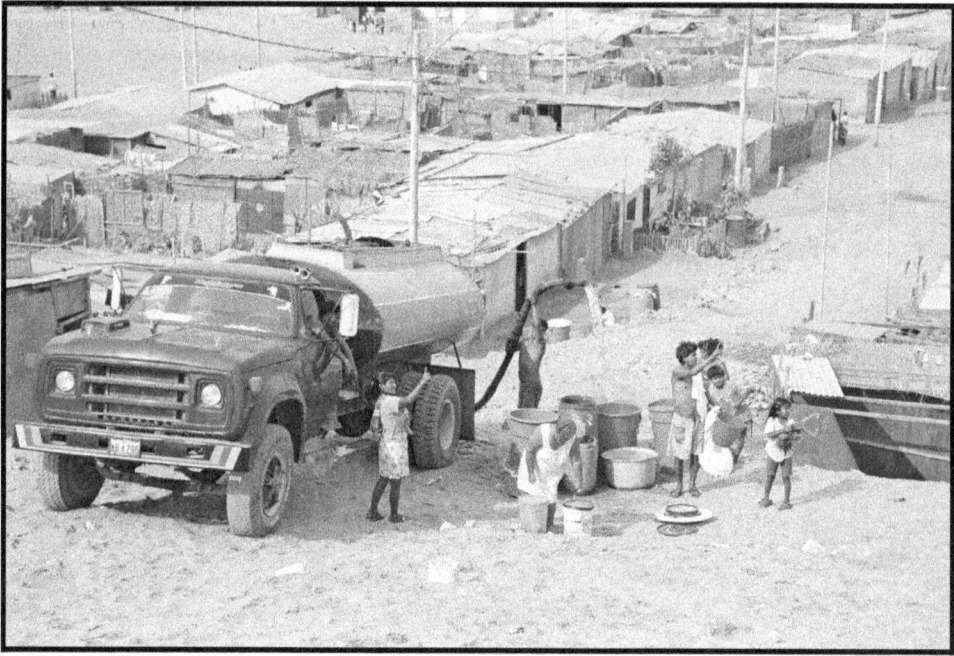

Initially, water provision takes the form of a truck that makes daily visits to informal settlements. Water quality is generally poor.

Villa El Salvador's famous yellow-and-blue buses were originally used in the city's founding invasion in 1971 but now provide district transit.

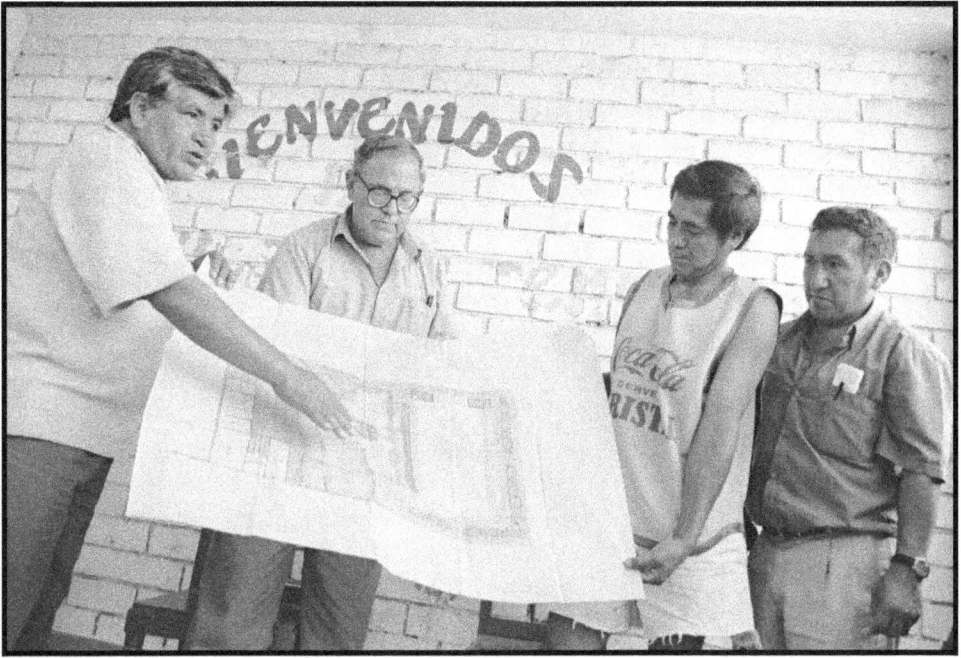

In 2002, former Villa El Salvador mayor Michel Azcueta launched an unsuccessful bid for the office of metropolitan mayor, but his heart remained at the neighborhood level. Even during an election year, Azcueta spent his Saturdays teaching settlers how to organize infrastructure projects, such as a new soccer field.

In 2002, Itchimbía settlers held their assemblies outdoors, on the site of the initial land invasion, which overlooks downtown Quito.

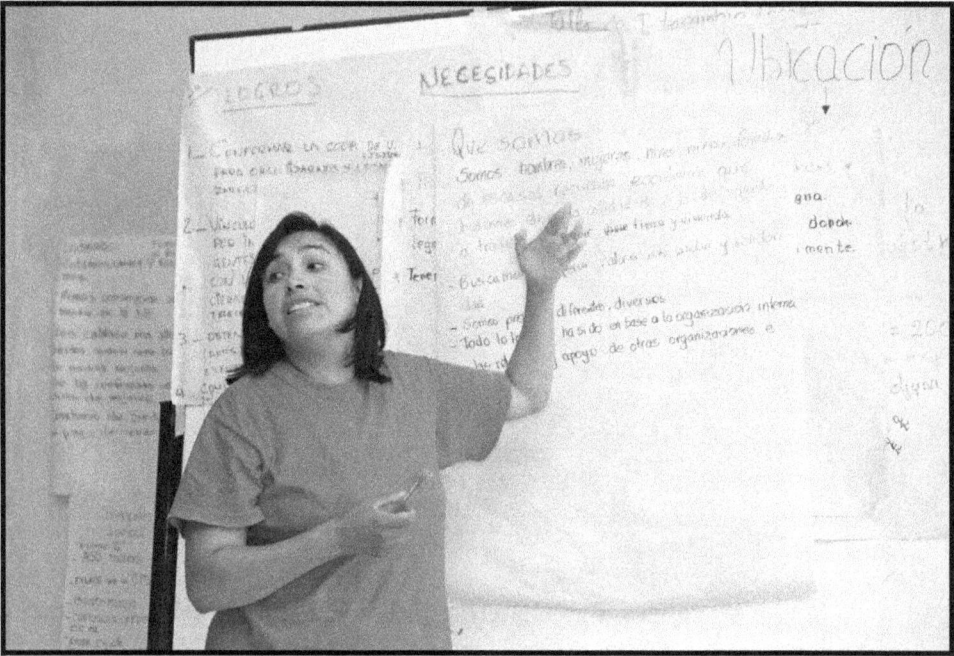

As president of both Itchimbía and Mujeres por la Vida, María Hernández tirelessly took care of her family, earned an income, and led over a hundred community events per year. In 2004, she was elected to Quito's secondary Metropolitan Council.

In 2002, Itchimbía settlers filmed community events, such as neighborhood elections, for a new video documentary. The cost of editing and production was supported by external donations.

Itchimbía benefited from having an in-house architect, who engineered a clandestine and illegal sewer system that provided excellent plumbing for the settlement.

With help from European NGOs, Mayor Paco Moncayo, and other allies, the Itchimbía settlers built their own condominiums at a greatly reduced cost.

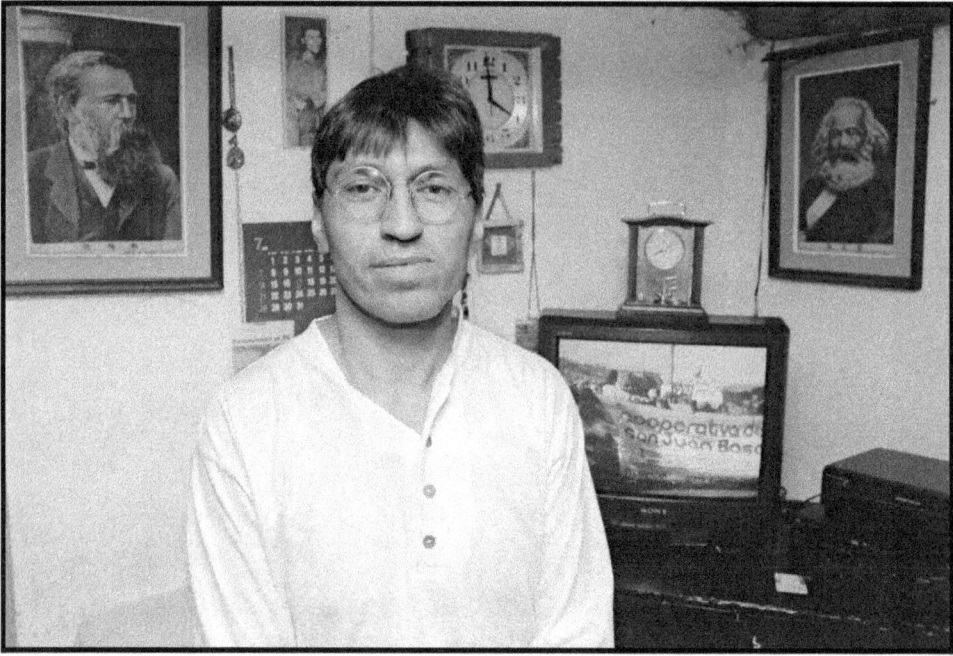

Itchimbía is remarkable for its use of technology, such as the Internet and home video photography. The vice president of the cooperative, Milton Chamorro, has produced three high-quality videos about this Quito neighborhood's political struggles.

Quito's poor are accustomed to ads for opportunities and entertainment that they could never afford.

Negotiated in April 2000, the pipes were fully installed and working by November, just seven months later. Such rapid service acquisition clearly hinged on full financing by Project Ala, but it also required Condori's outreach to both Project Ala and FOVIDA. Competitive neighborhood regimes can make long-term alliances difficult to maintain due to leadership turnover, but the speed of this project and Condori's long tenure as secretary general meant that Encantada's democratic regime was an asset, as Project Ala preferred to work with neighborhoods governed by democratic methods.

But this stunningly rapid accomplishment—by a settlement barely four years old—did not last. The infrastructure had been hastily built, resulting in poor water quality. Within months the pipes were shut off, as settlers preferred the moderately cleaner water from the trucks. Even before this service failure, however, Encantada faced an organizational crisis: with the arrival of land titles and the installation of piped water, participation dropped off sharply, leading the neighborhood into a moribund state.

Property Security Fuels Organizational Decline: Service Acquisition Stagnates

From November 2000 until October 2002, the *moribund* Encantada organization struggled to survive and its service acquisition agenda stagnated. During this two-year period, only a single service demand was initiated: a *bootstrap* attempt to install a new water system (and theoretically also a sewer system)—a failure. Despite favorable external conditions—a friendly mayor, a local ally, and a local participatory institution for the infrastructure project—the attempt failed because of low settler participation.

While participation in neighborhood meetings, protest marches, and other activities had remained above 90 percent between 1996 and 2000, the acquisition of land titles precipitated a steady decline in rates of attendance at meetings, until they reached a record low of 20 percent in October 2002 (P. Valencia 2002, interview). City Councilman Vivanco noted in a 2002 interview that this was consistent with the roughly 50 percent drop in attendance he observed in many invasion communities in the district following receipt of land titles.

When the existing water system was shut off in 2001 due to poor water quality, declining rates of participation dropped further as settlers grew frustrated over the loss of this important service victory. The popular Secretary General Condori concluded his second term and was replaced by Luis Garces (2001–2), who pledged to fix the water problem. Garces hoped to acquire both water and drainage through the cross-neighborhood Multisectoral Commission (see the Oasis case study), but the Multisectoral required major participation by the community both in terms of involvement and in actual construction.

Two up-and-coming community leaders, Carlos Ipanaque and Jesús Valencia, had hoped that the Multisectoral project would serve as a springboard for getting Encantada settlers to work with other communities, as the neighborhood had "always fought alone and with fierce independence" (P. Valencia 2002, interview). But with the decline of the neighborhood organization, Garces failed, and by October 2002 it seemed unlikely that the ailing Encantada organization would overcome low participation to deliver the needed services. And it probably would have failed, were it not for a deeply ironic turn of events: a new invasion of Encantada's remaining vacant lands.

A New Invasion Reinvigorates Encantada: Fresh Hope for Water and Drainage

Following the October 2002 invasion of land adjacent to Encantada, the neighborhood's moribund organization rapidly consolidated due to the influx of new settlers and the consequent invocation of a new activist mission for the entire community. During this period, three service demands were initiated: (1) *militant* demands for municipal recognition of the newly founded Groups 3 and 4—a success; (2) *rogue* construction of illegal electricity hookups for Groups 3 and 4—a success; and (3) ongoing *bootstrap* efforts to acquire piped water through the Multisectoral Commission—unresolved as of mid-2005. Why did an organization that was so recently incapable of even initiating demands suddenly rejuvenate and encounter renewed success?

While the sudden influx of new and vulnerable settlers provided a major boost to the Encantada organization, it was the activist mission of Secretary General Carlos Ipanaque (2002–3) and Secretary General Jesús Valencia (2003–5) that rejuvenated the participation of the more established 920 Encantada families. Without their successful reorientation of the organization toward a community mission of helping their new neighbors, Encantada would likely not have been able to resuscitate its participation in the Multisectoral Commission water and drainage project.

During this consolidated stage, the success of Encantada's demands hinged on both external factors—a friendly mayor, an influential ally, and a local participatory institution—and internal factors—good strategy choices, organizational resources, and Encantada's neighborhood regime type (see table 5.1). The key organizational resource was participation, which rose sharply as the more established settlers enthusiastically took on the task of teaching the newcomers the lessons of their own struggles in the 1990s.

This consolidated stage began on October 31, 2002, with the surprise invasion of vacant land adjacent to Encantada. The new invasion threw the neighborhood political structure into turmoil as incumbent leaders struggled to identify the newcomers as either allies or competitors. Between midnight and 6:00 A.M., the settlers arrived with wooden posts and ready-made walls. It was a chaotic scene, with people running frantically back and forth, trying to find an empty space to stake a claim. The district police tried halfheartedly to evict them but lacked the will to use their tear gas and clubs, and the invaders managed, once again, to retain "their land."

Within days, the Encantada membership voted to welcome the new settlers, substantially expanding their organization and stretching the physical boundaries of the neighborhood to include the newly designated Groups 3 and 4. Secretary General Garces, however, was not interested in governing the newly expanded organization, and he resigned, prompting the election of Carlos Ipanaque to a special one-year term. Encantada (all four groups) then marched to city hall, demanding that Mayor Pumar recognize the new groups of makeshift homes. With district elections (not coincidentally) just two weeks away, Pumar—who was in a tight race—agreed to recognition. On November 17, Pumar lost to Unidad Nacional (National Unity) challenger Jaime Zea (2002–present), but Groups 3 and 4 had gotten what they wanted—immediate municipal recognition.[8] Land titles would take considerably longer, but they would soon be contacting COFOPRI to begin this process.

Immediate recognition by Pumar galvanized participation by the new Groups 3 and 4 as well as the more established Groups 1 and 2. Encantada held a general assembly for all four groups, and more than one thousand people attended, an impressive turnout for an organization whose last major assembly had attracted fewer than two hundred.

Ipanaque scored two quick service victories: recognition and provisional electricity for Groups 3 and 4. The recognition march succeeded because of the participation of not only the new settlers but also the more established Groups 1 and 2. Timing was also crucial, as the November 2002 election put pressure on Pumar. Soon thereafter, the settlers of Groups 1 and 2 cooperated with Groups 3 and 4 to establish illegal electrical connections to Encantada's existing (privately provided) electrical infrastructure. Ipanaque also initiated a fresh attempt at acquiring a water and drainage system through the Multisectoral Commission. With settlers once again active in the neighborhood organization, it was possible for Encantada to participate in grassroots Multisectoral meetings and fund-raising activities, and to begin working with FONAVI for financing.

8. Michel Azcueta also lost his 2002 bid for the office of metropolitan mayor of Lima. Notably, even his Encantada opponents supported his metropolitan candidacy; although they had become opponents by circumstance, the settlers still admired Azcueta as Villa's legendary first mayor.

The Multisectoral project and Ipanaque's mission of organizational outreach continued under his successor, Jesús Valencia (2003–5). Valencia created a network of domestic and international e-mail contacts and began documenting Encantada's struggles as a tool for recruiting new allies and donors (Encantada Cooperative 2005). In 2005, construction had not begun, but partial funding and financing was in place, technical assessments of the project were under way, and participation remained high.[9] The ideological continuity between the Ipanaque and Valencia administrations (as well as Valencia's work under Ipanaque) facilitated a continuous relationship with FONAVI, despite the change in leadership. Impressively, Encantada was attempting to bring the infrastructure project not only to the established Groups 1 and 2 but to the newcomers as well.

Importantly, Encantada's rejuvenated levels of participation were facilitated by Valencia's broader sense of mission. When a December 2003 fire destroyed nearly one thousand shantyhomes just a half mile from Encantada, Valencia seized the opportunity to get more settlers involved in helping their suddenly homeless neighbors (Valencia 2005, interview). Valencia's cyber networking also yielded gains in the status of his organization and his own leadership. In February 2005, an IMF delegation visited the neighborhood and met with Valencia and other leaders. In June 2005, former Peruvian president Valentín Paniagua visited, and Valencia emceed the public ceremony, introducing Paniagua to the crowd. Although such public honors do not translate directly into material gains for settlements like Encantada, they are important to understanding why Innovator leaders like Valencia are seen (correctly) as interested in the greater public good, and not just in their own neighborhood.

Summary of Encantada's Organizational Successes and Failures

Reviewing the case of Encantada, this Innovator organization made fourteen attempts to acquire services between 1996 and 2005. Of these fourteen, Encantada netted nine successes, three failures, and one short-lived success (piped water service was soon aborted due to poor water quality). In addition, it joined the Multisectoral water and drainage project, which was still in progress in 2005. This constituted an impressive record. When compared to the cases examined in chapters 3 and 4, Encantada clearly accomplished a great deal in just nine years, especially considering the obstacles it faced, including external opposition and, initially, internal division.

9. In May 2004, the SEDAPAL water company began rationing water in Lima by shutting off access for twelve hours during the evening and early morning hours. This move underscored the strained condition of Lima's water resources, but these events did not have any appreciable effect on Encantada's ongoing efforts to acquire piped water service.

Although Encantada's inauspicious founding was dominated by two Old Guard leaders, Angélica Salas and Arturo Laynes, the organization took shape as an Innovator under the creative leadership of Quispe and Condori, and later the activist leadership of Ipanaque and Valencia. Not only did Quispe's and Condori's innovative use of the media yield victory over business and mayoral opposition, but under Ipanaque and Valencia, Encantada began creating an e-mail network of international supporters to help the organization meet the needs of its original membership and the hundreds of newcomers. Yet while Encantada did not begin using new technologies until several years into its development, another Innovator made such tactics an integral part of its strategic repertoire from the very beginning.

INNOVATIVE TACTICS AND ACTIVISM WIN BOTH SECURITY AND CONSOLIDATION: THE CASE OF ITCHIMBÍA

National and Metropolitan Context

Relative to the tumultuous 1996–2005 period in Ecuador, the politics of the early 1990s were fairly routine, despite daunting economic problems. In 1992, Ecuador exchanged the populist leftist president Rodrigo Borja (1988–92) for Sixto Durán Ballén (1992–96) of the conservative Partido Unido Republicano (United Republican Party) (Gerlach 2003, 45, 81). At the metropolitan level, Quito elected the congressman Jamil Mahuad to his first four-year term as mayor (1992–96, and later 1996–98). A member of the DP, Mahuad was considered center-left on social policy but an economic conservative (118). Unlike the intense hostility that characterized relations between Fujimori and Villa El Salvador in Peru, relations between Durán Ballén and Mahuad were amiable, and Mahuad accepted Durán Ballén's aggressive neoliberal program (88).

But as Ecuador's political establishment swung to the Right, Ecuador's leftist indigenous movement picked up speed (Van Cott 2005, 115–22). In 1990, as part of a broader uprising, indigenous activists seized the capital city's main cathedral as a protest in support of concurrent land invasions, and numerous indigenous-based organizations were created (Selverston-Scher 2001, 58–61; Yashar 1998, 25). In 1994, they fought to defend campesino social security from privatization. These and many other mobilizations would culminate in the 2000 indigenous-led coup to oust and exile Ecuador's president (Gerlach 2003, 163–203).

The story of Itchimbía begins in 1989 with one such organization, the Coordinadora Popular de Quito (People's Coordinating Committee of Quito, or CPQ). The CPQ was not explicitly an indigenous organization, but most of the struggles with which it dealt exhibited a distinctly indigenous character. The CPQ founders were a tight-knit group of university students who had participated in various social justice struggles in the 1980s, and had helped occupy the cathedral in 1990. Few of them were able to finish college due to financial limitations, but their diverse areas of study—law, journalism, architecture, and communication—would later prove an exceptional resource for developing their own invasion community. The key leaders were Juan Carlos Manzanillas, María Hernández, and Milton Chamorro, and in 1994 they organized sixty families and formed the Cooperative of San Juan Bosco, with Manzanillas as president (*Últimas Noticias*, 9/25/95).

In Search of Land

The cooperative initially planned to buy land and create a small community.[10] It conducted an extensive search, but most empty sites were either commercially zoned or owned by land speculators, making them too expensive for the cooperative. Banks refused to even discuss the possibility of loans. Most sites were also too far away. The families were from La Tola, one of Quito's oldest downtown neighborhoods, where they lived in miserable conditions with dozens in each large house, many surviving on as little as fifty dollars a month (a standard basket of goods cost four hundred dollars for a family of five; *Hoy*, 10/13/95). Most of the settlers relied on informal jobs in the downtown district.

Exploring an alternative idea, the group conducted research on Itchimbía "Park," a steep hill overlooking downtown that had become a garbage dump for central Quito and the nearby hospital. In 1949, the municipality had ordered that the half square kilometer of land be used for a park, and in the 1980s the municipality had proposed developing the land as a park, but nothing was done until 1993, when Mayor Mahuad and the Durán Ballén government negotiated a joint plan to develop the land. In 1994, Mahuad rezoned the land, ostensibly for public use, but he simultaneously began to negotiate a commercial deal with the Metropolitan Touring development corporation (*Hoy*, 10/13/95).[11] But despite Mayor Mahuad's zoning authority (and entrepreneurial streak), the land was owned by the national Instituto Ecuatoriano de Seguridad Social (Ecuadorian Institute of Social Security, or IESS) and the local Catholic church (*La Hora*,

---

10. The following sections draw on interviews with founding leaders María Hernández (2002) and Milton Chamorro (2002, 2005). Unlike the Next Generation case of Camino, which pretended to attempt purchase of land as a prelude to invading, Itchimbía's effort to find an affordable site was sincere, though in the end they still invaded.

11. This was consistent with earlier patterns of park development in Quito. To build La Carolina, Quito's massive central park, the government used eminent domain to expropriate 240 hectares for the project, but then sold 75 percent of the land to developers through sweetheart deals. The park ended up being only 60 hectares, surrounded by commercial real estate (*Últimas Noticias*, 1/23/96).

10/12/95). By 1995, aside from a small flower garden begun by the local Nature Foundation, no work was done on the supposed park, and the Cooperative of San Juan Bosco saw an opportunity (*Últimas Noticias*, 10/18/95).

Skeptical of the mayor's intentions, the would-be settlers crafted an innovative proposal for an "ecological community." They would clean up the park, including all the garbage and hospital waste, build homes made of alternative materials on less than 10 percent of the land, and employ themselves as custodians and security guards of the park. They would make the park safe from crime, provide an enjoyable destination for Quiteños and tourists, and provide themselves housing and employment.

Proposal in hand, the cooperative leaders visited municipal and church offices dozens of times, but neither the bishop nor mayor would meet with them, although the national Ministry of Urban Development and Housing did hear them out. Mayor Mahuad was particularly resistant to meeting with the settlers because his negotiations with Metropolitan Touring had yielded a plan to build a five-star hotel on the precise acres sought by San Juan Bosco, as this area had the best view of the city (*Últimas Noticias*, 10/18/95).

Preparing to Invade

Convinced that direct action would succeed where diplomacy had failed, Manzanillas, Hernández, and Chamorro began preparing their membership for a land invasion. Nominally, the invasion was merely "a pressure strategy," but no one had any doubts that the group was crossing a major societal and legal boundary. In September 1995, the entire membership spent a week preparing for the invasion. Each night they had four hours of mandatory training with near-perfect attendance. Manzanillas had studied successful and failed invasions of the past, and he told the settlers what to expect (militarized police) and how the group would respond (with nonviolence and submission). Chamorro also warned the settlers of the threat of land traffickers, who would surely materialize and try to insinuate themselves into the cooperative. As a precaution, Manzanillas announced that for the initial months, absolutely no settler would pay any money to anyone (*Últimas Noticias*, 10/18/95). He hoped that this rule would lead prospective traffickers to lose interest in their invasion, as there would be no opportunity to swindle settlers out of their money.

An Innovative Invasion

Confident that their innovative approach would succeed, the sixty families arrived just before midnight on September 23, 1995. They chose the time of the spring equinox as a symbol of their "planting" of a new community. Whereas most such groups would promptly set up makeshift housing, the Itchimbía settlers brought not shelter, but cleaning supplies! They began cutting grass and hauling trash. Thus, when fifty National Police arrived at 7:00 A.M. with body armor and tear gas bombs, they were perplexed to find not makeshift homes, but nine well-organized groups of men and women peacefully cleaning. When ordered to disperse, the settlers docilely complied, slumping their shoulders and bowing their heads as Manzanillas had taught them. On the far side of the park, a picnic awaited them, right on schedule. The baffled officers remained and patrolled the garbage dump until dusk, when they finally departed. With the police gone, the settlers returned to their cleaning.

But by the next morning, word had spread, and three thousand additional settlers had spontaneously arrived with the classic plastic shelters that characterized most land invasions. Many came from nearby, but some were from the farthest reaches of Quito. A huge march for recognition soon paraded through the city, forcing Mayor Mahuad to move cautiously. But although the surprise arrival of three thousand more people helped keep the National Police from immediately returning, their sheer numbers presented a great problem for the original settlers. If everyone stayed, there would be no vacant land left over, which would make their unique "eco-park" proposal irrelevant; they would be "just another land invasion." Said one founding settler, "We came to clean up the land. They came with plastic houses" (Cocha 2002, interview).

Eventually Manzanillas and the other leaders decided to limit the settlement to a total of three hundred families, with the new arrivals earning spots on a "first come, first served" basis. If they could restrict each lot to one hundred square meters, this number of families would allow them to respect their original goal of settling less than 10 percent of the available land (*Últimas Noticias*, 10/18/95). Through difficult negotiation, a clear and persistent message, and stubborn refusal to admit any more settlers into the cooperative, the original group convinced most of the newcomers to leave, and the remaining families began to build their illegal neighborhood.

The First Year: An Innovative Struggle for Organizational Survival

From its founding invasion in September 1995 until it acquired tacit municipal recognition in July 1996, Itchimbía struggled as a *nascent* organization. During this difficult period, six attempts to acquire urban services can be identified: (1) *militant* protest marches for municipal recognition from Mahuad—a failure; (2) *rogue* theft of electricity through informal hookups—a success; (3) *militant* demands for water truck service—a failure; (4) *rogue* theft of water through clandestine hookups—a failure; (5) *militant* use of nonviolence to pressure for recognition—a failure; and (6) another *militant* use of nonviolence to pressure for recognition—a success. Why did Itchimbía's rogue and militant strategies either succeed or fail?

During Itchimbía's nascent stage of development, the key determinants of organizational success were mayoral hostility, influential allies, the pressure of metropolitan elections, strategy type, and organizational resources such as leadership and technology (see table 5.2). While these factors would contribute to two important successes during this period, Itchimbía's major nascent victory would simply be its survival in the face of repeated threats of eviction.

In the wake of the three-thousand-person march for recognition (though 90 percent of these settlers did not stay in Itchimbía), the police did not immediately return, but Mahuad made it clear that the settlers would not be permitted to stay. The settlers held many militant protest marches demanding recognition, but without any results. They put most of their efforts into building, reasoning that more permanent structures would enhance the validity of their claim. Within two weeks they were building such structures, purposely choosing recycled materials consistent with their "eco-proposal." While nearly all shantyhomes, almost by definition, include reused materials, at least one "flagship" house in Itchimbía would soon incorporate enough unusual materials (e.g., recycled cans and bottles) to practically appear as a work of modern, eco-friendly art. These efforts paid off, and although Mahuad demanded that the IESS and the Ministry of Government evict the settlers, the mayor could not force the National Police to take action when popular sentiment was broadly opposed to violence (*La Hora*, 10/12/95).

The settlers also moved quickly to establish a strong organizational structure, with eight residential blocks of twenty-five to thirty families each. A schedule developed wherein each Monday night, the five-member Itchimbía neighborhood council met to plan for the week and give instructions to eight block captains. On Tuesday nights, each block captain met with his or her own five-member block council to prepare them for Wednesday, when 100 percent of Itchimbía settlers met in their respective block meetings. For major issues and crises, the Wednesday block meetings were replaced by a general assembly of most of the one thousand settlers.

But the meetings did not stop there. Each block council consisted of the block captain and four officers for security, sports, women, and youth. Hence, each week all eight block security officers, for example, would meet together with the head security officer from the Itchimbía council to manage their respective responsibilities. So in a community of only three hundred families, forty-five

Table 5.2 Itchimbía data matrix

Stage of development	Neighborhood leader	Service demand	External factors				Internal Factors			
			District mayor	Service provider	Allies	Avenue of participation	Strategy type	Key resources	Neighborhood regime type	Outcome
Nascent (95–96)	Manzanillas (95–96)	Recognition	Hostile	Metro			Militant	Large group	Consensual	Failure
		Electricity	Hostile	Metro			Rogue	Architect	Consensual	Success
		Water truck	Hostile	Metro			Militant	High participation	Consensual	Failure
		Piped water	Hostile	Metro			Rogue	No money	Consensual	Failure
		Recognition	Hostile	Metro	Many*		Militant	Leadership	Consensual	Failure
		Recognition	Hostile	Metro	Many*	96 Election	Militant	Leadership	Consensual	Success
		Piped water	Hostile	Metro			Rogue	Architect	Consensual	Success
Mature (96–00)	Hernández (96–05)	Sewers	Hostile	Metro			Rogue	Architect/Minga	Consensual	Success
		Land titles	Hostile	Metro			Militant	High participation	Consensual	Failure
		Land titles	Hostile	Metro		00 Election	Conformist		Consensual	Failure
		Piped water	Friendly	Metro			Conformist		Consensual	Success
Consolidated (00–05)		Condo electric	Friendly	Metro	Many**		Conformist/Bootstrap	Leadership	Consensual	Success
		Condo water	Friendly	Metro	Many**		Conformist/Bootstrap	Leadership	Consensual	Success
		Condo sewers	Neutral	Metro	Many**		Conformist/Bootstrap/Militant	Leadership	Consensual	Success
		Condo titles	Neutral	Metro	Many**	04 Election	Conformist/Bootstrap	Leadership	Consensual	Failure

*The Confederation of Indigenous Nationalities of Ecuador, the Political Front of Women, the National Campesino Coordinating Committee, the Coordinating Committee of Social Movements of Ecuador, and domestic NGOs. The second of these two demands for recognition was also supported by a European religious order.

**The Ministry of Public Health, the Ministry of Urban Development and Housing, and domestic and international NGOs.

people were elected officers, and many more belonged to endless committees and working groups. These numbers only grew as the organization added posts like office manager, secretary, and chief architect. In addition to generating substantive results, one additional effect was record participation in all activities and political actions.

Despite high participation in regular protest marches, however, militant demands for water and recognition went unmet due to intense mayoral hostility. When pressure was high, Mahuad would temporarily relent and permit the water truck to visit Itchimbía, but this would not last. Service would soon halt, often for two to four weeks at a time, forcing settlers to rely on hauling water up the steep hill or collecting water in cisterns.

Since their demands got them nowhere, in November 1995 the settlers tried to steal water through clandestine water pipes, but the attempt failed due to limited resources. Their efforts did generate a small supply of water, but without adequate pressure the water could not get up the steep hill, so the secret pipes remained largely unused—yet another failure.

Meanwhile, a large number of external political actors quickly took sides in the growing conflict. The settlers encountered staunch opposition from Mahuad, the Metropolitan Council, and many established La Tola neighbors who lived around Itchimbía. News coverage during the first year also went against them. Various indigenous-based groups backed them, however, including the Confederación de Nacionalidades Indígenas del Ecuador (Confederation of Indigenous Nationalities of Ecuador, or CONAIE), the Frente Político de Mujeres (Political Front of Women), the Coordinadora Nacional de Campesinos (National Campesino Coordinating Committee), and the Coordinadora de Movimientos Sociales de Ecuador (Coordinating Committee of Social Movements of Ecuador). The settlers also soon received the unofficial support of several NGOs, as well as a few politicians opposed to Mahuad, such as representatives from the indigenous Movimiento Unido Pluricultural Pachakutik (Pachakutik Movement of Pluricultural Unity). But one of the settlers' biggest early wins was the neutral stance of IESS, which refused to side with Mahuad despite considerable pressure.

As predicted by Manzanillas, the settlers also received offers of "help" from one group they did not embrace: land traffickers. Famous invasion veterans from Quito's legendary Comité del Pueblo settlement arrived on the scene, as did representatives from Edgar Coral in Pisulli and the infamous Segundo Aguilar, formerly of Roldós (see chapter 3 for details on Coral, Pisulli, Aguilar, and Roldós).

The tensions among these various actors ebbed and flowed until the end of 1995, when the threat of violent eviction resurfaced. Recent settlement evictions on the outskirts of Quito, including Conocoto, Amaguaña, and the violent Christmas Eve eviction in Collaloma (see chapter 2), demonstrated that the Itchimbía settlers were no longer safe from Mahuad's threats. A spy for the cooperative learned that an eviction was planned for January 15, 1996, leaving the group only one day to prepare. Manzanillas recognized that this time they could not simply walk away in submission, as their homes would be bulldozed, but he announced that they would maintain their commitment to nonviolent resistance. "Not one drop of blood," the settlers declared (Mera 2002, interview).

And so the next day the National Police found not violent resistors, but men and women literally chained to their homes, surrounded by journalists. They announced that they would not resist, but neither would they leave. The newspapers were soon filled with memorable pictures, including one of a woman standing in chains, head slumped and arms outstretched in a crucifixion pose (*La Hora*, 1/16/96; *El Comercio*, 1/16/96; *El Universo*, 1/17/96). This nonviolent, media-driven approach put pressure on Mahuad, who was up for reelection and did not want a massacre, so Itchimbía was left alone.

In early 1996, the settlers legalized their status as a cooperative. Formally this was unrelated to the land dispute, but their status as a legal political entity put even more pressure on Mahuad to recognize them in relation to the land. To emphasize this shift in status, Manzanillas ended his role as president of what had technically been known as a "pre-cooperative," and María Hernández and Milton Chamorro were elected as the "first" president and vice president of the cooperative's consensual regime. They would hold these positions throughout at least nine years of annual neighborhood elections.

On July 9, 1996, Mahuad formally asked the Ministry of Government to proceed with the standing eviction order on July 15 (*El Comercio*, 7/17/96). This time, by sheer luck, the settlers again got one day's warning of the eviction, and Hernández decided that they had to try something new. So when the army arrived, they found Chamorro and five other Itchimbía leaders *buried* up to their chests, blocking the road! A painted sign read, "You can drive in, but you'll have to go over us."[12] At this the police hesitated, but they did not retreat until the mayor had received as many as one hundred e-mail messages from an order of nuns in France, shaming Mahuad for his refusal to negotiate.

This was a turning point for Itchimbía. Although Mahuad would never cede the land to the settlers, he abandoned the use of force and began to urge their voluntary relocation to some other site; this constituted de facto municipal recognition. The struggle for the land would continue, but the Itchimbía organization had survived its nascent stage of development and now had a place at the bargaining table.

---

12. On July 16, 1996, photographs and articles of this dramatic standoff appeared in *El Comercio*, *La Hora*, *Últimas Noticias*, *Expreso*, *Extra*, and other smaller papers.

Reviewing the demands of this nascent period, the hostile metropolitan mayor clearly made externally dependent strategies extremely difficult, and lack of money made bootstrap options initially impossible, leaving only the rogue approach. Theft worked for acquiring electricity, but not for piped water, and certainly not for municipal recognition. Mahuad's intransigence also held out against most militant strategies, but when these Innovators persisted with their nonviolent protest tactics, including international, Internet-based political support, the pressure of upcoming metropolitan elections earned them tacit recognition. While the timing of elections revealed the important role of local participatory institutions in acquiring services, their effect did not, in this case, seem to causally interact with Itchimbía's consensual neighborhood regime, though the group's consensus-based decision making had already begun to form the backbone of what would become an extraordinary streak of self-sufficient service initiatives.

Itchimbía's Cold War with the Mayor: Clandestine Acquisition of Most Services

Following tacit recognition by Mahuad in July 1996, the *mature* Itchimbía organization entered a four-year period of clandestine service acquisition in which the mayor eschewed direct confrontation in favor of proxies employed to harass the settlers. In addition to their continued theft of electricity and illegal dumping of garbage at nearby collection points, new settler initiatives included: (1) *rogue* theft of water through illegal pipes and water pumps—a success; (2) *rogue* theft of drainage through a clandestine sewer system—a success; (3) *militant* demands of Mayor Mahuad for land titles—a failure; and (4) *conformist* negotiations with Mayor Roque Sevilla for land titles—a failure. The success or failure of these rogue, militant, and conformist demands depended mainly on continued mayoral hostility and the internal factors of strategy type, resources, and neighborhood regime, as noted in table 5.2.

With legal recognition, Mahuad had abandoned efforts to evict the settlers by force, but he continued to stonewall them, and his administration funded the Comité Prodefensa del Parque Itchimbía (Committee for the Proactive Defense of Itchimbía Park, or "Prodefensa"), an organization of middle- and working-class neighbors opposed to the invasion. Prodefensa president Angel Costa initially presented his group to Hernández and Chamorro as nominal allies interested in helping the settlers relocate "to a more appropriate site," but their "proactive defense" of the neighborhood translated into regular harassment and pressure for the settlers to leave. Prodefensa filed complaints against the settlers, alleging that their presence resulted in "skyrocketing" crime rates, and also organized a signature drive to petition for an eviction (*Hoy*, 8/96).

Itchimbía responded with a petition of its own, doubling the number of signatures collected by Prodefensa, but Hernández and Chamorro put most of their energy into capitalizing on the favorable press generated by their "buried alive" stunt.[13] While earlier news coverage favored Mahuad, a fresh wave of newspaper articles provided balanced coverage or even highlighted the merits of the settlers' innovative eco-proposal.[14]

The settlers soon secured a meeting with IESS director Raúl Zapatier and laid the groundwork for their proposal to be considered by both IESS and the Ministry of Social Welfare. Mahuad refused to attend the meeting, but IESS expressed cautious optimism regarding park proposal details like bike lanes, a car-free pedestrian zone, and information booths with exhibits about the different parts of Quito. Hernández also used their momentum to bolster their partnership with the Ecological Action Foundation, which had helped them plant one thousand trees during their first year, a figure they now doubled as a mature invasion organization (*El Comercio*, 8/19/96).

The Sevilla Mayoral Administration: New Face, Same Old Hostility

In 1998, following the ouster of President Abdala Bucarám (1996–97) and the interim presidency of Fabio Alarcón (1997–98), Jamil Mahuad was elected president of Ecuador (1998–2000) and the vacant mayor's office was filled by Vice Mayor Roque Sevilla (Gerlach 2003, 115–23). But for Itchimbía, the change to Mayor Sevilla (1998–2000) made little difference. As another entrepreneurial mayor intent on downtown development, Sevilla proposed that the settlers relocate to land in distant Quitumbe, almost beyond Quito's southern boundary, despite the fact that the settlers worked downtown (*Últimas Noticias*, 10/14/97). Itchimbía held a public forum to discuss Sevilla's offer and eventually held a neighborhood referendum. The settlers voted overwhelmingly to reject the offer, both because of the location and because giving up their homes for empty land was a poor trade. Sevilla promised to build infrastructure on the proposed site, but the settlers had no reason to believe him.

But Sevilla would not be deterred and, as a pressure tactic, he ordered that the settlers begin paying rent to the metropolitan government until the conflict

---

13. *Hoy* reported a margin of ten thousand signatures for Itchimbía to five thousand against (11/9/95).

14. In one January 1996 comic strip, for example, a well-dressed man berates a tent settlement labeled "Itchimbía": "City Hall is so busy building the trolley . . . that it doesn't realize that the rest of the city is becoming the inheritance of invaders!" Another article alleged that the Itchimbía invasion was just a political stunt, evidenced by the "fact" that "80%" of the houses were uninhabited, a claim that turned out to be incorrect (*El Comercio*, 8/19/96). A report by *Hoy* (8/96), however, discussed at length the environmental benefits of Itchimbía's proposal and noted that the park had remained unused for decades.

was resolved. Guessing that outright refusal to pay might fail, Hernández instead cleverly proposed that the settlers pay the amount demanded but put it into a third-party savings account, ostensibly to help them pay for their own relocation, though the settlers had no intention of moving. In this way, Sevilla was able to claim progress on the relocation of the settlers, and the settlers of Itchimbía generated modest savings accounts rather than paying rent. These accounts would later prove a crucial resource during Itchimbía's consolidated stage of development.

Despite the ebb and flow of the conflict over the land, Sevilla sustained Mahuad's ironfisted denial of all services to Itchimbía (*Últimas Noticias*, 8/17/99). To allay suspicions, Itchimbía continued to make halfhearted requests for streetlights, water, and sewer drainage, but Hernández and Chamorro had actually abandoned the hope of extracting such services from Sevilla. Instead, Itchimbías settlers found innovative ways to develop their own infrastructure. They upgraded their illegal electrical hookups. They secretly installed an electric pump to pressurize their defunct network of uphill water pipes, and in 1998 they built a high-quality, clandestine sewer system. After gradually acquiring pipes and building materials, they began work each night at midnight. They would spend four hours digging up a ten-foot section of the road, lay down pipe, and rebury everything by morning. After four months and over one thousand feet of pipe, Itchimbía had the best sewer system of any invasion settlement on record. And since it was a secret, the settlers never had to pay service bills.

Reviewing the demands of this mature period, internal factors as well as mayoral hostility were most important. With respect to land titles, Itchimbía did not have the resources to succeed with either militant demands (Mahuad) or conformist bargaining (Sevilla). With respect to other services, however, mayoral resistance eliminated the feasibility of both legal strategies and externally dependent strategies, but allowed rogue strategies a chance of success. Even so, the extraordinary success of Itchimbía's service thefts clearly relied on unusual resources like creative leadership, an in-house architect, and a consensual decision-making structure whose inclusiveness galvanized nearly 100 percent of the membership to record levels of participation and commitment. Without these factors, it is doubtful that the quality or secrecy of Itchimbía's service infrastructure could have been attained.

An Extraordinary and Innovative Solution: Self-Help Condominiums

The mayoral administration of Paco Moncayo (2000–2008, Izquierda Democrática) briefly threatened to prolong Itchimbía's conflict with city hall, but creativity on the part of both Moncayo and the settlers instead led to organizational *consolidation* and an almost fairy-tale ending in the form of a complicated *conformist* and *bootstrap* project to build high-quality self-help condominiums with legal ownership titles for all Itchimbía settlers. During this five-year period, Itchimbía made five service demands: (1) *conformist* negotiations with Moncayo for improved water service to the original settlement location—a success; (2) a *conformist* and *bootstrap* collaboration for electricity service in the new condominiums—a success; (3) a *conformist* and *bootstrap* collaboration for water service in the condominiums—a success; (4) a varied *conformist, bootstrap,* and briefly *militant* demand for working drainage in the condominiums—a success; and (5) a *conformist* and *bootstrap* bid for individual condominium property titles—thus far, a failure. The dramatic success of these largely conformist and bootstrap strategies resulted from a friendly mayor, economically influential allies, organizational resources such as leadership and labor, and Itchimbía's consensual neighborhood regime (see table 5.2).

Moncayo, a former general and congressman, arrived in office eager to offer a solution to "the Itchimbía problem" (Gerlach 2003, 90–91). Where Sevilla had proposed relocation, Moncayo offered relocation to Quitumbe *and* free housing (*El Comercio,* 7/17/00). The settlers were not impressed. Itchimbía's leaders were still flush with excitement from their participation in the January 2000 ouster of the hated President Mahuad, and they were feeling powerful. They had heard honeyed promises before, and even if Moncayo was serious, no one wanted to live in distant Quitumbe.

But when Itchimbía's clandestine water and drainage system burst and flooded the road, revealing the settlers' years of service theft, Moncayo made no move to punish them. Daring to hope that this mayor might be different, cooperative president María Hernández decided to test Moncayo by requesting improvements in their illegal water service (which, of course, was not supposed to exist in the first place). Moncayo surprised the settlers by promptly granting their request. His administrator stated his position clearly: the settlers absolutely could not stay on the invaded land, but while a solution was negotiated, the mayor had an obligation to provide basic human necessities to the settlers.

Now the settlers were impressed . . . but they still refused to relocate. Moncayo then pitched a new idea. While Moncayo's plans for Itchimbía Park would not permit space for 220 houses, sufficient land was available on the other side of the park to build 220 units of condominium housing. It was a tempting offer, especially considering the economic straits the settlers faced in the wake of Ecuador's dollarization in April 2000, which devastated the purchasing power of their already meager incomes (Gerlach 2003, 213–17). In a 2002 interview Itchimbía manager Alba Mera described the economic situation: "People's debts are suddenly even more unpayable. Dollarization is killing us today. Salaries have stayed exactly the same as prices skyrocket. The news is a big lie. The economists are clueless. Salaries have maybe tripled, while prices go up one-hundred times or more." Moncayo also now had some credibility, so his pledge to work with the settlers to find reasonable financing and service provision resonated with the struggle-weary settlers. In the end, it came down to a blind neighborhood ballot, and the assenting votes carried the day 160–40 (with 20 abstentions): they would accept Moncayo's condominium proposal (Mera 2002, interview).

The following months were a whirlwind of meetings and proposals involving the settlers, the Moncayo administration, the Ministry of Public Health, the Ministry of Urban Development and Housing, several domestic NGOs, the EU Project "Paso a Paso" ("Step by Step"), volunteer architects from Quito's universities, and the competing bids of several construction companies. Negotiations dragged, as Hernández and Chamorro held out for financing terms that the poor settlers could actually manage, and in the end the settlers got their way.

The savings accounts the settlers had been forced to create under Mayor Sevilla provided each of the 220 families with $600 as a down payment. Beyond this, each family would contribute $62 per month for six years (a total of $4,464), plus they would provide most of the labor for construction. The Ministry of Urban Development and Housing and the EU-financed Project Paso a Paso would subsidize any remaining costs. The downside was that the condominiums would be completely "unfinished," meaning that each apartment's fixtures and even internal walls would not exist until that family managed to build them for themselves. But this was still an incredible accomplishment. In 2002, comparable fully finished condominiums in the area had a market value of at least $30,000, and the settlers were acquiring theirs for about $5,000 plus a major investment of personal labor (Aceles 2002, interview).

Ground was broken in June 2001, and in December 2002 and January 2003 the 220 families took possession of their rough but legally owned condominiums. The process took two months, but it was well organized. As each house was emptied by the settlers, a bulldozer waited nearby, demolishing the house immediately to ensure that new settlers from other parts of Quito would not claim the vacant structure. The negotiation and installation of electricity and water service in the new condominiums had gone smoothly, helping to build settler confidence in the move, but problems with the drainage system nearly derailed the whole process. When settlers discovered that the drainage system did not work due to construction defects, many settlers got cold feet, initially refusing to vacate their houses. To keep the project on track, the settlers organized a protest, which was embarrassing to Mayor Moncayo, who had been claiming credit for resolving the Itchimbía conflict, but the small demonstration was effective: the city fixed the plumbing (Chamorro 2005, interview).[15]

The minor conflict cooled relations with Mayor Moncayo, however, which may have contributed to subsequent challenges over individual property titles. In April 2005, city hall notified the Itchimbía leaders that settlers would have to pay not only for the square footage of their individual dwellings but also for a fair share of the open space around the condominiums. City hall's initial estimate of this additional cost was $1,050 per family, or about a 20 percent increase (Chamorro 2005, interview). With this challenging new sticking point, the process of assigning individual titles stalled, leaving the settlers frustrated, though arguably still secure.

The move from illegal houses to legal condominiums had significant effects on the Itchimbía organization, primarily through changes in the environment, membership, and leadership of the organization. The new condominium environment thrust settlers into close quarters with each other, and the lottery system of assigning dwelling units meant that many settlers suddenly did not know their immediate neighbors and were more apt to complain about their loud music, habits, or guests. Compounding this, many newcomers—typically cousins and their families—came to live in the complex, crowding two or three families into some single-family apartments. These newcomers uniformly lacked the organizational zeal of Itchimbía's core population, meaning that overall rates of participation dropped from the 80–100 percent range down to as low as 50 percent (which was still quite good compared to other cases).

With the condominium project secure, if not completely finished, leaders like Milton Chamorro and María Hernández devoted less time to Itchimbía, instead turning to long-deferred plans. Chamorro took eight months' leave from his post as cooperative vice president to finish his university degree in journalism. Hernández continued to serve as cooperative president but also ran successfully as a Pachakutik candidate for Quito's Secondary Metropolitan Council (Chamorro 2005, interview; Hernández 2008, interview). These kinds of commitments left Itchimbía leaders with less time to organize workshops. That said, Itchimbía's intense meeting schedule continued at least until 2005, with as many as a dozen meetings happening every Monday, Tuesday, and Wednesday night, and with continuing weekend workshops in other parts of Quito.

---

15. In addition, the settlers' demand for a pedestrian bridge (a service not analyzed in this study) over the adjacent Avenida Oriental highway was not successful until the settlers organized a July 2003 human blockade of the major traffic artery, stalling thousands of cars. Following the protest, the bridge was built in three short months. Thus, during this period the Innovators of Itchimbía continued to be flexible in their strategy choices, even if they relied principally on conformist and bootstrap methods.

Although in 2005 the living conditions in many of the condominiums were not yet equal to those the settlers had possessed in their original invaded community, it is fair to call the acquisition of the condominiums—complete with electricity and full plumbing—an extraordinary success. Though the settlers never acquired title to the original invasion site, they made the move to the condominiums by choice. In time, it seems likely that their quality of life will exceed that which they achieved in 2002, before the move. Further, the settlers are now considered the legal owners of their condominiums, though they could ultimately fail to receive titles through default on their loans or a failure to successfully negotiate the issue of paying for the surrounding land.

During Itchimbía's consolidated phase, external factors like mayoral assistance, friendly national government ministries, and generous NGO allies were clearly pivotal. Yet two internal factors made it possible for Itchimbía to take advantage of these opportunities. First, Hernández and Chamorro possessed the leadership skills to forge successful relationships with a wide array of actors, including international allies. This and other unusual assets, such as an in-house architect, constituted organizational resources that most invasion organizations lack. Second, the consensual neighborhood regime provided the leadership continuity needed for long-lasting government partnerships, and also provided the democratic character required by the European NGOs (ironically, Itchimbía's annual neighborhood elections were never competitive, though they were always free and fair). Ultimately, however, a *lack* of resources led the settlers to forfeit their first choice of homes, as they were unable to pressure Moncayo into ceding the original invasion site. Although Itchimbía remains a case of extraordinary success, it is important to note that the settlers did not get everything they wanted.

Summary of Itchimbía's Organizational Successes and Failures

The Innovator organization of Itchimbía made fifteen attempts to acquire services between 1996 and 2005. Of these fifteen, Itchimbía scored seven failures and eight successes. Although Itchimbía was the only group of the ten case studies in chapters 3–5 to lose its land, I argue that it nonetheless constituted the most impressive success story of them all. As with the Next Generation case of Camino, which benefited from acquiring de facto property security but not actual land titles, the Itchimbía organization may have benefited from its unusual form of property security. With the election of Mayor Moncayo, it became clear that the settlers would never be forced off the land, but the mayor's insistence on an alternative solution kept the settlers engaged and active on the condominium project. With the settlers physically relocated to the condominiums, Itchimbía remains an important case to continue to study.

Itchimbía's population declined from 300 families in 1996 to only 220 in 2002. This decline, however, represented a strengthening of the organization, as the 220 that remained were stalwarts committed to the cause, while the 80 families that left had grown tired of endless committee meetings and activities. Yet between 2003 and 2005, the condominium population was augmented by perhaps 40 families crowded into the dwellings of their relatives. This latter increase can be seen as a modest weakening of the organization, because these newcomers showed no interest in participating in the community's activities and mission.

Such shifts in the community membership and leadership suggest that the newfound security could compromise settlers' commitment to their activist mission, but it seems equally possible that the mission will endure. Hence, this study anticipates that the Itchimbía organization has consolidated permanently and will not "regress" into a moribund state.

One major success that is not obvious given this study's focus on services such as electricity and water is that in 2005 the city of Quito had transformed the once garbage-strewn Itchimbía hill into a beautiful park used by thousands of Quiteños every weekend. Although the specifics of the settlers' eco-park never materialized, the events surrounding the Itchimbía settlement between 1995 and 2003 appear to have foreclosed on earlier plans to turn the park into a private hotel and resort. Although private businesses do run parts of the park's services and administration, it is fundamentally a public locale, with a well-equipped playground, a bike path surrounding a lagoon, a glass pavilion that can be rented for weddings and events, and a safe and clean environment that has become popular with families from near and far.

Visiting the site of the original Itchimbía settlement in 2005, there were few signs that a robust community of 220 family homes had been there just three years earlier. Middle- and working-class families picnicked on a grassy hillock, the former site of a health post and family home, and children on rollerblades skated down a paved path, oblivious to the defunct sewer system concealed beneath their feet.

THE INNOVATOR TYPE

Synthesis of the cases of Encantada and Itchimbía provides a composite picture of the identity traits, repertoire traits, and neighborhood regimes characteristic of the Innovator type. With respect to identity, Innovator organizations tend to have novice leaders whose pursuit of both material and activist objectives is driven by a sense of mission. With respect to repertoire, the Innovators exhibit strategic flexibility and generally follow the strategy life cycle. The specific tactics employed within each strategy type, however, are remarkable for their originality and creativity, including use of technology and the practice of non-violence. Finally, the Innovators have a preference for power-sharing neighborhood regimes, perhaps because of their commitment to democratic activism. They vary, however, in organizational competitiveness, meaning that Innovator regimes tend to be democratic or consensual.

Innovator Identity Traits: Sense of Mission, Activist, and Inexperienced

Innovator organizations are characterized by a sense of mission, mixed motives, and leaders with little or no experience in organizing land invasions. The Innovators arose in the mid-1990s in a fashion similar to that of the Next Generation, meaning that many had grown up in invasion communities and now sought to found settlements of their own. But Innovator imaginations had also been inspired by local and national struggles for democracy. Regular activity by domestic and international NGOs and human rights organizations fueled ideas and discourse about broader societal transformation, and led Innovators to see their invasion settlements not merely as functional, but as part of a democratic revolution; unlike other organizational types that focus solely on material incentives, Innovators also seek transformation, such as democracy building. In this respect, the Innovators' sense of mission is even bolder than the Next Generation's sense of entitlement.[16]

Yet the Innovator attitude of "we must be different or we will fail" points to a capacity for realistic assessment of political obstacles that is sometimes lacking in the more brash Next Generation. This attitude was clear in the founding moments of Itchimbía, when the settlers explicitly designed an ecology-oriented plan to differentiate themselves from other invasions, but in the Encantada case this attitude was manifested mainly under later leaders. Hence, Encantada leaders Ipanaque and Valencia had more in common with Itchimbía's Manzanillas and Hernández than they did with earlier Encantada leaders like Quispe and Condori. Despite their inexperience, Ipanaque, Valencia, Manzanillas, and Hernández all recognized the potential advantages of creating a unique mission and identity for their respective organizations.[17]

16. This finding echoes the work of Debra King; in her development of Melucci's (1988) work, she argued that activism is best sustained "when activists can maintain their passionate participation in creating social change, regardless of circumstances, rather than simply enhancing their commitment to a particular organization" (King 2004, 73).

17. Working in Brazil, Guidry (2003, 196) found that movement success depended in part on a group's capacity to build a sense of citizenship, rather than an exclusive focus on material needs.

In addition, Innovator organizations explicitly seek novice leaders, like Encantada's Máximo Quispe, with little or no prior experience organizing a land invasion. Like the anti–Vietnam War activists of the United States who warned "don't trust anyone over thirty," the young Innovators suspect older veterans—like Encantada's Angélica Salas and Arturo Laynes—of being corrupt land traffickers seeking to exploit settlers. The Itchimbía group managed to fend off offers of "help and assistance" from Quito's invasion veterans, like Edgar Coral and Segundo Aguilar, but Encantada was less successful, though they did attempt to expel suspected veteran leaders despite an initial lack of any concrete evidence of wrongdoing.

Innovator Repertoire Traits: Flexible, Original, and Nonviolent

The demand-making repertoire of Innovator organizations is characterized by strategic flexibility, tactical originality, and the use of nonviolence and technology. Like the Next Generation, the Innovators abandon the ideological rigidity of their Old Guard parents and instead follow the more flexible strategy life cycle. Encantada, for example, began with rogue and militant strategies, then employed a combination of militant and conformist demands, and finally shifted to a mix of conformist and bootstrap methods. The timing of Itchimbía's strategy cycle was different, but its general direction was similar. Itchimbía began with a prolonged period of rogue and militant strategies, and then moved into conformist and then bootstrap methods. In both cases, strategy choices revolved around estimations of a method's chance of success, rather than identity-based strategy preferences. For example, although Innovators often reject clientelism, they do so because they recognize its costs, not because they are ideologically precluded from considering conformist strategies. Thus, choosing a nonclientelist strategy for one demand does not preclude an Innovator from negotiating a clientelist deal to meet another demand.

Although the Innovators share the Next Generation's strategic flexibility, the Innovators sometimes appear to choose the "wrong" strategy, given existing political opportunities, but this is because Innovator objectives differ from those of conventional invasion organizations. Since Innovators do not care solely about their own material success, their activist mission sometimes leads to surprising choices that undermine their material demands, such as Itchimbía's wholesale rejection of the three thousand extra settlers who spontaneously tried to join their invasion. Thus, although we see cases of both Innovator success and failure, it is often not because of the strategy "mismatches" that characterize some Next Generation demands.

While Innovators mimic the Next Generation's strategic flexibility, they differ in all other repertoire traits. The Innovators explicitly seek to use original and innovative tactics, rather than the "tried-and-true playbook" of their parents. In Encantada, for example, Quispe and Condori pursued a novel public health strategy that used media attention to recast the land conflict as a case of victimized infants and children. And in Itchimbía, settlers sought to steal not only electricity but piped water and drainage as well, via high-quality, clandestine infrastructure.

The Innovators also avoid violence. The violence of Encantada's founding spurred Quispe to redirect Encantada away from physical confrontation and toward a public relations approach. In Itchimbía, settlers foiled three eviction attempts with Gandhian nonviolence, which has rarely been implemented in a rigorous way in either Lima or Quito.

Finally, the Innovators make use of technology. For example, Encantada made good use of the television media, created an e-mail network to contact international donors, and used Internet reports of their progress to attract support.[18] Itchimbía produced video documentaries of their struggles for use in organizing workshops, and also maintained an extensive e-mail network that delivered not only crucial opposition to their eviction by Mahuad but also lasting connections with Spanish and German NGOs that supported the condominium project.[19]

Innovator Neighborhood Regimes: Power-Sharing

Innovator neighborhood regimes vary in their competitiveness but are usually power-sharing, meaning that they are democratic or consensual. This makes sense since Innovators often have explicit democracy-building goals, and settlers might logically demand that their leaders "practice what they preach" by employing a power-sharing model of governance. Encantada had a competitive regime while Itchimbía's was noncompetitive, but both regimes were about equal in their degree of organizational inclusiveness.

Given these characteristics, we expect Itchimbía's noncompetitive regime to exhibit better alliance-building skills than the competitive Encantada regime.

18. See Keck and Sikkink (1998, 201–7) for a discussion of how international networks can facilitate organizational success.

19. In 2001, Spain's Instituto de Estudios Políticos para América Latina y Africa (Institute of Latin American and African Political Studies) and Germany's Center for Ecology and Development partnered to launch the Step by Step Successive Loans for Progressive Houses project in Peru and Ecuador. Sponsored by the European Union, the project aimed to help poor urban families obtain loans and technical support to buy or build housing.

While both organizations made ample use of allies, this theoretical expectation is supported by these two cases. In the noncompetitive Itchimbía case, Manzanillas and Hernández cultivated a host of diverse alliances, many of which lasted eight years or more. Itchimbía's more recent partnerships for the condominium project began in 2000 and were still strong in 2005. In Encantada, however, the more limited alliances were further compromised by leadership turnover. Quispe allied with Cambio 90, but this ended when his administration concluded. Condori cultivated successful relationships with the municipality and Project Ala, but these friendships both faltered under Secretary General Garces. Garces created a working relationship with the FONAVI housing agency, but this connection lapsed and had to be recreated by Valencia two years later.

With respect to participatory institutions and other local avenues of participation, we expect both power-sharing regimes to make good use of available opportunities. In Quito, no clear opportunities existed for examination, but in Encantada the Multisectoral Commission proved a welcoming framework for settlers. The organization's initial attempt to work with the Multisectoral failed due to declining participation and a moribund organization. Under the leadership of Secretary General Valencia, however, the consolidated Encantada organization resumed work with the Multisectoral.

Implications for the Innovator Type

The identity and repertoire traits common to the Innovator type have implications for the survival and success of other organizations. With respect to identity, the Innovators' sense of mission and organizational activism positions these groups to evade the security trap and consolidate. For example, Itchimbía avoided the security trap entirely by making activism the organization's founding principle. Even more persuasive, however, the creative but materialist Encantada organization fell prey to the security trap, but was able to move from a moribund condition to consolidation by transforming its organizational purpose. This implies that for long-term organizational survival, all invasion organizations—not just Innovators—should consider an alternative or supplemental mission. While the need for housing and services proves a powerful rallying cry for nascent organizations, the Encantada case demonstrates that organizations can still reinvent themselves in order to sustain collective action through mixed motives.

With respect to demand-making repertoire, strategic flexibility and tactical innovation were pivotal to the success of each group. In terms of strategy type and the strategy life cycle, Encantada and Itchimbía look similar to Next Generation cases like Camino and Oasis, but the tactical creativity and originality of the Innovators delivered high-quality infrastructure and an uncontested ownership claim for most settlers, a combination that no Old Guard or Next Generation case duplicated.[20] The implication is that while unoriginal tactics can deliver some services, acquiring all services occurs most quickly with innovative tactics and a sense of mission.

20. Pisulli acquired both infrastructure and land titles, but settlers could not obtain individual titles. Camino acquired land titles for one-third of its settlers, but this third lived on the most remote lots, where service provision was much poorer than in the Camino flatlands. It should also be repeated that despite their great success overall, Itchimbía settlers did forfeit their original invasion lands.

6

Analyzing Organizational Strategy, Success, and Survival

How well do the study's analytic tools explain variation in organizational strategy, success, and survival? Does the study accomplish its descriptive and analytic agenda with respect to each of these outcomes? And how does the empirical reality of the study's ten cases fit the expectations of the typology of Old Guard, Next Generation, and Innovator organizations? This chapter answers these questions through four sections that correspond to the analysis of the organizational typology and the study's three key outcomes. Each section delves into considerable analytic detail, but to begin the chapter, table 6.1 summarizes the major outcomes of organizational strategy, success, and survival for all ten cases.

Table 6.1 shows that with respect to organizational type, there is a clear pattern in terms of strategy, but no obvious pattern in terms of success or survival. This corresponds to earlier claims that while organizations tend either to exhibit strong strategy preferences or follow the flexible strategy life cycle, the success or failure of invasion organizations hinges on several other factors that vary both within and across organizational types. With respect to strategy pattern, the Old Guard clients strongly prefer legal strategies, while the Old Guard radicals strongly prefer extralegal strategies. By contrast, the newer types of organizations all follow the strategy life cycle, wherein an organization begins with extralegal strategies and gradually shifts toward legal methods.

With respect to the rate of success for service demands, the Old Guard (average of 46 percent, N = 56) is generally less successful than the Next Generation (average of 57 percent, N = 47) or the Innovators (average of 64 percent, N = 28),

Table 6.1   Overview of major organizational outcomes

Organization type	Invasion organization	Strategy pattern	Success rate*	Survival outcome**
Old Guard (clients)	Pro	Legal	54% (N = 13)	Moribund
	Sector C	Legal	38% (N = 13)	Moribund
Old Guard (radicals)	Rosales	Extralegal	33% (N = 18)	Mature
	Pisulli	Extralegal	67% (N = 12)	Consolidated
Next Generation (large, older)	Camino	Life cycle	86% (N = 14)	Consolidated
	Oasis	Life cycle	62% (N = 13)	Moribund
Next Generation (small, younger)	Villa Mar	Life cycle***	33% (N = 12)	Mature
	Paraíso	Life cycle***	38% (N = 8)	Mature
	Encantada	Life cycle	77% (N = 13)	Consolidated
Innovators	Itchimbía	Life cycle	53% (N = 15)	Consolidated

*Percentage reflects the raw number of successes out of total attempts, and does not reflect the scope or quality of services acquired. Hence, the figure overstates an organization's chance at success, but as this overestimate is consistent across cases, it still facilitates relative comparison.

**Stage of development refers to 2005 and may not reflect the organization's terminal stage.

***By 2005, the younger Next Generation cases had begun the strategy life cycle, but it remained unclear if they would continue to follow the cycle.

but the range of success rates for specific cases is so great that drawing any conclusions about this apparent difference requires more systematic analysis. For example, Old Guard success rates range from 33 to 67 percent, while the Next Generation success rates range from 33 to 86 percent. Further, these numbers reflect only the raw percentage of successful demands, and tell us little about the quality or scope of those services.

Finally, with respect to organizational survival, table 6.1 suggests the possibility that Innovators are better than other types at consolidating, but without systematic comparison, simply listing outcomes as of 2005 tells us little. For example, Rosales and Paraíso were both mature organizations in 2005, but Rosales was in its fourteenth year, while Paraíso was just four years old. Hence, examination of these cases at "closer range" is required.

A METHODOLOGICAL NOTE: EXTRACTING IDEAS AT CLOSE RANGE

The project's intensive and qualitative approach to fieldwork (see the appendix, which describes seventy interviews and other primary sources) resulted in an empirically rich body of "causal-process observations" (Brady 2004). The study's data matrices (see tables 3.1 to 3.4, 4.1 to 4.3, 4.5, 5.1, and 5.2) present more than one thousand data observations with respect to 132 service demands. Since these nonindependent observations are drawn from a nonrandom sample of ten invasion organizations, they are unsuitable for statistical methods such as multiple regression. Because of the study's efforts to "extract ideas at close range" (Collier, Brady, and Seawright 2004), however, this body of data is far richer empirically than the matrices suggest. As the qualitative case studies make clear, the study's analysis and findings are based on much more than a series of scores for each service demand on a handful of variables. Rather, those scores constitute a synthesis of in-depth causal-process observations whose details are described in the case study chapters. Since its theoretical framework emerged from intensive study of these cases, the study cannot be said to "test" the framework with those same cases, yet the extraction of these observations at such a close range that causal processes could be seen at work gives us greater confidence in the study's findings. The data matrices alone cannot possibly describe the collected information; rather, the matrices display an aggregate summary of a deep and rich body of new empirical data.

ANALYZING TYPES OF INVASION ORGANIZATIONS

How well does the study's organizational typology capture the identity, repertoire, and regime traits of invasion organizations? Comparative analysis of these factors reveals that the ideal-typical traits presented in the organizational typology in chapter 1 seem to be excellent "predictors" of organizational objectives, tactics, and technology use, as well as good predictors of organizational outlook, leadership experience, degree of strategic flexibility, and regime inclusiveness.[1] With respect to violence use, however, organizational type is only a fair predictor, and with respect to regime competitiveness, organizational type is not a predictor at all.

Analyzing Identity Traits

Looking first at identity traits, a group's classification as Old Guard, Next Generation, or Innovator appears to be an excellent predictor of organizational *objectives*, and also a good predictor of *outlook* and *leadership experience*. When scoring all ten case studies on these three identity traits, twenty-six of thirty

---

1. This "prediction" is based on a typology generated from study of these cases. Thus, it would be surprising if the overall fit were not quite good. At the same time, observing that certain traits vary together, even in a small set of cases, can be quite valuable.

Table 6.2   Identity traits by invasion organization

Organization type	Invasion organization	Outlook	Objectives	Leadership experience
Old Guard	Pro	Pragmatic	Material	Veteran
	Sector C	Pragmatic	Material	Veteran
	Rosales	Pragmatic/**Entitlement***	Material	Veteran
	Pisulli	Pragmatic	Material	**Novice**
Next Generation	Camino	Sense of entitlement	Material	**Veteran**
	Oasis	Sense of entitlement	Material	Novice
	Villa Mar	Sense of entitlement	Material	Novice
	Paraíso	Sense of entitlement	Material	Novice
Innovators	Encantada	**Entitlement**/Mission	Material/Activist	Novice
	Itchimbía	Sense of mission	Material/Activist	Novice

*"Deviant" scores are in **bold**.

scores (87 percent) are consistent with the typology's expectations. Table 6.2 reveals an excellent fit between the ten case studies and the typology's claim that Old Guard and Next Generation organizations pursue material objectives, while Innovator organizations pursue a combination of material and activist objectives (i.e., they have mixed motives). All cases corresponded to this expectation, though Encantada began with material goals and later shifted its agenda to include activist objectives.

We also observe a very good analytic fit with respect to outlook. The typology associates the Old Guard with a pragmatic outlook, the Next Generation with a bold sense of entitlement, and Innovators with a sense of mission. Eight out of ten cases conform to this expectation, and even Rosales and Encantada are only partial exceptions. In the case of Rosales, the organization's stubborn determination to make extralegal strategies work (despite years of failure) echoes the bold sense of entitlement of the Next Generation, yet its outlook also included the pragmatism of the Old Guard. In the case of Encantada, the settlers began with a sense of entitlement, but adopted a new mission when the organization had sunk into a moribund state. Thus, where Rosales straddled the conceptual line between different kinds of outlooks, Encantada made a qualitative shift from one outlook to another.

Finally, we see a good analytic fit with respect to leadership experience. The study argues that the Old Guard preferred veteran leaders, while the newer types tended to have novice leaders, and we see this trend confirmed in eight of the ten cases. The cases of Pisulli and Camino, however, clearly contradict expectations. In Pisulli, neighborhood boss Edgar Coral did employ several veteran settlers as his assistants, but Coral himself was unquestionably a novice and was unquestionably in charge. Whereas in Pisulli we see a novice in charge of an Old Guard organization, in the case of Camino we see a Next Generation leader who was an experienced veteran. Celso Meza was a classic Next Generation novice when he cofounded Comité del Pueblo #2 in 1978, but by the time he founded Camino in 1990, his years of land invasion experience were evident in his strategy choices and his generally savvy tactical decisions. Together these two exceptions confirm the standard caveat about any ideal type—there are bound to be exceptions—but more interestingly, they point to the finding that although leaders are crucial, they are not the sum total of an organization's identity. In some cases leadership may be the single most important factor, but in Pisulli, Camino, and other cases, traits such as objectives and outlook also play a major role in determining a group's identity.

Analyzing Repertoire Traits

Turning to repertoire traits, organizational type proves to be an excellent predictor of tactics and technology use, as well as a good predictor of degree of strategic flexibility, but only a fair predictor of violence use. Scoring the ten cases on these four repertoire traits, thirty-three out of forty scores (83 percent) conformed to expectations. Table 6.3 illustrates an excellent analytic fit between tactics and organizational type. As predicted by the typology, all Old Guard and Next Generation cases employ unoriginal tactics, while both Innovator organizations invented new tactics. Encantada, for example, deployed an innovative public health campaign to secure its land and services. In Quito, Itchimbía reached new heights of originality with its ecological park proposal and numerous media-oriented stunts.

Table 6.3 also shows an excellent fit with respect to *technology use*. While none of the Old Guard and Next Generation organizations made significant use of new technologies, both Innovator groups did. In Encantada, the public health campaign made clever use of the television media to embarrass the Villa El Salvador mayor and Agrosilves, and in 2002 Encantada began developing a web of Internet contacts to support its new mission of organizational activism. In Itchimbía, settlers produced educational documentaries and targeted Mayor Mahuad with international criticism online. Hence, not only did both Innovators use technology, but it was central to their success.

Comparative analysis also points to a strong correlation between organizational type and degree of *strategic flexibility*. Seven out of ten cases clearly support the image of a rigid and inflexible Old Guard contrasted with more flexible Next Generation and Innovator groups. Even the three exceptions are only deviations in degree, not in kind. Sector C and Rosales are not as rigid as Pro and Pisulli, but they are still more rigid than they are flexible. Similarly,

Table 6.3   Repertoire traits by invasion organization

Organization type	Invasion organization	Strategic flexibility	Tactics	Violence use	Technology use
Old Guard	Pro	Rigid	Old	Yes	No
	Sector C	**Fairly rigid***	Old	**No**	No
	Rosales	**Fairly rigid**	Old	**No**	No
	Pisulli	Rigid	Old	Yes	No
Next Generation	Camino	**Fairly flexible**	Old	**Yes**	No
	Oasis	Flexible	Old	No	No
	Villa Mar	Flexible	Old	No	No
	Paraíso	Flexible	Old	No	No
Innovators	Encantada	Flexible	New	**Once**	Yes
	Itchimbía	Flexible	New	No	Yes

*"Deviant" scores are in **bold**.

Camino's long stretch of conformist service demands indicates that it is not as flexible as other Next Generation cases, but considering Camino's entire strategy choice trajectory, it remains an example of strategic flexibility. Hence, none of the ten cases actually contradicts the typology, even if three of them exhibit slightly less clear classifications of strategic flexibility.

Finally, table 6.3 appears to show an irregular analytic fit with respect to *violence use*. Although six cases are consistent with the image of a violent Old Guard, a Next Generation reluctant to use violence, and Innovators who are wholly nonviolent, four cases behaved otherwise. The Old Guard cases of Sector C and Rosales almost never used violence at the behest of the neighborhood organization, yet the Next Generation case of Camino did. Further, although Encantada made a strategic decision to avoid violence, the settlers did engage in one serious fight during the neighborhood's founding. What can we make of these clear deviations from the typology?

The presence of several cases whose level of violence use contradicts the organizational typology makes it tempting to discard the violence use hypothesis or to look for a broader or different set of cases, but the typology can be defended on the basis of the current sample of cases. Although Sector C and Rosales used almost no violence during their fourteen years of struggles for services, neither did they intentionally avoid violence. The typology does not predict that Old Guard organizations are bloodthirsty, but rather that they have no objection to using violence. While it might be more analytically convincing if these two groups were as aggressively violent as Pro and Pisulli, the lack of violence does not pose the kind of analytic threat of, say, an example in which Sector C eschewed a service opportunity because it would have required violence.

The outright contradictory behavior of Camino and Encantada is more analytically challenging, but the status of these two organizations as borderline cases provides space for an interpretation of broad consistency with the typology. Since most attempts at classification will have exceptions, should we not expect these exceptions to occur in the Next Generation case, which flirts with Old Guard traits (Camino), and the Innovator case, which began as part of the Next Generation (Encantada)? I think we should, and while the number of deviations should moderate our confidence in the violence use hypothesis, the particular distribution of those deviations sustains the claim of the typology, albeit with somewhat less confidence than the trends claimed with respect to other repertoire traits.

Analyzing Neighborhood Regime Traits

Finally, turning to neighborhood regimes, organizational type is shown to consistently predict degree of inclusiveness, but not degree of competitiveness. Considering first the latter claim, the *competitiveness* column in table 6.4 reveals no clear pattern with respect to organizational type. Instead, we observe both competitive and noncompetitive examples of all three types.[2] In addition to showing the lack of correlation between competitiveness and organizational type, table 6.4 also appears to illustrate the presence of a correlation between organizational inclusiveness and organizational type. Casual observation seems to point toward a strong correlation between power-concentrating regimes and Old Guard neighborhoods on the one hand, and power-sharing regimes and Next Generation and Innovator neighborhoods on the other. From this perspective, Camino appears to be a deviant case. Hence, table 6.4 lends itself to a dichotomous distribution of types, with the Old Guard on one side of the organizational inclusiveness fence and the Next Generation and Innovators on the other side. But Camino's apparent exceptionalism points toward an alternative explanation.

Replacing table 6.4's dichotomous approach with a continuous conceptualization of organizational inclusiveness reveals a more nuanced set of correlations wherein we find Innovator regimes to be highly inclusive, Next Generation regimes to be moderately inclusive, and Old Guard regimes to be noninclusive. Figure 6.1 presents a spatial distribution of neighborhood regimes with respect to competitiveness (the horizontal axis) and inclusiveness (the vertical axis), both of which are presented as continuous dimensions, permitting comparison of the relative position of cases within each quadrant. Note how the Next Generation case of

---

2. Although no pattern of organizational competitiveness emerges with respect to organizational type, recall the finding in chapter 2 that while informal neighborhoods in Lima tend to exhibit vibrant local democracy, informal neighborhoods in Quito are often ruled by local bosses.

Table 6.4   Neighborhood regime traits by invasion organization

Organization type	Invasion organization	Organizational inclusiveness	Organizational competitiveness
Old Guard	Pro	Power-concentrating	See below**
	Sector C	Power-concentrating	Competitive
	Rosales	Power-concentrating	Competitive
	Pisulli	Power-concentrating	Noncompetitive
Next Generation	Camino	Power-concentrating*	Noncompetitive
	Oasis	Power-sharing	Competitive
	Villa Mar	Power-sharing	Noncompetitive
	Paraíso	Power-sharing	Competitive
Innovators	Encantada	Power-sharing	Competitive
	Itchimbía	Power-sharing	Noncompetitive

*Camino's power-concentrating neighborhood regime appears to set it apart from the power-sharing regimes of other Next Generation cases. This apparent stark contrast, however, is actually an effect of the dichotomous conceptualization of organizational inclusiveness. In figure 6.1, a continuous conceptualization of this dimension demonstrates that with respect to inclusiveness, Camino has as much in common with other Next Generation regimes as it does with the Old Guard.

**Between 1990 and 1992, the neighborhood of Pro had a noncompetitive authoritarian regime, but between 1992 and 2002 it had a competitive electoral regime.

Camino is considerably more inclusive than the Old Guard regimes below it, even though they are all ultimately classified as power-concentrating.

Although figure 6.1 highlights one of the classic dilemmas of categorization (i.e., where to draw conceptual boundaries and how many of them to draw), it also confirms the capacity of organizational type to help predict regime inclusiveness. This serves as a reminder that while discrete categories such as veteran/novice leadership or old/new tactics serve valuable descriptive and analytic purposes, they remain imperfect labels for what is invariably a complex empirical reality.

Implications for Organizational Type

This section has shown that although organizational type varies in its capacity to predict specific characteristics, it remains a strong overall predictor of identity, repertoire, and neighborhood regime traits. The chapter's introduction noted that organizational type was highly correlated with strategy pattern, but showed no clear correlation with success rate or survival outcome. As the following sections make clear, however, although organizational type is most strongly associated with strategy choice patterns, it also remains a crucial analytic baseline for explaining organizational success and survival.

Power-sharing

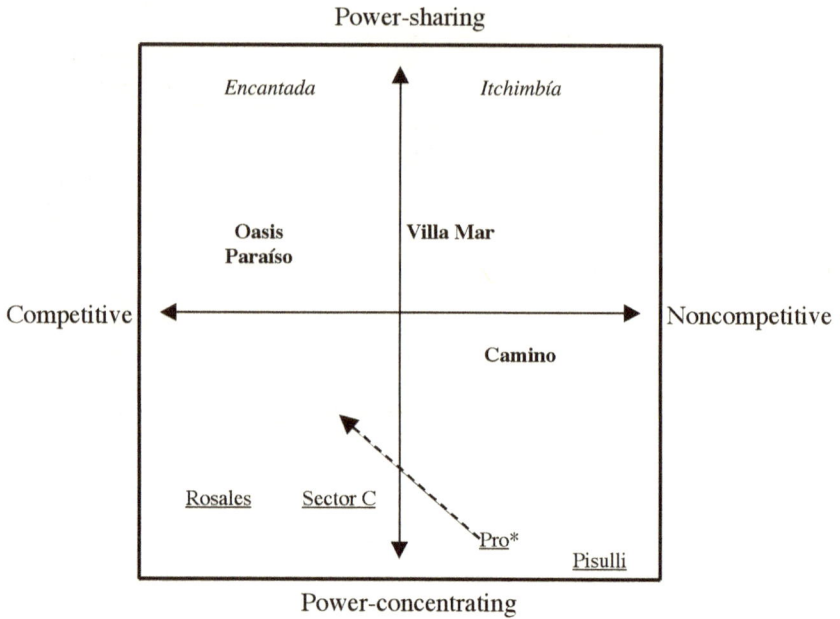

Fig. 6.1   Spatial distribution of neighborhood regimes

Note: Innovator regimes are italicized, **Next Generation** regimes set in bold, and <u>Old Guard</u> regimes underlined. Each quadrant contains cases of one regime type: democratic (upper left), consensual (upper right), electoral (lower left), and authoritarian (lower right).

*Pro began with an authoritarian regime in 1990 but changed to electoral regime in 1992.

ANALYZING ORGANIZATIONAL STRATEGY

How well do the strategy typology and strategy life cycle serve the descriptive and analytic goals of the study? With respect to description, the typology and life cycle concepts were introduced to facilitate conceptually useful differentiation among the strategy patterns of the three organizational types. With respect to analysis, organizational strategy was conceived as an important outcome in its own right, but also as an integral part of the causal analysis of organizational success (discussed in its own section below). Together, this descriptive and analytic agenda has laid the groundwork for an important theoretical contribution with respect to McAdam, Tarrow, and Tilly's concepts of contained and transgressive contention. This latter objective will be pursued in chapter 7, so I begin here with the tasks of description and analysis.

Analyzing Strategy Patterns: Old Guard Rigidity

Analysis of the individual demands for neighborhood services initiated by the ten invasion organizations demonstrates the conceptual utility of the strategy typology and confirms that Old Guard organizations exhibit strategic rigidity consistent with what Stokes (1995) labels "enduring mental templates." With respect to the straightforward applicability of the strategy typology, the strategies of 117 of 132 demands (89 percent) were classified as one of the four ideal types. Of the remaining fifteen demands, four were combination militant/conformist and eight were combination conformist/bootstrap, meaning that they did not match one of the ideal types but still fell somewhere on the strategy typology (if its legality and autonomy dimensions were considered continuous, rather than dichotomous). Only three demands—Pisulli's militant/bootstrap acquisition of land titles, Pro's militant/bootstrap attempt at titles, and Itchimbía's unusual conformist/bootstrap/militant demand for working plumbing in its condominiums—did not fit the typology at all.[3] The applicability of a typology to a set of cases is essential, but more important is the analytic leverage the typology offers toward the study's questions about organizational strategy.

Comparative analysis of the legality of service demands supports the study's claims about strategic rigidity and flexibility. Table 6.5 provides an aggregate view of the legality of the strategies used for all 132 of the service demands initiated.[4] Table 6.5 suggests that, as a whole, Old Guard clients and radicals have strong preferences for *either* legal *or* extralegal strategies, while Next Generation and Innovator organizations do not. Comparing all 132 demands, legal strategies were about as common (52 percent) as extralegal strategies (48 percent). Analysis of Next Generation and Innovator demands points to a similar distribution, with both appearing to slightly favor legal strategies (55 to 45 percent and 54 to 46 percent, respectively), but by and large, no strong preference is demonstrated.[5]

The Old Guard, however, offers a striking contrast. Old Guard clients strongly preferred legal strategies (73 percent), while Old Guard radicals strongly preferred extralegal methods (75 percent). This is important evidence in support of the study's claims, but it should not be overstated. Considering the two Old Guard radical cases separately, Pisulli used extralegal strategies 96 percent of the time, but Rosales relied on such methods only 61 percent of the time. Although Rosales still demonstrated a clear preference for extralegal strategies, this contrast points to the importance of understanding individual cases. Further, while the

3. Not only was the strategy of the Pisulli demand difficult to classify, but it was also unclear if the attempt at land titles succeeded or failed. The organization did acquire titles to all 1,800 lots, but they were never distributed to individual settlers (see chapter 3). Hence, I treat this demand as a failure.

4. Table 6.5 includes one demand by Encantada that was initiated but unresolved at the time of the study's conclusion. Since this demand was still in progress in 2005, it will be excluded from the later discussion of organizational success, resulting in a slightly smaller sample (N = 131).

5. Bear in mind that these quantitative statistics serve primarily as illustrations of the study's qualitative arguments.

Table 6.5   Legality of service demands by organizational type

Organization type	Legal	Extralegal	# Demands
Old Guard clients	73%	27%	N = 26
Old Guard radicals	25%	75%	N = 30
Next Generation	55%	45%	N = 49
Innovators	54%	46%	N = 27
Totals	52%	48%	N = 132

archetypal radicals of Pisulli were dogmatic in their pursuit of extralegal methods, Rosales's "deviant" experiments with legal strategies (39 percent) were crucial to chapter 3's categorization of Rosales as an Old Guard radical. Recall that the Rosales settlers punished or removed elected leaders who "dared" to deviate from the organization's primary identity. Hence, these apparent deviations actually constitute compelling evidence that Rosales strongly preferred extralegal methods. Similarly, Sector C's leaders occasionally initiated militant demands, but these attempts at services were hobbled by a lack of interest and support from the client settlers.

Straightforward counting of legal and extralegal demands is one indicator of strong strategy preferences, but examination of each case's strategy choices over time provides a more compelling depiction of Old Guard rigidity. Pro used conformist, militant, and bootstrap strategies, and Sector C used all four types of strategies, but despite experiments with militancy due to conformist failure, deviant leaders, or other circumstances, these settlers were clients at heart who repeatedly renewed their strong preference for legal petitioning and clientelist deals. In 1993, for example, Pro secretary general Donato Flores attempted to pressure Mayor Carmen Lezama into granting municipal recognition, but when this failed, Flores quickly reverted to conformist tactics, ushering in a four-year period based exclusively on clientelist deals. Only when the Pro organization experienced a drop in participation did its commitment to clientelism flag, at which point the moribund Pro cast about for alternatives, including militant and bootstrap bids for land titles, both of which failed.

Sector C also flirted with militant strategies, but three consecutive neighborhood leaders failed to mobilize the membership for these extralegal demands. In 1993, 1995, and 1998, Sector C leaders la Madrid, Ostros, and Vega each saw election-year opportunities and attempted to initiate militant demands, but each failed in part because of low participation. While Vega's failure in 1998 was primarily due to Sector C's then-moribund state, earlier attempts failed when neighborhood participation was still strong overall.

A similar story of strategic rigidity emerges with respect to the Old Guard radicals. Rosales relied heavily on extralegal methods, and when Jorge Encarnación

Sandoval (in 1998) and Claudio Tapia (in 2000–2001) attempted to initiate conformist demands, many settlers rebelled, undermining the demands as well as the organization itself. In 1997, Encarnación's bootstrap purchase of electricity did succeed, but he was "helped" by the privatization of electricity, which convinced the radical settlers that no other approach would work. The diehard radicals of Pisulli exhibited even stronger rigidity, virtually never deviating from militancy. Even their unusual acquisition of land titles was not a straightforward bootstrap purchase, but rather an odd militant/bootstrap hybrid with equally unusual results. Regardless, the trend is clear: all four Old Guard cases exhibited clear strategy preferences, and when they did dabble in alternative methods, their strategy choices did not follow any predictable pattern.

Analyzing Strategy Patterns: The Strategy Life Cycle

While Old Guard organizations exhibited strong or even rigid strategy preferences, the newer Next Generation and Innovator organizations exhibited remarkable strategic flexibility that is best captured analytically by the strategy life cycle. The aggregate numbers of legal and extralegal demands presented in table 6.5 suggested a relative indifference to strategy legality among Next Generation and Innovator organizations, but a chronological examination of strategy choices points not to indifference but to a predictable pattern.

All four Next Generation organizations followed strategy trajectories largely consistent with the life cycle concept. As younger organizations, Villa Mar and Paraíso had only begun the life cycle by 2005, but they were both consistent with the hypothesized progression from rogue to militant to conformist strategies. Recall that the framework does not expect a smooth path; instead, strategy trajectories tend to be messy, and organizations often move back and forth or simultaneously employ strategies from different quadrants of the typology. Despite several erratic turns in Villa Mar's trajectory, both young organizations moved through the early phases of the life cycle.

By 2005 Villa Mar and Paraíso had just begun experimenting with conformist strategies, but the older cases of Oasis and Camino provide a fuller picture of the Next Generation's strategy life cycle. Oasis began with a quick succession of rogue, militant, and conformist demands (1994–95), and then settled into a streak of militancy (1995–97) under Secretary General Campos, before progressing to a four-year period of conformist and bootstrap strategies (1997–2001) under Secretary General Goñe. Interestingly, Oasis then deviated from the life cycle into militancy once it became moribund, in a manner similar to that of Pro, whose Old Guard rigidity broke down as neighborhood participation dropped. This may point to the possibility that clear strategy patterns are most likely to break down when an organization is struggling to survive. In 2005, Oasis was still relying on conformist strategies and, other than their 1997 purchase of privately provided electricity, had not begun employing bootstrap methods.

Of the four Next Generation case studies, Camino best fits the strategy life cycle's expectations. Camino began in 1990 with rogue theft of electricity, quickly moved on to militant demands for recognition and water truck service, and then settled into three years of exclusively conformist demands. By 1995, Camino was taking tentative steps toward self-sufficiency through conformist/bootstrap acquisition of piped water and sewers, but it was not until 2001 that an initially hostile Mayor Paco Moncayo forced the community to adopt a pure bootstrap strategy for sewer installation, as direct municipal support came to an end. The case of Camino offers a clear picture of the strategy life cycle, but it also demonstrates why straightforward counting of demands, though important, is only one part of any complete analysis. Considering Camino's fourteen service demands, 79 percent of them were based on legal strategies, which is roughly comparable to the demands of the Old Guard clients in Sector C (69 percent) and Pro (77 percent). Yet the case studies in chapters 3 and 4 showed that the stories behind these deceptively similar numbers were quite different. Camino settlers pursued their militant and conformist demands with equal vigor, and likely would have employed greater militancy had their clientelist deals not delivered services so successfully.

The Innovator organizations also followed the strategy life cycle, although Encantada's strategy trajectory diverged wildly when it began pressing demands on behalf of the 2002 expansion invasion that added hundreds of new shanty-homes to the neighborhood. Nonetheless, prior to this shift, Encantada appeared to be a model Innovator, whose strategies steadily progressed through five phases: (1) rogue theft of electricity; (2) militant demands for recognition and water truck service; (3) a back-and-forth period of both militant and conformist demands; (4) a back-and-forth period of both conformist and bootstrap demands; and (5) bootstrap attempts at piped water and sewers.

Although Encantada's deviation to militant and rogue strategies in 2002–3 clearly disrupted its compliance with the life cycle, it also underscores the hypothesis raised in chapter 1 that the life cycle may be an effective response to a changing context wherein certain strategy types are best suited for demands associated with a particular stage of development. In the case of Encantada, we saw the unusual situation of a consolidated organization pressing rather basic demands, which makes it all the more interesting that this community reverted to extralegal methods for the initial tasks of the expansion invasion, such as electricity and municipal recognition.

Itchimbía was also a model adherent of the strategy life cycle. Although Itchimbía spent a long period (four years) relying on rogue and militant strategies, it nonetheless followed the cycle from rogue/militancy to conformist strategies to conformist/bootstrap methods. The final demands for condominium services were both complex and long lasting. They began as a conformist/bootstrap project, but by 2003, when the settlers took possession of their new homes, the installation of individual services had largely become the settlers' own responsibility. Hence, although the settlers flexibly augmented one demand with a militant protest march (leading to a service victory), their demands in this final 2003–5 period relied chiefly on conformist/bootstrap strategies.

Implications for Organizational Strategy

Considering the trajectories of all ten cases, this study has provided evidence that Old Guard organizations are likely to exhibit strong preferences for either legal or extralegal methods, while Next Generation and Innovator groups exhibit strategic flexibility and follow the contours of the strategy life cycle. But what explains the different behavior? Although both external factors (e.g., mayoral hostility, privatization of service provision) and internal factors (e.g., organizational resources) help shape strategy choices with respect to *specific* demands (see next section on organizational success), broader *patterns* of organizational strategy choices are driven by factors correlated with organizational type.

First, degree of *leadership experience* is an important indicator of likely strategy pattern. Recall that Old Guard groups tend to be led by veterans, who often bring with them ingrained ideas about "what works." By contrast, the newer types are led by novices, who seem open to a variety of strategies. The technology and media use that characterizes some Innovator demands might seem to suggest that the younger generation is simply more comfortable with changes wrought by technology, but this explanation falters when we consider the Next Generation organizations, which are also led by young settlers yet exhibit different identity and repertoire traits on several dimensions (see table 1.1).

Second, the *political context* also shapes strategy patterns. The newer generations of settlers grew up exposed not only to their parents' stories of founding their communities but also to the ongoing process of settlement formation and development based on a diverse array of strategies and tactics. These younger leaders became politically active during a period of both decreasing partisan affiliation as well as more widespread ideological moderation, all of which contributed to the formation of less rigid organizational identities. Although organizational type alone cannot predict how a group will act with respect to a specific service demand, it does appear to be a powerful predictor of overall strategy pattern.

ANALYZING ORGANIZATIONAL SUCCESS

How well does the neighborhood service acquisition model explain the success or failure of individual service demands? Does analysis of the model support the hypothesized causal relationships among external and internal factors? And does the model's application to the land invasion phenomenon contribute to opportunity structure theory while also validating the continuing relevance of political process theory to understanding urban popular movements in Latin America? To answer these questions, this section revisits and disaggregates the neighborhood service acquisition model and analyzes seven specific hypotheses with respect to 131 service demands.[6]

Identifying Causal Claims: Disaggregating the Service Acquisition Model

The neighborhood service acquisition model combines external and internal factors to explain organizational success outcomes through a series of causal relationships and interactions. Figure 6.2 again presents chapter 1's neighborhood service acquisition model, but *strategy type* is disaggregated into its component dimensions—strategy legality and strategy autonomy—and *neighborhood regime type* is split into organizational competitiveness and organizational inclusiveness. This disaggregation permits clearer articulation of the study's causal hypotheses, which are represented by the various arrows in figure 6.2. Six main hypotheses are illustrated:

1. *hostile/friendly mayor* affects *strategy legality*—hostile mayors make all demands less likely to succeed, but extralegal demands are especially likely to fail;
2. *public/private service provider* affects *strategy autonomy*—privatization of service provision makes externally dependent strategies much less feasible;
3. *influential allies* interacts with *organizational competitiveness* to affect *success/failure in service acquisition*—noncompetitive organizations produce more stable leadership, which can take fuller advantage of alliances;
4. *local avenues of participation* interacts with *organizational inclusiveness* to affect *success/failure in service acquisition*—power-sharing groups are

6. This excludes Encantada's final demand, which was still in progress in 2005 (see note 4).

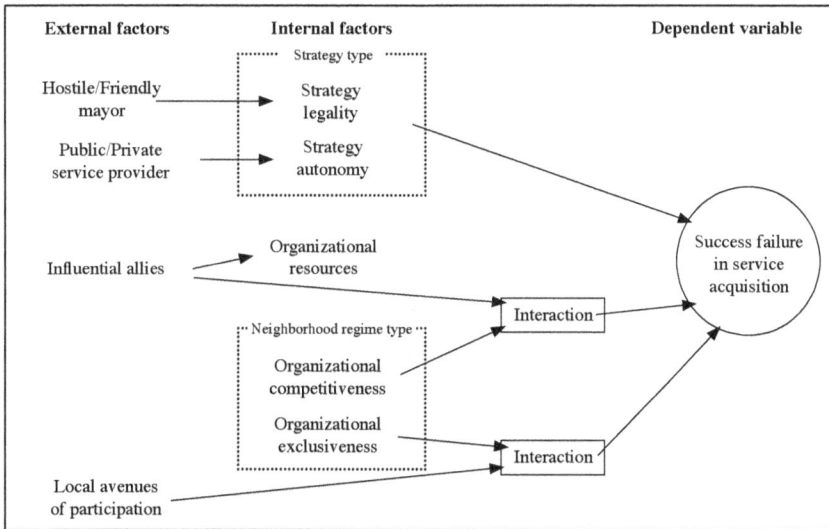

Fig. 6.2   Disaggregated service acquisition model

not threatened by new avenues of participation and are thus better able to take advantage of such opportunities;

5. *organizational resources* affects *strategy autonomy*—increased resources (e.g., membership participation) increases the feasibility of self-sufficient strategies; and

6. *strategy type* affects *success/failure in service acquisition*—certain strategies are more effective than others, depending on the specific service demanded.

In addition to these hypotheses illustrated in figure 6.2, a related hypothesis emerges from the sixth hypothesis. If certain strategies are more effective in certain situations, it stands to reason that strategic flexibility would permit an organization to pursue the optimal strategy in a greater number of situations. Hence:

7. *organizational type* affects *strategy type*—strategically rigid organizations will often fail to use the optimal strategy or will implement the optimal strategy poorly.[7]

The study does not advance a separate hypothesis with respect to the causal link between *influential allies* and *organizational resources*, but figure 6.2 nonetheless includes an arrow to acknowledge that in some cases, a generous

7. Note that organizational type does not appear in the model. This is because although certain strategies, resources, and neighborhood regimes typify different types of organizations,

patron party or NGO can dramatically increase an organization's available financial resources. Rather than develop an additional hypothesis, however, this phenomenon is discussed as part of the hypothesized interaction between allies and competitiveness.

Analyzing Organizational Success: External Dimensions of Opportunity

Factors external to land invasion organizations shape opportunities for successful service demands. Drawing partly on Tarrow's "dimensions of opportunity" (1998, 76–80), the model emphasizes the causal role of four external variables: *mayoral position* (hostile, neutral, or friendly), *service provider* (public or private), *influential allies* (partisan or nonpartisan), and *local avenues of participation* (local elections or participatory frameworks). All four of these factors affect the success or failure of individual service demands, but while the mayoral position and service provider affect strategy type, which in turn affects the outcome, the latter two variables—allies and avenues of participation—interact with neighborhood regime type to affect the outcome. The model thus advances four causal claims with respect to external factors, each of which will be analyzed separately.

Mayoral Hostility Forces Organizations to Rely on Risky Extralegal Strategies

Invasion organizations that face a hostile district or metropolitan mayor are more likely both to adopt risky extralegal strategies and to have those extralegal strategies fail. Table 6.6 shows the aggregate success rates of fifty-nine legal service demands and sixty-five extralegal demands, and also lists the success rates for each type of demand under hostile, neutral, and friendly mayors. Table 6.6 illustrates two claims: that mayoral hostility makes extralegal strategies more likely to be employed and that mayoral hostility makes such strategies more likely to fail—an unfortunate pair of effects for settlers on the wrong side of city hall. Of the thirty-two service demands made under a hostile mayor, twenty-three were extralegal (72 percent),[8] compared to twenty-six of forty-two demands (62

---

an organization's type is not the *cause* of these traits; rather it is a conceptual shorthand for such traits. In other words, an organization's rigid strategy choices, unoriginal tactics, and power-concentrating regime lead to its classification as a part of the Old Guard, not the other way around. Exclusion of organizational type as a distinct variable—rather than an implicit background factor—also results in a more parsimonious model that can offer a general causal road map for any service attempt, regardless of the organization that demands it.

8. To be clear, the 35 percent listed in the Hostile/Extralegal cell refers to the *success rate* of these twenty-three demands. Thus, the 72 percent figure in the text refers to the proportion of extralegal demands made under a hostile mayor.

Table 6.6   Success rates by strategy legality and mayoral position

Strategy legality	Mayoral position			
	Hostile	Neutral	Friendly	Total
Legal	67% (N = 9)	50% (N = 16)	59% (N = 34)	58% (N = 59)
Extralegal	35% (N = 23)	46% (N = 26)	56% (N = 16)	45% (N = 65)
Totals	44% (N = 32)	48% (N = 42)	58% (N = 50)	51% (N = 124)

Note: In this and subsequent tables, the percentages are success rates. The success rate in a Total cell for a given column or row represents the average of the corresponding percentages *weighted by the N of each relevant cell* (i.e., simply averaging the percentages irrespective of the N will yield a different and incorrect overall success rate). Percentages have been rounded. Table excludes seven demands that combined legal and extralegal strategies. Also, this and subsequent tables exclude one demand that was still in progress in 2005.

percent) under a neutral mayor and sixteen of fifty demands (32 percent) under a friendly mayor. A good example of this trend was Itchimbía. In the face of hostility from both Mayor Mahuad and Mayor Sevilla, Itchimbía relied exclusively on extralegal demands for five years. With the election of the (eventually) friendly Mayor Moncayo, however, Itchimbía switched to legal strategies.

Table 6.6 also shows that extralegal demands are more likely to fail with a hostile mayor. Under a hostile mayor, extralegal demands succeeded only 35 percent of the time, compared with 46 percent success under a neutral mayor and 56 percent under a friendly mayor. Pisulli provides a stark or even exaggerated illustration of this finding. Between 1984 and 1988, all three of Pisulli's extralegal demands failed in the face of government hostility, but between 1988 and 2005, all five of the organization's extralegal demands succeeded under a neutral metropolitan mayor. Hence, both by forcing settlers to adopt extralegal methods and by opposing those extralegal demands, hostile mayors often play an important role in blocking settler demands.

Privatization Condemns Externally Dependent Strategies to Failure

Although self-sufficient demands tend to succeed more often, externally dependent strategies generally remain important and more common, but privatization of service provision makes such methods almost certain to fail. Table 6.7's summary of the success rates of 120 service demands with respect to strategy autonomy and service provider reveals an unambiguous effect of privatization—that externally dependent strategies have almost no chance of succeeding when employed to demand privatized services. Although such strategies succeeded about half the time when targeting a publicly provided service, all nine such demands for private services failed. In northern Lima, for example, Pro

Table 6.7   Success rates by strategy autonomy and service provider

Strategy autonomy	Service provider		
	Private	Public	Totals
Externally dependent	0% (N = 9)	51% (N = 85)	46% (N = 94)
Self-sufficient	78% (N = 9)	76% (N = 17)	77% (N = 26)
Totals	39% (N = 18)	55% (N = 102)	53% (N = 120)

Note: Table excludes eleven demands that combined externally dependent and self-sufficient strategies.

Developers denied numerous externally dependent attempts by the neighborhoods of Pro, Sector C, and Rosales to acquire land titles. The impossibility of squeezing private goods out of corporations forces settlers to adopt self-sufficient methods, which are employed much less frequently: only 26 of 120 demands (22 percent) used rogue or bootstrap strategies (not shown in table 6.7). Encantada provides a good illustration. In early 1997, the community used a combination militant/conformist strategy to acquire publicly provided electricity for several city blocks. In late 1997, however, after privatization of electricity, Encantada used a bootstrap approach to buy service for the remaining blocks. Self-sufficient strategies like this are more likely to succeed (77 percent success versus 46 percent for externally dependent demands), but this is likely because settlers undertake self-sufficient attempts at services primarily when they believe they have the means to succeed.

Noncompetitive Organizations Maximize Alliance Benefits

Overall, noncompetitive organizations benefited more consistently from alliances than did competitive organizations, but closer inspection reveals that although this difference held true for nonpartisan allies, both noncompetitive and competitive groups were equally able to benefit from partisan alliances. Table 6.8 calculates the success rates of competitive and noncompetitive organizations with respect to influential allies. The table illustrates that although all organizations benefit from the presence of any type of ally, noncompetitive groups may do a better job taking advantage of alliances. For example, noncompetitive and competitive groups had about the same success rate without allies (43 percent versus 41 percent), but with an ally, noncompetitive groups succeeded 81 percent of the time, whereas competitive groups succeeded only 65 percent of the time. For example, noncompetitive organizations like Pro (1990–92), Pisulli, Camino, and Itchimbía all made excellent and consistent use of allies. This stands in stark contrast to the competitive Rosales organization, however, which could never forge a lasting relationship with local NGOs, in part due to frequent and polarizing leadership turnovers.

Table 6.8   Success rates by influential allies and organizational competitiveness

Organizational competitiveness	Influential allies				
	None	Any	Partisan	Nonpartisan	Totals
Competitive	41% (N = 49)	65% (N = 26)	90% (N = 10)	50% (N = 16)	49% (N = 75)
Noncompetitive	43% (N = 30)	81% (N = 26)	92% (N = 12)	71% (N = 14)	79% (N = 56)
Totals	42% (N = 79)	73% (N = 52)	91% (N = 22)	60% (N = 30)	54% (N = 131)

Note: "Partisan" refers to allies representing or affiliated with political parties. "Nonpartisan" refers to allies such as domestic and international NGOs, as well as other invasion organizations. The Partisan and Nonpartisan columns are subsets of the Any column. Hence, the Totals column is the sum of the None and Any columns.

Separating demands backed by partisan allies from those supported by nonpartisan allies, however, reveals that this difference between noncompetitive and competitive organizations is almost entirely accounted for by the latter set of demands. Among demands made with partisan help, competitive and noncompetitive groups both succeed close to 90 percent of the time. What does this mean? Does organizational competitiveness weaken a group's capacity for building certain kinds of alliances but not others, or is this simply a correlation that is not causally significant? This is an especially important question to answer because this study did not present any a priori theoretical expectation for this kind of difference.

Based on qualitative analysis of each individual alliance-backed demand, I conclude that the correlation is not causally significant. Although demands by competitive organizations with nonpartisan allies do have a lower success rate, this set of cases does not support the conclusion that this is representative of a recurring causal effect. The demands that failed within this subset of cases generally exhibited other factors that explained their failure. Oasis, for example, succeeded with its three partisan-backed demands and failed with most of its nonpartisan-supported demands, but this is because the latter occurred disproportionately during its moribund stage of development, when participation levels had sunk. Similarly, Encantada succeeded with a variety of demands supported by both partisan and nonpartisan allies, but when it entered its moribund stage, the community also happened to rely on a nonpartisan ally, further skewing statistics. In conclusion, while the sample does support the general claim that noncompetitive groups tend to gain maximum advantage from alliances, there is no clear support for arguments about specific types of alliances.[9]

9. Schönwälder (2002, 50–54) finds that popular movements have a variety of options, including autonomy, partisan partnerships, broader alliances, and the formation of multiple alliances. This study suggests that noncompetitive groups are more likely to excel at the latter three options.

Table 6.9   Success rates by local avenues of participation and organizational inclusiveness

	Local avenues of participation		
Organizational inclusiveness	No	Yes	Totals
Power-sharing	57% (N = 53)	67% (N = 21)	59% (N = 74)
Power-concentrating	55% (N = 38)	32% (N = 19)	47% (N = 57)
Totals	56% (N = 91)	50% (N = 40)	54% (N = 131)

Power-Sharing Organizations Benefit from Local Avenues of Participation

The opening of access to participation through local elections and other participatory frameworks creates opportunities for invasion organizations, but while power-sharing groups are able to take advantage of these openings, power-concentrating groups often cannot. Table 6.9 lists the service demand success rates by organizational inclusiveness and local avenues of participation.

Table 6.9 illustrates the claim that power-sharing groups succeed more often with local avenues of participation, while power-concentrating groups fare better without such avenues. Demands by power-sharing organizations succeeded 57 percent of the time without a local avenue of participation, and this figure increased to 67 percent with a participatory opportunity. The reverse was true for power-concentrating groups. Organizations like Pro, Rosales, and Pisulli succeeded 55 percent of the time without a local avenue of participation, but this figure dropped to 32 percent when settlers tried to exploit participatory opportunities. For example, the power-sharing Oasis organization made four election-year demands in 1995 and 1998, three of which succeeded. Oasis also successfully acquired electricity and land titles through the participatory Multisectoral Commission. Oasis's subsequent attempts to use the Multisectoral failed, but these demands were compromised by Oasis's moribund state, rather than a general inability to take advantage of the Multisectoral's participatory framework.

By comparison, the power-concentrating Sector C had an overall success rate of 38 percent (see table 6.1), but when making demands timed to coincide with the 1993, 1995, 1998, and 2002 elections, Sector C's demands invariably failed. How can this be? Election time does provide some of the best opportunities for land invasion organizations to press their demands, but Sector C's electoral regime concentrated decision-making power in the hands of each successive secretary general (la Madrid, Ostros, and Vega), and each experimented briefly with militant demands that the membership refused to support. In a power-sharing organization, leaders are less likely to make such unilateral decisions, which may position them to better exploit available avenues of participation.

Analyzing Organizational Success: Internal Mobilization of Resources

Although external factors dictate the landscape of the political opportunity structure, the capacity of invasion organizations to exploit particular opportunities often hinges on internal factors. The model emphasizes three internal variables: *strategy type* (rogue, militant, conformist, or bootstrap), *organizational resources* (assets, practices, or skills), and *neighborhood regime type* (authoritarian, electoral, democratic, or consensual). The study advances three specific causal claims related to these factors, each of which is analyzed separately.

High Organizational Resources Facilitate Success of Self-Sufficient Strategies

In general, higher levels of organizational resources make *all* strategies more likely to succeed, but self-sufficient strategies benefit in particular since they rely more heavily on the organization itself. This causal relationship is more difficult to theorize than most because organizational resources are so varied in form. In the present context, key resources can include: (1) organizational assets such as money and membership size, unity, or participation; (2) routinized practices such as obligatory *minga* community work projects or daily meetings; (3) leadership skills such as organization, cooperation, or negotiation; and (4) specialized skills in the fields of law, architecture, or journalism.

Since the multifaceted nature of organizational resources makes it difficult to analyze the claim that higher resource levels facilitate self-sufficient strategies, let me present several pieces of anecdotal evidence from the cases of Sector C and Encantada in support of the specific claim that the resource of *participation* has this kind of positive effect. As this method is less satisfactory than the more systematic evidence in support of other hypotheses, however, we must be especially cautious in drawing inferences from these examples.

While participation remained high, Sector C successfully stole and later purchased electricity service; once participation had fallen, however, its bootstrap attempt at land titles failed, both because of low financial resources and because low levels of participation gave Secretary General Vega little leverage to bargain for a better price. Encantada provides an even clearer example. In 1996 and 1997, high participation helped Encantada steal and then purchase electricity service, but in 2001–2, Encantada's bootstrap attempt at piped water failed. Between 2002 and 2005, however, Encantada emerged from its moribund state and consolidated, and a resurgence in participation helped its rogue theft of electricity succeed and rejuvenated its bootstrap attempt at piped water. These cases illustrate the trend, but exceptions also occur. In 1996, Itchimbía made its first attempt to install an illegal water pipe system, but failed despite near-total membership participation, as they could not yet afford to buy an electric water pump. Although this shows that high participation may not be enough, this was still a case where low organizational resources compromised a self-sufficient strategy.

Note that the model claims not only that high resources facilitate self-sufficient success but also that resource level affects strategy choice. In other words, organization leaders tend to correctly assess their capacity to implement self-sufficient strategies, and so they do not attempt them if they are likely to fail. This makes sense, as leaders usually have more information about their own organization's resources than those of, for example, a domestic NGO or local mayor. Still, leaders obviously miscalculate on both fronts, as shown by Sector C's attempts to use militant strategies with a membership that generally rejected extralegal methods.

Different Strategies Prove Optimal for Different Service Demands

Not only does the effectiveness of each strategy type vary with different external opportunity structure contexts, but it also varies according to the specific service demand; crucially, when ordered according to the common chronology of demands, the data suggest that shifts in the optimal strategy choice over time may correspond to the strategy life cycle. Table 6.10 lists the success rates of each strategy type with respect to the six major service demands (demands for water are split between demands for water truck service and demands for piped water). These data point to the likelihood that an optimal strategy may exist for certain service demands. In reading the table entries, note that some percentages may be unreliable due to a very small sample size. In some cells, the number of demands proves more instructive than the success rate. For example, the fact that 100 percent of rogue demands for sewer drainage succeeded tells us very little, since only one such demand occurred. The fact that this demand represents a mere 6 percent of the seventeen demands for sewers, however, tells us that it is very difficult to steal sewer drainage service, even if the one attempt (by Itchimbía) did succeed.

With respect to specific services, at least four observations can be made: (1) electricity was the easiest service to acquire, regardless of strategy employed, with fully 88 percent of all demands succeeding; (2) settlers did not even attempt to use self-sufficient strategies to acquire water truck service or municipal recognition because these services are inherently external in their provision; (3) most demands for piped water and sewer service relied on externally dependent strategies; and (4) extralegal demands for land titles appear to have had no chance of success, and land titles were also the most difficult service to acquire.

With respect to specific strategy types, four more trends are apparent: (1) rogue strategies were used mainly to steal electricity, but were occasionally employed for other demands; (2) militant strategies were the most common (N = 53) and the least reliable (34 percent success rate), but had a chance at

Table 6.10   Success rates by strategy type and service demand

Service demand	Strategy type				
	Rogue	Militant	Conformist	Bootstrap	Totals
Electricity	91% (N = 11)	60% (N = 2.5)	86% (N = 7)	100% (N = 4.5)	88% (N = 25)
Water truck		50% (N = 8)	100% (N = 2)		60% (N = 10)
Recognition		43% (N = 17.5)	68% (N = 9.5)		52% (N = 27)
Piped water	50% (N = 2)	29% (N = 8.5)	87% (N = 7.5)	50% (N = 2)	55% (N = 20)
Sewers	100% (N = 1)	45% (N = 5.5)	63% (N = 8)	100% (N = 2.5)	65% (N = 17)
Land titles		0% (N = 11)	23% (N = 11)	38% (N = 4)	15% (N = 26)
Totals	86% (N = 14)	34% (N = 53)	63% (N = 45)	73% (N = 13)	54% (N = 125)

Note: For this table only, hybrid strategies (e.g., conformist/bootstrap) are split between two columns and counted as 0.5 in each respective column. Empty cells indicate that no demands for that service were made with that type of strategy. The table excludes Villa Mar's theft and later purchase of water through a garden hose, as these instances cannot be considered demands for water truck or piped water service.

working for all services except land titles; (3) conformist strategies succeeded 63 percent of the time, but this figure rises to 76 percent if land title demands are excluded, making conformist methods almost twice as likely to succeed as militant demands; and (4) self-sufficient rogue and bootstrap strategies had 86 percent and 73 percent success rates, respectively, but were also the least common, with only 14 of 125 demands (11 percent) using rogue methods and 13 of 125 demands (10 percent) using bootstrap strategies.

Combining these descriptive observations leads to the analytically important insight that the strategy life cycle may, by accident or design, correspond to a highly effective progression of optimal strategy choices. Referring again to table 6.10, note that the services are listed in an order typical of the service demand trajectory of many invasion organizations. Many organizations begin with demands for electricity and water truck service and then, after acquiring municipal recognition, move on to demands for piped water and sewer drainage. Land titles are often the last service acquired.

Now consider how the life cycle does a fairly good job of optimizing strategy choices. The life cycle begins with rogue theft of electricity, then shifts to militant and conformist demands for most services, and concludes with conformist and bootstrap demands for land titles and major water and sewer infrastructure. Looking at the success rates in table 6.10, this progression finds some support in the numbers. Yet the idea of the life cycle being an optimal strategy pattern is appealing, since the Next Generation and Innovator cases were generally more successful than the Old Guard. In conclusion, table 6.10 does show that service-specific optimal strategies exist, but cannot offer clear support for the contention that strategic flexibility gives newer types an advantage over the rigid Old Guard. To pursue the latter claim, we turn to the section's final table.

Strategic Rigidity Results in Suboptimal Service Demands

Table 6.11 describes the success rates of each type of strategy by organizational type. Since the Old Guard sample includes both client and radical cases whose strategy preferences are different, these subtypes are also shown in order to disaggregate the Old Guard success rates. The rogue and bootstrap columns contain relatively few cases in each cell (samples range from two to six cases), but comparing the militant and conformist columns, it appears that all three types are about as good at using militant strategies, while conformist strategies are best used by the Innovators, followed by the Next Generation, followed by the Old Guard. Disaggregating the Old Guard type, however, shows that Old Guard clients are in the same league as the Next Generation when using conformist strategies, and that Old Guard radicals are the clear experts at using militant strategies.

Cautious of the fact that having a small number of cases in a given cell can yield dramatic swings in success rates, it is nonetheless notable that Old Guard clients always failed when using militant strategies (N = 5) and Old Guard radicals always failed when using conformist strategies (N = 4). Yet if Old Guard groups always fail when they "violate" their strategy preference, why deviate at all?

The finding that optimal strategies exist for certain service demands suggests that strategic rigidity ties the hands of Old Guard organizations and sometimes forces them to choose between a suboptimal strategy that may fail because it is the "wrong choice" and an optimal strategy that may fail because the organization leader or the membership oppose such methods. The clearest example of this trend was Rosales, where three consecutive demands for piped water failed despite a neutral or friendly mayor and high participation. The first two suboptimal militant demands failed, but when Rosales finally shifted to the optimal strategy of conformist negotiation, the membership rebelled against Secretary General Tapia and their demand failed yet again. Similarly, the 1993 municipal election in the district of San Martín de Porres presented Sector C with a good opportunity to press a militant demand for recognition, but when Secretary General la Madrid attempted just that, the membership did not turn out to march. Hence, Old Guard organizations are more likely to have demands that either use the "wrong" strategy or use the optimal strategy poorly.

Implications for Organizational Success

Combined in the service acquisition model, these seven hypotheses explain the success or failure of individual demands. Considering the model's implications

Table 6.11   Success rates by strategy type and organizational type

Organization type	Strategy type				
	Rogue	Militant	Conformist	Bootstrap	Totals
Old Guard	75% (N = 4)	35% (N = 23)	47% (N = 19)	60% (N = 5)	45% (N = 51)
Next Generation	100% (N = 5)	28% (N = 18)	60% (N = 15)	75% (N = 4)	52% (N = 42)
Innovators	83% (N = 6)	33% (N = 9)	83% (N = 6)	50% (N = 2)	61% (N = 23)
Totals	87% (N = 15)	32% (N = 50)	58% (N = 40)	63% (N = 11)	51% (N = 116)
Old Guard subtypes					
Clients	100% (N = 1)	0% (N = 5)	60% (N = 15)	33% (N = 3)	46% (N = 24)
Radicals	67% (N = 3)	44% (N = 18)	0% (N = 4)	100% (N = 2)	46% (N = 26)

Note: Table excludes fifteen demands that employed combination strategies (e.g., militant/conformist).

for an organization as a whole, the model predicts that a worst-case scenario for organizational success would be a rigid Old Guard organization with an electoral regime whose internal competition prevents it from forging alliances and whose power-concentrating leaders cannot take advantage of avenues of participation. Indeed, this describes Rosales, which by 2005 was the least developed neighborhood in the entire district of Los Olivos and had one of the poorest success rates (33 percent) within this study's sample of cases. On the other hand, the model's best-case scenario would be a flexible Next Generation or Innovator organization with a consensual regime whose lack of internal competition facilitates many lasting alliances and whose power-sharing leadership meshes well with local avenues of participation. This describes Itchimbía, the invasion organization superstar that in less than a decade secured low-cost condominiums with full services.

ANALYZING ORGANIZATIONAL SURVIVAL

How well does the security trap concept explain why some organizations become moribund while others evade the trap and consolidate? And how well do the organizational stages of development analytically capture the important junctures in an organization's survival trajectory? To answer these questions, this section examines the ten neighborhood cases across each stage of development and investigates the survival trajectories common to each organizational type. I then take a closer look at the cases that achieved property security in order to evaluate the study's causal explanation for organizational survival or decline.

Describing Survival Trajectories

In order to analyze contrasting outcomes in organizational survival, we must first have a comparative understanding of the survival trajectory of each case study. We begin with the broad developmental contours of each organizational type and then take a closer look at the impact of attaining property security.

New Organizational Types Reach the Security Trap More Quickly

Comparison of the stages of development of the ten cases reveals that the Next Generation and the Innovators arrive at the security trap more quickly than the Old Guard. While nascent periods were roughly similar in length across organizational types, lengths of mature periods varied. The nascent stage typically ranged from one to three years (Camino's was four years) for all three types. The mature stage, however, ranged from four to eleven years among Old Guard cases, but only a brief two to six years among organizations of the newer types (this excludes Villa Mar and Paraíso, which each only began their mature stage in 2002 and by 2005 had not yet attained property security). This trend is likely due either to a broad shift in how easily invasion organizations acquire property security or to the repertoire traits of the newer types. Since the trend held in both Lima and Quito, the capacity of each group to employ optimal strategies surfaces as a likely cause. Note that of the seven cases that achieved property security, only Oasis and Encantada did so through straightforward acquisition of land titles. Although several of the other five organizations did eventually acquire titles, the initial sense of security arose from either reliable and sustained service provision or from confidence that titles would eventually arrive. Consider also that Oasis and Encantada benefited from the enthusiasm of Peru's state titling agency, COFOPRI, though this provided little benefit to Pro and Sector C. Thus, rigidity-driven, suboptimal Old Guard strategies might prolong the struggle for property security, but do Old Guard demands really encounter increased resistance as such organizations mature?

Property Security Leads to Sharp Split in Success Rates

Comparison of service demand success rates by organizational type and stage of development provides supporting evidence for the claim that service demand failure by mature Old Guard organizations may prolong the struggle for property security. Table 6.12 shows the success rates of each organizational type by stage of development and tells a striking story about the contrasting fates of mature Old Guard, Next Generation, and Innovator organizations. Although nascent Old Guard organizations started out strong with a 65 percent success

Table 6.12   Success rates by organizational type and stage of development

Stage of development	Organizational type			
	Old Guard	Next Generation	Innovator	Totals
Nascent	65% (N = 17)	67% (N = 21)	50% (N = 12)	62% (N = 50)
Mature	37% (N = 30)	47% (N = 19)	75% (N = 8)	46% (N = 57)
Moribund	17% (N = 6)	25% (N = 4)	0% (N = 1)	18% (N = 11)
Consolidated	100% (N = 3)	100% (N = 3)	86% (N = 7)	92% (N = 13)
Totals	46% (N = 56)	57% (N = 47)	64% (N = 28)	54% (N = 131)

rate, suboptimal strategy choices spurred by strategic rigidity contributed to a low (37 percent) success rate as these organizations demanded piped water, sewer drainage, and land titles. For example, the mature radicals of Rosales and Pisulli refused to negotiate with neutral and hostile governments, and the mature clients of Sector C insisted on using ineffective conformist strategies despite an unreceptive government.

Collectively, the Next Generation organizations experienced a similar drop from a 67 percent success rate during their nascent stages to 47 percent during their mature stages, but this aggregate figure is driven partly by the string of failures encountered by the young Villa Mar and Paraíso cases, which had not yet concluded their mature stage in 2005. Camino and Oasis, by contrast, were very successful during this stage. The nascent Camino had begun with a cycle of rogue, militant, and conformist strategies, but then settled into a streak of conformist and conformist/bootstrap demands during its mature stage, all to excellent effect (all five such demands succeeded). The mature Oasis was similarly successful, setting aside the rogue and militant methods of its nascent stage in favor of militant, conformist, and bootstrap strategies, most of which succeeded (75 percent). Finally, the Innovators began with a 50 percent success rate, but *improved* to 75 percent during their mature stages as each organization "hit its stride," exploring creative methods of demand-making that generally proved successful.

While the newer types of organizations appear to have the upper hand during their mature stage of development, all three types exhibit similar success rates during their moribund stages (0 to 25 percent) and consolidated stages (86 to 100 percent). Why do all three types share this dramatic contrast? Is an organization's stage of development really such an all-powerful predictor, or is this simply a tautology, wherein periods of failure are labeled as moribund and, thus, moribund organizations tend to fail? Answering this question and testing the logic of the security trap requires analysis of the study's cases of moribund and consolidated organizations.

Analyzing Survival Outcomes: Explaining the Security Trap

Comparative analysis of moribund and consolidated organizations reveals the powerful—but escapable—logic of the security trap. This section excludes the cases of Rosales, Villa Mar, and Paraíso, which never attained property security, and focuses solely on the other seven organizations that became either moribund or consolidated. Table 6.13 summarizes select attributes of these eight cases (Encantada is listed twice as it had both a moribund stage and a consolidated stage).

Beginning with the right-hand column, table 6.13 reiterates the starkly contrasting success rates of moribund and consolidated organizations and implies a connection with highly correlated levels of participation. Earlier analysis in this chapter argued that organizational resources in the form of participation were one of several important causal factors, but table 6.13's correlation of low participation with demand failure and high participation with demand success points to a particularly strong causal role for organizational resources during an organization's moribund or consolidated periods. This finding fits both theoretical expectations and empirical data from earlier chapters, but what causes this striking correlation to emerge?

The remaining two columns in table 6.13 imply the importance of neighborhood regime and mixed motives in determining levels of participation and, thus, demand success rate. None of the four moribund cases had either an authoritarian regime or mixed motives, while all four consolidated cases had one or the other. I argue that these two factors constitute the crux of organizational survival for the latter set of cases, while the former groups' lack of either factor led them into the analytic framework's "default" path: the security trap.

Survival Outcome #1: Security Trap Snares Organization

When most organizations acquire property security and thus eliminate a key selective incentive, levels of participation immediately begin to drop, resulting in organizational decline and a general incapability of acquiring other needed services even under favorable conditions. In some sense, this outcome requires no additional explanation beyond the ideal-typical trajectory introduced in chapter 1. With respect to the security trap, Pro, Sector C, Oasis, and Encantada all present a similar story. Pro and Sector C attained a sense of security through sustained delivery of most services, while Oasis and Encantada acquired land titles, but all four organizations then experienced a drop in participation that resulted in the failure of nine of their eleven service demands (a meager 18 percent success rate). In some cases, the drop in participation was so debilitating as to create failure in the most unlikely situations. In Sector C, for example, the

Table 6.13   Comparing moribund and consolidated organizations

Stage in 2005	Invasion organization	Authoritarian leadership	Mixed motives	Participation level	Demand success rate
Moribund	Pro	No	No	Low	0% (N = 4)
	Sector C	No	No	Low	50% (N = 2)
	Oasis	No	No	Low**	25% (N = 4)
	Encantada*	No	No	Low	0% (N = 1)
Consolidated	Pisulli	Yes	No	High	100% (N = 3)
	Camino	Yes	No	High	100% (N = 3)
	Encantada*	No	Yes	Fairly high	100% (N = 2)
	Itchimbía	No	Yes	High	80% (N = 5)

*In 2002, Encantada made the unusual shift from a moribund to a consolidated stage of development.

**Participation was low in most of Oasis, but in Group 3 levels of participation increased under Efraín Huamán, leading to Oasis's lone victory during this period: sewer drainage for about half of Group 3 settlers (about 12 percent of the total population).

moribund neighborhood organization presided over a sewer system that, rather unbelievably, was completely built but not activated due to poor relations with the neighborhood of San Diego.

Likewise, when Oasis acquired land titles in 2000, it experienced a sharp drop in participation and membership, as many settlers sold their land and abandoned Oasis. For the nascent and mature stages of Oasis's trajectory, a lack of property security had motivated high levels of participation, while in its moribund stage, the disappearance of this key selective incentive was to blame for low participation and the failure to install sewer drainage even though the friendly district mayor had agreed to pay for it. This was a clear-cut illustration of Olson's (1965) logic of collective action: with no mechanism to enforce participation or punish free riders, remaining incentives such as water and drainage were insufficient to sustain even a modest level of mobilization. Other examples can be found in all four cases where organizations that had proved adept at navigating rugged political and geographic terrain suddenly appeared incompetent, as apparently satisfied settlers abandoned the organization. These organizations had been snared by the security trap and showed few signs of escaping.

Survival Outcome #2: Trap Evaded Through Authoritarian Mobilization

With the arrival of property security, the Old Guard settlers of Pisulli and the Next Generation settlers of Camino might have chosen to stop participating in neighborhood meetings, mobilizations, and work projects, but their authoritarian leaders did not permit them to quit. In Pisulli, Edgar Coral secured monopoly control over the settlement's land titles, giving him an effective blackmail tool with which to enforce the "permanent mobilization" of all settlers (Coral 2002, interview). Though he wielded power more subtly, Camino's Celso Meza was no less effective in sustaining settler participation. Through the implementation of weekly *mingas*, Meza kept all settlers working on neighborhood infrastructure well beyond the attainment of property security. The 33 percent of Camino settlers who received land titles in 2002 had even more incentive to abandon the organization, but as with a powerful home owners association that retains some authority over residents, these settlers still found themselves vulnerable to Meza's power to impose fines for nonparticipation. The settlers owned their homes, but they remained accountable to the organization and accountable to the boss. Despite these similarities, Coral and Meza differed in how settlers perceived their leadership. In numerous interviews, Pisulli settlers complained about Coral while looking over their shoulder, while Camino settlers praised Meza as a hero who went to jail for the community. Analytically, however, the two cases illustrate one clear method of evading the security trap.

Survival Outcome #3: Trap Evaded Through Mixed Motives

Although Innovators are unlikely to have authoritarian regimes, both the moribund Encantada and the mature Itchimbía found that their mixed motives helped revive or sustain settler participation in a period of property security. Itchimbía was characterized by tactical innovation, democratic governance, and mixed motives, and despite winning an impressive array of services and condominium titles was able to avoid the security trap and sustain participation. Although Itchimbía had a mixed agenda from the start, during its nascent and mature stages the selective incentive of property security alone might have been sufficient to motivate participation, though headline-grabbing tactics and deeply democratic governance probably helped boost participation to extraordinary levels. When property security arrived in 2000, however, Itchimbía had a long-established mixed agenda to fall back on, and participation remained high. The case of Itchimbía thus highlights the specific moment when the mixed motives emphasized by Elster and Udéhn begin to matter more than selective incentives.

Encantada initially relied on innovative tactics, democratic governance, and a material agenda to sustain very high participation and win services and then land titles, but this led to the security trap and a moribund organization. Only when Encantada shifted to a mixed-motives agenda could it overcome the security trap and rejuvenate participation. In many ways, the case of Itchimbía is more flamboyant, with its eye-catching Gandhian stunts and clandestine infrastructure, but analytically Encantada may be the more compelling case because it allows comparison of the 2000–2002 period of property security and material motives (low participation) with the 2002–5 period of property security and mixed motives (high participation).

Admittedly the Encantada case is not clear-cut. During its moribund stage, Encantada's tactics were equally moribund, so perhaps that contributed to low participation. And during its consolidated stage, the neighborhood grew in size and the newcomers had different needs, complicating the picture. Nonetheless, a process can be observed in which a disengaged community found inspiration in a fresh cause that also materially benefited its families with dramatic results, including leading an infrastructure project for fifty-four thousand people and hosting high-level dignitaries in a neighborhood that in 2005 did not yet appear on many city maps. At the conclusion of the study, the consolidated stages of the two Innovator cases were perhaps too new to assess their durability, but as of 2005, participation remained sufficiently strong for each organization to continue to press the demands of its members.

Implications for Organizational Survival

The survival outcomes observed in this study's eight cases of secure organizations point to two possible methods of evading the debilitating effects of the security trap. Authoritarian organizations sustained participation through enforced mobilization, while Innovator organizations kept participation up through mixed-motive agendas. For invasion organization survival, however, the bottom line is not whether an organization is authoritarian or activist, but whether it can find some means to sustain settler participation beyond attainment of property security.

Considering the Innovator cases, it may appear that the interplay of selective incentives and mixed motives is sufficient to explain organizational survival, suggesting that other factors such as innovative tactics and democratic governance are analytic deadweight. Indeed, if settlers rely on mixed motives, that alone may be sufficient for them to evade the security trap, but what makes an invasion organization likely and perhaps able to have mixed motives? The stories of Itchimbía and Encantada show that articulating and sustaining mixed motives in a context of economic desperation is challenging. In neighborhoods where settlers frequently go hungry, getting people to pursue ecological or community service work usually relies on educated and passionate leaders who can meaningfully integrate such a mission with the material agenda settlers so urgently need to accomplish. In these two cases, this integration was accomplished through an Innovator identity that supported mixed motives with tactical innovation and democratic governance. How do the roles of tactics and governance compare across cases? Consider the examples of Oasis, Encantada, and Itchimbía.

In the case of Oasis, high participation helped standard (noninnovative) tactics succeed, but there is no evidence that the nature of the tactics boosted participation levels. If anything, Oasis's clientelist partnerships may have dampened participation because little was expected of the settlers other than to vote for Cambio 90. And when the European Union built the Oasis water tanks, there was little role for the settlers, reinforcing the belief that such services were collective goods, which would always benefit free riders.

Winning services with innovative tactics (or any tactics) can hasten an organization's arrival at the security trap, but since the use of creative tactics is part of the Innovator identity, this effect can be partially offset by settler enthusiasm for being part of a unique and important mission. In Encantada, the settlers pursued a novel public health strategy that used television to recast the land conflict as a case of victimized infants and children. Such creative tactics helped lay the foundation for the organization's eventual articulation of a greater community mission. In 2002, when the Encantada settlers began focusing on helping other neighborhoods, they had stories to tell of the "legendary" founding of Encantada and the "epic" struggle they waged against Agrosilves and city hall. Encantada also created an e-mail network to contact international donors and led a huge coalition to develop the zone's infrastructure. And in Itchimbía, excitement for tactical innovation was palpable. The settlers foiled three eviction attempts with nonviolence and built a high-quality, clandestine service infrastructure. They produced video documentaries of their struggles for use in organizing workshops, and also maintained an extensive e-mail network that delivered crucial opposition to an eviction attempt by the mayor, as well as connections with Spanish and German NGOs that supported the condominium project.

Like tactical innovation, democratic governance plays a supporting role in explaining participation and organizational survival. Democratic governance can lead to a factionalism that renders some organizations ineffective, but members of Innovator organizations (which are focused on democratic transformation) logically expect neighborhood governance to also be democratic, and having opportunities to participate (e.g., committees, assemblies) can facilitate sustained participation. In Oasis and Encantada, this meant regular elections, some of which were hotly contested. In Itchimbía, Athenian democracy reigned, supported by a modest neighborhood size that made consensus feasible. Itchimbía's top leadership rarely changed, but this reflected widespread enthusiasm for leaders like María Hernández, not electoral authoritarianism. In all three case studies, democratic neighborhood institutions provided many opportunities for involvement, but only in Itchimbía and Encantada was democratic governance a pillar around which an Innovator identity coalesced.

The case of Oasis suggests that democratic governance is insufficient to sustain participation in the face of the security trap, and the 1996–2002 period in Encantada suggests that even the combination of innovative tactics and democratic governance can do little to foil the trap's logic. The experiences of Itchimbía as well as of Encantada between 2002 and 2005, however, indicate that tactical innovation and democratic governance can play important supporting roles when combined with a mixed-motives agenda, which helps organizations evade or escape the security trap. An organization need not be an Innovator to harness the power of mixed motives, but these cases suggest that the synergy of Innovator traits is an especially promising route for sustaining participation in the face of reduced selective incentives.

SUMMARY

The chapter began with an analysis of the study's central organizational typology and then separately analyzed the study's three main outcomes: organizational strategy, organizational success, and organizational survival. Overall, organizational type was shown to be a crucial baseline for understanding the struggles of land invasion organizations. Ideal-typical identity, repertoire, and neighborhood regime traits for each organizational type generally exhibited good or excellent fit with specific organizational traits.

Through comparative analysis of 132 demands initiated by Old Guard, Next Generation, and Innovator organizations, this chapter also demonstrated a strong correlation between organizational type and strategy pattern, and showed how repertoire traits like degree of strategic flexibility are driven in important respects by identity traits such as the leadership experience and the political context in which the newer types emerged. Longitudinal analysis supported the claim that Old Guard groups exhibit strong strategy preferences, while newer, more flexible types follow the strategy life cycle, though two of the Next Generation cases were too young in 2005 for me to fully evaluate their compliance with the life cycle. Moving beyond strategy patterns to look at strategy choices with respect to specific demands, however, revealed that despite strong identity-driven strategy patterns, particular strategy choices were constrained or affected by external and internal factors.

Through comparative analysis of 131 successful and failed service demands, a series of hypotheses was advanced in the form of the neighborhood service acquisition model. Within the model, four external variables acted on and interacted with three internal variables to determine the success and failure of service demands. The model not only presented a road map of how demands succeed or fail, but also provided insights into why some organizations make seemingly foolish or irrational choices. Although the service acquisition model served as a powerful tool for analyzing the success of individual demands, it could not assess the long-term prospects of the organizations themselves.

Through a longitudinal comparison of neighborhood organization survival trajectories, the concepts of the organizational stages of development and the security trap were introduced to explain the consolidation or decline of invasion organizations that had attained property security. The study found that while most organizations declined as security dampened participation, some groups were able to sustain settler participation and evade the security trap, via either authoritarian coercion or mixed motives. Hence, through detailed comparison of causal-process observations in neighborhood case studies, this chapter articulated causal mechanisms for the three major outcomes of organizational strategy, success, and survival.

7

Conclusions:
Contention, Political Process, and Mixed Motives

What are the theoretical implications of the study's analysis of organizational strategy, success, and survival? Chapter 1 introduced a series of analytic tools intended both to answer substantive questions about these three outcomes and to probe each outcome's relevance to social movement theory. With respect to organizational strategy, this study sought to explore McAdam, Tarrow, and Tilly's concepts of contained and transgressive contention (2001), with specific attention to the conceptual boundary where the two meet.

With respect to organizational success, the study posited an original theoretical model for explaining movement success in the context of invasion organizations, and also pursued two additional theoretical goals. First, I aimed to demonstrate the sustained relevance of political process theory to the Latin American context while commenting on its particular application to urban popular movements in the region. Second, I attempted both to apply and to improve Tarrow's dimensions of opportunity as one important—but still developing—component of political opportunity structure theory.

Finally, with respect to organizational survival, the study adopted McAdam, McCarthy, and Zald's recommendation for dynamic analyses of social movements not at their emergence (1988), but during their subsequent development or decline. By delivering important causal insights about mixed motives and collective action with respect to one specific empirical context, this contribution underscored the challenge to McAdam, Tarrow, and Tilly's assertion that the classic social movement agenda now constitutes a closed chapter in the study of contentious politics. In this chapter I first discuss the study's implications with respect to all three parts of this theoretical agenda, and then summarize the key conclusions of the study.

THEORIZING ORGANIZATIONAL STRATEGY: NO COMMON DYNAMIC
BETWEEN CONTAINED AND TRANSGRESSIVE CONTENTION

What are the theoretical implications of the study's analysis of organizational strategy? This study problematizes the observation that transgressive contention often emerges from contained contention across a variety of political settings, including the struggles of social movements. Recall that while Gamson provides only minimal conceptual footing for understanding land invasion organizations, McAdam, Tarrow, and Tilly's distinction between contained and transgressive contention offers a more appropriate conceptual starting point. Gamson (1990, 41–49) identifies the crucial movement choice between contained conformist demands and transgressive militant demands, but it is McAdam, Tarrow, and Tilly who reconceptualize this dichotomy as a dynamic process.

McAdam, Tarrow, and Tilly observe that episodes of transgressive contention routinely (though not always) emerge from contained contention (i.e., existing social networks and organizations). Contrary to their observation that contention moves from contained to transgressive, however, in this study's analysis of specific organizations (a related but distinct unit of analysis) we see every possible pattern represented *except* the one they observe as the norm. We see Old Guard clients who rely on contained contention, Old Guard radicals who rely on transgressive contention, and Next Generation and Innovator organizations who move from transgressive to contained contention. Yet no type routinely begins with contained or legal methods and then shifts to transgressive or extralegal strategies.

Why do we see such divergence from the expectations of McAdam, Tarrow, and Tilly? At least three possibilities could excuse this divergence. First, as suggested in the previous paragraphs, it is not clear that they expect movement *organizations* to follow the same pattern as overall episodes of contention. Yet if so many such organizations confound the overarching trend, this suggests that the trend should be examined more closely. Second, their finding could apply only at the national level, and not at the local level. As explained earlier, however, McAdam, Tarrow, and Tilly argue that their "analytic program . . . also applies to local, sectoral, international, and transnational contention" (2001, 8).

Third, with a broader perspective, McAdam, Tarrow, and Tilly might consider all ten of these neighborhood organizations a single "case," as they are all part of the same invasion "movement." Hence, they might argue that just as Pro's brief deviations into militancy do not undermine its clientelist identity, similarly a "single" contrary finding regarding direction of change in contention poses little threat to the general relationship, especially since they do not make all-or-nothing deterministic claims. This perspective deserves some sympathy, as the ambitious scope they propose for their study may require this kind of macro-perspective. Even so, if this study's findings in Lima and Quito are replicated in other Latin American cities, McAdam, Tarrow, and Tilly would then be confronted with one quite major social movement case whose component parts behaved in three different ways, but not in the fourth way that they find to be most common—that is, we see exclusively contained contention, exclusively transgressive contention, and contained contention emerging from transgressive contention, but never the opposite. Given all this, I contend that their particular selection of national-level cases of transgressive contention may be misleading and demands closer scrutiny. Despite McAdam, Tarrow, and Tilly's laudable objective of seeking common "dynamics of contention" across a wide sweep of social conflicts, this study points to the plausible alternative that no common pattern exists and that the dynamics of contained and transgressive contention routinely go in both directions in different contexts.

Hence, my analysis supports O'Brien's supposition that boundary-spanning contention constitutes a worthy and fruitful area of inquiry. This is especially true since in many contexts, the location of the boundary between contained and transgressive contention is dynamic, and "what is forbidden one year, is tolerated the next, and is readily accepted the third" (2003, 58). In this respect, Old Guard organizations clearly laid the groundwork for subsequent generations of settlers, who encounter an already modified "terrain of contention" in which land invasions, in Lima especially, are seen increasingly as the norm rather than as aberrations.[1]

With respect to the study's secondary theoretical referent—Stokes's work on settler identity (1995)—analysis of the three types of organizations suggests both that her work may have broader significance than she takes credit for and that the temporal scope of her findings warrants investigation to see if they still apply in the 1990–2005 period. Specifically, analysis of Old Guard organizations showed that Stokes's client/radical dichotomy is useful not only at the level of the individual but also at the level of the organization. Analysis of Next

1. The study's description and analysis of the three types of organizations also offers some support for the evolutionary approach introduced by Koopmans (2005), which was discussed briefly in chapter 1 (see note 3). This approach reminds us that the promise of the Innovator type is dependent, in part, on the failures and relative successes of the other types of invasion organizations, because those examples provided vital information on which the Innovators could base effective decisions.

Generation and Innovator organizations, however, showed that Stokes's rigid "mental templates" are much less likely to apply to the younger types of organizations, suggesting that they might not apply to younger individual settlers either, though this is beyond the scope of this study.

More generally, my analysis suggests that a core portion of Stokes's findings was not tied to a particular period in Peru, but in fact had a remarkably enduring salience. After all, Stokes focused on a period prior to party system collapse, the authoritarian leadership of Alberto Fujimori, and Peru's internal conflict of the 1990s. With Peru having changed dramatically on all these fronts, it is notable that Stokes's study continues to be relevant in a new political context. Though neoliberalism helped reshape partisan politics and clientelism in Peru, it did not eliminate them, and Stokes's approach continues to help us discern how Peru's reformulated politics relies on clientelism as one of several types of relationships between urban popular movements and state actors.

THEORIZING ORGANIZATIONAL SUCCESS: REFINING POLITICAL PROCESS AND OPERATIONALIZING POLITICAL OPPORTUNITY

What does the study's analysis of organizational success imply for social movement theory? To explain the success or failure of 131 service demands, I introduced the neighborhood service acquisition model, which involved the causal interaction of several factors external and internal to land invasion organizations. Disaggregation of the model permitted assessment of specific causal claims through comparative analysis, but this analysis required the operationalization of Tarrow's dimensions of opportunity with respect to the land invasion context. Further, the application of this facet of the theory of political opportunities, in conjunction with attention to internal variables, demonstrated the sustained importance of McAdam's political process approach to the task of uncovering important causal mechanisms affecting urban popular movements in Latin America.

McAdam's critique of resource mobilization theory and his consequent political process model remain potent theoretical tools for grasping the enormous power differential between elites and excluded groups in Latin America, while allowing analytic space for the conclusion that excluded groups nonetheless wield some influence over their own fates. In the land invasion context, this translates into neighborhood organizations whose opportunities for success are powerfully constrained by external factors, but whose acquisition of urban services within those constraints hinges in important respects on internal factors and decisions. But although McAdam's (1982, 51) two core variables—political opportunities and organizational strength—prove pivotal in the invasion context, his third key variable—cognitive liberation—deserves special note.

In McAdam's model of movement emergence, changes in the opportunity structure trigger "cognitive cues" that trigger the initiation of cognitive liberation. In the present context, however, the Next Generation and Innovators are, in some sense, "born liberated," as these newer types of organizations emerged from a younger generation of settlers who take the entire land invasion process for granted. This is a key distinction for understanding the organizational typology, but as I am centrally concerned with the evolving struggle for services, rather than the initial emergence or founding of organizations, this factor is less important.

The core contribution of the political process model, however, is its combination of external and internal factors. As chapter 6 demonstrated, this proves to be central to understanding organizational success, as external factors do shape and constrain the causal effects of internal organizational factors, despite the continued causal relevance of the internal factors themselves. In order to articulate the specific impact of external opportunities on internal resources, my framework made use of Tarrow's (1998, 76–80) dimensions of opportunity.

That theoretical framework also contributed to political opportunity structure theory by specifying how four of these dimensions can be measured and how, in the land invasion context, these dimensions either hinder or facilitate organizational success. These dimensions of opportunity include *shifting alignments*, *repression and facilitation*, *influential allies*, and *increasing access*.[2] To analyze invasion organization service demands, the study combined the first two dimensions—shifting alignments along with repression and facilitation—into the *mayoral position* variable. Mayoral position was scored as hostile, neutral, or friendly toward the specific invasion organization in question. While some mayors proved hostile or friendly to all invasion neighborhoods, many selected particular organizations to support or oppose. With respect to allies, I followed Tarrow in the adoption of Gamson's (1990, 64–66) finding that influential allies enhance chances of movement success. Unlike Tarrow's emphasis on political parties, however, my *influential allies* variable also included nonpartisan allies such as domestic and international NGOs, nonpartisan public agencies, and allied social movements. This proved to be an interesting distinction, as different types of neighborhood regimes were more or less able to forge lasting relationships with different types of allies; ultimately, however, this was not a causally significant distinction in this particular context (at least not with the data analyzed).

2. Tarrow's fifth dimension of opportunity, *divided elites*, was occasionally a factor—such as during Fujimori's political conflict with Villa El Salvador mayor Michel Azcueta—but was not a central recurring cause of success or failure that merited inclusion in the model.

Finally, I operationalized Tarrow's increasing awareness dimension—which empha- sizes elections—with the broader variable of *local avenues of participation*, which includes both local elections and nonelectoral participatory frameworks, such as the Fraternidad housing program in Lima. This proved to be an important addition, as different neighborhood regimes benefited or suffered from this kind of avenue of participation.

In addition to operationalizing these dimensions of opportunity, the study's theoretical framework also advanced a series of causal assertions about how these external factors shape organizational success and failure.[3] These seven hypotheses not only explained the organizational success or failure of specific service demands by land invasion organizations in Latin America but also pro- vided a fresh set of hypotheses, grounded in Tarrow's dimensions of opportunity, that can be tested in other contexts. In this way, the study of land invasion organization service demands demonstrated that, supported by new innovations in political opportunity structure theory, political process theory continues to provide powerful analytic tools for answering substantive questions. Far from a closed chapter, political process theory demands fine-tuning in order to maxi- mize its effectiveness in empirical contexts such as Latin America.

THEORIZING ORGANIZATIONAL SURVIVAL:
MIXED MOTIVES SUSTAIN COLLECTIVE ACTION

Examining popular neighborhoods founded by land invasion, a puzzle emerges: why does the acquisition of land titles usually cause participation to plummet, though in a minority of cases it can lead to continued high participation? I argue that the common outcome of movement collapse is explained by the dis- appearance of the key *selective incentive*—property security. Some groups, how- ever, evade this "security trap" through *mixed motives*—an agenda that combines material and nonmaterial objectives—which maintain participation in the face of reduced selective incentives.

Stepping away from the context of land invasions, this study thus engages the broad question of why many movements collapse while others prove resilient. Exploring this puzzle through case studies generates hypotheses related to the work of Olson (1965), Elster (1989), Udéhn (1993), McAdam (1983), and Levine (1992). Why do movements collapse? In the context of land invasion organiza- tions, the initial answer appears simple: Olson is correct; selective incentives

---

3. The model also includes a fourth external variable—*service provider*—but this is not drawn from Tarrow's framework.

are the initial driver of participation, and when the key selective incentive disappears, participation plummets unless a mechanism exists to enforce participation or punish free riders. But then why do some movements defy Olson's logic and prove resilient? Because mixed motives pick up where selective incentives leave off. My findings echo Elster and Udéhn in arguing that Olson's (1965, 51) emphasis on self-interest is important but insufficient to explain sustained participation of rank-and-file members for initiatives that do not specifically benefit them. Mixed motives not only help explain such instances of collective action but may also be increasingly important as a movement organization matures. This study thus generates a hypothesis that mixed motives matter more at later stages of development.

Given the hypothesis that mixed motives are most important to popular movements immediately following achievement of their key selective incentive, what type of organization is best able to motivate its membership with a mixed agenda? In the present context, it is the Innovators, who benefit from a synergy among their tactical innovation, democratic governance, and transformative mission. McAdam (1983) showed that tactical innovation was continually needed to overcome the challenges posed by interaction between insurgents and opponents. This raised the possibility that innovative organizations would more quickly fall prey to the security trap, leading to stagnation and service demand failure. Thus, the security trap appeared to undermine McAdam's claim because of a sequence that could result in innovation harming a movement instead of helping it. This is precisely what happened in Encantada, where the organization achieved land titles in record time—and became moribund in record time as well. But the more important finding is that tactical innovation can undergird an Innovator identity characterized by mixed motives, helping it evade the security trap. In both Itchimbía and Encantada, innovation not only helped win specific demands but supported the crucial mixed agenda of each organization. This study thus supports the hypothesis that tactical innovation can facilitate organizational survival not only through overcoming challenges as proposed by McAdam but also through support for an identity grounded in mixed motives, which Levine has shown to be an effective combination for religious popular organizations.

In addition to the similarities between CEBs and Innovators mentioned above, another parallel is clear: for both types of popular organizations, egalitarian and participatory practices are important to sustaining a mixed-motives agenda (Levine 1992, 202–12). That the mixed motives of religious popular organizations also rely on democratic governance supports this study's claim that Innovators not only are democratic but *need* to be democratic.

Despite such parallels, CEBs and Innovators differ in their agenda sequencing, underscoring the importance of testing hypotheses in a variety of popular movement contexts. CEBs began as religious organizations and progressed to a material and political agenda (Levine 1992, 46), whereas invasion organizations always begin with a material agenda and Innovators appear to either parallel this with a nonmaterial agenda from the start (Itchimbía) or add one later (Encantada). Despite the success stories of Itchimbía and Encantada, this difference in sequencing suggests that Innovators could be less resilient in the face of disappearing selective incentives than religious popular organizations and perhaps other types of popular organizations as well. Since CEBs are initiated with a nonmaterial agenda, they are more likely to withstand the disappearance of selective material incentives, whereas land invasion organizations, however innovative their supplemental mission, are fundamentally focused on material needs and without such incentives will struggle to survive.

This raises a question for popular movements throughout Latin America: should a movement organization that anticipates material setbacks not only develop mixed motives but perhaps even create an alternative agenda or unifying identity (e.g., women's empowerment) to establish a lasting purpose *before* seeking material improvement? Given economic deprivation, this may be impossible for many groups, but these cases make clear that popular movements ought not be underestimated. Whatever the sequence, the clear lesson for popular movement organizations is to develop mixed motives that include an altruistic mission. This study has illustrated several types of supplementary missions, including Itchimbía's ecological park proposal, Encantada's relief efforts for fire victims, and the mentoring of other popular movements in which both organizations engaged. Another example comes from the land invasion settlement of Kawachi. Founded in 1995 in the Lima district of San Juan de Lurigancho, the Innovators of Kawachi made preservation of archaeological ruins their special mission. The settlers intentionally chose a valuable part of the Canto Chico archaeological zone and made plans for a neighborhood museum, arguing that their community was best prepared to care for the neglected site (*El Peruano*, 5/7/97).

One aspect of organizational survival that deserves further attention is the benefits and costs of organizational consolidation. My research has explored what might be called the "short-term" costs and benefits of consolidation, but what effects might consolidation bring in another five or ten years? For example, in the longer term, might consolidation help bridge the disconnect between urban popular movements and the formal political process (Schönwälder 2002)? Edgar Coral of Pisulli ran for office but lost, and María Hernández won a seat on Quito's sub-Metropolitan Council, but these examples do not yet teach us what more established settlements might gain or lose from political victories by their neighborhood leaders. Yet Haber's (2006) work suggests that such developments will probably come in time for some of these settlements, and with substantial benefits, despite some pitfalls.

As tactical success eliminates key selective incentives, many popular movements find themselves caught in the steel jaws of Olson's logic of collective action. The example of the Innovators, however, suggests that when aided by tactical innovation and democratic governance, the key of mixed motives can unlock the trap and set settlers free to participate and develop a resilient organization and community.

CONCLUSIONS

On the periphery of Latin American cities, poor settlers have for decades founded illegal settlements and then employed a variety of strategies to demand basic services. Until the 1990s, invasion organizations exhibited rigid strategy preferences, but in the wake of neoliberalism and the decline of partisan ideology, new organizational types have emerged, characterized by tactical flexibility and innovation, resulting in agile organizations better able to navigate the dynamic political terrain.

Metropolitan-level analysis revealed six surprising trends that differed by metropolitan context. Specifically, invasion organizations tended to differ with respect to building materials, original land ownership, the difficulty and consequences of acquiring land titles, strategies for acquiring electricity, and types of neighborhood regimes. A more general contrast also emerged: Lima organizations were more likely to encounter quick initial success followed by gradual decline, while the success of Quito organizations was often more gradual, resulting in long-term organizational survival. These citywide trends were explained by three factors—public policy, local democratization, and geography and climate—but most relevant outcomes varied not only across cities but also within each metropolitan context. To examine these differences, the study then focused principally on neighborhood-level analysis of three key outcomes: organizational strategy, organizational success, and organizational survival.

First, grounded in two new typologies of invasion organizations and of strategies for demanding services, analysis of ten neighborhood cases in Lima and Quito helped us understand *organizational strategy* preferences that may appear random, but that in newer types of organizations actually follow a predictable strategy life cycle. Importantly, this life cycle *begins* with strategies that transgress institutional norms and shifts *toward* legal strategies deemed acceptable by established institutions. This finding seemed at odds with the observation by McAdam, Tarrow, and Tilly (2001, 7–8) that episodes of contained contention routinely precede transgressive contention. Obviously in some contexts this pattern applies, but this study suggests a reconsideration of the broad scope of their finding.

What drives the strategy patterns of invasion organizations? The rigid strategy patterns of the Old Guard type are driven by the "enduring mental templates" identified by Susan Stokes (1995), but recent variations in leadership experience and political context have resulted in the formation of the Next Generation and Innovator types, which follow the flexible strategy life cycle. Unlike the strategic rigidity of the Old Guard, where "clients" prefer contained contention and "radicals" rely on transgressive contention, the strategy life cycle begins with extralegal strategies and steadily moves toward legal strategies. Although organizational type alone cannot predict how a group will act in a specific instance, this factor does appear to be a good predictor of overall strategy pattern.

Given both the increasingly uncertain benefits of cooperating with political parties—which can make legal strategies unreliable—and the growing privatization of urban services—which can make extralegal strategies unworkable—the strategy life cycle may offer invasion communities a more versatile strategic menu for demanding services. With service acquisition opportunities slimmer now than during the decades-past zenith of Latin American land invasions, many young invasion leaders are embracing strategic flexibility. Their Old Guard parents viewed ideological commitment as a source of strength, but younger settlers are more likely to see it as a liability that inhibits adaptability. Importantly, Innovators are not merely an exception to enduring practices, but may signal a break from the decline of urban movement activity in the 1990s. Certainly Ecuador's remarkable upsurge of popular movement activity in the 2000s, culminating in a new constitution in 2008, seems consistent with this observation (Dosh and Kligerman 2009a).

Second, in order to understand *organizational success*, we looked both at external factors—the political opportunity structure—as well as internal factors like strategy and neighborhood regime, both of which connect again to the three types of invasion organizations. Here the study made a contribution to political process theory by operationalizing four of Tarrow's dimensions of opportunity and demonstrating a set of seven interrelated causal relationships. Not only can these particular specifications be tested in other contexts, but the study's use of this operationalization to help answer questions of substantive and analytic importance points to the continued relevance of such an approach.

The seven causal claims used to explain outcomes in my case studies were as follows: (1) mayoral hostility forces organizations to rely on risky external strategies; (2) privatization makes it almost impossible for externally dependent strategies to succeed; (3) noncompetitive organizations are more likely to benefit from alliances; (4) power-sharing organizations are more likely to benefit from local avenues of participation; (5) organizational resources facilitate the success of self-sufficient strategies; (6) different strategies prove optimal for different service demands; and (7) strategic rigidity is more likely to result in suboptimal service demands. Although further testing of these claims in other cases and contexts will surely refine them, the study suggests that the integrated external-internal nature of the claims will endure.

And third, in order to understand *organizational survival*, we needed to recognize that successful acquisition of services can actually *weaken* an organization before its goals are fully accomplished, but also that different types of organizations have different methods of evading the security trap. Here McAdam, Tarrow, and Tilly (2001), as well as McAdam, Mayer, and Zald (1988), are justified in their call for dynamic analyses.

The study revealed two organizational trajectories in which success comes at a high price. In the first "costly" path, successful acquisition of property security led to a moribund and largely useless neighborhood organization. In the second costly path, organizational consolidation was achieved, but only through the authoritarian tactics of a neighborhood boss. Only in the case of the Innovators, whose mixed motives permitted them to become truly secure *and* to consolidate, was the attainment of organizational success unambiguously worth the cost.

What determines movement success? External factors beyond the control of organizations do invite and curtail mobilization in a variety of ways, but this study shows that whatever the array of external variables, certain types of organizations, characterized by specific strategies, resources, and leadership structures, are better able than others to exploit those external factors. In short, organizations do in fact exert control over key aspects of their own process of acquiring resources.

Although this analysis focuses on neighborhood-level cases in two Latin American cities, its empirical and theoretical findings raise important issues for social movements in nonurban contexts and in other world regions. Through a macro-longitudinal conceptualization of the evolution of invasion organizations, the study demonstrates that a historical dimension may be required to fully grasp how opportunities for mobilization change. More important, however, the fact that the main causal model for movement success relies critically on the study's micro-longitudinal framework for predicting organizational strategy selection indicates that the success and failure of social movements in general can only be understood through both an evolutionary conceptualization of invasion organizations and a dynamic and operationalized deployment of political process theory.

Epilogue:
From Scholarship to Activism

In 2005, my research team and I concluded our follow-up interviews in each of the ten neighborhood case studies; between 2007 and 2009, I revisited eight of the ten neighborhoods. In this section I provide snapshots of the post-2005 development of some of these communities, but this does not constitute an extension of the research project for two reasons. First, the 2007–9 interviews were not systematic, and I did not rigorously examine post-2005 service demands. Whereas the previous chapters rely on a detailed set of original qualitative data, this epilogue is anecdotal. And second, since 2008 my collaborators and I have become involved in social justice and development work in the Villa El Salvador communities of La Encantada and Oasis. We are privileged to have shifted our role in these communities from that of scholars to activists, as described below, but this also means that on some level we have ourselves become a "causal factor," making it impossible to independently analyze changes in these neighborhoods from 2008 onward.

In Ecuador, fieldwork in 2008 confirmed that the Quito neighborhood of Itchimbía remained an exceptional case in terms of both organizational consolidation and political ambition. After more than five years of living in condominiums, settlers' participation levels remained high and the group had steadily pursued a community agenda of improved on-site health care, more employment for settlers in Itchimbía park, and paying off the condominium mortgages. Most settlers made their final mortgage payments in August 2008. Founding Itchimbía president Juan Carlos Manzanillas did not get to witness that milestone, however, as he died in a car accident on July 14, 2007. The community subsequently renamed the neigh-borhood's main avenue in his honor (Chamorro 2008, interview).

With most of Itchimbía's material needs met, the residents expanded the scope of their political ambitions. In 2004, the Coordinadora Popular de Quito merged with fourteen smaller popular organizations and became Foro Urbano (Urban Forum). In 2008, neighborhood president María Hernández—already an elected official for Quito's metropolitan government and the president of Mujeres por la Vida (Women Struggling for Life)—left Itchimbía's governing council in order to work full-time for Foro Urbano (Hernández 2008, interview). Neighborhood vice president Milton Chamorro was elected to fill Hernández's post as president.

Led by a six-member executive council, most of whom still live in Itchimbía, Foro Urbano includes three principal popular organizations: Mujeres por la Vida, which comprises five territorial organizations within Quito; the Red de Vivienda (Housing Network), which includes two thousand families searching for land to build communities); and the Red de Barrios (Neighborhood Network), which encompasses fifty poor neighborhoods (Mera 2008, interview). Foro Urbano scored quick victories by placing two of its leaders on Quito's Metropolitan Council in 2004 and four of its leaders on the 2007–8 constitutional assembly called by Ecuadorian president Rafael Correa (2007–present) (Dosh and Kligerman 2009b). In 2008, Foro Urbano articulated plans to seek the Quito mayoralty and extend its reach into every province in the country (Endara 2008, interview).

In Peru, a 2007 visit to the northern Lima neighborhoods of Pro, Sector C, and Rosales suggested that little had changed in the previous two years. The clientelist neighborhoods of both Pro and Sector C had not improved their infra-structure and appeared to still be in a moribund state of limited and unsatis-factory progress on community objectives. The militants of Rosales were no better off, according to a 2007 interview with Rosales secretary general Marcelo Hizo (2006–8). Hizo indicated that infighting continued to keep Rosales from catching up with its neighbors, and that no support was forthcoming from the APRA government of President Alán García, who returned to power in 2006.

By contrast, visits to Villa El Salvador in 2007, 2008, and 2009 gave me the opportunity to observe dramatic progress in Encantada, Oasis, and Paraíso, as well as the dissolution and relocation of Villa Mar. By 2009, after thirteen years of struggle, Encantada had transformed itself from a shantytown on the brink of eviction to a resilient neighborhood leading the surrounding area in the construction of a water and sewer infrastructure project that will serve fifty-four thousand settlers in Encantada, Oasis, Paraíso, and more than a dozen other contiguous neighborhoods. In terms of selective incentives, this project offers Encantada residents the same divisible benefits as before—running water and indoor plumbing. But whereas that promise alone had been insufficient to motivate participation during Encantada's moribund stage, now that the neighborhood has taken the lead in a larger project of great importance, people believe both in their greater mission and in their greater chance of success. For example, spearheaded by Encantada settlers, mass mobilizations in support of this infrastructure project have blocked the Pan-American Highway five times, leading to a dozen arrests (Valencia 2007, interview).

The Encantada settlers also responded to a 2007 earthquake that leveled buildings in Villa El Salvador by providing clothing, blankets, and emergency supplies to victims. Encantada's cyber networking also yielded gains in the status of the organization and its leadership, including 2007 visits to the community by President García of Peru and Bolivian president Evo Morales (2006–present) (Valencia 2007, interview). Jesús Valencia emceed these presidential visits, each of which drew many thousands of settlers. It seems clear that Encantada's moribund stage has been put to rest.

But while Encantada, Oasis, and Paraíso benefited from the large-scale water and sewer infrastructure project, Villa Mar was left out. Villa Mar residents continued to believe their exclusion was motivated by a desire to build a road through their neighborhood, which would directly connect the district of Villa El Salvador with the Pan-American Highway. A more likely proximate cause of their exclusion, however, was Villa Mar's extremely rugged physical terrain. By April 2009, a decade of occupation by settlers had not made the Villa Mar hillside any less steep, nor made its sandy foundation any more stable, and installation of water and sewer infrastructure on such terrain was unrealistic.

The exclusion of Villa Mar from a project that included nearly every surrounding neighborhood was a message of rejection so unmistakable that even the enduring optimism of the Villa Mar settlers faltered, and the community relocated in April 2009 (Martínez 2009, interview). With no sufficiently large site available in Villa El Salvador, the community had to choose between breaking up and scattering their families, or moving en masse to the adjacent district of Pachacamac, a distant thirty minutes by bus.

The settlers of Villa Mar chose the latter, relocating to Pachacamac and integrating with the existing neighborhood of Santísimo Salvador. In a government-approved deal, the settlers abandoned their hillside of shifting sands and accepted three hundred new lots of flat and usable terrain. The community thus became removed from employment and community connections they had built up in Villa El Salvador, but it was an excellent move for the settlers, who immediately had access to running water (though not yet in their houses). Former secretary general Modesta Martínez, now retired from neighborhood governance, continued to serve as an informal senior adviser, and in this capacity led the establishment of a new market, which was bustling with activity within three months of the move to Pachacamac. For now, the Villa Mar group maintains its subgroup identity, but by August 2009 it already seemed integrated with the neighborhood of Santísimo Salvador.

During and after field research, I shared the project's findings with both academic and community audiences. In Lima and Quito, these audiences ranged from groups of settlers to affluent families whose lands had been threatened or seized by land invasions. These presentations gave way to long-term relationships with various groups and, in the case of La Encantada and Villa El Salvador, to a new commitment to supporting community activists.

In September 2008, my colleague Emily Hedin and I founded Building Dignity, a Minnesota-based nonprofit focused on supporting and empowering neighborhood activists in poor communities in Peru (http://www.buildingdignity.org/). In December 2008 we worked with Encantada leaders Jesús Valencia and Martha Huamán to create a grassroots organization called the Centro para el Desarrollo con Dignidad (Center for Development with Dignity). In the subsequent months we constructed an innovative community building to house the center, which we inaugurated in August 2009. Free and open to the public, it includes a public meeting space, a library, a museum of La Encantada's social justice activism, a technology center, and a public kitchen and bathrooms. It houses grassroots development projects, leadership development, community education, and resources for La Encantada's human rights activists. Between 2001 and 2005, our research benefited immensely from the generosity of hundreds of Peruvian and Ecuadorian settlers who have demanded both land and dignity. It is a great privilege to now shift from studying these resilient settlers to collaborating with them to craft fresh models of community activism and development.

Appendix:
Sources of Data and List of Interviews

In approaching the subject of land invasion organizations, I benefited from
previous scholarship focused principally on the 1960s, 1970s, and 1980s. In the
1990s, although the urban land invasion phenomenon continued—and in Lima,
even accelerated—attention shifted to related, but distinct, topics such as the
MST of Brazil (e.g., Wright and Wolford 2003). Yet the manifestations and challenges of the urban invasion phenomenon continued to evolve, in part due to
democratization and neoliberalism, and in part due to the development of the
invasion communities: as the invasion phenomenon "came of age," it gave birth
to successive generations of settlers who followed their parents' example in some
respects and forged new paths in others.

The present research sought to examine these changes through data collection and analysis of newer settlements, primarily those founded in the 1990s.
During a period of six months in Peru (2001–2), six months in Ecuador (2002),
and follow-up research in all ten research sites (2005), I conducted semi-
structured interviews with forty past and present settlement leaders, as well
as open-ended interviews with more than thirty political officials, municipal
and service agency bureaucrats, landowners, state and paramilitary security
forces, NGOs, and other relevant parties. A number of these seventy individuals
were interviewed multiple times. The study also benefited from informal interviews with about fifty individual settlers who are not listed below.

The semi-structured interviews followed a series of questions about the history of the neighborhood and the neighborhood governance structure, and

detailed questions about each attempt to acquire urban services. Although interpretations varied widely, comparison of factual claims by different (and sometimes opposed) settlement leaders revealed strong consistency in most respects, with the exception of chronological ordering and time frame. Interview subjects at all levels often proved unreliable in identifying specific dates and years, and sometimes recalled occurrences in the wrong order. To eliminate as many of these inaccuracies as possible, I relied on the paper archives that virtually all former and current settlement leaders maintain. Settlement leaders rarely discard any document no matter how minor, and these leaders along with their landowner opponents generously shared these archives, which provided reliable chronologies and dating of events.

Periodicals and newspaper archives were of great use in cases that received sustained media attention (e.g., Camino and Itchimbía), but many settlements never received media coverage in even the most local publications. Hence, news sources were used when available, and proved to be a valuable additional way of confirming portions of the interview data.

Details on interview dates and locations, periodicals consulted, and archival letters cited are provided in the "Interviews by Author," "Letters," and "Periodicals" sections of the references. In the following list, the use of asterisks denotes that the name given is a pseudonym.

LIST OF INTERVIEWS

Semistructured Interviews with Past and Present Settlement Leaders

Aceles, Freddy. Founding settler and architect of the Itchimbía cooperative.

Andrade Rodriguez, Juvenal. President of the Pisulli cooperative (1996) and leader of the opposition Frente Cívico Democrático para la Dignidad de Pisulli (2003–5).

Arturo Vega, Miguel. Secretary general of the Sector C cooperative (2000–2002).

Bustamente, Victoriano. Secretary general of the Pro cooperative (2001–3).

Campos, Victor. Secretary general of the Oasis cooperative (1995–97).

Chamorro, Milton. Vice president (1995–2008) and president (2008–present) of the Itchimbía cooperative.

Chávez, María. Secretary general of the Sector C cooperative (1998–2000).

Chupingahua, Santiago. Secretary general of the Jardines de Paz cooperative (1998–2002).

Condori, Nestor. Secretary general of the Encantada cooperative (1997–2001).

Coral, Edgar. Manager and boss of the Pisulli cooperative (1983–2005).

Encarnación Sandoval, Jorge. Secretary general of the Rosales cooperative (1995–98).

Galarga, Carlos. President of the Asedim cooperative (2000–2002).

Geronimo, Victoria. Secretary of women for the Oasis cooperative (2000–2002).

Goñe, Macario. Secretary general of the Multisectoral Commission and spokesperson for the Oasis cooperative (1997–2005).

Hernández, María. President of the Itchimbía cooperative (1996–2008).

Hilarios de Peña, María Ariza. Secretary general of the Sector C cooperative (2005–7).

Hizo, Marcelo. Secretary general of the Rosales cooperative (2006–8).

Huamán, Efraín. Secretary general of Group 3 of the Oasis cooperative (2000–2006).

Lara, José. Paraíso block captain and employee of the Fernández Concha family (2001).

la Madrid, Diego. Secretary general of the Sector C cooperative (1991–94).

Martínez, Modesta. Secretary general of the Villa Mar cooperative (1999–2005).

Mera, Alba. Manager of the Itchimbía cooperative (1995–2005).

Meza, Celso. Manager and boss of the Camino cooperative (1990–2005).

Montenegro, Herbert. Founding sub-secretary general of the Encantada cooperative (1996–98).

Montesinos Morales, Lino Teclo. Secretary general of the Rosales cooperative (2003–6).

Muesmueran Imbaquingo, María Lupe. Camino block captain (2002).

Peña, Elvira. Secretary general of the Rosales cooperative (2002–4).

Pérez, Ruben. Organizer of the failed five-thousand-person "20 de Enero" invasion of 2002 in the district of Carabayllo.

Remuzgo, Elvis. Secretary general of the Pro cooperative (2003–5; 2007–9).

Rojas, Willy. Secretary general of the Rosales cooperative (1993–95).

Ruíz, Abrahím. Secretary general of the Paraíso cooperative (2001–5).

Tapia, Claudio. Secretary general of the Rosales cooperative (2000–2002).

Valencia, Jesús. Secretary general of the Encantada cooperative (2003–5).

Valencia, Pilar. Manager of the Encantada invasion.

Varas, Jorge. Secretary general of Group 2 of the Oasis cooperative (2000–2002) and city councilman for Villa El Salvador (1996–98).

Vasquez, Pedro. Leader in the Pro cooperative (1992–97).

Villavicencio, Wilson. Vice president of the Frente Cívico Democrático para la Dignidad de Pisulli (2003–5).

Yabar, Celia. Founder of the *comedor popular* in Paraíso.

Yaranga, Wilfredo. Secretary general of the Laureles cooperative (2000–2002).

Yataco, José. Secretary of urban development for the Encantada cooperative (1999–2001).

*Yicate, Luis. Paramilitary henchman of Chito Rios and neighborhood leader, settlement of Pro.

Open-Ended Interviews

*Avelino, Elias. Pro settler.
*Avendaño, Diana. Villa Mar settler and victim of arson.
Azcueta, Michel. Mayor of Villa El Salvador (1984–89, 1996–98).
Barrera, José. Researcher at the Centro de Estudios y Promoción del Desarrollo.
Cabana, Máximo. President of the Frente Lomo de Corvina (2001–3).
Casas, Isaías. Attorney representing the Villa Mar cooperative.
*Cocha, Gabriela. Itchimbía settler.
Cotler, Julio. Senior scholar at the Instituto de Estudios Peruanos (Institute of Peruvian Studies).
de Riobamba, Luz. Camino settler.
de Soto, Hernando. Founder and president of the Instituto Libertad y Democracia in Lima.
*Domínguez, Justo. Villa Mar settler.
Endara, Patricio. President of the Coordinadora Popular de Quito (1996–2004) and coordinator of Foro Urbano (2004–present).
Jaimes, Eusebio. Office of Neighborhood Participation, Municipality of Los Olivos.
López, Rommel. Manager of the Cucho Hacienda ranch before it was occupied by settlers.
Mejia, Alcides. President of the Frente Unitario de los Pueblos de Perú (United Front of the Peoples of Peru) (2000–2002).
*Meneses, Blanca. Itchimbía settler.
*Morales, Olga. Oasis settler.
Muñoz, Isabel. Oasis block captain (2001–2).
Pazmiño Navas, Jorge Humberto. Retired catholic priest and legal (though contested) owner of the invaded Cucho Hacienda ranch.
Polo Burga, Julio. Treasurer of the Frente Unitario de los Pueblos de Perú (2000–2002).
Pumar, Martín. Mayor of Villa El Salvador (1998–2002).
*Ramírez, César. Longtime Pisulli resident.
Romero, Eric. Land disputes researcher at COFOPRI.
Santos, Nelli. Asociación Latinoamericana para Desarrollo regional coordinator, district of Los Olivos.
*Silva, Isabel. Pisulli settler.
*Solar, Jesús. Paraíso settler.
*Tamaca, Carla. New Pisulli settler.

Thomas, Robert. Catholic priest from the Archdiocese of Boston, Massachusetts.

Toche Lara, Miguel. Chief engineer for Villa El Salvador at SEDAPAL.

Vásquez Solano, Harold. President of the Public Works Committee, Los Olivos (2000–2002).

Velásquez, Yuri. Director of Villa El Salvador Municipal Development Agency (2000–2003).

Villavicencio Carrasco, Isabel. Founder of the Commission for the Defense of Human Rights, Villa El Salvador.

Vivanco, Alfredo. City councilman for Villa El Salvador (1999–2002).

Zuñiga, Oscar. Attorney representing the Encantada cooperative.

References

Alcázar, Lorena, Lixin Colin Xu, and Ana M. Zuluaga. 2002. "Institutions, Politics, and Contracts: The Privatization Attempt of the Water and Sanitation Utility of Lima, Peru." In *Thirsting for Efficiency: The Economics and Politics of Urban Water System Reform*, ed. Mary M. Shirley. New York: Pergamon Press, 103–38.

Araoz, Mercedes, and Roberto Urrunaga. 1996. *Finanzas municipales: Ineficiencias y excesiva dependencia del gobierno central*. Lima: CIUP.

Arce, Moisés. 2006. "The Societal Consequences of Market Reform in Peru." *Latin American Politics and Society* 48 (1): 27–54.

Arias, Enrique Desmond. 2004. "Faith in Our Neighbors: Networks and Social Order in Three Brazilian Favelas." *Latin American Politics and Society* 46 (1): 1–38.

Arnao Rondán, Raymundo, and Maritza Meza Carey. 1990. *Economías municipales en la Provincia de Lima: Retos de un problema nacional*. Lima: Instituto de Investigaciones Económicas.

Arnillas, Federico. 1999. "Organizaciones comunitarias de base en el Cercado de Lima: Formas de organización y participación en la gestión municipal." In *Lima Megaciudad*, ed. Jaime Joseph. Lima: Alternativa, 229–42.

Assies, William, Gerrit Burgwal, and Ton Salman, eds. 1990. *Structures of Power, Movements of Resistance: An Introduction to the Theories of Urban Movements in Latin America*. Amsterdam: CEDLA.

Auyero, Javier. 2001. *Poor People's Politics: Peronist Survival Networks and the Legacy of Evita*. Durham: Duke University Press.

Ballón, Eduardo. 1986. "Los movimientos sociales en la crisis: El caso Peruano." In *Movimientos sociales y crisis: El caso Peruano*, ed. Eduardo Ballón. Lima: DESCO, 9–44.

Barry, Brian. 1970. *Sociologists, Economists, and Democracy*. Chicago: University of Chicago Press.

Bennett, Vivienne. 1992. "The Evolution of Urban Popular Movements in Mexico Between 1968 and 1988." In *The Making of Social Movements in Latin America*, ed. Arturo Escobar and Sonia E. Alvarez. Boulder, Colo.: Westview Press.

Brady, Henry E. 2004. "Data-Set Observations Versus Causal-Process Observations: The 2000 U.S. Presidential Election." In *Rethinking Social Inquiry: Diverse Tools, Shared Standards*, ed. Henry E. Brady and David Collier. Lanham, Md.: Rowman and Littlefield, 267–71.

Brooke, James. 2004. "An Ex-president of Peru Plots His Return." *New York Times*. 24 February.

Bruneau, Thomas C., and W. E. Hewitt. 1989. "Patterns of Church Influence in Brazil's Political Transition." *Comparative Politics* 22 (1): 39–61.

Burga, Jorge, and Claire Delpech. 1989. *Villa El Salvador: La ciudad y su desarrollo: Realidad y propuesta*. Lima: CIED.

Burgwal, Gerrit. 1990. "An Introduction to the Literature on Urban Movements in Latin America." In *Structures of Power, Movements of Resistance,* ed. William Assies, Gerrit Burgwal, and Ton Salman. Amsterdam: CEDLA, 163–75.

———. 1993. *Caciquismo, Paralelismo, and Clientelismo: The History of a Quito Squatter Settlement.* Amsterdam: Institute of Cultural Anthropology, Vrije Universiteit.

———. 1995. *Struggle of the Poor: Neighbourhood Organization and Clientelist Practice in a Quito Squatter Settlement.* Amsterdam: CEDLA.

Burt, Jo-Marie. 1997. "Political Violence and the Grassroots in Lima, Peru." In *The New Politics of Inequality in Latin America: Rethinking Participation and Representation,* ed. Douglas A. Chalmers et al. Oxford: Oxford University Press, 281–309.

Campbell, Tim. 2003. *The Quiet Revolution: Decentralization and the Rise of Political Participation in Latin American Cities.* Pittsburgh: University of Pittsburgh Press.

Caniglia, Beth Schaefer, and JoAnn Carmin. 2005. "Scholarship on Social Movement Organizations: Classic Views and Emerging Trends." *Mobilization* 10 (2): 201–12.

Carrión, Diego. 1996. "Ecuador." In *The Changing Nature of Local Government in Developing Countries,* ed. Patricia L. McCarney. Toronto: University of Toronto Press, 253–82.

Carrión, Fernando. 1987. *El proceso urbano en el Ecuador.* Quito: Instituto Latinoamericano de Investigaciones Sociales.

———. 1995. "Gobierno locales y descentralización en Ecuador." In *Democracia: Descentralización y política social,* ed. Luis Perrano. Lima: Grupo Propuesta Ciudadana, 132–62.

COFOPRI. 2000. COFOPRI arbitration documents for the settlement of Oasis. 13 December.

Collier, David. 1976. *Squatters and Oligarchs: Authoritarian Rule and Policy Change in Peru.* Baltimore: Johns Hopkins University Press.

Collier, David, Henry E. Brady, and Jason Seawright. 2004. "Critiques, Responses, and Trade-Offs: Drawing Together the Debate." In *Rethinking Social Inquiry: Diverse Tools, Shared Standards,* ed. Henry E. Brady and David Collier. Lanham, Md.: Rowman and Littlefield, 195–227.

Collier, Ruth Berins, and David Collier. 1991. *Shaping the Political Arena: Critical Junctures, the Labor Movement, and Regime Dynamics in Latin America.* Princeton: Princeton University Press.

Cornelius, Wayne A. 1975. "Introduction." In *Latin American Urban Research: Urbanization and Inequality,* ed. Wayne Cornelius and Felicity Trueblood. London: Sage, 9–25.

Corrales, Javier. 2002. *Presidents Without Parties: The Politics of Economic Reform in Argentina and Venezuela in the 1990s.* University Park: Pennsylvania State University Press.

Dalton, Russell, and Manfred Kuechler, eds. 1990. *Challenging the Political Order: New Social and Political Movements in Western Democracies.* New York: Oxford University Press.

de Soto, Hernando. 1989. *The Other Path: The Invisible Revolution in the Third World.* New York: Harper and Row.

———. 2000. *The Mystery of Capital: Why Capitalism Triumphs in the West and Fails Everywhere Else.* New York: Basic Books.

Dietz, Henry A. 1998a. "Urban Elections in Peru, 1980–1995." In *Urban Elections in Democratic Latin America,* ed. Henry A. Dietz and Gil Shidlo. Wilmington, Del.: Scholarly Resources, 199–224.

———. 1998b. *Urban Poverty, Political Participation, and the State: Lima, 1970–1990.* Berkeley and Los Angeles: University of California Press.

Dietz, Henry A., and Gil Shidlo, eds. 1998. *Urban Elections in Democratic Latin America*. Wilmington, Del.: Scholarly Resources.

Dietz, Henry A., and Martín Tanaka. 2002. "Lima: Centralized Authority vs. the Struggle for Autonomy." In *Capital City Politics in Latin America*, ed. David J. Myers and Henry A. Dietz. Boulder, Colo.: Lynne Rienner, 193–225.

DiGaetano, Alan. 1989. "Urban Political Regime Formation: A Study in Contrast." *Journal of Urban Affairs* 11 (3): 261–81.

DIGESA. 1997. Report on environmental inspection of Encantada settlement, Villa El Salvador. 6 May.

Dosh, Paul. 2006. "Surprising Trends in Land Invasions in Metropolitan Lima and Quito." *Latin American Perspectives* 33 (6): 29–54.

———. 2009. "Tactical Innovation, Democratic Governance, and Mixed Motives: Popular Movement Resilience in Peru and Ecuador." *Latin American Politics and Society* 51 (1): 87–118.

Dosh, Paul, and Nicole Kligerman. 2009a. "Correa vs. Social Movements: Showdown in Ecuador." *NACLA Report on the Americas* 42 (5): 21–24.

———. 2009b. "Women's Leadership and Anti-privatization Movements in Bolivia and Ecuador." Paper presented at the international congress of the Latin American Studies Association, Rio de Janeiro, Brazil, 11–14 June.

Driant, Jean-Claude. 1991. *Las barriadas de Lima: Historia e interpretación*. Lima: DESCO.

Driant, Jean-Claude, and C. Grey. 1988. "Acceso a la vivienda para la segunda generación de las barriadas de Lima." *Boletín del Instituto Francés de Estudios Andinos* 17 (1): 19–36.

Eckstein, Susan. 1989. "Power and Popular Protest in Latin America." *Power and Popular Protest: Latin American Social Movements*. Berkeley and Los Angeles: University of California Press, 1–60.

———. 1990. "Urbanization Revisited: Inner-City Slum of Hope and Squatter Settlement of Despair." *World Development* 18 (February): 165–81.

Eckstein, Susan, and Timothy Wickham-Crowley. 2003. "Struggles for Social Rights in Latin America: Claims in the Arenas of Subsistence, Labor, Gender, and Ethnicity." In *Struggle for Social Rights in Latin America*, ed. Susan Eckstein and Timothy Wickham-Crowley. New York: Routledge, 1–56.

Elster, Jon. 1989. *The Cement of Society: A Survey of Social Order*. Cambridge: Cambridge University Press.

Encantada Cooperative. 1996. Petition to COFOPRI. 6 November.

———. 2005. Internet bulletins on the progress of the Encantada settlement. Various dates.

Energy Information Administration. 2004. "Ecuador Country Analysis Brief." Washington, D.C.: EIA. Available at http://www.eia.doe.gov/emeu/cabs/ecuador.html#elec. Visited 20 July 2004.

Escobar, Arturo, and Sonia E. Alvarez, eds. 1992. *The Making of Social Movements in Latin America: Identity, Strategy, and Democracy*. Boulder, Colo.: Westview Press.

Flores, César, Jeannet Lingán, and Blanca Cayo. 2002. "Juego de actores de la producción del espacio urbano de Carabayllo: Invasiones del 2002." Typescript, Universidad del Pacífico, Lima.

Foweraker, Joe. 1990. "Popular Movements and Political Change in Mexico." In *Popular Movements and Political Change in Mexico*, ed. Joe Foweraker and Ann L. Craig. Boulder, Colo.: Lynne Rienner, 3–22.

Fox, Jonathan. 1997. "The Difficult Transition from Clientelism to Citizenship: Lessons from Mexico." In *The New Politics of Inequality in Latin America: Rethinking*

Participation and Representation, ed. Douglas A. Chalmers et al. New York: Oxford University Press, 391–420.

Franceschet, Susan. 2004. "Explaining Social Movement Outcomes: Collective Action Frames and Strategic Choices in First- and Second-Wave Feminism in Chile." *Comparative Political Studies* 37 (5): 499–530.

Friedmann, John. 1989. "The Latin American Barrio Movement as a Social Movement: Contribution to a Debate." *International Journal of Urban and Regional Research* 13 (3): 501–10.

Gamson, Joshua. 1995. "Must Identity Movements Self-Destruct? A Queer Dilemma." *Social Problems* 42 (3): 390–407.

Gamson, William. 1990. *The Strategy of Social Protest*. 2nd ed. Belmont, Calif.: Wadsworth.

Gangotena, Raúl. 1994. "El proceso de descentralización en el Ecuador." In *Municipalidades y descentralización*, ed. Fabio Velásquez et al. Lima: Centro de Investigaciones de la Universidad del Pacífico, 37–48.

Ganz, Marshall. 2000. "Resources and Resourcefulness: Strategic Capacity in the Unionization of California Agriculture, 1959–1966." *American Journal of Sociology* 105 (4): 1003–62.

George, Alexander, and Timothy McKeown. 1985. *Advances in Information Processing in Organizations*. Vol. 2. Santa Barbara: JAI Press.

Gerlach, Allen. 2003. *Indians, Oil, and Politics: A Recent History of Ecuador*. Wilmington, Del.: SR Books.

Gilbert, Alan. 1998. *The Latin American City*. 2nd ed. London: Latin American Bureau.

Gilbert, Alan, and Josef Gugler. 1992. *Cities, Poverty, and Development: Urbanization in the Third World*. Oxford: Oxford University Press.

Gilbert, Alan, and Peter Ward. 1978. "Housing in Latin American Cities." In *Geography and the Urban Environment*, ed. David Herbert and R. J. Johnston. New York: John Wiley, 285–318.

Glasser, David. 1988. "The Growing Housing Crisis in Ecuador." In *Spontaneous Shelter: International Perspectives and Prospects*, ed. Carl V. Patton. Philadelphia: Temple University Press, 147–67.

Godard, Henry R. 1988. *Quito, Guayaquil: Evolución y consolidación en ocho barrios populares*. Quito: Centro de Investigaciones.

Gómez, Nelson. 1995. *Pasado y presente de la ciudad de Quito*. Quito: I. Municipio Metropolitano de Quito.

Guidry, John. 2003. "Trial by Space: The Spatial Politics of Citizenship and Social Movements in Urban Brazil." *Mobilization* 8 (2): 189–204.

Haber, Paul. 1996. "Identity and Political Process: Recent Trends in the Study of Latin American Social Movements." *Latin American Research Review* 31 (1): 171–87.

———. 2006. *Power from Experience: Urban Popular Movements in Late Twentieth-Century Mexico*. University Park: Pennsylvania State University Press.

Harrigan, John, and Ronald Vogel. 2000. *Political Change in the Metropolis*. 6th ed. New York: Longman.

Hershberg, Eric, and Fred Rosen. 2006. "Turning the Tide?" In *Latin America After Neoliberalism: Turning the Tide in the Twenty-first Century*, ed. Eric Hershberg and Fred Rosen. New York: The New Press, 1–25.

Hidalgo, Sofía. 1999. *Cono Norte de Lima Metropolitana*. Lima: Alternativa.

Hirsch, Eric. 1990. "Sacrifice for the Cause: Group Processes, Recruitment, and Commitment in a Student Social Movement." *American Sociological Review* 55 (April): 243–55.

Hirschman, Albert. 1970. *Exit, Voice, and Loyalty*. Cambridge: Harvard University Press.

Holzner, Claudio A. 2004. "The End of Clientelism? Strong and Weak Networks in a Mexican Squatter Movement." *Mobilization* 9 (3): 223–40.

Huamán, María Josefina, Gloria Cubas, and Juan Pedro Mora. 1999. "Los nuevos desafíos de la ciudad para las mujeres y la visibilidad de su participación en la construcción del hábitat: El caso del Cono Norte." In *Lima: Megaciudad*, ed. Jaime Joseph. Lima: Alternativa, 169–99.

Inter-American Development Bank. 2004. "The Power Sector in Ecuador." Washington, D.C.: IDB. Available at http://www.iadb.org/sds/doc/2019eng.pdf. Visited 20 July 2004.

Jasper, James M. 2004. "A Strategic Approach to Collective Action: Looking for Agency in Social-Movement Choices." *Mobilization* 9 (1): 1–16.

Kay, Bruce H. 1996. "'Fujipopulism' and the Liberal State in Peru, 1990–1995." *Journal of Interamerican Studies and World Affairs* 38 (4): 55–98.

Keck, Margaret, and Kathryn Sikkink. 1998. *Activists Beyond Borders: Advocacy Networks in International Politics*. Ithaca: Cornell University Press.

Kenney, Charles D. 2004. *Fujimori's Coup and the Breakdown of Democracy in Latin America*. Notre Dame: University of Notre Dame Press.

King, Debra. 2004. "Operationalizing Melucci: Metamorphosis and Passion in the Negotiation of Activists' Multiple Identities." *Mobilization* 9 (1): 73–92.

Kitschelt, Herbert P. 1986. "Political Opportunity Structures and Political Protest: Anti-nuclear Movements in Four Democracies." *British Journal of Political Science* 16 (January): 57–85.

Klandermans, Bert. 1997. *The Social Psychology of Protest*. Oxford: Blackwell.

Koopmans, Ruud. 2005. "The Missing Link Between Structure and Agency: Outline of an Evolutionary Approach to Social Movements." *Mobilization* 10 (1): 19–33.

Leeds, Anthony, and Elizabeth Leeds. 1970. "Brazil and the Myth of Urban Rurality: Urban Experience, Work, and Values in 'Squatments' of Rio de Janeiro and Lima." In *City and Country in the Third World*, ed. Arthur Field. Cambridge, Mass.: Schenkman Publishing, 229–85.

Levine, Daniel H. 1992. *Popular Voices in Latin American Catholicism*. Princeton: Princeton University Press.

Levine, Daniel H., and Brian F. Crisp. 1999. "Venezuela: The Character, Crisis, and Possible Future of Democracy." In *Democracy in Developing Countries: Latin America*, ed. Larry Diamond et al. 2nd ed. Boulder, Colo.: Lynne Rienner, 366–428.

Levine, Daniel H., and Scott Mainwaring. 1989. "Religion and Popular Protest: Contrasting Experiences." In *Power and Popular Protest: Latin American Social Movements*, ed. Susan Eckstein. Berkeley and Los Angeles: University of California Press, 203–40.

Linz, Juan, and Alfred Stepan. 1996. *Problems of Democratic Transition and Consolidation: Southern Europe, South America, and Post-Communist Europe*. Baltimore: Johns Hopkins University Press.

Lipsky, Michael. 1968. "Protest as a Political Resource." *American Political Science Review* 62 (December): 1144–58.

Mainwaring, Scott. 1987. "Urban Popular Movements, Identity, and Democratization in Brazil." *Comparative Political Studies* 20 (2): 131–59.

Matos Mar, José. 1966. *Estudio de las barriadas Limeñas: Informe presentado a Naciones Unidas en diciembre de 1955*. Lima: n.p.

———. 1968. *Urbanización y barriadas en América del Sur*. Lima: IEP.

———. 1986. *Desborde popular y crisis del estado: El nuevo rostro del Perú en la década de 1980*. 2nd ed. Lima: IEP.

McAdam, Doug. 1982. *The Political Process and the Development of Black Insurgency.* Chicago: University of Chicago Press.

———. 1983. "Tactical Innovation and the Pace of Insurgency." *American Sociological Review* 48 (December): 735–54.

McAdam, Doug, John McCarthy, and Mayer Zald. 1988. "Social Movements and Collective Behavior: Building Macro-Micro Bridges." In *Handbook of Sociology*, ed. Neil Smelser and Ron Burt. Beverly Hills: Sage, 695–737.

McAdam, Doug, Sidney Tarrow, and Charles Tilly. 1997. "Toward an Integrated Perspective on Social Movements and Revolution." In *Comparative Politics: Rationality, Culture, and Structure*, ed. Mark Irving Lichbach and Alan Zuckerman. Cambridge: Cambridge University Press, 142–73.

———. 2001. *Dynamics of Contention.* Cambridge: Cambridge University Press.

McCarthy, John D., and Mayer N. Zald. 1977. "Resource Mobilization and Social Movements: A Partial Theory." *American Journal of Sociology* 82 (6): 1212–41.

McClintock, Cynthia. 1999. "Peru: Precarious Regimes, Authoritarian and Democratic." In *Democracy in Developing Countries: Latin America*, ed. Larry Diamond et al. 2nd ed. Boulder, Colo.: Lynne Rienner, 308–65.

Melucci, Alberto. 1988. "Getting Involved: Identity and Mobilization in Social Movements." In *From Structure to Action: Comparing Social Movement Research Across Cultures*, ed. Bert Klandermans, Hanspeter Kriesi, and Sidney Tarrow. Greenwich, Conn.: JAI Press, 329–48.

Munck, Gerardo L. 1995. "Actor Formation, Social Coordination, and Political Strategy: Some Conceptual Problems in the Study of Social Movements." *Sociology* 29 (4): 667–85.

Municipality of Villa El Salvador. 2002. Resolution granting municipal recognition to the cooperative of Villa Mar. Lima, 15 March.

Murakami, Yusuke. 2000. *La democracia según C y D: Un estudio de la conciencia y el comportamiento político de los sectores populares de Lima.* Lima: IEP.

Myers, David J., and Henry A. Dietz, eds. 2003. *Capital City Politics in Latin America: Democratization and Empowerment.* Boulder, Colo.: Lynne Rienner.

Nickson, R. Andrew. 1995. *Local Government in Latin America.* Boulder, Colo.: Lynne Rienner.

Norris, Pippa, Stefaan Walgrave, and Peter Van Aelst. 2005. "Antistate Rebels, Conventional Participants, or Everyone?" *Comparative Politics* 37 (2): 189–205.

O'Brien, Kevin J. 2003. "Neither Transgressive nor Contained: Boundary-Spanning Contention in China." *Mobilization* 8 (1): 51–64.

O'Brien, Kevin J., and Lianjiang Li. 2005. "Popular Contention and Its Impact in Rural China." *Comparative Political Studies* 38 (3): 235–59.

Oliver, Pamela E., and Daniel J. Myers. 2003. "The Coevolution of Social Movements." *Mobilization* 8 (1): 1–24.

Olivera, Oscar, with Tom Lewis. 2004. ¡*Cochabamba! Water War in Bolivia.* Cambridge, Mass.: South End Press.

Olson, Mancur. 1965. *The Logic of Collective Action: Public Goods and the Theory of Groups.* Cambridge: Harvard University Press.

Ondetti, Gabriel. 2006. "Repression, Opportunity, and Protest: Explaining the Takeoff of Brazil's Landless Movement." *Latin American Politics and Society* 48 (2): 61–94.

Panfichi, Aldo. 1997. "The Authoritarian Alternative: 'Anti-politics' in the Popular Sectors of Lima." In *The New Politics of Inequality in Latin America: Rethinking Participation and Representation*, ed. Douglas A. Chalmers et al. New York: Oxford University Press, 217–36.

Pease, Henry. 1994. "Mesa redonda: Experiencia de descentralización en el Perú." In *Municipalidades y descentralización: Presente y futuro*, ed. Fabio Velásquez et al. Lima: Centro de Investigaciones de la Universidad del Pacífico, 109–14.

Pease, Henry, with Pedro Vargas-Prada. 1989. "Los gobiernos locales en el Perú." In *Descentralización y democracia: Gobiernos locales en América Latina*, ed. Jordi Borja et al. Santiago: CLACSO, 337–78.

Pecorella, Robert. 1987. "Fiscal Crises and Regime Change." In *The Politics of Urban Development*, ed. Clarence Stone and Heywood Sanders. Lawrence: University Press of Kansas, 52–72.

Pedraglio, Santiago. 1995. "Perú: Políticas sociales, desarrollo, y reforma del estado." In *Democracia: Descentralización y política social*, ed. Luis Perrano. Lima: Grupo Propuesta Ciudadana, 220–32.

Piven, Francis Fox, and Richard A. Cloward. 1977. *Poor People's Movements: Why They Succeed, How They Fail*. New York: Pantheon Books.

Portes, Alejandro. 1989. "Latin American Urbanization During the Years of the Crisis." *Latin American Research Review* 24 (3): 7–44.

Portes, Alejandro, and John Walton. 1976. *Urban Latin America: The Political Conditions from Above and Below*. Austin: University of Texas Press.

Power, Margaret. 2002. *Right-Wing Women in Chile: Feminine Power and the Struggle Against Allende, 1964–1973*. University Park: Pennsylvania State University Press.

Powers, Nancy R. 2001. *Grassroots Expectations of Democracy and Economy: Argentina in Comparative Perspective*. Pittsburgh: University of Pittsburgh Press.

Rice, Roberta, and Donna Lee Van Cott. 2006. "The Emergence and Performance of Indigenous Peoples' Parties in South America: A Subnational Statistical Analysis." *Comparative Political Studies* 39 (6): 709–32.

Riofrío, Gustavo. 1978. *Se busca terreno para próxima barriada: Espacios disponibles en Lima, 1940–1978–1990*. Lima: DESCO.

———. 1986. *Habilitación urbana con participación popular: Tres casos en Lima, Perú*. Eschborn, Germany: GTZ.

———. 1991. *Producir la ciudad (popular) de los '90: Entre el mercado y el estado*. Lima: DESCO.

Riofrío, Gustavo, and Jean-Claude Driant. 1987. *¿Qué vivienda han construido? Nuevos problemas en viejas barriadas*. Lima: CIDAP.

Roberts, Bryan, and Alejandro Portes. 2006. "Coping with the Free Market City: Collective Action in Six Latin American Cities at the End of the Twentieth Century." *Latin American Research Review* 41 (2): 57–83.

Roberts, Kenneth M. 1995. "Neoliberalism and the Transformation of Populism in Latin America: The Peruvian Case." *World Politics* 48 (October): 82–116.

———. 1997. "Rethinking Economic Alternatives: Left Parties and the Articulation of Popular Demands in Chile and Peru." In *The New Politics of Inequality in Latin America: Rethinking Participation and Representation*, ed. Douglas A. Chalmers et al. New York: Oxford University Press, 313–36.

———. 1998. *Deepening Democracy? The Modern Left and Social Movements in Chile and Peru*. Stanford: Stanford University Press.

———. 2006. "Populism, Political Conflict, and Grass-Roots Organization in Latin America." *Comparative Politics* 38 (2): 127–48.

Roberts, Kenneth M., and Moisés Arce. 1998. "Neoliberalism and Lower-Class Voting Behavior in Peru." *Comparative Political Studies* 31 (2): 217–46.

Sawyer, Suzana. 2004. *Crude Chronicles: Indigenous Politics, Multinational Oil, and Neoliberalism in Ecuador*. Durham: Duke University Press.

Schönwälder, Gerd. 2002. *Linking Civil Society and the State: Urban Popular Movements, the Left, and Local Government in Peru, 1980–1992*. University Park: Pennsylvania State University Press.

Selverston-Scher, Melina. 2001. *Ethnopolitics in Ecuador: Indigenous Rights and the Strengthening of Democracy*. Miami: North-South Center Press.

Sen, Amartya. 1999. *Development as Freedom*. New York: Knopf.

Skinner, Reinhard. 1983. "Community Participation: Its Scope and Organization." In *People, Poverty, and Shelter: Problems of Self-Help Housing in the Third World*, ed. Reinhard Skinner and Michael Rodell. New York: Methuen, 125–50.

Snow, David, and Robert Benford. 1988. "Ideology, Frame Resonance, and Participant Mobilization." In *From Structure to Action: Social Movement Participation Across Cultures*, ed. Bert Klandermans, Hanspeter Kriesi, and Sidney Tarrow. Greenwich, Conn.: JAI Press, 197–217.

Snow, David, E. Burke Rochford, Jr., Steven Worden, and Robert Benford. 1986. "Frame Alignment Processes, Micromobilization, and Movement Participation." *American Sociological Review* 51 (August): 464–81.

Sosa, José, and César Flores. 2002. "El capital intelectual como determinante de la riqueza: Un caso de estudio—asentamiento humano Los Olivos de Pro." Typescript, Universidad del Pacífico, Lima.

Stokes, Susan C. 1991. "Politics and Latin America's Urban Poor: Reflections from a Lima Shantytown." *Latin American Research Review* 26 (2): 75–102.

———. 1995. *Cultures in Conflict: Social Movements and the State in Peru*. Berkeley and Los Angeles: University of California Press.

———. 2001. *Mandates and Democracy: Neoliberalism by Surprise in Latin America*. Cambridge: Cambridge University Press.

Stone, Clarence. 1987. "Summing Up: Urban Regimes, Development Policy, and Political Arrangements." In *The Politics of Urban Development*, ed. Clarence Stone and Heywood Sanders. Lawrence: University Press of Kansas, 269–90.

———. 1989. *Regime Politics: Governing Atlanta, 1946–1988*. Lawrence: University Press of Kansas.

Swyngedouw, Erik A. 1995. "The Contradictions of Urban Water Provision: A Study of Guayaquil, Ecuador." *Third World Planning Review* 17 (4): 387–405.

Tanaka, Martín. 1999. "La participación social y política de los pobladores populares urbanos: ¿Del movimientismo a una política de ciudadanos? El caso de El Agustino." In *El poder visto desde abajo: Democracia, educación, y ciudadanía en espacios locales*, ed. Martín Tanaka. Lima: IEP, 103–53.

Tarrow, Sidney. 1989. *Democracy and Disorder: Protest and Politics in Italy, 1965–1974*. Oxford: Oxford University Press.

———. 1998. *Power in Movement: Social Movements and Contentious Politics*. 2nd ed. Cambridge: Cambridge University Press.

Tilly, Charles. 1995. *Popular Contention in Great Britain, 1758–1834*. Cambridge: Harvard University Press.

Tovar Samanez, Teresa. 1982a. *Movimiento barrial: Organización y unidad (1978–1981)*. Lima: DESCO.

———. 1982b. *Velasquismo y movimiento popular: Historia del movimiento popular, 1968–1975*. Lima: DESCO.

———. 1986. "Vecinos y pobladores en la crisis (1980–1984)." In *Movimientos sociales y crisis: El caso Peruano*, ed. Eduardo Ballón. Lima: DESCO, 113–64.

Tuesta, Fernando. 2001. *Perú político en cifras: 1821–2001*. 3rd ed. Lima: Fundación Friedrich Ebert.

Udéhn, Lars. 1993. "Twenty-five Years with the Logic of Collective Action." *Acta Soci-ologica* 36 (3): 239–61.

Unidad de Suelo y Vivienda. 2002. "Asentamientos ilegales, Quito, 2002." Internal report of the Unidad de Suelo y Vivienda, Quito.

Van Cott, Donna Lee. 2005. *From Movements to Parties in Latin America: The Evolution of Ethnic Politics.* Cambridge: Cambridge University Press.

Vanden, Harry E. 2007. "Social Movements, Hegemony, and New Forms of Resistance." *Latin American Perspectives* 34 (2): 17–30.

Villalón, Roberta. 2007. "Neoliberalism, Corruption, and Legacies of Contention." *Latin American Perspectives* 34 (2): 139–56.

Wildavsky, Aaron. 1987. "Choosing Preferences by Constructing Institutions: A Cultural Theory of Preference Formation." *American Political Science Review* 81 (March): 4–21.

Willis, Eliza, Christopher da C. B. Garman, and Stephan Haggard. 1999. "The Politics of Decentralization in Latin America." *Latin American Research Review* 34 (1): 7–56.

Wolff, Jonas. 2007. "(De-)Mobilising the Marginalised: A Comparison of the Argentine *Piqueteros* and Ecuador's Indigenous Movement." *Journal of Latin American Studies* 39 (1): 1–29.

Wolford, Wendy. 2003. "Families, Fields, and Fighting for Land: The Spatial Dynamics of Contention in Rural Brazil." *Mobilization* 8 (2): 157–72.

Wright, Angus, and Wendy Wolford. 2003. *To Inherit the Earth: The Landless Movement and the Struggle for a New Brazil.* Oakland: Food First Books.

Yashar, Deborah J. 1998. "Contesting Citizenship: Indigenous Movements and Democracy in Latin America." *Comparative Politics* 31 (1): 23–42.

Zapata, Antonio. 1996. *Sociedad y poder local: La comunidad de Villa El Salvador, 1971–1996.* Lima: DESCO.

INTERVIEWS BY AUTHOR

Aceles, Freddy. 2002. Quito, 8 September. Tape recording.

Andrade Rodriguez, Juvenal. 2005. Quito, 9 June.

Arturo Vega, Miguel. 2002. Lima, 16 February. Tape recording.

Avelino, Elias. 2002. Lima, 12 March.

Avendaño, Diana. 2002. Lima, 10 January.

Azcueta, Michel. 2002. Lima, 24 February. Tape recording.

Barrera, José. 2002. Lima, 15 February.

Bustamente, Victoriano. 2002. Lima, 3 March. Tape recording.

Cabana, Máximo. 2001. Lima, 25 November and 1 December.

Campos, Victor. 2002. Lima, 9 March and 17 March. Tape recordings.

Casas, Isaías. 2001. Lima, 9 December.

Chamorro, Milton. 2002. Quito, 2 September, 9 September, and 11 September. Tape recordings.

———. 2005. Quito, 8 June. Tape recording.

———. 2008. Quito, 20 July. Tape recording.

Chávez, María. 2002. Lima, 3 March. Tape recording.

Chupingahua, Santiago. 2002. Lima, 10 February.

Cocha, Gabriela. 2002. Quito, 10 September.

Condori, Nestor. 2002. Lima, 9 March. Tape recording.
Coral, Edgar. 2002. Quito, 5 September. Tape recording.
Cotler, Julio. 2001. Lima, 15 November.
de Riobamba, Luz. 2002. Quito, 2 September.
de Soto, Hernando. 2002. Houston, 10 January.
Domínguez, Justo. 2001. Lima, 16 December.
Encarnación Sandoval, Jorge. 2002. Lima, 10 March. Tape recording.
Endara, Patricio. 2002. Quito, 7 September.
———. 2008. Quito, 25 July. Tape recording.
Galarga, Carlos. 2002. Quito, 20 August.
Geronimo, Victoria. 2002. Lima, 9 March.
Goñe, Macario. 2002. Lima, 2 January. Tape recording.
Hernández, María. 2002. Quito, 16 September. Tape recording.
———. 2008. Quito, 30 July. Tape recording.
Hilario de Peña, María Ariza. 2005. Lima, 26 June. Tape recording.
Hizo, Marcelo. 2007. Lima, 21 July.
Huamán, Efraín. 2002. Lima, 9 March.
———. 2005. Lima, 25 June. Tape recording.
Jaimes, Eusebio. 2002. Lima, 8 March. Tape recording.
la Madrid, Diego. 2002. Lima, 2 March. Tape recording.
Lara, José. 2001. Lima, 23 November.
López, Rommel. 2002. Quito, 15 September. Tape recording.
Martínez, Modesta. 2002. Lima, 12 March, 17 March, and 24 September. Tape recordings.
———. 2005. Lima, 18 June. Tape recording.
———. 2009. Lima, 13 August.
Mejia, Alcides. 2001. Lima, 21 December.
Meneses, Blanca. 2002. Quito, 16 September.
Mera, Alba. 2002. 10 September. Tape recording.
———. 2008. Quito, 24 July. Tape recording.
Meza, Celso. 2002. Quito, 1 September and 6 September. Tape recordings.
———. 2005. Quito, 8 June and 9 June. Tape recordings.
Montenegro, Herbert. 2002. Lima, 10 February. Tape recording.
Montesinos, Lino. 2002. Lima, 16 March. Tape recording.
———. 2005. Lima, 22 June. Tape recording.
Morales, Olga. 2002. Lima, 9 March.
Muesmueran Imbaquingo, María Lupe. 2002. Quito, 6 September.
Muñoz, Isabel. 2002. Lima, 12 March.
Pazmiño Navas, Jorge. 2002. Quito, 11 September. Tape recording.
Peña, Elvira. 2002. Lima, 16 February. Tape recording.
Pérez, Ruben. 2002. Lima, 21 January. Tape recording.
Polo Burga, Julio. 2001. Lima, 17 December.
Pumar, Martín. 2002. Lima, 20 February. Tape recording.
Ramírez, César. 2002. Quito, 8 September.
Remuzgo, Elvis. 2005. Lima, 22 June. Tape recording.
Rojas, Willy. 2002. Lima, 3 March. Tape recording.
Romero, Eric. 2002. Lima, 13 March. Tape recording.
Ruíz, Abrahím. 2001. Lima, 23 November.
Santos, Nelli. 2002. Lima, 14 March. Tape recording.
Silva, Isabel. 2002. Quito, 2 September.
Solar, Jesús. 2002. Lima, 12 February.

Tamaca, Carla. 2002. Quito, 8 September.
Tapia, Claudio. 2002. Lima, 2 March 2002. Tape recording.
Thomas, Robert. 2002. Quito, 15 August. Tape recording.
Toche Lara, Miguel. 2002. Lima, 15 March. Tape recording.
Valencia, Jesús. 2001. Lima, 15 November. Tape recording.
———. 2002. Lima, 24 February. Tape recording.
———. 2005. Lima, 22 June. Tape recording.
———. 2007. Lima, 25 July. Tape recording.
Valencia, Pilar. 2002. Lima, 5 February.
Varas, Jorge. 2002. Lima, 17 March. Tape recording.
Vásquez, Pedro. 2002. Lima, 2 March. Tape recording.
Vásquez Solano, Harold. 2002. Lima, 14 March. Tape recording.
Velásquez, Yuri. 2002. Lima, 12 February. Tape recording.
Villavicencio, Wilson. 2005. Quito, 9 September.
Villavicencio Carrasco, Isabel. 2001. Lima, 20 October.
Vivanco, Alfredo. 2002. Lima, 31 January. Tape recording.
Yabar, Celia. 2001. Lima, 23 November and 30 November.
Yaranga, Wilfredo. 2002. Lima, 24 February.
Yataco, José. 2002. Lima, 10 February.
Yicate, Luis. 2002. Lima, 2 February.
Zuñiga, Oscar. 2002. Lima, 13 March. Tape recording.

LETTERS

Azcueta, Michel. 1997. Letter to the INC. 29 April.
COFOPRI. 1996. Letter to the Encantada cooperative initiating the land titling process. 7 November.
Figueroa, Gustavo. 1999. Letter to the Oasis cooperative. 3 October.
INC. 1997a. Letter to the Luz del Sur electricity company. 20 November.
———. 1997b. Letter to Secretary General Macario Goñe, Oasis de Villa. 21 October.
———. 2002. Letter to the Villa Mar cooperative. Lima, 22 March.
Zuñiga, Oscar. 1996. Letter to COFOPRI on behalf of the Encantada cooperative. 6 November.
———. 2000. Letter to the Appellate Court of Lima on behalf of the Encantada cooperative. 24 August.

PERIODICALS

Ajá (Lima)
El Comercio (Lima)
El Comercio (Quito)
Debate (Lima)
Expreso (Quito)
Extra (Guayaquil)
La Hora (Quito)
Hoy (Quito)

El Peruano (Lima)
La República (Lima)
Reto (Lima)
El Tío (Lima)
Últimas Noticias (Quito)
El Universo (Quito)

Index

and Paraíso, 139, 141
and Pisulli, 59, 91, 93–94, 96, 101, 213–14
and Pro, 67, 70, 71
and Rosales, 79, 82, 85–86, 99, 101
and Sector C, 74, 75, 77
and Villa Mar, 133, 134, 144
and organizational survival, 11
Moncayo, Paco, 44
and Camino, 116–19, 196
and Itchimbía, 173–77, 201
and Pisulli, 96, 98
Montesinos, Lino, 85–87, 100, 101
Montesinos, Vladimir, 66 n. 8
Morales, Evo, 232
Morales, Marcelino, 60–61, 63, 74
moribund stage of development, 29, 32–34,
  185, 211–15, 229
of Encantada, 23, 48, 147–48, 159–60, 182,
  205, 225, 232
of Oasis, 2, 104, 105, 126–27, 128, 195,
  203, 204
of Pro, 69–71, 103, 194, 231
of Sector C, 77–78, 103, 194, 231
motives, mixed
and collective action, 9, 28–31, 219,
  224–27, 229
of Innovators, 8, 17, 34, 148, 179, 182,
  187, 217
and participation, 212, 218
and security trap, 214–15
movement resilience. See survival,
  organizational
Movimiento Popular Democrático (Popular
  Democratic Movement), Ecuador, 88
Movimento dos Trabalhadores Rurais Sem
  Terra (MST, Movement of Landless Rural
  Workers), Brazil, 16 n. 5, 26 n. 15, 234
MPD. See Movimiento Popular Democrático
MST. See Movimento dos Trabalhadores Rurais
  Sem Terra
Multisectoral Commission, 125–28, 130, 145,
  159–62, 182, 204
municipal government. See local government
municipal recognition, 20, 33, 53–54, 72
definition of, 53 n. 23
and level of service provision, 54
and organizational survival, 33
strategies for acquiring, 206–7
and strategy life cycle, 21, 207
success rates of demands for, 207

nascent stage of development, 32, 210–11
of Camino, 110–15
of Encantada, 152–56
of Itchimbía, 166–71, 214

and mixed motives, 182
of Oasis, 122–24, 213
of Paraíso, 138–39
of Pisulli, 90–91, 102
of Pro, 64–67
of Rosales, 79–81
of Sector C, 72–74
and universe of cases, 52
of Villa Mar, 129–33
National System for the Support of Social
  Mobilization. See Sistema Nacional de
  Apoyo a la Movilización Social
neighborhood regimes, 24–25
and alliances, 223
and avenues of participation, 224
authoritarian, 24, 27, 41, 102, 103, 104,
  106, 116, 145
consensual, 25, 27, 28, 105, 170, 174, 177,
  209
democratic, 25, 26, 28, 41, 105, 145, 157,
  159
electoral, 24–25, 64, 68, 75, 78, 87, 102
and land titling, 47
metropolitan trends of, 41, 50–51, 227
and neighborhood service acquisition
  model, 26–27
and organizational competitiveness, 50
organizational trends of, 190–91, 217
and organizational success, 205, 209, 212,
  228
and type of previous land ownership, 55
neighborhood service acquisition model,
  25–28, 51, 60, 198, 208, 217–18, 222
neoliberalism
in Ecuador, 5, 49, 53, 107, 163
in Latin America, 5, 6, 22, 30, 49, 227, 234
in Peru, 5, 22, 49, 53, 61–62, 156, 222
and privatization, 49 n. 17, 50 n. 18
Next Generation organizations, 2, 104–46. See
  also Camino; Oasis; Paraíso; and Villa Mar
identity traits of, 18, 143, 145–46, 186–88
neighborhood regimes of, 144–45, 190–91
repertoire traits of, 18, 143–44, 146,
  188–90
strategy preferences of, 20–22, 195–97, 228
success of, 207–9
summary of, 7–8, 16, 145–46, 104
survival of, 210–11, 213–14
tactics of, 16, 20, 21, 142–46
NGOs. See also Project Ala
as allies, 27, 199–200, 203, 223
international, 81, 86, 156, 157, 169, 175,
  177, 179, 181, 216
local, 84, 202, 206
non-governmental organizations. See NGOs